GOVERNANCE AMID
BIGGER, BETTER MARKETS

Visions of Governance in the 21st Century

Why People Don't Trust Government
Joseph Nye Jr., Philip Zelikow, and David King
(1997)

democracy.com? Governance in a Networked World
Elaine Ciulla Kamarck and Joseph Nye Jr.
(1999)

Governance in a Globalizing World
Joseph Nye Jr. and John D. Donahue, editors
(2000)

Governance amid Bigger, Better Markets

John D. Donahue
Joseph S. Nye Jr.
Editors

VISIONS OF GOVERNANCE
IN THE 21ST CENTURY
Cambridge, Massachusetts

BROOKINGS INSTITUTION PRESS
Washington, D.C.

Library of Congress Cataloging-in-Publication data
Governance amid bigger, better markets / John D. Donahue and Joseph S. Nye, Jr., editors.
    p.   cm.
Includes bibliographical references and index.
    ISBN 0-8157-0200-0 (cloth : alk. paper)—ISBN 0-8157-0201-9 (pbk. : alk. paper)
    1. Capitalism.   2. Corporate governance.   3. Political culture.   I. Donahue, John D. II. Nye, Joseph S.
    HB501 .G6275 2001   2001005928
    322'.3'0973—dc21   CIP

9 8 7 6 5 4 3 2 1

The paper used in this publication meets minimum requirements of the American National Standard for Information Sciences—Permanence of Paper for Printed Library Materials: ANSI Z39.48-1992.

Typeset in Adobe Garamond

Composition by R. Lynn Rivenbark
Macon, Georgia

Printed by R. R. Donnelley and Sons
Harrisonburg, Virginia

Preface

HARVARD'S JOHN F. KENNEDY School of Government launched the Visions of Governance in the Twenty-First Century project in 1996 in order to better anticipate, account for, accommodate, and appropriately influence major trends in the missions and in the means of governance. The Visions project concentrates the school's scholarly resources on the large and medium-term questions of governance, with the proximate goals of better understanding and more effective teaching and the ultimate goal of better professional practice. It establishes a forum for collaborative faculty discussion and research, honoring and advancing the Kennedy School's tradition of cross-disciplinary intellectual endeavors applied to practical problems of governance. This volume is the latest product of that enterprise.

Support for the research from which these essays grew has been generously provided by the Ash Fund for Research on Democratic Governance; the Christian A. Johnson Endeavor Foundation; the Daniel and Joanna S. Rose Fund; the Parker Gilbert Montgomery Endowment; Mr. Kenneth G. Lipper; and the Smith Richardson Foundation. We gratefully acknowledge their assistance. We also thank the participants in the 2000 Visions of Governance Bretton Woods faculty symposium, at which drafts of these essays were presented and refined through critical (but collegial) discussion. And we note, with gratitude, the contributions of many scholars within and beyond the Kennedy School who participated in Visions of Governance gatherings during the year and a half over which this book took shape.

Special thanks are due to Christoper Kelaher, Janet Walker, Janet Schilling Mowery, and Susan Woollen of the Brookings Institution Press; to Elaine Kamarck, whose earlier stewardship of the Visions project set the stage for this book; and to Lynn Akin, the project's coordinator, whose energy, resourcefulness, and cheerful competence make this work possible and make it pleasant.

JOHN D. DONAHUE
Raymond Vernon Lecturer in Public Policy
Director, Visions of Governance
    in the 21st Century

JOSEPH S. NYE JR.
Don K. Price Professor of Public Policy
Dean, John F. Kennedy School of Government

Contents

PART THREE
Governing Well When Markets Rule

GOVERNANCE AMID
BIGGER, BETTER MARKETS

1

JOHN D. DONAHUE
JOSEPH S. NYE JR.

Market Ascendancy and the Challenge of Governance

A PHENOMENON THAT HAS been discernible (at least dimly) for two decades or more is becoming vividly clear as we settle into the twenty-first century. Changing markets are challenging governance. The growing scale, reach, complexity, and popular legitimacy of market institutions and market players are reopening old questions about the role of the public sector and redefining what it means to govern well. Bigger, better markets bring both good news and bad news for the pursuit of cherished public goals like equity, community, stability, security, progress, and growth, but the operant word here is *news*. Twenty-first century markets confront us with fresh possibilities, unaccustomed challenges, and tripwires for traditional habits of mind.

Governance is the organization and regulation of our collective lives—the things we do with other people. Governance means making rules that matter. Often authoritative rule-making is performed by formal structures of government, but sometimes not. (For example, private clubs or industrial associations create their own authoritative rules.) Every market occurs within some framework of rules, but the architecture may or may not be governmental—witness barter among tribes in the Amazon, international black markets, or the "robber baron" governance of security markets in Russia. The relation between governments and markets varies greatly by place and also (the key point for this book) by time. As Susan Strange has argued, the balance between states and markets shifted after the 1970s in a way that made the state just one source of authority among several and left "a yawning hole of non-authority or non-governance."[1]

What do we mean by "bigger, better markets"? Some distinctions are in order. For over two centuries an influential school of Western thought has held that market solutions (even at their worst) are almost always superior to anything government (even at its best) can pull off. We are not adding our voices to that chorus. "Bigger, better markets" is meant to be descriptive rather than celebratory. It emphasizes, against the contrasting backdrop of laissez-faire fundamentalists' faithful constancy, the variation over time in what we can expect from market arrangements.

Nor do we simply mean economic health. This book was written, and many of the phenomena it explores took form, during an extraordinary period of prosperity. The American economy grew at an annual pace approaching or exceeding 4 percent during the last several years of the 1990s—a winning streak of rapid growth, low unemployment, and surging productivity unseen since the 1960s.[2] But a nice stretch of good times does not amount to market ascendancy. Even a small and primitive market system can deliver its own version of prosperity. Even without fundamental change, markets can expand along well-mapped paths. Growth has something to do with the trend at issue here, to be sure. The relatively sunny economic climate predominating after World War II was a favorable environment for the stepped-up evolution of market mechanisms. Business cycles persist, even if for the past half-century or so the torque they impose on the economy has been dampened by good public policy. A plain old cyclical downturn, if sufficiently sharp and prolonged, could slow or reverse market ascendancy for a time. But if "good enough" economic conditions are necessary to breed bigger, better markets, they are not sufficient. The phenomenon flows from a complex of factors that can be summarized as *scope, sophistication*, and *legitimacy*.

SCOPE. Markets have become more extensive, more integrated, and more intricately interwoven into the fabric of life. This is partly a matter of growth, of course. More production means more transactions, and even "more of the same" would make for bigger markets. It is also partly a matter of economic globalization—the growing number of market economies and the rising pace of international exchange. Jeffrey Frankel has marked some milestones: the precipitous fall in the cost of international transportation and communication during the twentieth century; the resurgence (after the setbacks of the World Wars) in global trade and investment; the expansion (to a 1998 level of $1.5 trillion per day) in foreign-exchange transactions.[3]

But the growing scope of markets is also a matter of greater transactional "density" within nations, especially in the United States. Aspects of life that were once held at some distance from the market system have become integrated into the cash economy. The most intimate example is people's time. Each year, the average working American now sells nearly 2,000 hours of his or her time for pay, according to public data cited by former secretary of labor Robert B. Reich. The average middle-income couple with children marketed 3,918 hours of their time in 1998, up seven work weeks from a decade earlier. Families balance the boost in time rendered to the market by delegating to the market domestic functions—cooking and cleaning, child care, entertainment, and fitness—that were once familial, rather than commercial, undertakings.[4] Another evocative example involves public order and personal security. By 1996 there were three times as many private as public security officers in the United States.[5] These illustrations of the price system's deepening (and the many other instances they exemplify) inform our theme of "bigger" markets. Whether they make things better, on balance, is a topic that warrants (and gets) extensive debate, including in these pages.

SOPHISTICATION. The abstract aggregate of "the market" is built up of concrete individual transactions. A buyer scans for goods and services that meet her requirements. As she identifies purchases that promise to deliver value, she gathers information on the quality of the product and the reliability of each purveyor. Once she makes her choice, she negotiates terms with the seller—the timing of delivery, the manner of payment, any warranties or contingencies. The seller, meanwhile, may check out *her* credibility, and measure her willingness to pay against other potential buyers'. Once both parties are confident they will gain from the exchange, the transaction is finalized. Nearly all of these functions have become easier to perform than they were twenty years ago and promise to become easier still. As a recent essay in the *Economist* observed, "the textbook model of perfect competition . . . assumes abundant information, many buyers and sellers, zero transaction costs, and no barriers to entry. Information technology makes these assumptions a bit less far-fetched."[6]

Better markets are largely a function of the information revolution, but not entirely. They also reflect the evolution and elaboration of old-fashioned mechanisms like contracts, insurance, franchises, branding, and alliances. For example, until recently one's views about the good society—

the morality of international arms sales, the ethics of homosexual rights, the relative priority of economic growth and environmental protection— were expressed (at least authoritatively expressed) chiefly through politics. But the development of various "socially responsible" investment vehicles allows individuals to exercise their social voice—at a decibel level proportionate to stock holdings, to be sure—through the market. The Social Investment Forum, a trade group for such funds, reports that the dollar value of portfolios deployed in line with explicit social criteria tripled, to around $1.5 trillion, between 1997 and 1999.[7]

Related areas where the growing sophistication of market mechanisms expands the repertoire for collective action outside formal government are discussed in this book. Akash Deep and Guido Schaefer's chapter traces the refinement of financial instruments by which banks manage the mismatch between the time structure of their main assets and liabilities, and asks whether the decades-old tradition of public deposit insurance may be approaching obsolescence. John Meyer and José Gómez-Ibáñez analyze the role of long-term contracts in reducing the vulnerability of shippers and haulers alike as transportation markets evolve. Joseph Newhouse traces the growing depth and complexity of market mechanisms in health care. John Donahue and Richard Zeckhauser suggest that a long period of relative social and economic stability has permitted the institutions and instruments of nongovernmental coordination to flourish economywide, as collective mastery of the mechanics of transaction progresses. Better *markets*, again, may not make for a better society, as Mark Moore warns us in this book's final chapter. But taken on their own terms—the best possible allocation of resources across alternative uses, as guided by individual choices constrained by initial resource distribution—significantly upgraded market mechanisms appear to be emerging on a wide front.

LEGITIMACY. Throughout much of the twentieth century "the market" tended to be politically suspect. The gross inequities and cultural disruptions unleashed by untrammeled commerce in nineteenth-century Europe, Karl Polanyi has argued, triggered the mass movements of communism and fascism, which (though strikingly dissimilar on other ideological planes) both featured close governmental control over markets.[8] Emerging in midcentury from the trauma of depression and war, most industrial democracies forged a new social contract marked by a large governmental role in regulating economic activity and narrowing the range of market outcomes. The United States, insulated from the worst of the previous century's traumas, never broke so fully with laissez-faire, but wariness about unregulated markets reigned here as well.[9] Although there has been no sharp sea change toward popular faith in markets, the tide seems to have turned. The palpable failure of planned economies, stagflation in the member economies of the Organization for Economic Cooperation and Development (OECD), and the rehabilitation of market ideas led to a shift toward the right in most industrialized democracies, with the most dramatic manifestation being the "Thatcher-Reagan revolution" that set the political tone for the century's final fifth in much of the English-speaking world. By the end of the century, citizens in most countries were open to market solutions to a degree that would have been unthinkable a few decades earlier. Over three-fourths of respondents to a 1999 Pew survey saw business success as central to America's strength.[10] In the 2000 version of the Gallup Organization's annual survey of confidence in major American institutions, a quarter or more of respondents reported a great deal or quite a lot of confidence in "big business"—traditionally the least popular avatar of the market principle.[11] More subtly, popular culture seems to be casting a somewhat more favorable light on market players and institutions in recent years. Business people in the movies (once standard-issue scoundrels) are sometimes heroes, or at least quirkily cool, while public officials tend to be portrayed in the media more harshly than was common in earlier decades.[12]

How Should Government Respond?

"Governance where there is no government" can serve as a Zen-like definition of the market. As markets expand and improve, what are the implications for electoral politics, law and regulation, public investment and spending, and other aspects of government? How is government's mission altered in an era of ascendant markets? One possible broad-gauged response starts from the presumption that government and the market are strictly competing blueprints for social organization. Where one advances, the other gives way. When markets extend their reach and remedy their flaws, we can get by with less government, as the market occupies formerly public ground. Alternatively, government can be cast not as a substitute for markets but as a counterweight. From this viewpoint, ascendant markets call for a parallel expansion in government's reach and potency. Bigger markets mean more terrain to patrol, and markets are "better" only according to the economist's cramped definition of the good society. The more effectively markets advance individualistic and utilitarian norms, the more vigorously government must assert and enforce other conceptions of value. As our construction of these parallel straw men suggests, our view is that neither "less government" nor "more government" will prove the best watchword (though, as further reading will reveal, there are times when each applies.)

"*Different* government" comes closer. Expansive, integrated markets pose different challenges for governance than those we sought to master when markets were simpler, more segmented, less audacious in their reach. Complex, sophisticated markets render obsolete intellectual and political habits formed when the mechanisms of private transaction were less elaborately evolved, more readily comprehensible, and prone to fail in familiar ways. Gaining some purchase on the meaning of good governance in this transformed context is the goal of this book. Before moving to the individual essays, however, a bit more attention to the rudiments of market governance is required.

There are three categories, or perhaps more precisely, *levels*, of the governance of a market system, building from relatively primitive and uncontroversial functions to increasingly subtle and decreasingly unanimous missions.

MAKING MARKETS POSSIBLE. The first level of governance is providing the intellectual and institutional infrastructure of a market system. Property rights must be defined. Rules for private exchange must be put in place. Procedures must be established for enforcing commitments, resolving disputes, and sanctioning default. These foundation and housekeeping responsibilities of government are little noticed except in times (the aftermath of World War II in much of Europe), places (Russia and other countries enduring rocky transitions from communism), and sectors (wide swaths of the Internet economy at the turn of the century) where they are conspicuously absent. Like the humble creatures that build coral reefs hosting complex ecologies, the accretion of these unremarkable functions of governance is what makes markets possible.

FIXING MARKET FAILURES. In the best of all possible worlds, by the market theorists' metric, the invisible hand meticulously orders economic affairs so as to wring out the absolute maximum of human happiness that limited resources can provide. Waste is banished, progress hastened, and every ill eased up to the point that further remedy would cause greater problems elsewhere. But as economists know better than anyone, this theoretical idyll is never seen in practice. Markets are imperfect, and examples

of market failure (ranging from the rudimentary to the baroque) fill a volu-
minous literature. Joseph Stiglitz offers one of the most concise typologies
of market failure. Cases where the premise of market efficiency is faulty and
governance could potentially improve outcomes include:[13]

—*Market power.* Efficiency requires that market players confront actual
or potential competitors, to push them back to the point where marginal
cost equals marginal benefit. Absent competition, resources can be squan-
dered and innovation stifled. Intervention may be justified to increase competition or to compensate for its absence.

—*Public goods.* The logic of optimal outcomes through private exchange
requires that specific consumers pay for and use up every good; and by
paying, the consumers both attest to the value they place on the good and
motivate its provision. When this lockstep alignment of payment and benefit breaks down, the market delivers too little of the good, by the bench-
mark of maximum welfare. "Pure" public goods—where one person's
enjoyment doesn't diminish anyone else's, and where access cannot be
restricted to paying customers—are relatively rare (if important); clean air
and national defense are conventional examples. But many goods feature
some aspects of nonrivalry and nonexcludability, and a large number of
"impure" public goods challenge the efficient-markets framework and
invite consideration of public provision.

—*Externalities.* Analogous to public goods are cases where some important element of a market exchange escapes the framework of payment
received for value delivered. A transaction generates unpriced benefits to
outside parties (positive externalities) or imposes uncompensated costs on
them (negative externalities.) Efficiency breaks down, and intervention
may be warranted to fix the externality or counteract the distortion it
imposes.

—*Information gaps.* Perfect markets require perfect knowledge—information that is complete, accurate, and shared among all participants.
Where information is incomplete or unreliable or unevenly distributed, a
range of ills can arise. Government may act to encourage better information or to fix outcomes warped by bad data.

—*Incomplete markets.* Unless everything has its price—all goods and
services, in every imaginable contingency—markets can break down. If
some items are kept off the market, for good reasons or bad reasons (or-
gans, narcotics, embryos, marriage vows, the promise of future servitude)
the tapestry of efficiency through voluntary exchange begins to fray.

MACROECONOMIC DISRUPTIONS. Recessions, market crashes, panics and contagions, or inflationary surges can disrupt delicate market networks, creating serious (even if temporary) cases of various kinds of market failure.

—*Distribution.* The story of maximum happiness through voluntary exchange assumes that initial resource endowments are either equal, or unequal for some good reason. Handing your wallet to a gunman who demands "your money or your life" might be considered a voluntary selection of the best deal on the table but is a decidedly unequal exchange. Voluntarily providing your labor in lieu of starvation is not much better. The play of the market may produce "efficient" outcomes, but if the players enter the game with uneven piles of chips the tally at the end of play will, by all odds, be comparably tilted. Improving distribution is not what markets are good at.

—*"Merit goods."* Economists use the term "merit goods" as a linguistic wild card to cover cases where individuals make flawed judgments of value, mistaking wheat for chaff or dross for gold. We act (collectively) to countermand the flawed choices we (individually) would otherwise make. For example, school attendance is declared to be better than individual decisions would indicate; recreational drug use is declared to be worse.

Where one or more of these conditions prevail, markets cannot be expected to reach their theoretical ideal of maximum welfare from given resources. This starts the conversation about governance, rather than ending it. When markets alone are short of perfect (which is the usual case, not an aberration), intervention may or may not make things better. Governance can be short of perfect, too.[14]

ECONOMIC VERSUS NONECONOMIC CRITERIA. These last two categories of market failure—concerns about distribution, and merit goods— cover a lot of ground, comprising an aggressive and rather awkward foray by economists onto other disciplines' intellectual homelands. Market theory is mostly silent on what constitutes a fair distribution of resources, which is a matter many people find rather germane to governance. And "merit good" is cryptic shorthand for the large category of cases in which people are disinclined to accept economic logic as dispositive. Philosophers, lawyers, politicians, ministers, sociologists, novelists, and just about every person sitting around just about every kitchen table can and does talk about fairness, community, and the public good, generally unimpressed by economists' bid to relegate the conversation to a footnote on the theory of market failure.

These issues define an endlessly contested intellectual and political battleground. The debate over the public role in governing markets has raged for more than two centuries and will quite likely endure for another two centuries. We do not pretend to *settle* any important part of it here. Rather, this book (and the broader Visions of Governance enterprise from which it emerged) explores how evolving markets alter the terms of that debate.

Cases in Point

The first several chapters are "cases in point" of revised concepts, fresh evidence, or altered policies within specific areas of market governance, starting with the largest sector in America's economy: health care. The medical industry has undergone a maelstrom of change over the past two decades, driven in large part by an expanding role for market forces. Joseph Newhouse offers a concise and deeply informed account of ongoing innovation and experimentation with the organizations that structure medical services; the rules that choreograph the relationships among healers, patients, and funders; and the incentives that fuel the system. His chapter both clarifies what we have gained and what we have lost through more market-driven medicine and hints at generalizations that apply beyond health care.

In contrast to health care in some other countries, American medicine was never dominated, in any simple way, by government. Federal entities provide health care for selected subgroups (such as veterans and reservation Indians), pay the bills for a much larger part of the population (the elderly, the disadvantaged), and exercise considerable influence over medical research. State and local governments play roles in Medicaid and other major health programs as well as run their own enterprises (including public hospitals). But most health insurers, and the vast majority of physicians and other providers, have traditionally been private. Until recently, though, health care has occupied a special domain within the private sector. "The market," as we commonly interpret the term, operated in unconventional and circumscribed ways. Health care may never have been government-run, but this large and sensitive sector has been interlaced with multiple mechanisms of governance.

The shape of governance in the medical realm began to shift in the 1980s amid anxiety over the climbing costs of health care. Traditional health insurance—in which patients picked a physician, who prescribed and delivered the services he judged necessary and sent the bill to the insurance carrier of the patient's employer—rapidly lost ground to various models of "managed care." Cost-consciousness and incentives to economize, hallmarks of the market, applied to health care in a far less muted way. At the same time, insurers increasingly competed on the basis of price, transforming themselves from simple administrators to aggressive agents of cost control. Private bureaucrats in insurance companies took on increasingly consequential roles. Government joined in this transformation (albeit unevenly) both by encouraging or accommodating private players' new game plans and by adopting similar changes in public programs.

Newhouse carefully sifts the evidence on what this change has wrought, applying a variety of intellectual lenses. He finds strongly suggestive (if not quite conclusive) signs that managed care and managed competition have indeed reined in medical spending growth. The rate of growth in health-care costs is lower today, by something like 10 to 15 percent, than it would otherwise have been. Yet he suggests we may already have harvested many of the economic advantages to be expected from boosting the market role in health care. Costs will continue to climb at a shallower rate than they would have under the old rules, but he suspects they will not continue to decelerate.

Newhouse makes clear that the market transformation comes as a package. Harvesting the benefits of better cost discipline means accepting the market's downside as well. The traditional structure of American health care featured a complex network of cross-subsidies: some payers, some procedures, and some patients (those able or willing to pay more, or unable to dodge premium prices) bore a disproportionate burden of the system's overall cost (relative to the hypothetical market outcome), while others paid less than the full freight. The increase in price competition has eroded this system, and in so doing places growing strain on established procedures for insuring low-income populations, training new physicians, and safeguarding the solvency of hospitals and other provider institutions.

Objectively, the changes in health-care market governance have been a mixed blessing, Newhouse writes, though the balance on the economic dimension seems clearly positive. Popular perceptions are otherwise. Public opinion polls show that Americans are "profoundly unhappy with the changes." He notes, though, that Canadians—who have undergone a similar campaign of health-care austerity, but *without* the overt shift toward market mechanisms—are just about equally dissatisfied with health-care policy reforms, raising questions about whether the new types of market arrangements or belt-tightening itself accounts for the backlash.

Almost everywhere, almost always, and almost by definition, transportation involves a melange of markets and public policy. Hence the inquiry by José Gómez-Ibáñez and John Meyer into America's experience with transport deregulation affords lessons of special depth and resonance for the larger themes of this book. They offer an overview of the origins of railroad regulation as a response to both the peculiar economics of rail transport and the generic cupidity of rail barons, which brewed political pressures to deliver price relief to Western populations. The form of the response to these pressures—the concrete, and consequential, embodiment of governance—took a novel form. Rather than new responsibilities and offices woven into existing departments, or the establishment of state-owned corporations to take over from markets whose outcomes were objectionable, a new institution was tailor-made for the market forces it confronted: the Interstate Commerce Commission (ICC). Its mandate was to soften the transportation market's harsh edges without stifling the rail industry's development. Most contemporary observers know the ICC from its waning days, when the agency and its mission had drifted apart, but Gómez-Ibáñez and Meyer remind us of the care and creativity that attended the ICC's creation. This institutional innovation became the template for a new category of governance institutions, the "public regulatory commission." Over the next half-century or so, the ICC was joined by siblings or cousins including the Federal Communications Commission, the Federal Maritime Commission, the Federal Energy Regulatory Commission, the Civil Aeronautics Board, and a welter of analogous entities at the state level regulating power and gas utilities, water suppliers, telephone service, and transport.

Three factors eventually inspired a widespread rethinking of the relatively straightforward approach to market governance symbolized by the ICC and its kin. First, as Gómez-Ibáñez and Meyer relate, the Depression, the New Deal, and World War II and its aftermath all layered new or revised goals onto regulatory policy, rendering it more difficult to cleanly accomplish (or even cleanly define) the mission. Second, regulated markets mutated (often in response to regulation itself) more rapidly than the institutions of governance could adapt. Third, the glory days of confident initiatives to edit out the market's less welcome aspects gave way to a spreading realization that "regulating well is technically difficult." Less than a century after the ICC was launched, the conventional wisdom had switched from the view that sensible regulation was pretty easy to the view that it was pretty close to impossible.

Regulatory agencies were seen as "captured" by the interests they were meant to control. Relatively coarse regulatory instruments were either outflanked by growingly sophisticated market mechanisms or channeled market forces in wasteful directions. The last third of the twentieth century was marked by antiregulatory sentiment (in the transport industry as in other sectors, and especially, though not exclusively, in the United States). Some simply called for laissez-faire, surrendering many goals of regulation as ill-conceived or too costly when the price of lost efficiency was fairly reckoned. Others sought suppler, more sophisticated forms of governance, experimenting with new ways to advance regulatory goals—price caps instead of profit ceilings, and franchise arrangements to interject the discipline of competition episodically into industries where it is naturally weak. The efforts to rethink transport regulation over the past twenty years marked the overture to an era of governance amid bigger, better markets.

In their review of railroad deregulation, Gómez-Ibáñez and Meyer describe how radically the market context had changed as the ICC neared its hundredth birthday. The robber barons were dead and gone. The West had been won. Powerful corporations, not scattered homesteaders, were the railroads' main customers. Interstate highways and air freight offered alternatives. The imbalances of options, information, and resources that had brought government to shippers' rescue were far less stark. Private mechanisms (like long-term contracts) that could limit vulnerability without traditional governance had been refined. In 1980, Congress deregulated railroad tariffs and the ICC withered away (though it would linger on for fifteen more years.) And market transactions, operating without the regulatory safety net (or straightjacket, if you prefer) turned out to govern rail rather well. Average rates charged to shippers fell sharply. Rail freight volume surged, reversing what had looked like the railroad's inevitable replacement by truck shipping. Rail profits rose to financially respectable (but by no means extortionate) levels.

While judging rail deregulation a success, the authors take care to avoid depicting a free-market nirvana. Some interests (especially smaller "captive" shippers without realistic options) still do suffer under railroad market power. Waves of mergers have moved the industry even further from the textbook ideal of perfect competition. And the successor to the ICC still has regulatory weapons it can, and does, unsheathe when circumstances warrant.

Airline deregulation followed a more compressed timetable. Within a few years after industry and consumer interests and (especially) academic critics called into question the strictures of the Civil Aeronautics Board,

Alfred Kahn was appointed its head and set about dismantling most of its mission. America's healthy highway system offered alternatives to air travel over short distances, while the potential for new entrants almost anywhere was expected to discipline airline markets even if competition seemed slight at any particular point in time. Between 1976 and 1984, air travel shifted from a highly regulated sector to one in which the market mostly reigned. The outcome remains a work in progress, with many of the same benefits (lower average costs, expanded operations, reductions in obvious waste) and downsides (worrisome trends toward concentration, uneven benefits to customers, and clear losses for some suppliers, especially labor) as were seen in rail deregulation. Also like the case with rail, Gómez-Ibáñez and Meyer see an important government role in the modern air industry. But this role is not defined by rolling back deregulation and reconstructing the 1970s. It is a subtler set of responses—enabling private mechanisms to make the most of deregulation and limit vulnerability; deploying policy levers (such as control over landing slots) to promote competition; and using government's full complement of policy tools, from antitrust to information provision to safety regulation, in order to harness markets to the public interest. In short, they present the recent history of both rail and air transport as valuable test cases for the real (if imperfect) payoff from governmental pragmatism, flexibility, and respect (though not reflexive reverence) for market forces.

Few areas of market governance have attracted as much popular attention, provoked such fervent certainty, or inspired such richly diverse confusion as the deregulation of electricity utilities. William Hogan provides a calm and comprehensive guide to the issue in "Making Markets for Power." Electricity markets, he writes "are made; they don't just happen." New technologies for generating, transmitting, and pricing power, combined with a broader openness to market arrangements, have expanded the palette of possibilities for the electricity industry. Reopening established arrangements forces the issue of how to build a market. The results of experimentation with power markets have been richly instructive (if not always pretty), and Hogan harvests the lessons.

Without slighting the enabling factor of new technologies, Hogan casts the transformation of power supply as the replacement of one "big idea"— closely held control over vital infrastructure, whether by government agencies or regulated monopolies—with another. He underscores the temporal contingency of any good idea, a theme that arises repeatedly in this volume. In its time, "this old big idea delivered on its promise. . . . the miracle born of Edison became a necessity that we took for granted." But as the downside of close control became clearer, in electricity as elsewhere, a new "big idea" took hold: enlarge the role of markets, while focusing government's attention on tasks where markets fail. "This is easier said than done," Hogan notes. In particular, governing well in a more market-driven power system—perhaps counterintuitively—requires a finer-grained and more sophisticated understanding of the industry's details than does classic regulation. As market enthusiasts examined the power system, they learned that "it was not enough that all the gears would be turning. The gears also had to mesh, or the system would not work." Governing a market-based electricity system turns out to be a great deal harder than regulating monopolies, and Hogan finds that "we were unprepared for this new challenge of governance."

Making markets in electricity involves two special complications. One is the economic and technological interdependence of far-flung power grids. The other is the imperative (imposed by basic laws of physics) for supply and demand to be brought into balance—not in long-run equilibrium, but at every moment. It has proven surprisingly difficult for market architects to structure a system that "simultaneously respects the engineering reality and supports the market objectives." This is in part because of the novelty of the task, though the United Kingdom (and even earlier, Chile) cracked the basic problem in the first wave of reform. Hogan diagnoses the larger cause as ideological dissonance: the coordination required by blunt technical imperatives can't possibly be at the heart of a competitive market, can it?

This combination of technological intricacy and conceptual heterodoxy means that making markets for power presents ample opportunities for mistakes, and innovators have seized those opportunities. Hogan reviews some of these, including the "monstrous caricature of a market" in California that came to dominate popular thinking about electricity deregulation. The California meltdown was rooted in sloppy analysis, Hogan explains, yielding a system design whose failure was predictable and indeed predicted (though not, he concedes, in all its ghastly magnitude).

In a significant side note, Hogan highlights a safety net for this period of trial and error: the expertise and professional culture of the technical workers who run power systems. Echoing an old but recently neglected theme, he observes that the engineers' commitment to *making things work*—even when this requires editing or vetoing price signals—is a crucial and (he fears) temporary buttress for emerging electricity markets.[15]

Hogan concludes with a fundamental lesson drawn from the power market evidence but of broader relevance to the themes of this book. "Market efficiency" is broadly revered as an abstraction but in real-world markets has a limited constituency—especially among suppliers. Policy entrepreneurs may lobby for efficient markets, but business entrepreneurs (predictably and understandably) clamor for the kinds of *in*efficiencies that promise rich profits. Among the hardest challenges for market-makers is maintaining the discipline to support competition amid pressures to accommodate competitors. Good governance requires the wit to discern the ideal, amid the obscuring clutter of details surrounding any specific policy change, and the discipline to uphold it.

Experiments and Puzzles

Primary and secondary education in the United States has been an enclave of collectivism largely insulated from the market. Conventional public schools have long educated the majority of America's children. Private school attendance plummeted with the common-school movement of the mid-1800s and accounted for a bit more than 10 percent of students through most of the past half-century. Teachers and other education workers now form by far the largest category of government employees. (The number of government workers involved in education inched past the ranks of the armed services in the early 1960s, and educators now outnumber warriors by something approaching five to one.)[16] Any substantial incursion of market forces into this redoubt of collectivism is thus both consequential and controversial. Paul Peterson offers a guide to the landmarks on this changing terrain in "Choice and Competition in K–12 Education."

Marketlike arrangements in the education worlds are well developed, though sometimes not recognized as such. Some families, of course, have always opted out of the public school system and sent their children to religious or (far less commonly) secular private schools. But public education includes a substantial and growing degree of customer choice as well. Peterson notes the ubiquitous, albeit indirect, exercise of educational purchasing power as families choose to live where the schools are good. The large or dominant role of local finance in most states means that the richer the town, by and large, the better the school. Many parents' instinct to shop among towns and districts in search of the best schools they can afford is too familiar to gain much notice but puts an (arguably inappropriate) element of the market at the heart of American education.

Since the late 1960s, "magnet schools" and other forms of choice within or across districts have allowed at least some students in at least some areas to reach beyond the nearest public school without abandoning public education. The explosive growth of the charter school movement since its start in the early 1990s, meanwhile, has both widened the range of choice and stretched the definition of the "public" school. So the market has a well-established beachhead in the homeland of collective choice and public delivery. There are some signs of an imminent breakout. Two trends have heightened both the intellectual richness and the political voltage of the market's role in K–12 education. One is the extension of choice and competition to the "supply side" of the equation—the growing role of new entrants, including for-profit firms and (in the home-schooling movement) families themselves as suppliers of educational services. The other is the multifront campaign to amplify individual choice and challenge the common-school tradition through vouchers or tax preferences for private schools.

The for-profit education industry has become a growing presence on the school scene (and, intermittently, Wall Street's darling) as firms large and small emerge or enlarge to provide services ranging from special-education curricula to food services to the management of entire schools or school districts. Between the early 1980s and the early 1990s the majority of states enacted laws allowing parents to opt out of public schools and teach their children at home. Two states have already enacted tax-law provisions that let funds flow to private schools at the public fisc's expense; comparable arrangements have been proposed in many other states and at the federal level, with varying odds of success. Three jurisdictions—two large cities and the state of Florida—have launched hotly controversial and fiercely challenged experiments with tax-financed private school vouchers. Privately financed voucher programs and proposals in other communities probe the boundaries of state and market in this fundamental function.

Two big questions are roiling the American conversation over education. First, do the market mechanisms that serve so well in the fast-food and automobile industries promise similar boons for education? Would competition among providers, disciplined by consumer choice, produce a desirable diversity of educational offerings, accelerated innovation, effective and accountable management, efficient operations, and superior outcomes? Or is there something special about education—the uneven sophistication of consumers, the long-term and diffuse payoff from the enterprise, the multiplicity of factors other than school performance determining educational outcomes—that undercuts the story of efficiency through choice and competition? Second, what would be the broader consequences of embracing the market on the "demand side" of education and diluting the common-school tradition? Would an erosion of Americans' sense of community and shared stakes in key institutions outweigh the gains from schools better tailored to parents' preferences?

Neither question is even close to settled. The evidence is accumulating; the arguments are evolving. Paul Peterson, while making no disingenuous claims to neutrality, walks us through the controversies these two questions summon and implicitly frames a third: What lessons can we draw from educational choice and competition for the broader debate over governance in an era of ascendant markets?

The education puzzle involves potentially revising the governance of a long-established and deeply familiar function in order to better exploit market options. Jean Camp examines the other end of the policy-issue life cycle: drafting a blueprint for the governance of economic *terra incognita*. The Internet offers up classic concepts in strange new guises and poses urgent challenges for the most rudimentary aspect of market governance—defining "property" and drawing up the initial rules of the game. We may one day manage to cobble together an architecture for Internet governance with the right blend of efficiency incentives, protections for free speech, motives to innovate, and popular accountability. But so far, Camp fears, we are making a hash of it. Policy, like engineering, is "invisible when successfully and gracefully designed, and dramatically visible during failure." An engineer herself, Camp discerns some coming drama on the policy front.

The Internet "has no 'nature.' It is entirely constructed." Its construction is a melange of enterprise and policy, and looming policy choices may exercise great leverage over the trajectory of the Internet's development. The Internet originally took form in a setting of cheerful anarchy or (more precisely) a highly informal governance regime in which the engineering ethos prevailed. Technical beauty was a central desideratum; professional reputation was a major motivator. But many of the Internet's midwives also endorsed a vision of what Camp terms "democratic pluralism," embodied in design specifications promoting "content neutrality, consumer voice, and synchronous information flow." In the current, crucial era of market-making, in which authoritative rules replace conventions backed by informal norms, she fears these features (and the values they advance) are in jeopardy. She examines emerging design features in three areas: code, content, and conduit.

Code is a generic term for the family of languages permitting communication among machines, and between machines and humans. If code were considered simply "speech," established copyright law might settle its governance. If it were clearly a "machine," patents might do the trick. But code is in some ways both, Camp writes, and in some ways neither. Unlike text, pivotal pieces of code may have ambiguous parentage and hybrid authorship. Unlike machinery, "possession" of code is a fuzzy concept on the technical plane, even if legal decrees can clarify it. Camp charges that our dim understanding of code's nature (in a setting of potent commercial imperatives) is luring us toward an ill-considered system for defining property that "allows an excessive fencing off of the commons."

A significant plank in the framework of this emerging market, the Digital Millennium Copyright Act, meant to "enable a market," has instead allowed content producers to "control who uses the product, in what conditions, under what terms, and on what equipment." And what Camp views as the misguided application of the ancient concept of "chattel" to computer networks "creates property rights that allow network owners to reject content."

On conduit—the physical pathways along which data flow—Camp charges that "the banner of progressive 'un-regulation'" effectively surrenders the shaping of the still-plastic Internet to the most insistent commercial interests, "encouraging the creation of closed broadcast-style networks." Camp's passionate sense of the Internet's prodigious potential fuels her alarm over what she sees as hasty, underanalyzed, and generally reactive market-making. Her protest is, at base, an engineer's lament about flawed design, the awkward application of ill-fitting governance concepts that "will prevent the evolution of an Internet that maintains democratic principles in design." Realizing the Internet's immanent promise, by contrast, will "require a government that sees itself as the creator, not the handmaiden, of markets."

Public provisions to ensure the safety of consumer bank deposits offer an intriguing example of a disjuncture between rapidly evolving markets and comparatively slow and incremental legislative change. Only risk lovers or rash ideologues would challenge the logic of federal deposit insurance in the setting where it started. As economic foundations trembled in the 1930s, Americans hesitated to entrust their savings to banks, owing to the entirely rational, empirically validated fear that the bank might not be able to give them their money back when they asked for it. This was not a failure of good faith on the banks' part, but an upward spiral in economic complexity that rendered banks incapable of performing their accustomed alchemy of transforming safe, always-available deposits into risky, long-term investment capital. Nearly 9,000 American banks shut their doors between 1929 and 1933. The breakdown had already damaged the economy and threatened far worse. Though it is imaginable, perhaps, that the markets of the 1930s could have eventually engineered a remedy, even free-market fundamentalists would concede no such rescue was on the horizon. The Roosevelt administration designed a system of defense-in-depth for depositors' funds, organized around mandatory federal bank insurance covering most obligations of commercial banks and other savings institutions.

The improvised intervention was almost indisputably a good thing for America. And the dismissive caricature of policy on autopilot is not quite consistent with the facts. Federal deposit insurance has been continually, and for the most part intelligently, refined over the decades in response to new evidence, new ideas, and new market possibilities. Yet few are convinced—indeed, few have even entertained the possibility—that financial markets have improved enough to make deposit insurance superfluous. Akash Deep and Guido Schaefer raise the question: Could it be time to take off the training wheels?

There are two main thrusts to their inquiry. First, they ask whether conventional banks still form the foundation of American finance, as they did when deposit insurance was put in place. Are solid banks still the sine qua non, or has the emergence of new financial instruments and institutions undercut the predicate for federal deposit insurance—that bank deposits are the fountainhead of capital formation? Their second question is separable, and the answer would matter even if secure bank deposits remained an urgent concern. Is mandatory government insurance the best way to keep deposits safe, or have several decades of refinement in financial markets produced tools subtle enough and strong enough to ensure security through market means?

Why are these questions interesting? There is no groundswell of grassroots demand for revisiting deposit insurance. Banks seldom protest the requirement; consumers seem content to take the issue as settled. If deposit insurance isn't broken, why fix it? Deep and Schaefer suggest several reasons for suspecting quiet wastefulness in the status quo. Federal deposit insurance uses up real resources. The most obvious, perhaps, is the mundane expense of running and doing business with the Federal Deposit

Insurance Corporation (FDIC), but this may be the least important. (Any alternative would have such costs, too.) There are subtler but more weighty reasons for hopeful exploration into the possibility that the time for more market-driven deposit security is at hand.

Unless federal insurance is fine-tuned to fully reflect each bank's degree of risk, for example, banks are tempted to indulge in grand or petty reck-lessness, since the bank gains the profit edge from extra risk but diffuses the downside throughout the system. Both theory and evidence suggest that the FDIC hesitates to be as tough on banks, when toughness is required, as it would be on hypothetical (in the United States) profit-driven deposit insurers. And it seems silly to free depositors from *any* reason to pay atten-tion to the good sense and solidity of the institutions that steward their sav-ings. Although these concerns do not make the case against the current sys-tem, they hint at the potential merits of modernizing the system should market-geared updating turn out to be workable.

A "liquidity shortfall"—the problem to which deposit insurance is the solution—happens when depositors can demand (right away) more money from their bank than the bank can demand (right away) from its borrow-ers. As the financial system has matured, the scale and urgency of this prob-lem appear to have receded. Deep and Schaefer find ample evidence that banks, as a class, are no longer as preeminent as they once were within the financial system. Commercial banks account for a falling share of credit extended, while bank deposits form a sharply lower proportion of house-holds' assets. Viewed from the banks' perspective, deposits account for a declining fraction of total bank liabilities, and classic "demand deposits" have fallen even faster (in relative terms) as consumers have learned to accept some limits on access to their funds in exchange for higher returns. Loans have held fairly steady as a share of banks' assets. But these loans are far more likely to be liquid (or potentially liquid) because tactics like "secu-ritization" and repurchase agreements have proliferated over recent decades.

A careful (though preliminary) analysis of banks' contemporary expo-sure to liquidity shortfalls leads Deep and Schaefer to a startling conclu-sion: banks seem plenty liquid. Even in the unlikely event that depositors everywhere rushed to pull out their money; even invoking pessimistic assumptions about banks' ability to turn assets into cash to satisfy their depositors; and even ignoring deposit insurance altogether, the data suggest that very, very few banks are vulnerable to a run. It appears that only an improbable financial cataclysm would stress the system to the breaking point—a remarkable finding, if it holds up under more detailed scrutiny, and all the more remarkable because banks have had very little incentive to seek stability. Deposit insurance spares banks from the downside of extra risk and denies them most of the benefit from extra safety.

Have growingly sophisticated markets made it possible for America's banks and America's savers to dispense with governmental protection for deposits? Deep and Schaefer do not claim to have settled the issue. But they plausibly air the possibility, and they map the path for testing it.

The "free marketplace of ideas" is at once a venerated American tradition and, for some, a parable of the greatest possible collective good emerging from the least possible collective control. In "The Market for Truth," Frederick Schauer questions the reach of the parable while insightfully (and iconoclastically) examining the tradition. His point of departure is Oliver Wendell Holmes's famous dictum that "the best test of truth is the power of the thought to get itself accepted in the competition of the market." Interpreted aggressively, this simply defines the truth as whatever the peddler of some proposition can sell to the public (or some meaningful segment of the public). Schauer doesn't buy it—at least not the strong version of Holmes's dictum. The evidence of the marketplace shows, for example, that a great many people find truth in astrology. Yet "a panoply of ways of determining truth other than that of defining truth in terms of a market output" establish that "astrology is bunk."

But perhaps astrology exemplifies the special case of propositions amenable to some conclusive test separable from popular credence. Might market success be the best test of truth for that large class of assertions where science is short of dispositive—propositions that are either strictly normative or alloys of the normative and the empirical? Examples might include the overall justice of the minimum wage, the comparative merits of "mutually assured destruction" versus missile defense, and the legitimacy of requiring workers to save for retirement via Social Security.

One element to be considered, at least in a democracy, is the notion that respect for popular opinion can be valuable on its own, even when popular opinion happens to be wrong. So unless the right resolution of a public choice turns almost wholly on matters of fact, "when the issue is policy the claims of democracy and the claims of epistemology converge, even if on other issues they may at times diverge."

A related line of logic comes into play when the "truth" to be discovered is not some fact about the state of the world but rather an accurate calibration of citizens' preferences as they pertain to collective choices. Pro-life or pro-choice? Legalize gay marriage or ban it? The strong suit of market-style arrangements for divining the truth—the market's facility at registering preferences—matters most "in areas in which preferences are all there is."

There may well be a preserve harboring categories of truth that markets can best discern, but Schauer tracks Holmes onto more challenging terrain. Efficient market theory holds that the market has a wisdom its constituent players individually lack. A commodities exchange transforms the cacophonous bellowing of imperfectly informed traders into the right price for wheat. The scramble of competing innovators (not all paragons of insight or even common sense) propels technological progress. By analogy, even where "there are indeed truths out there to be found," not merely matters of preference or opinion, one could argue that "an unrestricted marketplace of ideas is the most reliable method for finding them."

But remember the rigorous assumptions embedded in market theory, Schauer cautions, and reflect that "implicit in modern marketing theory is that catchy music, clever dialogue, and Michael Jordan as an endorser may be far more important than the truth of a proposition in getting the public to accept it." The relationship between what emerges as credible from a market process and "the truth," he suggests, is "contingent, empirical, and possibly less reliable than has often been assumed."

Schauer ends by raising the possibility that speech might not be all that special after all. If we think of the "marketplace of ideas" as no metaphor but just one case of market organization, the conversation shifts from unreflective reverence to pragmatic assessment of the market's soundness. For some, the thrust of that conversation will be that "the same concerns for market failure, resource disparity, and capture . . . that pervade our thinking about markets should increasingly pervade our thinking about the marketplace of ideas." And for others, it will be that "the same libertarian assumptions that we have traditionally applied to the marketplace of ideas ought also to be applied to the market for goods and services." He thus strikes a heterodox note, by the American catechism, while ending his essay on an even larger theme than launched it.

Following Schauer's reflections on truth, Anna Greenberg takes up politics. Should we think of American politics as a "market"? The metaphor linking democracy to the market is an old one, and in some ways undeniably apt. Individuals signal their preferences by how they use their endowments—dollars in the one case, votes in the other. Rivals compete, innovate, and advertise to win individuals' favor. But at what point does the equation of politics with the market transcend metaphor and become simple description? Has the era of the permanent campaign—intensely professionalized, fragmented, and money-driven—taken us past that point? Greenberg poses this question and addresses it with appropriate caution and a wealth of historical perspective.

It is easy to overstate the novelty of marketlike politics, she reminds us, citing instances of mercenary politics in America's past far starker than those we see today—captive partisan newspapers, pervasive patronage, outright vote-buying. The advertising industry and party politics evolved in tandem, and the first president to turn to Madison Avenue for image-buffing television spots was not Bill Clinton or Ronald Reagan but Dwight D. Eisenhower. But has the accumulation of changes in degree led to a change in kind? Is turn-of-the-century politics markedly more marketlike than in the recent past? Greenberg examines several seemingly separate trends to cast light on the possible marketization of American politics.

Money may have always been the mother's milk of politics, but its flow has demonstrably freshened. Greenberg reviews trends that are no secret but remarkable nonetheless: the twentyfold increase in political action committee contributions since the early 1970s; average 2000 campaign spending of around $650,000 per House race and $5.5 million per Senate race; the $300 million spent by candidates in the 2000 presidential race; and the nearly uncontrolled rise in soft money contributions and independent advocacy efforts by business, labor, and other groups. All told, politics in 2000 was fueled by an estimated $3 billion.

Other developments both encourage the growing role of money in politics and amplify its impact. The new technologies that transform markets in other domains—ubiquitous telephones and television; cheap, powerful computers; the Internet—offer increasingly good substitutes for shoe leather and grass-roots political activism in assessing citizens' priorities and pitching campaign messages. Although there have long been full-time, mercenary political operatives, the maturation of a professional political industry seems like something new; the number of political consultants has tripled in a decade, and there are now around 3,000 political consulting firms.

The growing significance of ballot initiatives and voter referendums—pioneered in California but now a national phenomenon—both shifts politics into a market-style arena and widens the scope for money, technology, and professionalized politics. Commercialized polling, advertising, and strategy consulting, constants in modern politics, play an even larger role in political battles waged through referendum. For-profit firms forage for signatures, tightening the nexus between markets and politics. And wealthy individuals can launch policy initiatives that simply bypass stodgy old legislatures.

So does the cumulative effect of these developments mean that the market now reigns over American politics? Greenberg hesitates to declare any sweeping transformation but professes considerable concern that "the infusion of big money into electoral politics [and] ballot initiatives, and . . . the transformation of grassroots lobbying into a highly professional enterprise" are altering politics for the worse. The current dosage of market principles and practice "probably limits the diversity of voices in our political debate and inhibits greater citizen engagement."

Governing Well When Markets Rule

The press and the public have grown fascinated with the emergence of a "new economy" characterized by rapid technical change, skill-intensive production, unconventional organizational styles, and (at least some of the time, for some of the companies) glittering financial success. Has a "new politics" evolved in parallel—a different style of political action undertaken by and in the interests of new-economy market players? Political scientist David Hart examines the political playbooks of new-economy firms and ponders the implications for good governance.

Hart starts from the classic pluralist premise that "political power in the United States is divided . . . among a variety of institutions and actors," including politicians, elected officials, civil servants, and a host of interest groups of which business is only one, that "jostle for control of governmental authority and resources. Any emerging industry takes its place on an already crowded stage." Another key premise is that efforts to gain or use political power are largely overt and observable in the form of lobbying, campaign contributions, institutional infrastructure, and the like. And a third is that new-economy actors, like old-economy actors, are less than omniscient about where their interests lie and how to advance them.

Outlining a political science analogue to Schumpeter's economics of "creative destruction," Hart describes both the "offensive" political processes employed by disruptive economic newcomers and the "defensive" strategies of those whose interests are imperiled by change. Some firms are "born political," emerging in economic terrain with clear governmental landmarks and entrenched interests. (At the computer industry's dawn the government was the biggest customer for the costly, massive machines, and IBM learned its political moves early on.) Others only gradually learn in which direction a political offensive should advance. (Not until they became major employers of scarce technical labor did high-tech manufacturers discover their stakes in looser immigration rules.) Defensive strategies are even more diverse, not least because defenders tend to widen the political front whenever they hold weak ground, enlisting additional allies or invoking new classes of arguments to fend off threats to their interests. (For example, IBM's antagonists sought to hobble the dominant player by changing procurement rules, then by encouraging antitrust action.)

Employing these conceptual lenses and deep pools of fresh data, Hart examines how high-technology firms have forged and wielded five tools of political influence—corporate representation in the capital, trade associations, lobbying, political contributions, and congressional testimony. Weaving a tapestry of aggregate trends and telling anecdotes, he depicts the core features of high-technology firms as political actors. The political maneuvers of new-economy actors, Hart concludes, are complex, consequential, richly diverse, sometimes astute and sometimes ham-handed, frequently creative in their details—but in essence nothing new. Far from marking a sharp break with the politics of the past, the efforts of high-technology firms to shape policy to their liking are "as old as the marriage of capitalism and democracy that has distinguished the United States since its founding."

Viktor Mayer-Schönberger takes a finer-grained look at a narrow but vital slice of new-economy governance: information law. The law is the working edge of conventional market governance. By ensuring the broader community's aid in enforcing valid obligations, the law serves as a supplement to simple trust or personal leverage to make markets possible. Mayer-Schönberger identifies some special challenges that arise when *information* figures centrally in exchange.

First, he poses what he terms the "transactional challenge" to traditional law. It seems at first blush that the information revolution should systematically improve the mechanics of exchange. But Mayer-Schönberger argues it may usher in new problems with transaction costs. Electronic commerce multiplies the number of transactions between strangers, unbound by ties of trust and often under separate legal regimes. Even if they aggregate to staggering sums, each individual transaction may be of low value relative to the cost of conventional legal protection: "Having lawyers on both sides refine draft after draft of a contract to cover all possible options may be economical for a transaction involving a super-tanker full of crude oil, but is certainly not for an order of three paperback books from Amazon.com." The primacy of law as the linchpin of market governance thus seems imperiled. Resourceful transactors can develop alternatives, such as guarantees and remedies "governed" by credit card companies, or the binding dispute resolution process of the Internet Corporation for Assigned Names and Numbers (ICANN), the nongovernmental entity that regulates key features of the Internet. At the same time, Mayer-Schönberger suggests the law may well evolve to overcome the transactional challenge—by more systematic harmonization across borders to minimize conflicts, for example, or through tougher penalties to deter bad faith even with imperfect enforcement.

He next takes up the "structural challenge," citing work by Lawrence Lessig. In parts of the information economy, he suggests, "governance" is exercised neither formally through law nor informally through the market, but is embodied in the very structure of technology. E-mail services can be structured (and have been) to automatically filter out messages that fit the profile of junk—or that originate with a competing service. According to Mayer-Schönberger, "'Code is law' is the soundbite of a structural challenge to the traditional system of governance." He reviews a range of possible responses, some classically governmental, some as unconventional as the challenge itself.

The third challenge is substantive, dealing not with the information revolution's reshaping of market governance but with the governance of markets for information itself. Mayer-Schönberger's speculation from a lawyer's perspective on how to build a legal system robust and subtle enough to deal with information as a *product* parallels Jean Camp's engineer's perspective on the puzzles of defining rights to this increasingly important form of property. But he is rather more sanguine about the prospects for coming to terms with the challenge. The very information revolution that so sorely stresses governance, he suggests, may offer tools (such as digital watermarks, encryption, and sophisticated transaction and access control systems) that resurrect the relevance of classic legal concepts in this strange new world. Even if we can only dimly discern the possible shape of such solutions, Mayer-Schönberger expresses cautious confidence that with diligence, discipline, and creativity we can come to terms with the challenge of good governance in the information age.

The wary optimism of Mayer-Schönberger's conclusion is an appropriate segue to the penultimate essay. John Donahue and Richard Zeckhauser's chapter stresses both the perilous novelty of many policy challenges posed by bigger, better markets and the reasonable prospect that we will prove able to think our way through them. They do not discount the difficulties: "Intervening in fast-changing markets is akin to air-brushing a moving picture or editing an unfinished story. How can the agents of governance lower the odds of failure—of acting needlessly, or acting clumsily, or standing idly by while untrammeled markets wreak preventable damage—in such a setting?" They propose some guidelines that hinge on the watchword "diagnosis before therapy." By this they mean that "an interval of assessment and analysis . . . is more apt to improve policy today than in earlier eras when markets were less fluid, policy problems were more stable, and correct solutions had a longer shelf life." They concede that this calls for an unaccustomed and perhaps unnatural humility on the part of academics, pundits, and public officials and puts a similar strain on the public's patience. But the benefit from custom tailoring policy to fit emerging challenges (instead of grabbing solutions off the rack) increasingly warrants the wait.

"Rapidly changing markets strengthen the case for diagnosis before therapy in two ways," they contend, "both by tending to raise the payoff to incremental evidence and analysis, and (less obviously) by tending to reduce the cost of delay for diagnosis." To illustrate the trend of faster market change, they point to the accelerating pace of turnover in the Fortune 500 in the later decades of the previous century and to stepped-up turmoil in the ranking of top firms by the broader measure of market capitalization. Though they grant that this turn-of-the-millennium economic turbulence "may turn out to be a temporary phase—a jagged ridge connecting two placid mesas of relative stability," it strengthens the case for both creativity and caution in market governance. In such a setting it becomes more likely that "premature prescriptions will turn out to be misdirected" and that "underanalyzed interventions warp the trajectory of technological development and hobble future policy."

More subtly, they suggest, changing markets lower the cost of "diagnosis before therapy." Improvements in the mechanics of data gathering and processing make good analysis easier. Continuous economic change means adjustments to ill-fitting policies are less likely than in the past to disrupt a happily stable status quo. Perhaps most important is the prospect that market turmoil creates breathing room for well-considered governance.

Donahue and Zeckhauser note that "when economic interests are well-defined, concentrated, and self-aware, the option to intervene may bear a 'use it or lose it' label. Government must move with dispatch to counter a perceived clash between market dynamics and the public interest, even if the perception is murky, lest delay for diagnosis give special pleaders time to dominate the political terrain." The age of bigger, better markets, by contrast, features a political environment that is relatively complex, fragmented, and unstable. They point to the shift from industry associations to individual firms as the biggest contributors to political campaigns: "A sufficient degree of continuity in market shares and consensus on policy agendas, for a sufficiently long period, allows firms to overcome collective-action problems and coordinate their political activities through associations. When market segments blur, hierarchies topple, and interests splinter, conversely, the emphasis tips toward 'every firm for itself.'" This can lower the risk that special interests will entrench themselves while the agents of governance ponder how best to advance the public good.

Their call for careful diagnosis, they stress, is not "a backdoor counsel of conservatism" but rather underscores the virtues of "initial caution and ongoing intellectual diligence when constructing what eventually may turn out to be highly aggressive interventions." Heightened economic fluidity "means that objectionable market outcomes are apt to be imperfectly understood at any one point in time and likely to become less objectionable, or objectionable in different ways. Evidence and analysis are becoming more valuable, as is flexibility in the strategy and tactics of intervention." So a proper appreciation of government's role when markets rule is "likely to involve an unaccustomed, and doubtless uncomfortable, quotient of delay as evidence accumulates, cause and effect become better understood, and the mists of uncertainty dissipate."

In "The Market versus the Forum," Mark Moore strikes a deeper cautionary theme, richly developing a vital subtext touched upon (or conspicuously skirted) in many of these essays. What are the implications of bigger, better markets for governance broadly defined as a community's capacity to organize collective life in ways that promote its members' happiness? Do ascendant markets, in the aggregate, exact a steeper, subtler price than an issue-by-issue assessment reveals? Moore worries that even a sophisticated, eyes-open, scrupulously well analyzed embrace of the market invites the atrophy of our capacity for other kinds of collective action. Other authors implicitly view civic-mindedness and the capacity for collective deliberation as rare commodities to be preserved for the most crucial uses. Whenever better markets allow us to economize on these precious assets, according to this view, the substitution is all to the good. Moore proceeds from a different implicit analogy: Civic-mindedness is not an exhaustible stock to be husbanded, but more like a muscle that grows stronger with use and withers with neglect.

The refinement and extension of market mechanisms, he warns, tempt us to turn to markets for a growing extent of functions once reserved to the "forum" of politics, civil society, or the family—functions for which market arrangements, even at their glittering best, are fundamentally unsuited. At one level, citizens in an era of bigger, better markets are like the cook who acquires a magnificent new grill and enthusiastically learns to barbecue everything from hors d'oeuvres to baby food, instead of attending to the rest of the kitchen. But Moore's misgivings run even deeper than the potential atrophy of traditional habits of collective action. Improvements in markets and their spreading reach, he suggests, both flow from and feed the development of a "market ideology" that drains life and legitimacy from the very idea of common action outside the market. This ideology "changes the way individuals think about what they should value as individuals, how they might combine together to produce valuable social results, and how lines ought to be drawn in society between the private and the public, the individual and the collective, and the voluntary and the obligatory."

This occurs, Moore contends, by the alteration of values and preferences wrought by the market's very triumph on the material front, by its pervasive emphasis on the individual at the expense of the collective, and through the conceptual foundations of market theory that "undermin[e] confidence in the capacity of a group of individuals to form and achieve a collective purpose." In contrast to the crisp precision of market exchange, alternative models of cooperation involving public deliberation over shared goals "and an acknowledgment of shared responsibilities for achieving those goals, which are then pursued as a point of honor and social commitment, are deemed insufficiently reliable, too vulnerable to exploitation, and too threatening to individual liberty."

Moore challenges the internal consistency of this "market ideology" and probes the dynamic of its encroachment into civic and political life. In principle, the market and the forum can coexist. Harvesting the benefits of ascendant markets may not, as a logical entailment, require surrendering our mastery of political choice, civic deliberation, or the sense of a community as something beyond the plural of "individual." But as the market concept mutates from a tool to an ideology, Moore fears, this is precisely what occurs. If so—and even if markets become big to the point of all-encompassing, and better to the point of utter perfection—this loss puts a staggering price on the blessings the market can bestow, and any such prospect poses an intimidating challenge for governance.

The apotheosis of the market that some celebrate and others fear, to be sure, may be prematurely announced. To the extent that technology is at the root of the broad changes examined here, the refinement of markets may indeed be a long-term secular trend, though the details of that trend's unfolding will surely defy our capacity for prediction. To the extent that popular opinion and ideological fashion are driving the phenomenon, the balance between markets and politics may continue to oscillate cyclically.

Amid the richness of evidence, insights, and points of informed speculation assembled in these essays, a sobering theme can be seen. Whatever package of values and priorities one may bring to the debate over governance amid ascendant markets, it seems clear that the conversation has become more complex. Many defining episodes of policy change in the twentieth century—the Progressive Era, the New Deal, the Great Society, the Reagan revolution—could be organized, intellectually and politically, along relatively clean lines. Which goals do you cherish more? Which data do you see as sound? Which predictions are persuasive in light of past trends? Which examples seem compellingly general, and which can be discounted as sterile idiosyncrasies? Even: Which side are you on?

We may look back on our decades of obsession with comfortably familiar classes of "market failure" as an easy era for defining government's mission. Bigger, better markets promise to push us onto a new and uncharted path, where the economic footing is less secure and where other conceptual lanterns must be lit if we hope to clarify the hard questions about the public agenda.

Notes

1. Susan Strange, *The Retreat of the State* (Cambridge University Press, 1996), p. 121.

2. Council of Economic Advisers, *Economic Report of the President 2000*, tables B-4 and B-40 (GPO); 2000 GDP growth from Bureau of Economic Analysis news release, January 31, 2000.

3. Jeffrey Frankel, "Globalization of the Economy," in Joseph S. Nye Jr. and John D. Donahue, eds., *Governance in a Globalizing World* (Cambridge, Mass., and Washington: Visions of Governance/Brookings, 2000).

4. These trends are described in Robert B. Reich, *The Future of Success* (Alfred A. Knopf, 2001), pp. 111–12.

5. "Policing for Profit," *Economist*, April 19, 1997, pp. 21–24.

6. "Untangling e-conomics," *Economist* Survey on the New Economy, September 23, 2000, p. 8.

7. Danny Hakim, "On Wall Street, More Investors Push Social Goals," *New York Times*, February 11, 2001.

8. Karl Polanyi, *The Great Transformation: The Political and Economic Origins of Our Time* (Rinehart, 1944; Boston: Beacon Press, 1957).

9. The National Opinion Research Center discerned a "plateau" of mildly interventionist sentiment in the United States for much of the second half of the twentieth century. See Tom W. Smith, "Liberal and Conservative Trends in the United States since World War II," Report 63 (National Opinion Research Center, University of Chicago, 1989).

10. *Retro-Politics: The Political Typology 3.0*, Pew Research Center for the People and the Press, 1999, reported at http://www.people-press.org/typo99sec2.htm.

11. Gallup Organization, Confidence in Institutions, June 2000 survey and trends, reported at http://www.gallup.com/poll/indicators/indconfidence.asp.

12. See Joseph Nye Jr., Philip D. Zelikow, and David C. King, *Why People Don't Trust Government* (Harvard University Press, 1997).

13. Joseph E. Stiglitz, *Economics of the Public Sector* (Norton, 1988), pp. 71–83.

14. See Charles Wolf Jr., *Markets or Governments: Choosing between Imperfect Alternatives* (MIT Press, 1988).

15. Thorstein Veblen, *The Engineers and the Price System* (Viking, 1936).

16. As of 1998, state and local education workers—without counting federal or nongovernmental educators—accounted for about 6 percent of American employment, while uniformed military personnel accounted for 1.3 percent. U.S. Department of Commerce National Income and Product Accounts, table 6.5B, "Full-Time Equivalent Employees by Industry," *Survey of Current Business*, various issues.

PART I

Bigger, Better Markets— Cases in Point

2

JOSEPH P. NEWHOUSE

Lessons from the Medical Marketplace

OVER THE PAST two decades several countries have attempted to increase the role of markets in the medical care sector. The changes have generally taken the form of either moving away from administratively set prices or allowing prices a greater role in resource allocation. In the United States managed competition is well known, but countries as diverse as the Netherlands, Switzerland, Great Britain, Germany, and Israel have all attempted reforms of various sorts. The result has been a continuing worldwide debate about the role of the market in health care delivery. In this essay I attempt to take some stock of what has been learned and not learned thus far from the American experience. I focus on the United States, because that is what I know best and because data are more readily available than they are for other countries. I make no effort, however, to attempt a comprehensive answer, even for the United States.

I make the following points:

—There is a variety of somewhat soft evidence that the explosive growth in managed care and managed competition has reduced medical spending. My rough estimate of the savings, using several different methods of calculating them, is on the order of 10 to 15 percent.

—It is too soon to judge the effect of managed competition on the steady-state rate of increase in medical costs, but the reduction in the annual rate of growth of health care costs is probably transitory; in other words, the 10 to 15 percent savings are likely to be one-time-only savings.

—The system of cross-subsidization of the uninsured in the United States has been somewhat undone by the increase in price competition, placing more stress on the publicly financed direct delivery system or safety net.

—Managed care—which is not the same as managed competition— could in principle improve the quality of care, but most of the evidence to date suggest that its effects on quality of care have been mixed and mostly minimal.

—American consumers, judging by opinion polls, are profoundly unhappy with the changes in their health care financing system. I interpret this partly as a reaction to "paradise lost" and partly as a reaction to the perceived loss of some control over the services patients receive. To provide some perspective, however, Canadians, who have neither managed care nor managed competition but have also experienced tighter budgets, have comparable levels of unhappiness with their health care system.

What Have Been the Changes?

In the United States two principal changes in health care financing have occurred in the past two decades. First, purchasers have become more sensitive to the price of care. The typical private insurance plan of the 1950s through the early 1980s was provided through the place of employment. It was an indemnity plan, meaning that it reimbursed any medically necessary service a physician ordered that was covered by the contract.[1] Employees typically did not have a choice of insurance plans, although those living on the West Coast and in a few other places sometimes could choose a health maintenance organization (HMO). For the insured population any rationing of services was accomplished by demand-side cost sharing, meaning any deductibles and coinsurance specified in the policy. Physicians tended to practice in small groups or alone and were paid a fee for service, with fees above marginal cost, so there was generally a financial incentive for them to do more. Experience rating prevailed among large and midsize employers, meaning that the costs of services were passed on to the employer, who in turn shifted them to other forms of employee compensation, most notably cash wages.

Importantly, price competition among insurance companies was over the size of the loading, meaning the amount not paid out in claims by the insurer. There were some nonprice aspects of competition as well, such as how fast claims were paid. But competition did *not* take place over the amount paid out in medical benefits. In other words, the cost of the medical services themselves, about 90 percent of the cost of a large-group insurance policy, was not subject to standard market forces. After 1974 most large and midsize employers began formally to self-insure, meaning that the "insurer" was used for administrative services only—that is, to process claims.[2] In effect, the insurer wrote checks to medical providers on the employer's checkbook. This formalized the notion that the insurer took the cost of the medical services themselves as a given, and that the insurer's function was simply to partially or fully reimburse the cost in a passive fashion under all circumstances called for in the contract.

Insured patients could choose among almost all physicians, often by law, and could be admitted to any hospital to which their physicians had admitting privileges. Blue Cross and Blue Shield insurance plans paid physicians through an agreed fee schedule, which was set at a high enough level that virtually all physicians were happy to participate.[3] Commercial insurance, which had the other half of the private market, paid billed fees up to a rather high limit, subject to any coinsurance in the policy. Medicare was patterned on the Blue Cross and Blue Shield policies that were in place at the time of its enactment in 1965. It too set fees at a high enough level to ensure that almost all physicians would see Medicare patients. Medicaid fee policies varied from state to state but typically paid fees that were well below market, especially outside the southern states. As a result, many physicians would not accept Medicaid patients or sometimes not accept new Medicaid patients. Hospitals generally accepted both Medicare and Medicaid patients.

Two principal changes have occurred in these financing arrangements. First, indemnity insurance policies have in many cases been replaced by managed care policies, which provide incentives to consumers to use certain physicians and to physicians to reduce or ration the quantity of services. Managed care has spread rapidly: between 1987 and 1995 the percentage of the privately insured population in managed care increased by about 50 percentage points.[4] Likewise low-income women and children on Medicaid, the former Aid to Families with Dependent Children (AFDC) population, have been largely enrolled in managed care. Second, price competition in the insurance market now takes place over both the quantity and the price of the underlying medical services, as well as loading charges. The two changes are linked because the advent of managed care, or health plans with limited networks and incentives for reductions in the quantity of services, was a necessary precondition for price competition among insurance plans over the entire premium, not just the loading or retention by the insurer, as described in more detail below.

Price Competition in the Employer Market

By 1997, 43 percent of health plan enrollees had a choice among one or more competing health care plans at their place of work.[5] About a third of the time employers paid a lump-sum subsidy toward the premium, in which case price competition among insurance plans is driven by the choices of individual employees because they pay any incremental costs.[6] Even where employees do not have a choice of plans, however, the decline of indemnity insurance means that the price of the insurance plan, including the cost of the covered medical services, is a factor in the employer's choice of a plan.

Managed Care

Managed care has brought competitive forces to medical care services through several devices. First, freedom of choice of physicians has been abandoned. Managed care plans offer their enrollees a choice among physician networks. The threat to exclude a physician or hospital from a network means the plan can bargain for lower prices from physicians, hospitals, and other providers. Indeed, some types of managed care plans, so-called preferred provider organizations (PPOs), largely confine themselves to this type of discounting. Thus the unit price of services has been lowered.

Second, a reduction in the quantity of services has occurred in part through price incentives on the demand (patient) side, but especially on the provider (physician) side. Consider the patient side first. Although most managed care plans require patient co-payments, they are modest if services are received from a provider or physician in the plan's network.[7] Although co-payments may serve a modest rationing function, prices to the consumer mainly serve the function of channeling patients toward the plan's network.

Unlike indemnity plans, most managed care plans offer some price incentives to physicians to reduce the utilization of services. That is, plans contract with physicians or physician groups in ways that delegate some risk to the physicians. The risk that physician groups accept may be for certain services only, such as primary care physician services, or it may be for all services. Even if it is for primary care services only, there may be financial incentives for reducing referrals to specialists or hospital use. Whereas in the indemnity insurance world fees paid by insurers tended to be marked up over cost, sometimes substantially, physicians who accept risk now earn more by delivering fewer services.

Insurers have also intervened directly to reduce the quantity of services. Although the insurance contract continues to state that insurance should cover medically necessary services, this has been reinterpreted to mean that the insurer can review the service, either before the fact or concurrently, in order to "authorize" it. In other words, utilization review techniques have employed command-and-control type methods to reduce the quantity of medical services. In practice, however, services are rarely denied, and utilization review techniques are now beginning to be abandoned in favor of financial incentives.[8]

The Medicare program has largely remained in the earlier mode of indemnity insurance, although 16 percent of its beneficiaries are now in HMOs. It has, however, shifted its method of paying institutional providers away from its earlier use of cost reimbursement: in 1984 it introduced the prospective payment system for inpatient hospital services, and it is now in the process of introducing similar changes for skilled nursing facilities, home health agencies, and hospital outpatient departments. Under these methods of payment providers may be financially better off by delivering fewer services.

Have There Been Savings from Managed Competition and Managed Care?

A literature that goes back more than thirty years, including one well-known randomized trial, the Rand Health Insurance Experiment, suggests that health maintenance organizations can deliver medical care of equivalent technical quality for less money.[9] Establishing even this much, however, has been hampered by difficulties in controlling for potentially different health risks in HMOs and whatever comparison group is used (selection), as well as difficulties in measuring cost, quality of care, and health care outcomes. And even if one accepts that managed care or HMOs save money, that is not the same as establishing the effect of increased price competition.

To complicate the problem of establishing the effect of managed care, old-style indemnity insurance is in the process of disappearing, except in the Medicare program. Thus defining the comparison group against which any savings should be measured has also become an important method-ological issue. (For many reasons the Medicare group cannot be used.)[10] Nonetheless, data of several sorts suggest that the savings from the upsurge of managed care and increased price competition may have been on the order of 10 to 15 percent.

Overall Managed Care and National Spending Trends

A natural place to begin evaluating the effect of the managed care revolu-tion on cost is with trends in medical spending. Figure 2-1 shows the annual rate of increase in spending on medical care by decade since the 1940s. Except for the 1960s, which were the decade of large one-time increases from the enactment of Medicare and Medicaid, spending increases were in the 4 to 5 percent range in each decade except the 1990s. Figure 2-2 shows the rate of annual increase in the 1990s. The period from 1993 to 1997 is anomalous in its low rate of spending increase; there is no other five-year period like it in the post–World War II era. Specifically, from 1940 to 1992 the average annual rate of increase in spending was 4.7 percent, whereas from 1993 to 1997 it was 2.1 percent, or 2.6 per-centage points less. Compounded over five years, a 2.6 percentage point annual savings is 13.7 percent.[11] Although one hesitates to say that this decrease in the growth of spending was entirely attributable to the spread of managed care and managed competition, it is hard to identify any other factor that might have been responsible.[12]

Spending Trends in the Far West

A roughly similar number emerges from a comparison of spending in the Far West region with spending in the remainder of the country in the 1980s. In 1983 California passed legislation permitting health plans to contract only with certain providers. This so-called selective contracting law made possible the rapid growth of managed care in California and more generally in the Far West relative to the rest of the country in the mid- and late 1980s. (California had 75 percent of the Far West population in 1985.) I have data only on spending trends rather than managed care enrollment trends, but they are striking.

Figure 2-1. *Real Increases in per Capita Medical Care Spending, 1940s–90s*

Percent

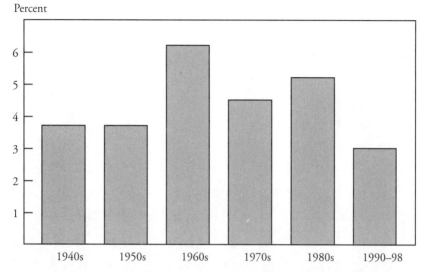

Sources: Joseph P. Newhouse, "Medical Care Costs: How Much Welfare Loss?" *Journal of Economic Perspectives*, vol. 6, no. 3 (1992), pp. 3–21; Katherine Levit, Cathy Cowan, Helen Lazenby, and others, "Health Spending in 1998: Signals of Change," *Health Affairs*, vol. 19, no. 1 (2000), pp. 124–32. Population from U.S. Bureau of the Census, *Statistical Abstract of the United States* (GPO). GDP deflator used to convert to real spending.

In 1980 the Far West region spent 12 percent more per capita on health care than the national average, more than any other census region. In 1991 the region spent 1 percent less than the national average. Spending in other regions relative to the national average was stable; that is, no other region looked like the Far West. There appears to have been about a 13 percent savings in the Far West, and again it is difficult to know to what to attribute such findings other than the spread of price competition there.

Care of Heart Attacks in Massachusetts

David Cutler, Mark McClellan, and I have compared the treatment and price of heart attacks (acute myocardial infarctions) in the state of Massachusetts among those enrolled in HMOs and in an indemnity insurance plan.[13] For this specific disease we found savings consistent with the macro trends just cited. Moreover, these savings appeared to have no or minimal consequences for outcomes.

Figure 2-2. *Annual Real Increases in per Capita Medical Care Spending,*
1991–98

Percent

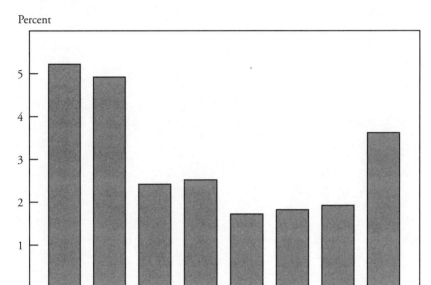

Sources: Katherine Levit, Cathy Cowan, Helen Lazenby, and others, "Health Spending in 1998:
Signals of Change," *Health Affairs*, vol. 19, no. 1 (2000), pp. 124–32. Population from U.S. Bureau of
the Census, *Statistical Abstract of the United States* (GPO). GDP deflator used to convert to real terms.

Because we condition on the fact of a heart attack, our comparisons
should be little affected by the better (or worse) risks of those enrolled in
HMOs. The cost of treating a heart attack is dominated by its severity;
because severity cannot be predicted, the distribution of severity should be
similar in HMOs and indemnity plans.

We obtained complete claims data from one large employment group for
the period July 1993 to December 1995. This enabled us to compare the
treatment of 554 patients with heart attacks who had indemnity insurance
with 299 other heart attack patients who were enrolled in HMOs. In addition, we had inpatient treatment data on all patients with heart attacks in
Massachusetts hospitals. These two data sources yielded consistent findings.

Although there are a variety of treatments for a heart attack, we grouped
patients into four categories: those who were managed medically (that is,
with drugs) and who had no major procedure; those who had cardiac
catheterization but no other major procedure; those who had coronary

Table 2-1. *Reimbursement of Heart Attack Treatment Costs, by Insurance Type*

Insurance	Average	Medical management	Cardiac catheterization	Coronary artery bypass graft (CABG)	Percutaneous transluminal coronary angioplasty (PTCA)
Indemnity	$38,502	$26,601	$38,848	$97,347	$41,597
HMO	$23,632	$16,318	$17,604	$55,826	$24,181
(percent of indemnity)	(61%)	(61%)	(46%)	(57%)	(58%)

Source: David M. Cutler, Mark McClellan, and Joseph P. Newhouse, "How Does Managed Care Do It?" *Rand Journal of Economics,* vol. 31, no. 3 (2000), pp. 526–48.

artery bypass graft (CABG); and those who had percutaneous transluminal coronary angioplasty (PTCA).[14] Table 2-1 shows that the overall payment for treating heart attacks was nearly 40 percent less among the HMO patients and that this difference held for each of the four major treatment options. Controls for covariates, such as age, sex, and whether the person had a prior admission to the hospital, did not change these results.[15] Table 2-2 shows that distribution of patients among the four types of treatment that we defined was almost the same among HMO and indemnity patients. Indeed, treatment was slightly more intensive among HMO patients. Consistent with the lack of treatment differences, outcome differences were small. Mortality (adjusted for age and sex) was 2 percent

Table 2-2. *Treatment of Heart Attacks, by Insurance Type*
Percent

Insurance	Medical management	Cardiac catheterization	Coronary artery bypass graft (CABG)	Angioplasty (PTCA)
Indemnity	63	9	12	16
HMO	55	12	14	9

Source: David M. Cutler, Mark McClellan, and Joseph P. Newhouse, "How Does Managed Care Do It?" *Rand Journal of Economics,* vol. 31, no. 3 (2000), pp. 526–48.

lower among HMO patients, whereas readmissions were an insignificant 1 percent higher.[16]

Large real savings, probably with improved outcomes, have also been achieved in the treatment of major depression, where inpatient treatment has been sharply diminished.[17] Using data from four large employers, Ernst Berndt, Susan Busch, and Richard Frank compared the price of treatments that followed guidelines for depression treatment. They found that between 1991 and 1995 prices paid to providers (unit prices) fell in real terms, and the proportion of effective treatments being provided to patients rose. This is likely attributable to the spread of managed behavioral health care.

A crude calculation shows that if managed care saves on average 40 percent for each disease, the savings in total national spending would be about 13 percent, similar to the values from the other two sources. The reason that the 40 percent and 13 percent figures differ is that not everyone is in managed care. As mentioned above, there was roughly a 50 percentage point increase in private sector managed care enrollment from 1987 to 1995, as well as increases in Medicaid enrollment in managed care.[18] I assume that approximately two-thirds of spending on personal health care that is not Medicare might have been affected by a 50 percentage point increase in enrollment.[19] Multiplying 40 percent by (0.50 x 2/3) yields 13 percent.

THE RAND HEALTH INSURANCE EXPERIMENT. The Rand Experiment is the one instance in which individuals were randomized to a well-established health maintenance organization. The rate of hospitalization for those who were randomized to the HMO was 39 percent lower than for those who were randomized to an indemnity insurance plan. Ambulatory use was similar. The imputed difference in spending, using fee-for-service price weights for the observed utilization, was 25 percent.[20] Because this value was calculated using the same prices for the two systems, it should be a lower bound on savings; in effect, no savings from lower prices or the substitution of lower-level personnel such as physician's assistants are incorporated.

The consistency of all of these numbers suggests to me that the savings to date from managed care and the concomitant increase in price competition in the United States may have been on the order of 10 to 15 percent; that is, spending currently is 10 to 15 percent lower than it otherwise would have been.

The Effects of Competition among Providers More Generally

The premise of managed competition is that competition among both health care providers and health plans is a good thing.[21] In contrast, an earlier literature held that it was a bad thing because it led to excess capacity and possibly worse clinical results from excessively small volumes per provider.[22] In this earlier literature competition among hospitals was said to be a "medical arms race" because each hospital competed through non-price means to attract physicians who would admit patients, just as airlines competed on a nonprice basis before airline fare deregulation.

In a groundbreaking study, Kessler and McClellan have shown that the earlier literature was correct for the period it studied but that after 1990 hospital competition appears to have had salutary effects on both costs and outcomes among elderly heart attack patients.[23] Their study has several methodological innovations, but essentially they estimate the likelihood that a given Medicare heart attack patient will use a given hospital based on the distance between that patient's zip code of residence and the zip code of the hospital. They thus generate an expected number of heart attack patients at each hospital and from that derive an expected market share for each hospital in each zip code. From this they compute the degree of competition each hospital faces. Their data span the period from 1985 to 1994.

Consistent with the medical arms race hypothesis, they find that before 1990 hospitals in the top quartile of competition had 2 percent higher costs for treating heart attacks than hospitals in the bottom quartile and insignificantly different one-year mortality rates. After 1990, however, hospitals in the top quartile had 8 percent lower costs, and their one-year mortality rate was also 1.5 percentage points (4.4 percent) lower. In other words, after 1990 competition appeared to both lower costs and improve clinical outcomes. These are striking findings, and again it is hard to know to attribute them to anything other than increased price competition among hospitals after managed care laid the basis for such price competition.

Kessler and McClellan find similar results for changes in hospitals' competitive positions. Hospitals whose markets become more competitive in the 1985–88 period either do not show changes in costs or have higher costs. Mortality rates show no evidence of change. By contrast, in the 1991–94 period hospitals whose markets become more competitive either have lower costs or lower mortality or do not show evidence of change.[24]

How Long Will These Savings Continue?

Many of the effects of managed care on costs should be one-time effects. Prices can only be discounted by a finite amount before they fall below costs. Length of stay can only be reduced by a certain degree without endangering the patient's health. Admissions and procedures can only be limited to the point that serious adverse outcomes and malpractice suits are not made more likely. Of course, these effects in reality play out over time as managed care enrollment continues to increase and hospitals and physicians adjust to it. A key question in projecting health care cost—as well as the length of time for which the Medicare Part A trust fund will be solvent—is how long the reduced rate of cost increase observed from 1993 to 1997 will continue.

The upsurge in costs for 1998 shown in figure 2-2, along with continuing anecdotal reports of substantial increases in private insurance premiums after 1998, suggest that we may have achieved most of the savings. If so, future rates of increase may be more in line with historical rates, provided that we are willing to continue allocating an ever larger share of our future (higher) income to medical care.

All the savings, however, may not be one-time-only. That is because the prior indemnity insurance system essentially abolished the usual market test of willingness to pay for a new innovation. In most other sectors of the economy a new product succeeds if its combination of improved capabilities and cost are deemed an improvement over existing products (the defense sector in the early Cold War period may have been an exception). In medical care, however, the presence of insurance that stood ready to reimburse any legitimate (covered) treatment expense gave entrepreneurs a very different incentive. In effect, the market test in medical care was whether the expected outcome from using the new product was better than that from using the old; the price of the new product was largely irrelevant.

That is no longer the case. Consider, for example, the marketing of pharmaceuticals.[25] Virtually every managed care organization utilizes a formulary with incentives to physicians, and patients use drugs that are on its formulary. In many insurance plans, for example, consumers have smaller co-payments if on-formulary drugs are used; in others, physicians may have financial incentives to use on-formulary drugs. The formulary may contain only a subset of drugs of a certain class, such as antihypertensives or antidepressants. The drugs on the formulary are determined by a committee from the insurance plan, generally made up of physicians, pharma-cologists, and pharmacists, who consider the therapeutic advantages of the drug as well as its cost. This is a very different situation from what obtained in the indemnity insurance world, when drug companies' marketing efforts were focused on individual physicians (for example, the use of detail men). In short, the demand curve facing pharmaceutical manufacturers has almost certainly become more elastic, with the result that some drugs that earlier would have recovered their development costs may no longer do so. As a result, some drugs may no longer be developed. A similar story could be told about medical devices.

Thus, whether the greater price sensitivity of the American market will much affect the long-run rate of growth of medical costs is problematic. Although it is widely known that the United States has the greatest absolute spending on medical care, countries with very different financing methods have had reasonably similar rates of (real) long-run medical cost increases (see figure 2-3). This suggests to me that there has been an under-lying willingness to pay for the technological advances that the medical establishment has had on offer, which I believe have been a major driver of the sustained cost increase shown in figure 2-1.[26] In other words, even if there is now a mechanism for taking cost into account when making deci-sions on the adoption of medical advances, a mechanism that largely did not exist in the American market in the four decades following World War II, it may not much matter to cost growth: countries may just be will-ing to pay the cost. If so, one would expect the increase in managed care to exert only a modest effect on steady-state growth rates.

The Uninsured and the Safety Net

The American financing system traditionally relied on direct public financ-ing, as well as cross-subsidization, to finance care of the uninsured and the underinsured. Cross-subsidies cannot survive with strong price competi-tion, and the cross-subsidies to the uninsured are no exception.[27] Gruber found that increased price shopping for hospital care in California in the 1984–88 period resulted in a large fall in net private revenue and income in the least concentrated (most competitive) markets and that care to the uninsured fell sharply in those markets.[28] Gruber estimates an elasticity of uncompensated care with respect to net resources between 0.4 and 1.0. Gruber did not examine changes in health outcomes, however.

Figure 2-3. *Increases in Real per Person Health Care Costs in the G-7 Countries, 1960–97*

Percent

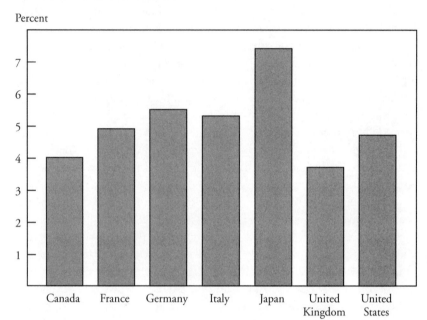

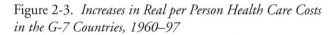

Source: Gerald F. Anderson and Jean-Pierre Poullier, "Health Spending, Access and Outcomes: Trends in Industrialized Countries," *Health Affairs*, vol. 18, no. 3 (1999), p. 179. GDP deflator used to convert to real costs.

Volpp found that the end of a regulated price system with cross-subsidies in New Jersey appeared to raise mortality from acute myocardial infarction. More important, almost all of the increase was among the uninsured.

The reductions in cross-subsidies and uncompensated care in turn have placed greater stress on the direct delivery or safety net system provided by local public hospitals and health centers. To date the safety net system appears to be coping, but it is under substantial stress.[29]

Another example of the end of the ability to cross-subsidize appears to be the end of cost shifting in the Medicare program (see figure 2-4). After the beginning of the prospective payment system in 1984, Medicare margins and private margins in hospitals had a negative correlation through 1998 (the $R^2 = 0.70$).[30] The data are consistent with the story that if Medicare cut prices hospitals insisted on higher prices from private payers. In 1998, however, both margins moved in the same direction for the first

Figure 2-4. *Private Payer and Medicare Revenue as a Percentage of Hospital Cost, 1980–98*

Percent

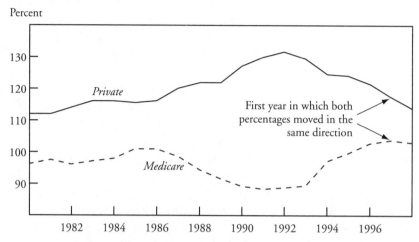

Sources: Prospective Payment Assessment Commission, *Medicare and the American Health Care System: Report to the Congress* (Washington, June 1997), p. 23; Medicare Payment Advisory Commission, *Report to the Congress: Selected Medicare Issues* (Washington, June 2000), table C-12.

time since the enactment of the prospective payment system. Whether this is a one-time anomaly remains to be seen.

What Has Been the Effect on Quality of Care?

Numerous studies have now been done that compare quality of care and clinical outcomes in managed care and indemnity insurance.[31] Studies can be found favoring both managed care and indemnity insurance, although the dominant finding is that for the average person there is no effect. This null result was the finding in the Rand Experiment as well.[32] Conflicting results across studies are not surprising, given that managed care is hardly a uniform treatment and that studies often use one or a small number of managed care plans. There are, however, a number of studies suggesting that managed care may have adverse effects for the chronically ill in disadvantaged or elderly populations.

The studies in the literature of patient satisfaction suggest that, on average, patients in managed care and indemnity insurance are about equally satisfied, with managed care having an advantage when it comes to financial matters and indemnity insurance with respect to nonfinancial matters. This is not surprising either, given that the marginal enrollee should be indifferent with respect to overall satisfaction conditional on any cost differences.[33] Consistent with this interpretation, in the Rand Experiment those randomized to the HMO were less satisfied than those randomized to an indemnity plan (with the same cost), but those who had self-selected the HMO were as happy as those in the indemnity plan.

In principle, managed care could solve some quality problems. It could, for example, offer incentives for physicians to adhere to clinical guidelines; coordinate care for individuals seeing multiple physicians, thereby alleviating such problems as one physician prescribing in ignorance of what another has prescribed; and follow up better after hospital discharge. In practice, however, managed care has sometimes done little more than seek price discounts. Nonetheless, by fostering more organization of the medical care delivery system, managed care has at least laid the infrastructure for initiatives to improve the quality of care.

So Why Is the Populace So Angry at Managed Care?

Managed care is one of the least popular industries in America today; it does manage to rank above the tobacco industry in public approbation, but not many others (see table 2-3).[34] If managed care is saving appreciable money with little or no reduction in the quality of care, why is the public so hostile? I speculate about several reasons:

—The cost savings are not widely appreciated. Employers almost invariably pay a substantial fraction of health insurance premiums. I would guess that only a handful of individuals, mainly those in the human resources departments of corporations, know the total cost of either their managed care health insurance or their old indemnity policies. Individuals know what their out-of-pocket costs for health insurance are, but those may have risen as employers shifted costs to employees. As a result, employers may be paying less in health insurance premiums and more in cash wages, but the somewhat larger cash wages may be lost in the noise of other factors affecting wages and not be seen as an effect of managed care.

—In the indemnity insurance world fully insured patients and fee-for-service physicians both had an interest in seeing that the patient received almost all medically beneficial services; cost was not much of an object.

Table 2-3. *Consumers' Ratings of Service by Industry, 1998*

Percent

Industry	Good	Bad
Computer software companies	78	7
Telephone companies	76	23
Pharmaceutical companies	73	23
Hospitals	73	23
Banks	72	26
Car manufacturers	69	25
Oil companies	64	26
Life insurance companies	48	47
Managed care companies	45	42
Tobacco companies	32	60

Source: Robert J. Blendon, Mollyann Brodie, John M. Benson, and others, "Understanding the Managed Care Backlash," *Health Affairs*, vol. 17, no. 4 (1998), pp. 80–94, from Harris poll.

Although out-of-pocket payments by consumers tend to be even lower in managed care, physicians now have financial and nonfinancial incentives to ration services. Indeed, a major raison d'être and potential value of managed care is to reduce the use of low but positively valued services by insured patients.[35] As a result, patients, if they know what they want, may be frustrated by physicians' failure to deliver the service.

—Perhaps even more important, unlike in a standard market, consumers have no financial way to express the intensity of their preferences. In a standard market, if I value something at more than its cost, I will buy it; otherwise I will not. If prices rise, almost by definition the goods and services I forgo are those I value least. Managed care does not necessarily work this way. If a physician determines that an expensive test is not worth running, the patient, who may have been willing to pay the actuarial cost of an insurance policy to cover the situation, may find himself or herself without recourse. This is surely a major reason behind the political demand for patient protection legislation. For both this and the prior reason, many patients no doubt feel a loss of control, and they certainly do not trust managed care companies to act in what they perceive to be their interests. Physicians, who have to discount their fees and also often feel a loss of control and professional autonomy, may encourage these views.

—Polling of the public by Robert Blendon and colleagues (1998) has also demonstrated that media coverage affects public views. Specifically,

Table 2-4. *Trends in Satisfaction with the Health Care System,*
Canada and the United States, 1988–98
Percent of public saying only minor changes needed

Country	1988	1994	1998
Canada	56	29	20
United States	10	18	17

Source: Karen Donelan, Robert J. Blendon, Cathy Schoen, Karen Davis, and Katherine Binns, "The Cost of Health System Change: Public Discontent in Five Nations," *Health Affairs,* vol. 18, no. 3 (1999), pp. 206–16.

although people report concern about whether they will be able to obtain care if they need it, few of them have any personal experience. Blendon and his colleagues suggest that well-publicized anecdotes—horror stories—have contributed to public distrust.

To provide some perspective, however, public satisfaction with health care in Canada has plummeted (see table 2-4). Whereas in 1988 satisfaction with the Canadian system among Canadians was much higher than satisfaction with the American system among Americans, a decade later satisfaction in the two countries was similar—and both publics were highly dissatisfied.[36] What happened in the interim was that the Canadian federal and provincial governments, in an austerity measure, reduced funding for health services.[37] The public noticed and reacted. Perhaps in an earlier time there was a view in both countries that all beneficial medical services were available to those who were insured, or at least to those insured in need, but this no longer appears to be the case. Paradise, which was probably not sustainable in either country, had been lost in both.

Notes

1. Some services, such as mental health care or drugs, may have been excluded contractually. There were also minor exclusions for services deemed experimental.

2. This change came about because of the Employee Retirement Income Security Act (ERISA), which exempted self-insured employers from state premium taxes and from state-mandated benefits.

3. Blue Cross and Blue Shield nationally had about half the private market, although percentages varied widely in local markets.

4. Jon Gabel, Steven Fink, and Gregory de Lissovoy, "Employer-Sponsored Health Insurance in America," *Health Affairs*, vol. 8, no. 2 (1989), pp. 116–28; and Gail A. Jensen,

Michael A. Morrisey, S. Gaffney, and D. K. Liston, "The New Dominance of Managed Care: Insurance Trends in the 1990s," *Health Affairs*, vol. 16, no. 1 (1997), pp. 125–36.

5. Stephen H. Long and Susan Marquis, "Trends in Managed Care and Managed Competition," *Health Affairs*, vol. 18, no. 6 (1999), pp. 75–88. In 1993 the percentage was 45 percent. I do not have comparable data from an earlier period, but the percentage was almost surely much lower, especially before the HMO Act was implemented in 1976. This act required that any employer with more than twenty-five employees offer a qualified HMO if an HMO desired to be offered. Initially, however, there were few qualified HMOs, so this clause had little effect. The repeal of freedom-of-choice laws in California in 1983 appeared to give the notion of competing health plans a large boost. This was partly because many existing HMOs thought that meeting the requirements to become a qualified HMO would impair their competitive position.

6. David M. Cutler and Sarah J. Reber, "Paying for Health Insurance: The Tradeoff between Competition and Adverse Selection," *Quarterly Journal of Economics*, vol. 113, no. 2 (1998), pp. 433–66. The practice of the employer's paying a lump sum toward any plan is likely more common than before, in which case insurance plans face a more elastic demand curve. Cutler estimates that when Harvard University changed from a percentage of premium to a lump sum, price quotes from insurance plans fell about 10 percent.

7. Jack Zwanziger and Rebecca Auerbach, "Evaluating PPO Performance Using Prior Expenditure Data," *Medical Care*, (February 1, 1991), pp. 142–51. Indeed, preferred provider plans may cost more than indemnity plans because the reduction in patient cost sharing increases demand by more than the price discount that the plan has generated.

8. Dahlia K. Remler, Karen Donelan, Robert Blendon, and others, "What Do Managed Care Plans Do to Affect Care? Results from a Survey of Physicians," *Inquiry*, vol. 34, no. 3 (1997), pp. 196–204.

9. Sherry Glied, "Managed Care," in Anthony J. Culyer and Joseph P. Newhouse, eds., *Handbook of Health Economics* (Amsterdam: North Holland, 2000).

10. These include the noncomparability of Medicare beneficiaries with the privately insured, as well as the administratively set prices of the Medicare program (see figure 2-4).

11. If one omits the decade of the 1960s, the long-term growth rate is 4.3 percent, which, if used in lieu of the 4.7 percent figure, yields a savings of 2.2 percent per year for five years, or 11.5 percent.

12. Kip Sullivan, "On the 'Efficiency' of Managed Care Plans," *Health Affairs*, vol. 19, no. 4 (2000), pp. 139–48. Highly skeptical that managed care produces cost savings, Sullivan offers the alternative hypothesis that the lower spending growth in the 1993–97 period can be attributed to an extended "three years up, three years down" insurance cycle. The problem with this explanation is that even if one accepts that there is a cycle in insurance premiums, there does not appear to be a similar cycle in total national health spending. Private insurance payments account for less than one-third of health care spending. Katherine Levit, Cathy Cowan, Helen Lazenby, and others, "Health Spending in 1998: Signals of Change," *Health Affairs*, vol. 19, no. 1 (2000), pp. 124–32.

13. David M. Cutler, Mark McClellan, and Joseph P. Newhouse, "How Does Managed Care Do It?" *Rand Journal of Economics*, vol. 31, no. 3 (2000), pp. 526–48.

14. A catheterization is a diagnostic procedure to determine the degree of obstruction of the coronary arteries. It has no therapeutic value in and of itself but is necessary before an angioplasty or a bypass graft can be performed. It also has minimal risk. A bypass graft

splices around the blockage; an angioplasty threads in a balloonlike device that then expands to open the artery.

15. In the regression results, we regressed the logarithm of reimbursement on whether the person was in the HMO and covariates, including dummy variables for treatment. The HMO dummy showed average reimbursement across the four treatments was 43 percent less in the HMO sample; the t statistic on the HMO variable was over 9.

16. The 2 percent value was statistically significant at the 5 percent level.

17. Richard G. Frank, Ernst R. Berndt and Susan Busch, "Price Indexes for the Treatment of Depression," in Jack Triplett, ed., *Measuring the Prices of Medical Treatments* (Brookings, 1999); and Ernst R. Berndt, Susan Busch, and Richard Frank, "Treatment Price Indices for Acute Phase Major Depression," in Ernst R. Berndt and David M. Cutler, eds., *Medical Care Output and Productivity* (University of Chicago Press, 2000).

18. This figure includes PPO enrollment. Our sample had too small a number of PPO enrollees to generate a reliable figure for savings from PPO treatment, but the point estimate of 31 percent was not far from the estimate of savings from HMOs.

19. Congressional Budget Office, "Predicting How Changes in Medicare's Payment Rates Would Affect Risk-Sector Enrollments and Costs" (March 1997); and Laurence C. Baker, "Association of Managed Care Market Share and Health Expenditures for Fee-for-Service Medicare patients," *Journal of the American Medical Association,* vol. 281, no. 5 (1999), pp. 432–37. Two-thirds is roughly the share of non-Medicare spending. In Medicare there were conflicting trends. Because of flaws in the way the Medicare program paid HMOs, Medicare paid HMOs more per enrollee than it would have paid had the individuals remained enrolled in traditional Medicare, on the order of 5 to 10 percent per enrollee. Potentially offsetting this effect, however, is that areas with increases in managed care penetration (both Medicare and non-Medicare) had slower growth of spending in traditional Medicare, a so-called spillover effect. Finally, there was a sharp increase in managed care enrollment among the Medicaid population, especially among low-income women and children, who account for about 5 percent of medical care spending. I will assume these factors roughly offset.

20. Joseph P. Newhouse and the Insurance Experiment Group, *Free for All? Lessons from the Rand Health Insurance Experiment* (Harvard University Press, 1993), chap. 8.

21. Alain Enthoven, *Theory and Practice of Managed Care Competition in Health Care Finance* (Amsterdam: North Holland, 1988).

22. For example, see James C. Robinson and Harold S. Luft, "The Impact of Hospital Market Structure on Patient Volume, Average Length of Stay, and the Cost of Care," *Journal of Health Economics,* vol. 4, no. 4 (1985), pp. 333–56.

23. Daniel P. Kessler and Mark B. McClellan, "Is Hospital Competition Socially Wasteful?" *Quarterly Journal of Economics*, vol. 115, no. 2 (2000), pp. 577–616.

24. Ibid. Kessler and McClellan also replicate Baker's finding (in "Association of Managed Care Market Share") that higher HMO enrollments are associated with lower costs in traditional Medicare (that is, they have a spillover effect).

25. For more detail see F. M. Scherer, "The Pharmaceutical Industry," in Culyer and Newhouse, *Handbook of Health Economics.*

26. Joseph P. Newhouse, "Medical Care Costs: How Much Welfare Loss?" *Journal of Economic Perspectives,* vol. 6, no. 3 (1992), pp. 3–21.

27. Jon Gruber, "The Effect of Competitive Pressure on Charity: Hospital Responses to Price Shopping in California," *Journal of Health Economics,* vol. 13, no. 2 (1994), pp. 183–212; and Kevin G. M. Volpp, "Market-Based Reforms and the Impact on Quality of Care: An Examination of the Quality Impacts of the Transition from Hospital Rate-Setting to Price Competition in New Jersey" (Ph.D. dissertation, University of Pennsylvania, 1998).

28. Ibid. Much of the adjustment was in outpatient care.

29. Institute of Medicine, "America's Health Care Safety Net: Intact but Endangered" (Washington: National Academy Press, 2000).

30. If the years 1980 through 1983 are included, when Medicare reimbursed hospitals a share of their costs equal to its share of patient days, the correlation falls to 0.47. Because of cost reimbursement, there was little need for cross-subsidization before 1983, so the fall in correlation is consistent with the interpretation in the text.

31. For reviews, see Robert H. Miller and Harold S. Luft, "Managed Care Plan Performance since 1980," *Journal of the American Medical Association,* vol. 271, no. 19 (1994), pp. 1512–19; and Robert H. Miller and Harold S. Luft, "Does Managed Care Lead to Better or Worse Quality of Care?" *Health Affairs,* vol. 16, no. 3 (1997), pp. 7–25.

32. Newhouse and the Insurance Experiment Group, *Free for All?* chap. 9.

33. The studies, however, compare the average and not the marginal enrollee.

34. Robert J. Blendon, Mollyann Brodie, John M. Benson, and others, "Understanding the Managed Care Backlash," *Health Affairs,* vol. 17, no. 4 (1998), pp. 80–94.

35. "Moral hazard" in the jargon of economics.

36. Karen Donelan, Robert J. Blendon, Cathy Schoen, Karen Davis, and Katherine Binns, "The Cost of Health System Change: Public Discontent in Five Nations," *Health Affairs,* vol. 18, no. 3 (1999), pp. 206–16.

37. C. David Naylor, "Health Care in Canada: Incrementalism under Fiscal Duress," *Health Affairs,* vol. 18, no. 3 (1999), pp. 9–26.

3

JOSÉ A. GÓMEZ-IBÁÑEZ
JOHN R. MEYER

Government and Markets in Transport: The U.S. Experience with Deregulation

GOVERNMENTS, IN VIRTUALLY all parts of the world and of all types, have long had an intense interest in transportation markets. That tradition lingers on, perhaps attenuated but nevertheless strong enough to justify the observation that few other industries have markets and operations more involved, for better or worse, with government. Government transport policy generally reflects the ruling consensus on national economic policy, determined in turn by the current conventional economic wisdom and political realities. The dominant ideology at the end of the twentieth century was that, on efficiency grounds, governments should intervene in markets as little as possible. Accordingly, governments around the world were reducing their roles in transport. In Europe and the developing world, many governments have been privatizing the state-owned enterprises that have historically provided their airline, railway, and other transport services. In the United States, where private provision has been the norm, government has been relaxing the regulatory controls on tariffs and services that have long existed.

This chapter examines only the "regulatory half" of this development, studying the evolution of transport policy in the United States and the recent U.S. experience with deregulating private railroads and airlines. In general, deregulation has proven to be reasonably effective in improving the performance of both industries. Nevertheless, some groups of railroad shippers and airline passengers feel that they have not benefited much from deregulation and are pressing government to intervene or even to reregulate. Moreover, waves of mergers have reduced the numbers of firms in both industries, adding to popular concern about whether competition is sufficient to be an effective substitute for regulation.

Though not explicitly evaluated in this chapter, similarly mixed but generally favorable results would seem to characterize the experiences of countries that privatized. In most of these countries, the relevant regulatory issue was usually whether regulation should be instituted when privatization occurred, so as to retain at least some government control. The emerging consensus about transport privatization seems to be that efficiency and innovation are enhanced, although at some cost in transition traumas and other negative externalities. Efficiency gains of 20 to 40 percent commonly seem achievable by privatization, although there appear to be some notable exceptions.[1] Private firms also seem to have better records of product and process innovation.

The Evolving Role of Government in Transport

The intense and early government interest in transportation in the United States reflected, to at least some extent, the pioneer role that railroads played in the development of big business. Railroads were usually the first nationally prominent big businesses to emerge from the industrial revolution.[2] As such they were almost automatically candidates for envy, suspicion, and government concern. The fact that almost "every ranking official of the earliest transcontinental rail systems could be labeled a crook, as most ultimately were," added to the public interest and attention.[3]

Despite much overbuilding and redundancy in nineteenth-century railroads, many railroad customers all over the world, but perhaps particularly in North America, felt that they were effectively served by only one railroad, which took advantage of a monopoly position by charging unfairly high tariffs. This is what economists call "natural monopoly," or a situation where the minimum efficient scale of plant is large relative to the size of the market and no close or plausible substitutes exist for the product or service. Nineteenth-century railroads seemed to fit this description fairly accurately, particularly when serving thinly populated farm areas; in such circumstances, one single-tracked railroad with a few sidings and primitive signaling might be more than enough to serve the available traffic. The fact that in the United States some railroads charged low rates or gave rebates to highly competitive traffic in the industrial Northeast did little to improve their acceptance by the public. Income transfers seemingly effectuated via differential rail tariffs from small farmers to John D. Rockefeller or Andrew Carnegie were not politically attractive.

A strong belief was also held that even though development of new transport systems involved problems—ranging, as noted, from corruption to politically objectionable income transfers—the problems were not as great as the benefits. Building a transcontinental railroad, for example, was widely regarded as essential to the United States' realizing its "manifest destiny . . . to overspread the continent allotted by Providence for the free development of our yearly multiplying millions."[4] In short, great "external benefits" flowed from building a transport system. These went well beyond anything that might be realized by private developers capturing only private market returns, thus "justifying" subsidization by governments.

In the early nineteenth century, before the railroad, government intervention, even in the United States, often took the form of government ownership and control. Some of these interventions were financed by tolls; some were not (and therefore, at least implicitly, were justified by beneficial externalities beyond capture in the market). For example, New York and several other states built barge canals. Many states and municipalities built plank roads to connect up to or fill in missing links in plank road arterials built by private investors. In short, by the time big business (as represented by the railroads) first confronted big government, the United States already had a well-established pattern of government involvement in transport development and markets.

Regulatory Commissions

Nevertheless, the railroad-government face-off in the last quarter of the nineteenth century in the United States involved something quite new: the creation in 1887 of a regulatory bureaucracy, the Interstate Commerce Commission (ICC). The ICC's role was to protect small shippers, particularly farmers, but not to the point of seriously inhibiting railroad development. Coupled with this was a general desire to redistribute income away from industrial to agrarian sectors and, in keeping with that, redistribute income geographically from east to west. To accomplish these goals, the ICC was given the authority to regulate virtually all aspects of rail management decisions on entry, mergers, routes, and tariffs. In essence, railroad

Table 3-1. *Regulatory Commissions for U.S. Transport and Utility Industries in the 1960s*

Commission (year established)	Industries regulated
State	
Public Utility Commissions (mostly between 1907 and 1939)	Electricity, gas, telephone, water, railroads, trucks, buses
Federal	
Interstate Commerce Commission (1887)	Railroads, trucks, buses (1935), and barges (1940)
Civil Aeronautics Board (1938)	Airlines
Federal Maritime Commission (1936)	Ocean shipping
Federal Communications Commission (1934)	Telephones
Federal Energy Regulatory Commission (1935)[a]	Electricity and gas (1938)

Source: Authors' tabulations.

a. The Federal Power Commission was renamed the Federal Energy Regulatory Commission in 1971.

management, as agents, had two principals to whom they had to answer: their private stockholders and the government as represented by the ICC.

The ICC had few immediate imitators elsewhere. Outside the United States governments were usually much more directly responsible for transport activities, managing them through ministries or government-owned corporations or some combination of both. With direct government ownership or control, special regulatory commissions did not seem as necessary. In the United States, however, the regulatory commission concept proved popular. As shown in table 3-1, by the 1960s (probably the high-water mark for U.S. regulatory commissions) regulatory commissions could be found at many levels of government and applied to many different activities. Commissions and agencies were eventually established to regulate the financial industry, food and drugs, safety, the environment, and other matters besides transportation and utilities.

The proliferation of regulatory activities in the United States carried the commissions well beyond their original rationale of protecting consumers from monopoly and effectuating income redistributions. For example, trucks and buses were brought under ICC regulation in 1935 and barges in 1940, as much for the purpose of establishing and protecting market shares among the modes as for protecting consumers.

Efficiency Considerations

Notably lacking throughout the first thirty years or so of formal commission regulation in the United States was any apparent concern with efficiency of operations. That oversight began to end with World War I, as railroads increasingly found themselves overburdened, partly because of a wartime surge in demand and possibly, too, because of the ostensible ineptness of wartime management under the temporary nationalization of the industry.

After World War I, national economic policy turned to "getting back to normalcy," in which normalcy meant rapid development of a consumer society based on broad middle-class participation. This goal emphasized growth and efficiency, and economic regulators reacted to those concerns. Transport policy focused on the construction of new highways and rationalizing and improving the efficiency of rail operations. The ICC developed a master plan of rail mergers and consolidations aimed at lowering railroad costs by eliminating excess capacity and extending the oversight and role of the industry's more competent managers, with prosperous railroads asked to take over the unprofitable. Perhaps not too surprisingly, the "rich" railroads did not volunteer for this duty easily and, for the most part, fought off all suggestions that they do so.

Any concern with efficiency issues was aborted by the advent of the Great Depression in the early 1930s. The major goal of economic policy became finding ways to reduce unemployment and to alleviate associated welfare problems. Broadly speaking, the ICC's major initiatives during the 1930s are best described as "cartelizing" the industry, with the market shares of the different modes stabilized at specified status quo ante levels. Only very limited lip service was paid to the efficiency notion that these market shares should be determined so that each mode did what it does best—that is, most efficiently.

This broad-based emphasis on stabilization of market share persisted into the period after World War II. The basic goal of economic policy in that period was to avoid any repetition of the stagnation and high unemployment of the Great Depression. In such an environment a little inefficiency might even be welcome (because, ceteris paribus, it would expand employment). A static cartel vision of the industry also helped maintain the established pattern of subsidies and redistributions effectuated through transport regulation. That, in turn, greatly simplified political problems for the regulators.

In the 1960s and 1970s the full-employment consensus began to slowly but surely disintegrate. The combination of Vietnam War spending and OPEC oil embargoes rekindled anxieties about inflation. That, in turn, led to reduced enthusiasm about adding or increasing employment regardless of the consequences. By the late 1970s, the search was for economic policies that would improve efficiency and reduce inflationary pressures. As this was happening, it was also becoming increasingly apparent that commission-style regulation was itself a source of considerable inefficiency.

Regulatory Problems

Policy analysts came to appreciate the technical challenges of regulating. To start, commissioners had to know what the costs of an efficient firm were in order to set the appropriate prices. But in complex network industries with ever-changing technologies and demand patterns, efficient costs and prices were often difficult to determine.

Many regulatory commissions also seemed to lack the political will to regulate well. Instead, they were allegedly "captured" by the firms they were supposed to regulate or, if not by the firms themselves, then by a combination of the firms and their labor forces.[5] Similarly, customer groups that derived particular advantages from a set of regulatory arrangements often became potent vested interests against change; benefits from regulatory subsidies were usually highly concentrated on a subset of the customers while the costs of creating those windfalls could be broadly and thinly spread over the rest of the market. Because there are winners and losers in almost any regulatory situation, regulators understandably often developed a strong preference for stability or maintaining the status quo ante.[6]

A taste or preference for stability also had a strong tendency to stifle innovation. Regulators often favored incumbent firms over new entrants or challengers and maintained the status quo almost regardless of cost and forgone innovation. Furthermore, because only the cognoscenti or "insiders" usually knew about possible innovations, regulation often seemed to have a "what-they-don't-know-won't-hurt-them" aspect.

Finally, perhaps in many ways most tellingly, evidence mounted that regulation as conventionally practiced almost never provided incentives for using the most productive practices. Commission regulation, with its emphasis on targeting a specified rate of return on invested capital, commonly led to either an inefficient over- or under-investment in capital relative to other factors of production.[7] This distortion occurred even without technological or other changes. It was "static" in character and difficult to avoid, even under the best of circumstances.

Alternatives to Commission Regulation

Rising political discontent with the inefficiency of transport provision, whether public or private or whether regulated or unregulated, generated a remarkable series of policy experiments with deregulation and privatization starting in the late 1970s. Initially, these were mainly in the United States, Britain, and a few developing countries, but they spread rapidly to most other parts of the world. Outside the United States, these innovations usually involved privatizing state-owned transportation companies. In the United States and elsewhere where private transport firms had been the norm or were being established, governments experimented with alternatives to commission-style regulation.

The British, for example, developed "price-cap" regulation as an alternative to the cost-of-service and rate-of-return regulation typically practiced by commissions in the United States. Under the price-cap alternative, regulators review tariffs only periodically (say, every three to five years) and make adjustments between reviews using a formula that automatically adjusts upward for inflation and downward for the estimated long-term rate of productivity improvement in the industry. This scheme motivates the regulated company to find ways to improve its efficiency because it can keep as profits any savings in excess of the expected rate of productivity improvement between review periods. In short, the idea is to deliberately insert "regulatory lag" into the process. Of course, taken to an extreme— say, a very long or infinite regulatory lag—private vendors would capture all the gains from technological innovation; as a result, price-cap regulation depends on the careful estimation of the formula's parameters and the frequency of reviews. Britain has applied price-cap regulation with at least a modicum of success—but not without problems—to most of its newly privatized utilities, and the concept is slowly spreading elsewhere.

Another alternative form of regulation, used extensively in developing countries, has been regulation by contract or franchise. The idea is to dispense with regulatory commissions altogether by awarding contracts of limited duration to provide monopoly services. If the contracts are awarded competitively to the bidder proposing the best price for a given service or the best service for a given price, then consumers should feel comfortable that they were receiving a fair deal. A government agency is still needed, but its role is largely limited to ensuring that the private firm complies with the contract.

Obviously franchises have their own problems, such as determining the appropriate length of a contract. Contracts that are too short limit the willingness of bidders to commit resources and realize the scale or other economies that might be available. Contracts that are too long are difficult to fully specify in advance, increasing the need for arbitration and other modes of adaptation.[8] Nevertheless, franchising is an attractive alternative in that it reduces the scope of the regulatory agency's discretion and thereby makes regulation less prone to errors or capture.

The most radical alternative, however, is to deregulate completely, as the United States more or less did with all of its intercity modes of transport, including airlines and railroads. Deregulation is best done with industries that are reasonably competitive, so that the need for regulation is less. But few industries are perfectly competitive—there are almost always some remaining elements or pockets of monopoly power. The U.S. experience with railroads and airlines suggests that these elements can sometimes threaten or undermine an otherwise successful policy.

Railroad Deregulation

Pressures for railroad deregulation in the United States grew slowly. In the 1950s, railroad passenger and freight traffic fell dramatically from the heights reached during World War II, and the railroads' financial situation deteriorated as well. Many factors contributed to the traffic and financial decline, perhaps the most obvious being the steady improvements to the U.S. highway and aviation systems during the postwar period. The railroads increasingly came to view regulation as an impediment to their efforts to adapt to their new environment.

Importantly, the ICC resisted railroad efforts to innovate in freight services, most famously in 1961 when the Southern Railway attempted to introduce modern 100-ton hopper cars so that it could offer lower rates and recapture bulk commodity traffic it had lost to barges and trucks. Responding to complaints from barge operators and from other railroads that did not have the new equipment (or the heavier welded rail that made heavier wheel loadings possible), the ICC disapproved the proposed rates. It eventually took a three-year legal battle, including an appeal to the Supreme Court, before Southern Railway forced the ICC to relent.[9] Even before the

Southern Railway battle, some academic economists had begun to argue that the ICC was forcing railroads to charge too much for freight and encouraging excessive diversion of traffic to trucks.[10]

The case for deregulation became more dramatic and compelling, however, when major eastern railroads started to go bankrupt. The failure of the New York, New Haven & Hartford in 1959 finally convinced Congress to pass legislation stripping state Public Utility Commissions (PUCs) of their power to force interstate railroads to continue to provide unprofitable commuter services. In 1970, Congress relieved the railroads of their obligations to provide intercity passenger service as well and created a government corporation, Amtrak, to take over that responsibility. But it took the bankruptcy of the Penn Central Railroad later that year to begin an earnest effort to limit the ICC's powers. The Penn Central had been formed only two years earlier when the two largest eastern railroads, the Pennsylvania and the New York Central, merged in the hope that together they could cut costs by eliminating duplicate facilities. Penn Central was so important to the economy of the Northeast that the federal government thought it wise to take over the collapsed carrier and keep it operating, at least temporarily, as part of a public corporation called the Consolidated Rail Corporation (Conrail). Congress was anxious that it not be forced to take over other carriers as well, and the search for measures that would improve the industry's profitability began in earnest. By that time, both academic studies and practical experience strongly suggested that the industry would have little chance of recovery unless regulatory restraints were loosened.

The Replacement of Government Regulation with Private Contracts

Congress limited some of the ICC's powers in 1976, but the key reforms were passed in 1980. The central innovations were to make contracts between railroads and shippers legal, exempt from ICC regulation, and confidential. Part of the motive was to give railroads more pricing flexibility. Contracts were also intended to reduce the potential for monopoly abuse and particularly the problem of "captive" shippers. A shipper can be captive to a railroad if the shipper invests in a valuable and immobile facility, such as a mine, power plant, or grain elevator, served by only that railroad and if there is no competition from other modes of transportation or from other products or locations. Similarly, a railroad can be captive to a shipper if the railroad invests in improving a line that is primarily needed for that shipper's traffic. Before deregulation, the ICC protected the shipper from opportunistic behavior by the railroad and vice versa. But after deregulation in 1980, long-term contracts were to protect them, just as they protected mutually interdependent investors in other types of fixed and specialized assets in a capitalist economy. Neither the shipper nor the railroad would be captive until it made its investments, and neither one would be likely to invest unless it could first agree on a long-term contract governing tariffs and services.

ICC review of rates was retained as a safety valve and to aid in the transition to the new contractual system, since initially there would be shippers and railroads with investments that were vulnerable but not protected by contracts. ICC intervention was limited in three ways, however. First, the agency could review a rate only if it exceeded 180 percent of a railroad's variable costs; rates below that threshold were presumed to be reasonable. Second, the ICC had to determine that the railroad had "dominance" over the shipper, or in the industry's parlance, that the shipper was captive. Finally, the ICC had to determine each year whether the railroads were making adequate returns and take their financial needs into consideration. If a railroad's returns were inadequate, the ICC would presumably allow it to charge higher rates.

In 1995, Congress replaced the ICC with a new Surface Transportation Board (STB), but this was largely a symbolic gesture. The STB was housed administratively in the U.S. Department of Transportation, but otherwise the board members enjoyed the same protections for independent decisionmaking that the old ICC commissioners had. The STB also retained the ICC's powers to approve entry, exit, and mergers, to calculate whether railroads were earning an adequate return, and to review tariffs that exceeded the 180 percent threshold.

Changes in Average Tariffs, Traffic, and Profitability

Deregulation brought about a remarkable improvement in the performance of the U.S. railroads that exceeded the expectations of most advocates. Between 1980 and 1997 average freight rates per ton-mile fell by 44 percent and total ton-miles carried increased by 55 percent, reversing decades of decline (see table 3-2). The railroads were also able to recapture some traffic from trucks, as indicated by the 196 percent increase in containers and trailers loaded. Profits increased despite the reduced tariffs, largely because the railroads managed to increase their average length of haul, cut back on underutilized track, and improve labor productivity. The

Table 3-2. *Performance of the U.S. Railroad Industry, 1950–99*

Year	Rail rates per ton-mile in constant 1999 dollars	Ton-miles carried (billions)	Containers and trailers carried (thousands)	Average haul-of-way length (miles)	Miles of right-of-way	Ton-miles per employee-hour
1950	n.a.	597	n.a.	454	223,779	n.a.
1960	5.57	579	n.a.	489	217,552	n.a.
1970	4.84	771	2,363	546	206,265	605
1980	4.34	932	3,059	587	179,000	863
1981	4.40	924	3,151	597	168,000	906
1982	4.27	810	3,397	600	163,897	927
1983	4.08	841	4,090	611	160,555	1,072
1984	3.96	935	4,566	614	156,558	1,167
1985	3.86	895	4,591	617	153,052	1,196
1986	3.76	889	4,997	613	152,666	1,302
1987	3.44	972	5,504	630	152,173	1,531
1988	3.35	1,028	5,780	633	147,833	1,683
1989	3.13	1,070	5,987	650	148,069	1,776
1990	2.97	1,091	6,207	628	145,979	1,901
1991	2.83	1,100	6,246	637	143,783	2,020
1992	2.79	1,138	6,628	634	141,064	2,176
1993	2.69	1,183	7,157	655	139,667	2,280
1994	2.64	1,275	8,128	670	137,973	2,509
1995	2.50	1,375	8,073	720	136,642	2,746
1996	2.38	1,426	8,154	722	136,115	2,965
1997	2.42	1,421	8,696	721	133,361	2,973
1998	2.38	1,442	n.a.	706	131,810	n.a.
1999	2.28	1,449	n.a.	712	122,027	n.a.
Percentage change 1980–99	−44.5	+55.5	+184.3 (to 1997)	+21.3	−31.8	+244.5 (to 1997)

Source: Rates and ton-miles from *Transportation in America 2000, with Historical Compendium 1939–1999*, 18th ed. (Washington: Eno Foundation, 2001). Traffic, length of haul, track, and employee productivity from Association of American Railroads, *Railroad Facts*, 2000 edition (Washington: 2000).

n.a. Not available.

railroads' average return on equity increased from less than 3 percent in the years 1971–80, to 5.3 percent in 1980–89, and to 10.7 percent in 1989–97.[11] According to the STB's calculations, rates of return were still short of those adequate to attract capital, although skeptics noted that the railroads seemed to be investing and that their share prices were rising faster than many stock market averages.[12]

Exactly how much credit deregulation should be given for the turn-around in the railroad industry is, of course, hard to tell. All things being equal, the growth in the economy during this period, for example, should have resulted in an increase in freight traffic. But the economy had grown in the 1950s and 1960s as well, and rail traffic had fallen then. Most observers believe that deregulation played a major role in the turnaround, if only because trends changed so dramatically once the industry was deregulated.

By the end of the 1990s, however, deregulation was being criticized for not providing enough protection to captive shippers. Although rates had gone down on average, not all shippers had benefited equally, and some were pressing Congress to strengthen the STB's powers to control rates, effectively reintroducing regulation. These complaints gained added impetus because of the consolidation of the industry into four very large railroads.

Railroad Mergers

From a public policy perspective, mergers involve a balancing of potential benefits and costs. A merger can allow the industry to cut costs and improve service, but it can also reduce competition and allow the industry to charge higher prices. The most desirable mergers are those that offer strong prospects for cost cutting and service improvements and minimal risks of reduced competition.

Transport economists distinguish mergers of carriers whose routes connect end-to-end from mergers of carriers whose routes are parallel. End-to-end mergers are deemed desirable because they usually increase benefits and reduce costs. End-to-end mergers should not reduce the number of carriers a shipper can choose from, as long as rail portals (interchange points) remain open. Moreover, end-to-end mergers can produce important cost savings and service improvements if there is a large volume of through traffic. Transferring a car from one railroad to another typically adds a day to the journey and is a major source of unreliability. Railroads with high volumes of interchange traffic can coordinate their schedules and take other steps to make transfers easier, but, as one railroad CEO explained, "there is nothing that is a substitute for one philosophy of management, one agenda, one operating plan, and a single implementation effort."[13]

Parallel mergers can generate substantial savings by eliminating duplicate lines and facilities. For example, the merged railroad can pick the most level and direct route between two points and concentrate enough traffic on it to justify improvements and exploit economies of traffic density. But parallel mergers also eliminate shipper choices and thus raise competitive concerns.

In the twenty years leading up to deregulation, mergers diminished the number of class I railroads from around seventy to around forty. (The definition of class I railroads has changed over the years, but generally the category includes all but the smallest short-line or local railroads.) Most of the mergers were parallel, like the one that formed the Penn Central, and were motivated primarily by the desire to cut costs. There was relatively little concern about the risk of increased market power at the time, however, because the ICC still tightly controlled railroad tariffs and because policymakers were more preoccupied with preventing bankruptcies than with the risk of monopoly.

After deregulation there were two waves of mergers. Most of these combined end-to-end and parallel elements, with the mixture varying from one merger to the next. The first wave occurred in the early 1980s and, for the most part, was approved enthusiastically by the ICC,[14] although it drew complaints from some shippers and helped prompt an effort to persuade Congress to reimpose regulation in 1986. The second wave occurred in the 1990s and generated more controversy because it resulted in the formation of four enormous railroads that together accounted for approximately 85 percent of all rail freight revenues in the United States.[15] Two of the railroads were located west of the Mississippi River and two were to the east. In the West, the Burlington Northern–Santa Fe (BNSF) was created when those two railroads merged in 1995. The Union Pacific (UP) responded in 1996 by absorbing the last remaining large railroad in the West: the Southern Pacific. In the East, there had been three large railroads until 1996, when the Norfolk-Southern (NS) and the CSX agreed to divide up Conrail, which by then had become profitable and was once again in private hands.

At the end of the 1990s, the industry seemed to be on the threshold of a third merger wave that would leave the country with two transcontinental railroads. The expectation was that the western and eastern railroads would pair up, perhaps as soon as NS and CSX had finished absorbing Conrail. But in January 2000 the BNSF expanded the possibilities by announcing its intention to merge with Canadian National (CN), one of Canada's two transcontinental railroads.

The Effectiveness of Contracts

Contracts seem to have been reasonably effective in protecting captive shippers from monopoly abuse even as rail transport became an increasingly concentrated industry. In 1998, when there were only four major railroads, Curtis Grimm and Clifford Winston estimated that only about 20 percent of all rail freight traffic met the STB's definition of captivity.[16] Most of the captive traffic was in coal, grains, and chemicals.[17]

The percentage of captive shippers would have been higher if the STB had not insisted on track rights as a condition for approving many of the mergers of the 1990s. In the BNSF merger, for example, UP was granted rights to use BNSF track in Kansas and Nebraska so that grain shippers in those states who had been served by both the Burlington Northern and the Santa Fe would still have a choice between two carriers. Similarly, when UP merged with Southern Pacific the STB required UP to grant BNSF track rights to the points that had been served by both UP and Southern Pacific. The division of Conrail between NS and CSX involved extensive track rights as well.[18] Moreover, the percentage of shippers served by only one railroad should not be affected significantly if future mergers create two transcontinental railroads because the transcontinental mergers would be almost purely end-to-end.[19]

Even where a shipper is served by only one railroad, competition from other modes, locations, or products is reasonably common. Trucks can be an effective alternative for containers and high-value, time-sensitive commodities, and barges are useful for bulk shippers located on a waterway. And many shippers, such as coal mines or chemical plants, face such strong competition from other plants and locations that the railroads cannot raise their rates too high without losing the shipment. For some large shippers, the "competition" may be internal to the company. A large chemical or auto company may have plants in several states and the option of shifting production from one site to another depending upon relative freight rates.

Captive shippers have two routes of relief: one private and contractual and the other public and regulatory. Most captive shippers rely on the contractual approach: 94 percent of the traffic classified by Grimm and Winston as captive moved under contracts. The contracts in their sample averaged two and one-half years, although some were for as long as ten years. But surprisingly, much of the traffic that is not captive moves under contract rates as well. Indeed, over 70 percent of all rail traffic moved under contract rates in the late 1990s.[20]

Contracts have proven attractive to noncaptive as well as captive shippers because they generate new opportunities for cost savings and service improvements. Negotiating the contractual arrangements between themselves, without interference or intervention by regulatory authorities, shippers and their railroads often identify and exploit efficiency opportunities that are not easily achievable by a regulatory agency. Shippers and the railroad can negotiate trade-offs at many different margins, such as volumes generated, volumes guaranteed, seasonal patterns of shipment, need for and availability of rolling stock, speed of delivery, and reliability of delivery. Indeed, these kinds of individually tailored adjustments and cost savings probably contributed importantly to the reduction in average railroad unit costs and rates since deregulation. By contrast, under regulation, equity, transparency, and other considerations often require that roughly similar rates be charged for apparently similar activities; this is more easily done by homogenizing the product or service than by allowing individual adaptations through negotiated contracts.

The alternative to a contract is for the captive shipper to appeal to the STB. The STB can decide if a tariff is roughly fair or not, usually compromising between the two final offers made by the parties involved. Clearly the scope, if not the possibility, of negotiating the various marginal valuations and costs of different service characteristics is greatly complicated, perhaps even foreclosed, with regulation. A "regulatory contract," often less than freely entered into by the participants, is also likely to be more difficult to enforce, certainly as contrasted with a contract derived through bilateral negotiations of the two parties involved. As a consequence, a regulatory solution may be less favorable to all concerned.

In fact, captive shippers operating under a contract may not be as interested in using the regulatory option to obtain a rate as they are in strengthening their negotiating position when their contracts come up for renewal. In effect, the threat to exploit regulatory relief becomes to the captive shipper what competitive relief is to the noncaptive shipper. In the long run, however, the best negotiating threat for the captive shipper is to cease operations at the captive site unless treated fairly enough so that it can be competitive with noncaptive shippers.

As a group, captive shippers appear to be better protected under deregulation than they were before, although perhaps not as well as they would be if they were not captive. On the basis of their 1998 sample, Grimm and Winston estimate that rail rates were 21 percent higher for captive than for noncaptive shippers, controlling for such factors as commodity type, length of haul, shipment volume, and corridor.[21] To put this in perspective, average rail rates fell by 44 percent between 1980 and 1997. Even allowing for the fact that the 44 percent figure is not adjusted for commodity mix and length of haul, the typical captive shipper probably paid less in 1998 than he would have under the old system of ICC regulation, although perhaps not as much less as his noncaptive peers.

Despite this favorable record, however, at least two problems persisted. The first was that small captive shippers were probably less well protected than large captive shippers, largely because the transaction costs of pursuing either contract or regulatory relief were relatively high for them. The second problem was that captive shippers were less and less impressed with comparisons to the regulatory regimes of twenty years earlier. The fact that captive shippers were paying more than their noncaptive colleagues seemed far more salient than the fact that they were paying less than they would have under the old regulatory regime.

By the end of the 1990s, complaints about captive shippers were becoming a rallying cry for efforts to reimpose regulation. Consumers United for Rail Equity (CURE), a group backed by coal and electric utility interests, was lobbying Congress for more protection for captive shippers. The Alliance for Rail Competition (ARC), which represented agricultural, manufacturing, chemical, and other trade associations, was lobbying not just for pricing constraints but also for the more radical idea of forcing the railroads to provide open access to all of their tracks. Open access would likely require some form of regulation, particularly to protect the rights of the remaining small railroads or of shippers who wanted to operate their own trains.[22]

The STB responded to shipper pressures in December 1999, when it simplified the test of whether a shipper was captive by eliminating the railroad's defense that there could be competition from other products or locations. From then on a shipper would be presumed captive if it did not have a choice of railroads and if there were no barge or truck alternatives. In

March 2000, shortly after BNSF announced its intention to merge with Canadian National, the STB also announced a fifteen-month moratorium on all merger approvals while it studied the future of the industry.

In October 2000, the STB went further by proposing new guidelines for the review of future mergers. In the past the STB had required merger applicants to "cure" specific reductions in competition that a merger might bring. If the merger reduced the number of railroads serving a point from two to one, for example, the STB would typically expect the applicants to grant track rights to a third railroad so that shippers at the location would still have a choice of two independent railroads. Under the proposed guidelines, applicants would have to demonstrate that the proposed merger would "enhance" competition, presumably by granting rights to points that were not affected by the merger. Shippers applauded the proposal, but the railroads feared that the effect would be to encourage rent-seeking behavior on the part of the shippers and to reintroduce regulation in the form of controls over the prices that railroads could charge for access to their tracks.

The problem of small captive shippers is less serious than it was 100 years ago, when the ICC was first formed, and probably can be addressed by other means. Far fewer small shippers use railroads today; trucks have captured almost all of the merchandise that is not shipped in bulk. Even for bulk commodities, trucks are often competitive for smaller shipments moving short distances. In addition, small shippers sometimes can and do join associations or cooperatives in order to increase their bargaining power with railroads. Freight forwarders or consolidators might also serve that purpose. Finally, the STB might reduce the transactions costs of the current system by creating an office to assist small shippers in their appeals. Such an office would seem a more sensible and measured response than arbitrarily eliminating one of the three criteria established for defining shippers as captive.

Airline Deregulation

The airline industry had not been declining under regulation, and thus most of the early criticism of the Civil Aeronautics Board (CAB) came from the academic community rather than the industry. By the 1960s, scholars were arguing that the CAB was excessively concerned with ensuring that the industry was financially strong enough to buy the most modern planes and to extend service to small communities.[23] The CAB awarded a disproportionate share of the more lucrative new routes to the financially weaker carriers, a strategy that was designed to prevent bankruptcies but that also seemed to reward poor management and create inefficient route networks. Fares were thought to be too high, as evidenced by the fact that the intrastate airlines, which were not under the CAB's control, charged less than those that provided interstate service.[24] High fares often resulted in wasteful service rather than large airline profits, moreover, because airlines on routes served by multiple carriers often competed for passengers by offering in-flight amenities—such as fancy meals and even piano bars—that passengers did not value much.[25]

By the 1970s a few airlines began to feel that the CAB's tight controls over routes and fares hampered the ability of the industry to respond to economic problems and opportunities.[26] The CAB set fares using a cost-based formula called the "standard industry fare level," or SIFL. Discounts off the SIFL were sometimes allowed, but only with restrictions such as advance purchase and Saturday-night stays. Because fuel is a large airline expense, the energy crisis of the early 1970s greatly increased airline costs, and it also contributed to a worldwide recession that cut airline traffic. The airlines were left with serious excess capacity, and some companies wished they had more flexibility to respond with pricing and other strategies.

Airline deregulation began in 1976, when a forward-looking CAB chairman, John Robson, began to relax controls over fares and routes. The big changes came after 1978, under chairman Alfred Kahn, when Congress passed a law immediately eliminating most controls and phasing out the CAB. In 1984 the CAB was closed and the U.S. Department of Transportation assumed the CAB's few remaining functions, most notably its authority to review mergers and other inter-airline agreements and to negotiate international aviation treaties. The regulation of airline safety was not affected by the reforms and remained the responsibility of the Federal Aviation Administration, a separate agency within the U.S. Department of Transportation.

The architects of airline deregulation did not conceive of much need for promoting private contracts or providing some residual form of tariff regulation, as in the railroad industry. Most observers thought the industry had characteristics that would ensure intense competition.[27] The automobile had long been a fairly effective competitor on short routes. The economies of flying larger aircraft were not so great that most busy routes could not support multiple departures by reasonable size planes. Finally, on routes where autos were not effective competition and that were served by only one airline, the mere threat of entry by another airline might be sufficient to make the incumbent show restraint. Airline routes were often cited as an example of a "contestable" market in that most airline assets were highly mobile and could be redeployed quickly from one market to another.[28] If the sole carrier serving a route raised its fares significantly above costs, it was likely to soon be joined by a competitor.

Changes in Traffic, Average Fares, Service Quality, and Profitability

The overall performance of the airline industry improved significantly with deregulation, although not to the same extent as the performance of the railroad industry. Airline travel had grown rapidly in the two decades before deregulation, in part because of the widespread introduction of jets in the 1960s and wide-bodied aircraft in the 1970s. Travel continued to grow rapidly after deregulation, and by 1999 U.S. airlines were carrying more than twice as many passengers as they had in 1978 (see table 3-3).

The growth in passenger traffic was not surprising because, over the same years, average fares declined by more than 50 percent (see table 3-3). Just how much of the fare decline was attributable to deregulation and how much would have occurred anyway owing to technological and other improvements is not obvious. The best available estimates are by Steven Morrison and Clifford Winston, who compare the average fares with the likely regulated fares calculated by applying an updated version of the CAB's old SIFL formula.[29] They estimate that the average fare savings climbed from 16 percent in the first year of deregulation to 31 percent in 1982 and have hovered around 25 percent since then (see figure 3-1).

Service quality increased as well, although not by all measures. Planes became more crowded as airlines reduced the cost per passenger in part by filling more seats. Load factors (the industry's term for the percentage of seats occupied) increased from the high 50s typical during the years of CAB regulation to the mid-60s and low 70s in the years after (see table 3-3). Flight times increased slightly owing to growing congestion at the nation's airports and airways. Passengers were also more likely to have to connect flights to complete their trips, as the airlines began to rely on hub-and-spoke route networks. People traveling on discounted fares often had to put up with the inconvenience of fare restrictions, such as advance purchase, cancellation penalties, and Saturday-night stays. And some small communities

Table 3-3. *Performance of the U.S. Airline Industry, 1950–99*

Year	Passengers enplaned (millions)	Passenger miles carried (billions)	Revenue per passenger mile (in 1999 cents)	Average trip length (miles)	Load factor (percent)	Estimated return on investment (percent)
1950	19.2	10.2	47.5	431	60.8	n.a.
1960	57.9	38.9	36.8	671	59.3	3.3
1970	169.9	131.7	24.7	775	49.6	1.5
1975	205.1	162.8	23.4	794	53.7	2.5
1978	274.7	226.8	21.1	825	61.5	13.0
1979	316.7	262.0	19.9	827	63.0	7.0
1980	296.9	255.2	22.2	860	59.0	5.8
1981	286.0	248.9	22.5	870	58.6	5.3
1982	294.1	259.6	20.3	883	59.0	2.7
1983	318.6	281.8	19.4	885	60.6	5.9
1984	344.7	305.1	19.4	885	59.2	10.0
1985	382.0	336.4	18.1	881	61.4	10.0
1986	418.9	366.5	16.6	875	60.3	5.0
1987	447.7	404.5	16.3	903	62.3	7.2
1988	454.6	423.3	16.0	931	63.0	11.0
1989	453.7	432.7	15.8	954	63.2	6.3
1990	465.6	457.9	15.7	984	62.4	-6.0
1991	452.3	448.0	15.1	990	63.0	-0.5
1992	475.1	478.6	14.4	1007	64.0	-9.3
1993	488.5	489.7	14.7	1002	64.0	-0.4
1994	528.8	519.2	13.7	982	66.2	5.3
1995	547.8	540.4	14.1	987	67.0	12.0
1996	581.2	578.7	13.8	996	69.3	12.0
1997	599.1	605.6	13.6	1,011	70.3	15.0
1998	612.9	618.1	13.4	1,008	70.7	12.0
1999	635.4	651.6	12.9	1,025	71.0	11.5
Percentage change, 1978–99	+131	+187	–39	+24	+15	–12

Source: Air Transport Association, *Air Transport: The Annual Report of the Scheduled U.S. Airline Industry*, various editions (Washington).

Figure 3-1. *Percentage Reduction in Average Airline Fares due to Deregulation, 1978–98*

Percent

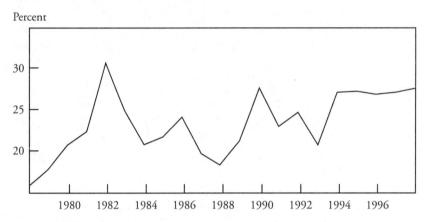

Source: Steven A. Morrison and Clifford Winston, "The Remaining Role for Government Policy in the Deregulated Airline Industry," in Sam Peltzman and Clifford Winston, eds., *Deregulation of Network Industries: What's Next?* (Brookings, 2000), p. 2.

saw their jet service replaced with smaller, slower, and noisier turboprops. These service quality reductions were offset, at least in part, by quality increases. The frequency of service between city pairs increased significantly, which was of particular benefit to business travelers with busy schedules. Although there were more connections, most of them were on the same airline rather than between airlines, so that the connections were tighter and anxieties about making them lower. Small communities may have lost jet services, but their prop replacements flew more often and at more convenient times.

As a whole, travelers appear to be substantially better off. Morrison and Winston estimate that the flying public gained $18.4 billion from airline deregulation in 1993. Of this, $12.4 billion was due to the savings in lower fares and the remaining $6.0 billion to benefits from higher service quality. In the case of service quality, they argue that the values travelers placed on added frequencies and on-line connections far outweighed the losses suffered from higher load factors, fare restrictions, and added connections.[30]

Whether the airline companies were better off or not is a little more difficult to determine. The industry's profitability has always been highly cyclical because both business and pleasure traffic are very sensitive to the ups and downs of the overall economy. Initially the industry was concerned that postderegulation profits might prove too modest to attract investment, particularly after returns on airline equity hit a record low during the recession of the early 1980s. By the late 1990s, however, this concern seemed to be put to rest as airline profits reached record highs by most measures.[31]

As in the case of the railroads, the generally happy story hid some problems. Although the average traveler was better off, some consumer groups did not feel they had benefited, particularly business travelers and travelers who resided in a dozen cities where most air service was provided by a single carrier. These concerns were heightened by increasing concentration in the industry.

Another stakeholder group that experienced mixed results under deregulation was labor. Organized labor on the whole was probably adversely affected. Opportunities to capture "rents" on monopoly activities protected or created by regulation were severely curtailed. Deregulation, and the attendant need to be efficient in the face of new competition, became the excuse or occasion for eliminating many featherbedding or make-work practices. To some considerable extent, however, the impact of these adverse developments was mitigated by various buy-out, grandfathering, and two-tier arrangements that protected the incumbent unionized labor force. For labor as a whole, as distinguished from organized labor, the probability of lower average wages was substantially, and possibly totally, offset by the prospect of greater growth and employment in this traditionally high-wage industry.

Changes in Airline Industry Structure

The airline industry can be divided into two groups: the "old guard" of major carriers that existed before deregulation and the new airlines that have entered the business since deregulation. Immediately after deregulation the old guard was largely preoccupied with developing hub-and-spoke route networks, and some smaller carriers disappeared quietly in the process.[32] A wave of important mergers also occurred later, in the mid-1980s, heavily motivated by the desire of carriers to develop stronger hubs or a more comprehensive national network.[33] At the end of the decade, other carriers were eliminated by bankruptcy, most notably Eastern and Pan Am (both in 1990).[34] By the end of the 1990s the old guard had been reduced to seven important airlines plus a handful of minor players. Of the seven, three (United, American, and Delta) were very large, and four (Northwest, Continental, US Airways, and TWA) were somewhat smaller but still national in scope and with important international routes.[35] In May 2000, United announced its intention to take over US Airways but abandoned the effort a year later because of the skepticism of antitrust authorities. Had the merger gone through, it probably would have provoked the remaining five large carriers to consolidate into two, leaving the country with three mega-carriers.[36]

While the old guard consolidated, the new entrants have had only mixed success. Morrison and Winston report that only one of the fifty-eight new companies that entered the scheduled airline business between 1978 and 1990 survived into this millennium.[37] A new crop of start-up carriers did enter though, during the 1990s. The pace of new entry slowed after 1996, however, when a plane of one of these new airlines, Valujet, crashed into the Florida Everglades and all aboard died. Almost all of the new entrants compete with the old guard by offering lower fares and no-frills service, but only Southwest Airlines has successfully used this strategy to develop into a large carrier.[38] Southwest technically should not be considered a new entrant, although it had avoided CAB regulation by operating only intrastate routes in Texas before deregulation. Southwest achieves extraordinary productivity by using only one type of aircraft, avoiding congested major airports in favor of secondary airports, and specializing in medium- and short-haul direct flights instead of developing a hub-and-spoke network. By the end of the 1990s, the low-fare, new-entrant airlines accounted for approximately 20 percent of the passengers carried in the United States, and approximately two-thirds of those passengers were carried by Southwest alone.[39]

The consolidation of the industry has meant a decline in head-to-head competition between airlines. Table 3-4 combines figures from two studies to show the percentage of city pairs served by three or more carriers from 1979 to 1989 and the percentage of passengers on city pairs with three or more carriers in 1992 and 1997. The percentage of city pairs with three or more carriers increased from 20 percent in 1979 to 53 percent in 1984 but has declined since. By 1997 the percentage of passengers on routes with three or more carriers had fallen to 35 percent, and the percentage of routes had probably fallen even further (since heavily traveled routes are more likely to have three or more carriers). By the end of the 1990s there were a dozen hub airports where a single airline carried over 50 percent of local passengers or two airlines carried over 60 percent, as shown in table 3-5.

Table 3-4. *City Pairs by the Number of Carriers Serving Them, 1979–97*

Number of carriers[a]	Percent of city pairs			Percent of passengers in city pairs	
	1979	1984	1988–89	1992	1997
One	n.a.	n.a.	n.a.	18	19
Two	n.a.	n.a.	n.a.	43	46
Three or more	20	53	40	39	35

Sources: The data for 1979–89 are from Transportation Research Board, *Winds of Change* (Washington: National Academy of Sciences Press, 1991), p. 106; the data for 1992 and 1997 are from Transportation Research Board, *Entry and Competition in the U.S. Airline Industry* (Washington: National Academy of Sciences Press 1999), pp. 68–71.

a. Only carriers with at least a 10 percent market share in the city pair are counted, because carriers with a lower share are unlikely to be effective competitors.

Table 3-5. *Hub Airports Dominated by One or Two Carriers*

Airport	Dominant carrier	Dominant carriers' 1997 share of	
		Enplanements (percent)	Flights (percent)
Atlanta	Delta	80	61
Charlotte	US Airways	92	89
Chicago O'Hare	United and American	47 and 34	39 and 31
Cincinnati	Delta	94	76
Dallas–Fort Worth	American	66	52
Denver	United	69	57
Detroit	Northwest	78	69
Memphis	Northwest	78	40
Minneapolis–St. Paul	Northwest	80	69
Pittsburgh	US Airways	90	78
Salt Lake City	Delta	77	66
St. Louis	TWA	71	54

Source: Transportation Research Board, *Entry and Competition in the U.S. Airline Industry* (Washington: National Academy of Sciences Press, 1999), pp. 74–77; shares from Federal Aviation Administration data as reported by Don H. Pickrell, "Air Fare Premiums at Hub Airports: A Review of the Evidence," Volpe Center, U.S. Department of Transportation, draft February 18, 2000, table 1.

a. Dominance is defined as a single carrier having over 60 percent of enplanements or two carriers having over 80 percent combined.

Are Some Passengers Worse Off?

Considerable attention has been given to the question of whether the growing concentration in the airline industry has harmed some groups of passengers. The studies are not conclusive, but they suggest a pattern similar to that in railroads: some passengers enjoy fewer benefits from deregulation than others, but even they are still probably better off than they would have been under the old regime.

One piece of evidence that suggests a possible "unfair" sharing of the benefits of deregulation is that the dispersion between the lowest and highest fares has grown enormously. Before deregulation, discounts rarely exceeded 25 percent off the standard coach fare. By 1992, as table 3-6 shows, the 10th percentile fare (that is, the fare 10 percent of passengers pay less than) was only half the median fare and one-quarter to one-fifth the 90th and 95th percentile fares. By 1998 the gap had widened further and the 90th and 95th percentile fares, which are typically paid by business people traveling at the last minute, were three to four times the median fare and six to eight times the 10th percentile fares.

Fare dispersion can reflect cost differentials as well as market power. The demand for air travel peaks at certain hours of the day and seasons of the year, and it is costly to maintain extra planes and crews to serve the peak. To accommodate last-minute travelers the airlines must hold some empty seats up until departure instead of releasing them to travelers looking for discount fares.[40] As a result, a higher proportion of the seats reserved for full fares depart empty, while the seats reserved for discount fares are sold out. Nevertheless, some of the restrictions placed on discount fares have no obvious basis in cost. Requirements to stay over a Saturday night serve no clear purpose, for example, except to separate less price-sensitive business travelers from more price-sensitive leisure travelers. And price differences that are not based on cost can only be sustained where competition is not completely effective.

Empirical studies of price dispersion suggest that a combination of cost and noncost factors are involved. The most careful study to date found that price dispersion was higher on routes served with two or three carriers than with one, suggesting that the introduction of competition had led to more cost-based differences in price.[41] But that same study also found that dispersion was higher for fares to airports with capacity limitations, which indicates that limitations on competition encourage dispersion as well. The study used data from 1986, which was close to the high point of competi-

Table 3-6. *Dispersion of Airline Coach Fares, 1992–98*[a]

Length of flight	Fares by percentile (median = 100)					
	10th	25th	50th	75th	90th	95th
Short haul (750 miles or less)						
1992	44	68	100	150	200	250
1995	46	71	100	150	250	300
1998	47	67	100	170	270	330
Medium haul (751–1,500 miles)						
1992	50	68	100	150	210	250
1995	65	77	100	150	250	300
1998	60	75	100	140	270	370
Long haul (over 1,500 miles)						
1992	50	67	100	140	210	240
1995	65	80	100	140	260	330
1998	56	77	100	150	290	400

Source: Transportation Research Board, *Entry and Competition in the U.S. Airline Industry* (Washington: National Academy of Sciences Press, 1999), p. 31.

a. Excludes frequent-flyer tickets.

tion within the industry when measured by the numbers of routes served by multiple carriers (see table 3-4). It is striking that fare dispersion increased during the 1990s even as the level of competition seemed to be declining (see table 3-6).[42] The pattern suggests that price dispersion increased for different reasons at different times. In the 1980s, price dispersion may have increased primarily because the relaxation of CAB fare controls and the introduction of competition in previous monopoly markets forced carriers to introduce more discount fares based on costs. In the 1990s, however, dispersion may have continued to increase because competition subsided a bit and carriers became more sophisticated at exploring differences in passengers' willingness to pay.

Other studies have concluded that passengers traveling to and from dominated hubs pay premium fares. In an early and widely reported study, for example, the General Accounting Office (GAO) estimated that during the 1985–89 period fares at fifteen dominated hubs were an average of 27 percent higher than fares at thirty-eight comparison airports.[43] The airlines argued that the GAO's comparison was unfair because the cities picked for hubs have a high proportion of short-haul and business traffic that is more expensive to serve per passenger-mile. Indeed, later studies showed that if one controlled for trip length the premium was cut roughly in half, to about 15 percent. Statistics on the percentage of business travelers by route are not readily available, but controlling for service qualities normally associated with business travelers cut the premium even further.[44] In addition, if the presence of Southwest at some airports is also controlled for, the hub premium disappears for all but a few airports.[45]

Finally, since the early days of deregulation, studies have consistently shown that the number of carriers on a route affects the fares they charge. In other words, the airline market is not perfectly contestable and the threat of entry is not as powerful as actual competition. Estimates of how much additional carriers reduce fares vary from one study to another, but an increase in the number of carriers from two to three can reduce fares by 4 to 21 percent.[46] By the late 1990s, the presence of Southwest on a route seemed to be particularly important in holding fares down. According to one estimate, entry by Southwest reduced fares on a route by roughly 20 percent, and the effects of Southwest accounted for 40 percent of the total fare savings attributable to deregulation in 1998.[47]

Collectively, this research suggests that there may be some truth to the popular impression that passengers on business trips and traveling to and from dominated airports are not benefiting as much as others. Moreover, actual competition matters, so the effects of past and proposed mergers and the survival of low-cost carriers like Southwest should be a matter of public policy concern.

Nevertheless, as in the case of railroads, it is probably true that even the travelers on business and from dominated hubs are probably better off because of deregulation. Not all of the observed fare differentials are due to limited competition; a good portion are cost-based. If only half of the premium paid by travelers from dominated hubs is due to lack of competition, for example, then these travelers are paying perhaps 10 percent more than other flyers. But this may still be less than before deregulation because deregulation reduced average fares by 25 percent.

Again, as in the case of railroads, some fare dispersion may be needed and even advantageous. Specifically, charging the highest fares to customers with the least sensitivity to price may be the best way of recouping the fixed costs and overhead of airline operations: such a pattern of price discrimination would yield the minimal diversion from a "socially optimal" marginal cost pricing solution (which is otherwise deemed unacceptable because, for example, it does not cover all the costs of airline operation, including overhead and fixed costs).

Sources of Market Power

The ability to charge customers more than cost depends on the presence of some barrier to entry that prevents competitors from entering and undercutting prices. In the case of airlines there are at least five such suspected barriers.

One suspect is the hub-and-spoke networks that airlines have developed since deregulation. A hub-and-spoke system allows an airline to provide frequent and low-cost service between many city pairs by concentrating traffic bound for many destinations on each spoke. An airline that wishes to serve a city pair served by a hubbing carrier has the unattractive choice of either building its own hub or charging a lower fare. Building a hub is a major investment, but without it the challenger will find it difficult to offer as frequent service at a reasonable cost and may be forced to drop its fares to attract traffic. The fact that hub fare premiums do not appear to be based entirely on costs suggests that hubs serve as barriers.

A second barrier most industry analysts consider important is constraints on access to airports. For a variety of reasons—congestion, noise, environmental concerns, and others—the Federal Aviation Administration limits the number of takeoff and landing "slots" per hour at four U.S. airports (Dulles, Kennedy, O'Hare, Reagan National). The large incumbent airlines own the rights to most of those slots, and attempts to force them to transfer the slots to challengers or to create a market in slots have been only partially successful. In addition, at many airports the major airlines have long-term leases on most of the gates and have resisted efforts to force them to lease gates to challengers at reasonable rates.

A third barrier may be airline marketing practices, such as frequent-flyer programs and travel agent incentives. Frequent-flyer programs give large airlines a competitive advantage because it is easier for passengers to accumulate enough mileage to earn free flights and special preferences at check-in or boarding by traveling on an airline with an extensive route network. One study estimated, for example, that American Airlines would have lost significant market share if frequent-flyer programs had been eliminated in 1990, when American had the largest and best developed frequent-flyer program. If all frequent-flyer programs had been abolished, American was projected to lose 18 percent of its market share, mostly to small airlines. If only American's program had been eliminated, American's market share might have fallen by 50 percent.[48]

Predatory behavior by large airlines against small start-up carriers may also be creating a barrier, although industry analysts disagree about the prevalence and importance of predation. The usual test of predatory behavior is whether an incumbent responds to entry by dropping its prices below the short-run marginal cost. Because airline costs and pricing strategies are so complex, applying the test is particularly difficult in this industry. Many economists believe, for example, that higher returns forgone (because of diverting more aircraft to fly on a contested route) should be included as an opportunity cost in calculating the relevant short-run opportunities. Measuring these opportunity costs can be exceedingly difficult. Nevertheless, by 1999 the Department of Justice's Antitrust Division had become sufficiently concerned that it brought a case against American Airlines for driving a start-up airline from American's Dallas–Fort Worth hub.[49]

Finally, international airline alliances also may reduce competition. During the 1990s, the U.S. Department of Transportation approved a number of agreements between U.S. airlines and foreign carriers that allowed them to share codes for flights and coordinate schedules and capacity. For example, United and Lufthansa concluded an agreement to coordinate and code-share both their flights over the North Atlantic and the feeder flights to their various gateways in the United States and Germany. Participating airlines argue that these alliances will improve connections for traffic originating or terminating beyond the gateway airports. But the danger, of course, is that this type of "coordination" will ultimately be used to reduce effective competition on the main gateway-to-gateway routes. Furthermore if only a few "world alliances" emerge, this may limit the number of major U.S. airlines that are able to survive (because a U.S. airline that is not a member of one of the world alliances will not get as much international feeder traffic).

Possible Remedies

Perhaps one should not be surprised that private contracts have emerged spontaneously, without government encouragement, as practical remedies to the airline industry's competitive shortcomings. One form these contracts have taken is fare discounts negotiated by large corporations with big travel budgets. It is not uncommon for an air carrier to agree to give a large corporation a special discount of 10 percent or more off all published fares for travel by its employees. These negotiated discounts should offset, at least in part, any price discrimination that the airlines attempt to practice against business travelers.

A second form of private contract is agreements by local corporations to support new airlines. The most prominent example is ProAir, which was established in 1997 to provide short-haul flights between Detroit and other business centers such as Pittsburgh, Atlanta, and New York. Local businesses had been complaining that Northwest was charging high fares at its Detroit hub and that Northwest had driven away at least one start-up airline that attempted to offer service out of Detroit. General Motors and other large Detroit-based corporations decided to back the creation of ProAir with multiyear contracts guaranteeing the airline a minimum amount of travel by employees and their families.[50]

Private contracts are unlikely to solve as much of the residual monopoly problems in the airline industry as they have in the railroads, however, simply because the airlines have many more small customers so the contractual solution is harder. Large corporations use airlines extensively, but they do not dominate airline traffic in the way they do railroad freight traffic. Thus the transaction costs of a contractual solution are too high for many of the businesses and travelers that rely on airlines.

The advantages of private contracts in tailoring services to the needs of individual customers are also probably smaller for airlines than they are for railroads. To a large extent the airlines have done this tailoring already with their proliferation of fares and sophisticated systems of capacity controls for customer reservations. Airlines offer passengers a wide range of service quality and pricing options in which, for example, travelers willing to book far ahead or travel outside peak hours and seasons are offered cheaper seats. When passengers select from this menu, they enjoy many of the cost savings of customized service that railroad shippers gain through contracts.

Given the limitations of private contract solutions, airline passengers may have to rely more on the government to resolve the residual problems of monopoly power. Luckily, there is much government can do, in essence completing the task of deregulation. The government might do more to make gates and landing slots more readily available to challengers, for example, particularly at concentrated hub airports. A more active antitrust policy can and has been used against predatory behavior by incumbent airlines. The Department of Transportation might be more sensitive to the competitive implications of international alliances that have recently emerged, much as it has already shown greater sensitivity to the potential for reduced competition from travel agent incentive plans and abuses of computer reservation systems. As for railroads, all potential avenues for increasing or enhancing competition should be explored.[51]

Conclusions

The provision of transport services has long been a major concern of governments around the world, in part because the proper provision of transport is almost invariably deemed a sine qua non for economic development. However, these government interventions have often led to considerable inefficiency in the provision of transport services. The emphasis in public policy for some time was on nonefficiency considerations, such as income redistribution and development for its own sake. The realization only slowly crept into the governing wisdom that efficiency deserves some attention as well. That realization, in turn, has led to considerable experimentation with privatization and deregulation in the past two decades, representing a systematic but still highly selective reduction of government involvement in the transport sector. Even restricting the survey to the U.S. experience with deregulation, as this chapter does, some remarkably strong policy conclusions emerge.

To start, if efficiency is the goal, deregulate if at all possible. Deregulation was strongly associated with improved performance in the U.S. railroad and airline industries. Some of the improvement in profitability might have been attributable to other sources, particularly in the case of the railroads.[52] Nevertheless, in both industries costs and tariffs went down and traffic and profits went up after deregulation.

The opportunities for deregulation may be greater, moreover, than originally thought possible. Many regulated activities combine separable and identifiable activities, some of which are competitive and some of which are not. Little seems gained from imposing the inefficiencies of regulation on subsidiary activities that are competitive and separable.[53] However, separability may not be obvious or easily identified; for instance, it may not be wise for railroads to separate the operation of passenger and freight trains (which are potentially competitive) from the provision of the stations, yards, track, and other infrastructure (which is deemed to be noncompetitive or monopolistic).[54] Again, once the separation has been made, different policies can be pursued such that competitive sectors are deregulated while the monopoly sectors remain regulated.

Many transport activities, of course, do not have to be restructured or unbundled before being deregulated because they were never natural monopolies. In many cases they came under regulation, not so much to control monopoly as to develop, promote, and perfect the industries' growth. That commonly seems to have been the case with airlines, buses, and trucking.

Finally, if some residual government regulation is unavoidable, then thought should be given to procedures other than those based strictly on conventional rate-of-return regulation as practiced by U.S. commissions. Among the interesting alternatives are franchise or concession contracts used in many developing countries and price-cap regulation as it has emerged in the United Kingdom.

In this regard, the potential of contracts is striking, particularly in the case of railroads. Railroads still retain elements of natural monopoly, despite the substantial inroads of trucks and barges over the past century. It is often efficient for only one railroad to serve a given route. And shippers may not have alternatives, for example, if they are moving bulk products not suitable for trucks and they have a substantial investment in a specific location. In these situations, however, long-term contracts may be sufficient to protect shippers (and railroads) from opportunistic behavior and make private markets more workable. Contracts have the added and critical benefit of allowing suppliers to tailor their services to the needs of particular customers and thereby save costs for all.

But contracts do not work in every situation, particularly where there are, as in airlines, many small customers for whom the costs of negotiating the contract could be high. In such cases, the only remedy may be government interventions to promote competition, particularly, but not exclusively, through antitrust laws. Government needs to review mergers, alliances, and other interfirm agreements to make sure that they do not threaten competition unnecessarily and that any cost is at least offset by the benefits of efficiency or service improvements.

Without vigilance to promote competition, in fact, deregulation may turn out to be a relatively short-lived fad. Memories are short, and after twenty years of railroad and airline deregulation the public is more mindful of the problems of the present than the problems of the past. It is good to remember that those who complain seriously about deregulation's adverse effects in the United States remain a small minority, say 5 to 10 percent, of all shippers or passengers. But an intensely unhappy minority can be very influential.

Formal commission-style regulation has been mainly an American phenomenon, supplemented by some limited experiences elsewhere. For the rest of the world, the most relevant question may not be what might be gained from deregulation but what might be gained from avoiding regulation. In particular, when countries undertake privatization of their transport industries, how much formal regulation should they introduce to ensure that the newly privatized activities do not excessively exploit monopolistic positions?

Obviously the answer will depend upon the particular circumstances. What the American experience suggests is that where efficiency is the goal, regulation should be avoided whenever possible—that is, when competitive markets can be created or transaction costs are not excessive and contractual solutions will suffice. Of course, competitive situations are less likely to develop or occur in smaller developing economies than in the huge and already developed U.S. economy. By the same token, however, if economic underdevelopment is also associated with a limited development of commercial and administrative law, then formal commission-style regulation might be more difficult to implement in developing economies than in the United States. In such circumstances, the American experience can provide only limited guidance.

In short, reducing the role of government in transportation markets seems to have had beneficial effects almost everywhere it has been tried. Typically, operating costs, fares, and tariffs are down, while traffic volumes and profits are up. That is a powerful combination of advantages. Competition, however, often appears to be an important enabling condition for achieving these positive results, a condition that may require continuing oversight to maintain. The key seems to be a vigilant, perhaps even sometimes threatening, government but not an overbearing or controlling government.

Notes

1. There are many broad reviews of the potential savings and pitfalls of privatization; see, for example, John D. Donahue, *The Privatization Decision: Public Ends and Private Means* (Basic Books, 1989). Studies specific to transport also abound, including José Gómez-Ibáñez and John R. Meyer, *Going Private: The International Experience with*

Transport Privatization (Brookings, 1993); or Peter R. White, "What Conclusions Can Be Drawn about Bus Deregulation in Britain?" *Transport Reviews*, vol. 17, no. 1 (1997), pp. 1–16.

2. Alfred D. Chandler Jr. *The Visible Hand: The Managerial Revolution in American Business* (Harvard University Press, 1977), esp. chaps 3–5.

3. Robert M. Utley in a *New York Times* (December 12, 1999) review of *Empire Express* by David Howard Bain (Viking, 1999).

4. John Louis O'Sullivan as quoted in ibid., pp. 22.

5. For a review of the early literature on capture, see Thomas K. McGraw, "Regulation in America: A Review Essay," *Business History Review*, vol. 49, no. 2 (1975), pp. 159–83.

6. Robert A. Leone, *Who Profits? Winners, Losers, and Government Regulation* (Basic Books, 1986).

7. For the classic discussion of this point, see H. Averch and L. Johnson, "Behavior of the Firm under Regulatory Constraint," *American Economic Review* (December 1962), pp. 1052–69.

8. See, for example, José A. Gómez-Ibáñez, "Commitment and Flexibility: Strategies for Regulating Private Infrastructure," Discussion Paper, Taubman Center for State and Local Government, Kennedy School of Government, Harvard University, January 1999.

9. This story is told in Aaron J. Gellman, "Surface Freight Transportation," pp. 166–96, in William M. Capron, ed., *Technological Change in Regulated Industries* (Brookings, 1971); and "Southern Railway System: The Big John Investment," Harvard Business School case no. 9-677-244, 1977.

10. The early studies of this type included John R. Meyer, Merton J. Peck, John Stenason, and Charles Zwick, *The Economics of Competition in the Transportation Industries* (Harvard University Press, 1959); and Ann F. Friedlaender, *The Dilemma of Freight Transportation Regulation* (Brookings, 1969).

11. U.S. General Accounting Office, *Railroad Regulation: Changes in Rates and Service Quality since 1990*, report GAO-RECD-99-93, April 1999, p. 40.

12. U.S. General Accounting Office, *Railroad Regulation*, p. 45; and John H. Winner, "The Future Structure of the North American Rail Industry," report to the Office of the Secretary, U.S. Department of Transportation, June 1998, p. 11.

13. BNSF chairman Robert D. Krebs, as quoted in Winner, "Future Structure," p. 13. Winner cites as his source Daniel Machalaba, "Railroads Merging to Give Trucks a Run for the Money," *Wall Street Journal*, August 11, 1994.

14. A major exception was the disapproval of a proposed merger of the Southern Pacific and the Santa Fe railroads.

15. The four accounted for 89 percent of all the revenues collected by Class I railroads in the United States in 1999; American Association of Railroads, *Railroad Facts, 1999 Edition* (Washington, 1999), pp. 65 and 67.

16. The STB considered shippers to be captive if they met three conditions: (1) only one railroad serves either the origin or destination of their shipment; (2) they have no barge or rail alternative, at least at reasonable cost; and (3) they do not face significant competition from other products or from companies producing the same product at other locations.

17. Curtis Grimm and Clifford Winston, "Competition in the Deregulated Railroad Industry: Sources, Effects, and Policy Issues," in Sam Peltzman and Clifford Winston, eds., *Deregulation of Network Industries: What's Next?* (Brookings, 2000), pp. 63–64.

18. For a summary of the track rights, see Paul D. Larson and H. Barry Spraggins, "The American Railroad Industry: Twenty Years after Staggers," *Transportation Quarterly*, vol. 54, no. 2 (2000), pp. 35–36.

19. These transcontinental mergers might generate important cost savings and service improvements by eliminating the delays at Chicago and the Mississippi River crossings where the eastern and western railroads meet. Although only 6 percent of car loadings are transcontinental, this traffic represented roughly 37 percent of the remaining interchanged cars as of 1998 and included transfers at some notorious bottlenecks, including Chicago, where it often takes as many as three days to transfer a car from one railroad to the next. Winner, "Future Structure," pp. 17 and 20.

20. Grimm and Winston, "Competition in the Deregulated Railroad Industry," pp. 64 and 56.

21. Ibid., p. 65.

22. Regulation would be needed because neither group would be able to offer the large railroads the prospect of reciprocal access to their own track.

23. Richard E. Caves, *Air Transport and Its Regulators* (Harvard University Press, 1962).

24. For the classic analysis of this evidence, see Theodore Keeler, "Airline Deregulation and Market Performance," *Bell Journal of Economics and Management Science*, vol. 3 (August 1972), pp. 399–424.

25. Several analysts made and developed this argument about service quality, but among the earliest and most influential were George W. Douglas and James C. Miller III, *Economic Regulation and Domestic Air Transport: Theory and Policy* (Brookings, 1974); Arthur S. DeVany, "The Revealed Value of Time in Air Travel," *Review of Economics and Statistics*, vol. 56, no. 1 (1974), pp. 77–82; and George C. Eads, "Competition in the Domestic Trunk Industry: Too Much or Too Little?" pp. 13–54, in Almarin Phillips, ed., *Promoting Competition in Regulated Markets* (Brookings, 1975).

26. See Ivor Morgan, "Government and the Industry's Early Development" and "Toward Deregulation," chapters 2 and 3 in John R. Meyer and Clinton V. Oster, eds., *Airline Deregulation: The Early Experience* (Boston: Auburn House, 1981).

27. For example, see Douglas and Miller, *Economic Regulation and Domestic Air Transport*.

28. William J. Baumol, John C. Pauzen, and Robert D. Willig, *Contestable Markets and the Theory of Industry Structure* (Harcourt, Brace, Jovanovich, 1982).

29. Steven A. Morrison and Clifford Winston, "The Remaining Role for Government Policy in the Deregulated Airline Industry," in Sam Peltzman and Clifford Winston, eds., *Deregulation of Network Industries: What's Next?* (Brookings, 2000), pp. 1–2.

30. All figures are in 1993 dollars. Morrison and Winston estimate that the consumer benefits from added frequencies and on-line connections were $10.3 and $0.9 billion, respectively; the estimated losses suffered from higher load factors, fare restrictions, added connections, and slower flight times were $0.6, $1.1, $0.7, and $2.8 billion respectively. See Steven Morrison and Clifford Winston, *The Evolution of the Airline Industry* (Brookings, 1995), p. 82.

31. See for example, Transportation Research Board, *Entry and Competition in the U.S. Airline Industry: Issues and Opportunities* (Washington: National Academy of Sciences Press, 1999); and Transportation Research Board, *Winds of Change* (Washington: National Academy of Sciences Press, 1991), p. 74.

32. For example, Southern absorbed North Central (1979) and Hughes Airwest (1980) to become Republic; American took over Air California; Continental absorbed Texas International; and Eastern absorbed the new entrant People Express.

33. In 1986, Northwest absorbed Republic, Delta took over Western, and TWA absorbed Ozark; in 1987, US Air took over Piedmont.

34. Continental, TWA, and America West were also driven into bankruptcy between 1990 and 1992, although all three carriers emerged from bankruptcy and continued to operate.

35. Of the other surviving old guard carriers, Alaska Airlines also has an important presence although it is confined mainly to the West Coast.

36. Late in 2000, American made bids to take over TWA and to split parts of US Airways with United in ways that seemed to lessen the antitrust objections to United's original proposal.

37. That airline is America West; see Morrison and Winston, "The Remaining Role," p. 9.

38. Two exceptions to the low-fare, no-frills strategy were Midway Airlines and Midwest Express.

39. Transportation Research Board, *Entry and Competition*, p. 5.

40. The airlines attempt to control their costs by overbooking and then holding auctions to make seats available if too many travelers show up.

41. Severin Borenstein and Nancy Rose, "Competition and Price Dispersion in the U.S. Airline Industry," *Journal of Political Economy*, vol. 102, no. 4 (1994), pp. 653–83.

42. Using 1995 data, Joanna Stavins found that the dispersion in posted fares increased as the level of competition increased, suggesting that the high dispersion in the 1990s was still a sign of the presence of competition rather than the lack of it. Stavins's data are for posted fares rather than actual fares paid, however, and thus do not reflect the effect of capacity controls on the availability of deeply discounted fares. This may help explain why she finds that even the discounts for Saturday-night stays, which are almost surely not cost-based, increase with competition. Joanna Stavins, "Price Discrimination in the Airline Market: The Effect of Market Concentration," *Review of Economics and Statistics*, vol. 83, no. 1 (2001), pp. 200–202.

43. General Accounting Office, *Airline Competition: Higher Fares and Reduced Competition at Concentrated Airports*, report GAO/RCED 90-102, July 1990.

44. See Morrison and Winston, *Evolution of the Airline Industry*, pp. 44–49; and the review of other studies in Don H. Pickrell, "Air Fare Premiums at Hub Airports: A Review of the Evidence," Volpe Center, U.S. Department of Transportation, draft February 18, 2000, pp. 9, 11–13.

45. Pickrell, "Air Fare Premiums," pp. 9 and 15; and Morrison and Winston, "The Remaining Role," p. 7.

46. For early studies that reach these results, see Elizabeth Bailey, David R. Graham, and Daniel P. Kaplan, *Deregulating the Airlines* (Cambridge, Mass.: MIT Press, 1985); and Steven A. Morrison and Clifford Winston, *The Economic Effects of Airline Deregulation* (Brookings, 1986); and Steven A. Morrison and Clifford Winston, "Evaluating the Performance of the Deregulated Airline Industry," *Brookings Papers on Economic Activity: Microeconomics* (1989), pp. 73–75.

47. Morrison and Winston, "The Role of Government," pp. 33–35 and table 5.

48. Morrison and Winston, *The Evolution of the Airline Industry*, pp. 58–59.

49. The airline driven out was Vanguard. For a fuller discussion of the definition of pre-dation, see Transportation Research Board, *Entry and Competition*, pp. 86 and 87.

50. Local business interests in Iowa backed the establishment of Access Air in 1998, although more because of poor service than high fares. See Transportation Research Board, *Entry and Competition*, p. 61.

51. As a recent National Academy of Sciences panel concluded, the "basic aim of pre-serving and expanding opportunities for competition should remain the principal goal of aviation economic policy"; Transportation Research Board, *Entry and Competition*, p. 14.

52. Simultaneous with or shortly after deregulation in 1980 railroad profits benefited from changes in the tax law that allowed railroads to depreciate long-lived assets in much the same way that other industries do. In addition, in the 1980s railroads achieved reduc-tions in crew manning requirements and elimination of cabooses, which reduced their oper-ating costs by 5 to 10 percent. These tax and labor savings might or might not have been achieved without deregulation. See Theodore E. Keeler, *Railroads, Freight, and Public Policy* (Brookings, 1983).

53. By far the largest-scale separation of competitive from monopolistic activities in a regulated industry was that achieved in the AT&T antitrust settlement in the United States in 1984. In that case, competitive intercity long-distance activities were separated from monopolistic intracity or local service. Interestingly, technological changes since then have increasingly opened up local service to competition as well, inducing a slow but steady reduction in the regulation of local telephone services.

54. See, for example, José A. Gómez-Ibáñez, "Regulating Coordination: The Promise and Problems of Vertically Unbundling Private Infrastructure," Discussion Paper, Taubman Center for State and Local Government, Kennedy School of Government, Harvard Uni-versity, December 1999.

4

WILLIAM W. HOGAN

Making Markets in Electric Power

THE UNDERPINNINGS OF our organization of energy markets often are invisible, obscure, or at least unexamined. Yet energy markets are important. Energy production and delivery constitute huge industries in every developed economy. These energy industries touch the lives of all, both directly, through heating and lighting, and indirectly, through the provision of everything from apples to zucchini. Even the so-called new economy, driven by information, floats on a river of electrons that irrigate the giant farms of computer servers.

Electricity is the most ubiquitous form of energy delivery, with a constantly expanding variety of applications. And the case of electricity and society can be seen as part of a larger tapestry that includes other developments in our economies and societies. The new trends in power markets create a challenge for governance.

This paper revises and extends a lecture prepared for the Cantor Lecture Series 2000: Energy and Society, The Royal Institute for the Encouragement of Arts, Manufactures & Commerce, London, February 21, 2000. The author draws on work from the Harvard Electricity Policy Group and the Harvard-Japan Project on Energy and the Environment.

Government and Business

Markets in power, more than most markets, are made; they do not just happen. The intent here is to illuminate the highlights of this unfolding story and to speculate a little on what may yet develop. The world experience is diverse and complex, but a few common themes stand out from the perspective of the interaction between business and government.

Where you stand depends on where you sit. For example, prospective students at Harvard's Kennedy School of Government should note at least one simple difference between the Kennedy School and Harvard's eminent Business School on the opposite side of the Charles River. At the Business School, my colleagues teach their students how to seek out or create market advantage to find protection from competition, all this in the interest of maximizing profits and shareholder value. At the Kennedy School, we teach our students how governments can structure the rules of the game so that these businesses succeed individually in the short run but fail collectively in the long run in avoiding competition. Government seeks rules to promote greater economic efficiency, where competition eats away excess profits while leaving intact the improvements in products and services.

This tension between public and private, between government and business, between regulation and markets, is the background for a continuing interest in the public policy issues woven through the story of making markets in power.

Technology Transformation

In part, the development of power markets illustrates the role of technology in shaping our economy. New technology has been central to the plot. The information revolution has affected energy and electricity markets in ways that are already significant and yet are only beginning to be exploited. It will not be long before the hyperbole of the Internet becomes a commonplace, when invisible computers at home will infer our intent and manage the purchase of energy while paying our bills and letting out the cat.

One step away from the revolution in personal computers and wireless communications, the enormous improvement in turbine design has seemingly overnight nearly doubled the energy efficiency of the machines that burn oil and natural gas to produce electricity. With supercomputers and greatly improved seismic analysis, petroleum geologists make it ever more economic to produce the fuel that drives the turbines. The combined effects completely reversed our relatively recent prognostications of scarcity. Not that long ago in the United States, during the oil crisis of the 1970s, the government forbade the use of natural gas to produce electricity, for fear of running out. By the end of the century, in many parts of the United States it was cheaper to tear down a perfectly functional power plant that used an older technology and replace it with a new gas-burning plant. The new plant would be both environmentally cleaner and so energy efficient that the savings in operating costs would pay for early retirement of the old and construction of the new. Hence new suppliers have shocked the electricity industry.

So technology is important. But new technology only sets the stage for the changes under way in the electricity industry. Furthermore, the most important feature of technology and electricity is more obscure and has more to do with the old real world of Thomas Edison than with the new virtual world of Bill Gates.

While giving technology its due, the more interesting aspects of the story of making markets in power concern society, ideas, and ideology. The changes under way in the markets for power derive more from the contributions of the likes of Prime Minister Margaret Thatcher than from the contributions of either Edison or Gates.

Electricity Revolution

Around the world there is an amazing and broadly contemporaneous revolution taking place in the organization of electricity markets. Consider a partial list prominent in policy discussions: England and Wales, Norway, Germany, Spain, Russia, Ukraine, several regions in the United States, Latin America—from Mexico in the north to Chile in the south, Canada, New Zealand, and Australia. In 2000, Japan took a first step. Even the French may not be able to resist the market liberalization directives from the European Union. The breadth of the revolution impresses. The rapid spread of the idea cannot be explained by technology alone. Norway, with its abundance of falling water, is quite unlike England, with its coal and gas. Australia is unlike England or Norway, and so on.

There is a big idea here, however, and the big idea has deep roots. The old way of organizing the electricity market grew from an old big idea of the century just ended, namely in the development of vital infrastructure under natural monopoly. The idea, probably valid in its time, was that electrification was a strategic asset for an economy, and the nature of electricity production made it economic to have one entity build the power plants and develop the network of wires. People did not want different companies with multiple sets of wires running down their streets. And the large investments in power plants would enjoy great economies if their development could be integrated with the expansion of the transmission network; engineers would guide the process and shield regular citizens from the complex details. Some countries, such as the United States, fostered large vertically integrated monopolies under government regulation. In other countries, such as England, the government took on direct responsibility for managing the electricity industry.

Making and Unmaking Monopolies

This general argument was not restricted to electricity, and the same history, with different details, can be found in telephones, airlines, trucks, rail, natural gas, oil, and more. The results were large monopolies, with government ownership or regulation, and little to challenge the conventional wisdom. And this old big idea largely delivered on its promise. The infrastructure developed and matured. Services expanded and penetrated virtually every sector of the economy. In the case of electricity, the miracle born of Edison became a necessity that we took for granted. When we flipped the switch, the lights went on. Furthermore, as the infrastructure matured and companies exploited larger and larger scale, the costs went down. For example, at inflation-adjusted rates, the price of electricity in the United States dropped by 60 percent between 1940 and 1970. More or less the same thing happened in telephones, and so on.

By the 1970s, however, the scene had begun to change. The great cost reductions began to disappear or even to reverse, at least in the energy sector. Some of this reversal could be explained by turmoil in the oil market (which is another interesting story), with higher costs and greater insecurity. Perhaps a little of the oil-related shock applied to airlines and trucks. But it could not be relevant for telephones. However, what we did see across these diverse industries was a new set of common circumstances. The many years of protection and government regulation had resulted in large, sometimes bloated, slow-moving institutions that were hostile to innovation, having grown accustomed to the "quiet life" that, as Sir J. R. Hicks famously observed, is one the privileges of monopoly power.

However, the quiet life began to vanish once the hallmarks of large scale and monopoly mutated from the early promise of better service and lower costs to the later experience of supplier arrogance and higher costs. The details were different in different industries. For telephones, the Bell Company determined the one style of phone we could connect, and new technology was delayed or suppressed. Airlines became a bureaucratic morass, with competition in the quality of meals but not in prices. In the case of electricity, the difficulties were compounded by high inflation and seemingly endless delays in construction, particularly of nuclear plants. In the worst cases, huge power plants were built with price tags of billions of dollars and, in the end, produced no electricity.

In countries like England, where the government owned many of the companies, the new mantra became privatization and marketization. Break up the monopolies, sell off the assets, and rely on market forces to drive innovation forward and costs down. In countries like the United States, which already had private companies operating as regulated monopolies, the move was to break up and deregulate, with the common thrust to rely more on the discipline of market forces. This move to greater reliance on markets is the new big idea that has animated sweeping and sometimes dramatic changes in policy across many industries, in many countries, and all in the same historical period at the end of the twentieth century. The new big idea, extolled by Mrs. Thatcher, was to leave to markets what they do best and narrow the focus of government to the arenas where markets typically fail, where government may be necessary.

Making Markets

As has become clear, this is easier said than done. When the government is in charge from soup to nuts, policymakers can avoid the problem of delineating what the market can do and what the government must do. However, seldom can virtually everything be left to the market, with government simply receding to familiar tasks such as enforcing the general rules of commerce.

Far more often the public retreat is only partial, and a number of critical services, such as setting the rules for air traffic control and access to airports, remain with the government. Certain elements of the old industry, such as the local loop from the central telephone switch to the individual telephones, continue as practical monopolies. In the case of electricity, the most obvious example of a continuing monopoly is the integrated transmission network, of which there is, and generally should be, only one. In theory, some might argue that eventually even this could be subject to competition, but the practical reality is that some form of government oversight is seemingly unavoidable.

This self-evident fact is not a surprise. What surprises is a somewhat subtle problem that follows. Before, government regulators or managers did not have to trouble themselves too much with the details of how the business really worked. To be sure, the regulatory process could be highly intrusive, but most of the time and effort focused on adding up the total costs of the delivered product or on the often zero-sum battle to allocate the costs among the various "ratepayers," as customers used to be known. The details of designing the production and delivery systems were usually left to professionals, typically talented engineers who honored a high ethic of efficiency and quality, a subject to which we shall return. To a surprising degree, even the senior management in the companies, not to mention the government overseers or regulators, had precious little understanding of critical details of how the pieces fit together.

In the case of electricity, this meant that the face of the industry was quite simple. Plug the appliance into the wall socket and the power would flow. Flip the switch and the lights would go on. Customers were expected to pay at the end of the month, with a simple bill that was silent on the many steps needed to deliver the power.

However, when marketization arrived, the call was to break up the companies and unbundle the many products and services needed to produce and deliver electricity. Power generation could be separated from the wires and subject to competition. Likewise, retail services and energy supply could be separated from the wires and competition could reign. New players emerged, the marketers and brokers, seeking out niches and repackaging services to meet the demands of customers, demands that were more diverse than the monopoly could ever acknowledge or see.

Behind the simple face of electricity, we began to recognize that, as in the other industries, there was more to the machine than most people had realized. It has many moving parts, and control of the gears was being transferred from the hands of one to the hands of many. But especially in the case of electricity, it was not enough that all the gears turned; the gears also had to mesh, or the system would not work. A coordination problem, submerged in the old monopolies, surfaced in the new design for a market that relied on competition.

Coordination for Competition

Hence, the immediate challenge for government and everyone else was to undertake a quick study of how the parts worked, and had to work together. At the same time, both government and the industry had to agree on new rules for connecting the competitive players with the remaining monopoly elements to promote the efficient outcomes that stood as the principal justification for the inevitable trauma that would accompany massive change.

The collective record suggests that everyone was unprepared for this new challenge of governance. The transition in most industries has taken longer and been costlier than expected. In some cases, such as telephones in the United States, real competition in local service does not yet exist, more than fifteen years after the breakup of "Ma Bell." In the case of electricity, frustration has set in, and there are even rumblings of a counterrevolution. There is at least one example of a major policy meltdown.

The electricity problem is especially challenging because of the particular nature of the remaining monopoly services. In the wholesale market, with some leap of faith, one can argue that the generation sector is or could be competitive and largely deregulated. Companies are unbundling their products and services and separate companies are being formed to provide them. But everyone recognizes that the transmission and distribution wires will continue to be regulated. The task then, is to set the rules and prices for access to the wires.

Given current technology—a collection of machines and networks, much like that designed by Edison and his contemporary Charles Steinmetz—this task is complicated by at least two features of the electricity system. The first is instantaneous balancing. The well-known Japanese innovation in automobile manufacturing known as "just-in-time production" is the practice of closely matching production and use in order to reduce or eliminate expensive inventories and facilitate changes in product design. Of course, in the case of automobiles, such tight scheduling is not without problems for the poor supplier operating on a very short leash, and could never be more than a goal. Manufacturers could reduce but not eliminate inventories.

For electricity, however, just-in-time production is more like a physical law than a management goal. There are very few effective storage media for bulk electricity, and measured over more than a few seconds, it is essentially true that what is consumed must be produced at the same moment. Throughout the entire interconnected grid there must be virtually instantaneous balancing of production and consumption. Any deviations from this rule cause power frequency fluctuations that can damage equipment or bring down the entire system, fast.

The second and related feature is in the complex interactions of all the elements of the electric system. Sometimes referred to as the world's largest machine, the interconnected system of electric power plants, wires, and appliances must operate synchronously within a variety of close tolerances for power flows and voltages. For everyone but electrical engineers, the details are mind-numbing. But the net result is that, more than for most systems, everything affects everything else. It is somewhat like broadcasting many competing video channels with only one volume control, one color control, and one schedule for commercial interruptions. The many hands of the competitive market must work within an environment where changes for one are changes for all.

The combined effect of just-in-time production and complex interactions means that coordination is another important necessity of the electricity market. It was always clear that operation of the competitive market would require that generators and customers be able to connect to the wires. There would have to be "Gridcos" and "Discos" that build and maintain the transmission grid and distribution systems, and grid access terms should somehow establish a level playing field. But equally important, and far less obvious, was the need for a system operator that would pool or coordinate the actions of the many competitive hands to respect the relatively brittle limits of the electric system. Over short horizons of minutes or hours, where the interactions would be critical, there must be a "Poolco" that provides unavoidable pooling or coordination services in support of a competitive market. (Note: this is not the vertical coordination often cited as justification for the firm. This is horizontal coordination across an entire industry, quite another matter.) As counterintuitive as it seems to some, coordination is necessary to support competition. And this need has been there since the time of Edison. For decades, the engineers handled the problem and hid it from our view. But the move to markets and separation of the components have exposed coordination services as another essential monopoly.

In every country, and for everyone new to the debate, it takes a while to come to terms with the implications of this reality of the electric system. One of the great surprises has been how difficult and contentious is the process of designing the coordination services in a way that simultaneously respects the engineering reality and supports the market objectives. Happily, we know how to do it, and the best working models have enough of a record to be judged quite good, as in the case of the Pennsylvania–New Jersey–Maryland Interconnection, New York, and similar systems elsewhere. Unhappily, there is a vocal segment of the industry that sustains and reinvents campaigns to defeat this sensible design.

Why has there been such opposition and debate? By now the arguments are familiar. An extreme but not unrepresentative argument is that central coordination is antithetical to markets and decisions should be left to the many hands of the competitive market. Were it possible to fully decentralize the decisions, this argument might carry some force. However, as outlined herein, this is simply not possible under current technology. Therefore, a close look at such proposals—through the fog of empty claims about who shows the greater commitment to real markets—always reveals a system operator who provides the coordination services. Hence, despite the rhetoric, the debate is not over the merits of centralized or decentralized operation; rather the debate is over who exactly will determine the rules for centralized coordination.

We can have good rules, or we can have bad rules. We don't have the option of having no rules.

This presents an immediate challenge for government. On the one hand, the government could require a set of rules that would support the public interest, setting the stage for the operation of a competitive market. On the other, the government could defer to a stakeholder process that seeks the least common denominator in setting the rules. At best, the latter approach is an abdication of responsibility. At worst, defective rules threaten the reliability of the system and undermine the whole enterprise.

In much of the debate that occurs in various countries, the process of formulating the market rules has some of the elements of the foxes designing the henhouse, with some stakeholders demanding flawed designs. In the end, the best models for organizing the coordination services under the Poolco framework solve the hardest problems and make it easy for small players to enter and participate in the market. Load balancing services, provisions for losses, emergency responses, and so on can be handled naturally and efficiently, with market participants bearing the costs of their own actions. There is scope for large aggregators and other middlemen, but a limited need for their services in providing the basic commodity. In retrospect, it should not have been a surprise that some of these middlemen would be unhappy with such an efficient market design. And it should not be surprising that when confronted with the arguments their usual response is to try to change the subject or denigrate the ancestry of the ideas.

A Poolco by Any Other Name

The debate continued into the beginning of the twenty-first century. The source of much of the early enlightenment on the subject was England and Wales. At the end of the 1980s the British wrestled with an electricity reform directive from the Thatcher government, with a strict deadline. To make a long story short, nearly two years were spent in a futile effort to avoid the inevitable need for active coordination of the short-run electricity market. In the end, the participants threw up their hands in frustration and in a few months put together a completely different approach that resulted in a "pool" with explicit responsibilities for such market coordination. The organizing idea was that the market participants would submit bids for producing and using electricity, and the pool operator would find the balanced equilibrium with its market-clearing price. The pool would combine the functions of market exchange with those of managing the complex physics of the electricity system.

It was a brilliant innovation, and the whole world was watching. Or at least the whole world that was close to England in geography or culture. (It turned out that reformers in Chile had anticipated many of the basic ideas by several years. But this is only a quibble.) Theirs was a remarkable achievement that included reinventing the idea from commodities markets that, for most business purposes, financial contracts could stand in the place of physical transactions, with only a final settlement at the price revealed in the spot market. And here the essential spot price would be readily available from the pool.

Soon Norway, New Zealand, Australia, and others adopted and improved on the basic ideas, all the while giving credit to the vanguard in England and Wales. Eventually, even the former colonies in the United States took up the task, and the trade balance in England was helped by the constant parade of visitors on the required tour to see how an electricity market could work and keep the lights on at the same time.

Unfortunately, the underlying debates are never far from the surface, and in every region there has been a long and not always successful process of educating all the parties to the essential facts of the electricity system: Government could not recede completely. There are remaining natural monopolies, including the complex requirements of coordination services. There must be a system operator. And in the end there is a natural division of labor. Market competitors can compete, and governments can decide on the rules that will produce a workable market with a level playing field.

At the end of the century past, such conversations in the United States culminated with the Federal Energy Regulatory Commission issuing its "Order 2000," elucidating the need for and design of regional transmission organizations that would be the coordinating institutions. The millennium signature number for this order was a signal of the importance of the rule and its intent. The subject of this substantial tome is the lineal descendant of the pool in England and Wales. Order 2000 built upon that innovation and subsequent experience to craft a framework that recognizes the reality of electricity systems, sets the primacy of public interest in establishing a workable and efficient competitive market, and makes a major contribution to the delineation of the boundary between the public and the private sectors.

As with the pool in England and Wales, the order relies on a coordinated spot market, within the limits of security constraints, using the bids of market participants to find the most economic use of the system consistent with market equilibrium. Learning from one of the few mistakes in the initial pool design, the broader framework recognizes that market-clearing prices can and will be different at every location. Financial contracts of the same type as found in England and Wales play a prominent role, as do financial transmission rights that extend the idea to cover the difference in prices at different locations. Costs for the grid are collected through regional access charges, and investments are pursued in large part through the incentives of the marketplace. This is a state-of-the-art design. Progress has been slow, but there is progress nonetheless. However, the cost has been high, with the expense compounded by taking the occasional step backward. And there are no guarantees of success.

Mistakes and Meltdowns

The sometime failures in this process illustrate many lessons. First, there is the human failing that it is difficult to learn from the mistakes of others;

people have to make their own mistakes. England and Wales made a mistake in setting up too few competing generators, so competition was slow in coming through entry. This is still a problem elsewhere, such as in Brazil, Ontario, and parts of the United States. New Zealand has gone through at least two rounds of separation and disaggregation.

Second, paraphrasing a harsher formulation often attributed to Nietzsche, there is the common mistake of forgetting what one is trying to accomplish. We want marketers and brokers to provide new products and simplify the process of capturing the benefits of a competitive market. But we do not want marketers and brokers per se. The argument is often made that with an efficient design of wholesale and retail markets there may be little, perhaps no, need for marketers and brokers who cannot provide real added value. The resulting absence of many traders and much visible trading is often mistaken as a problem, not as evidence of a solution, and the move is then on to break what is not broken, in order to give more middlemen something to fix.

The recent turn of policy in England and Wales suggests learning the wrong lesson. There were problems in the original wholesale market design, as witnessed by the improvements that have been adopted elsewhere. The design with too few competitors in generation results in an obvious problem for competition. Furthermore, aggregation to an artificial single market price, rather than the locational reality, creates bad incentives but could be easily fixed.

However, at the end of 2000 the regulator of England and Wales was about to fix what wasn't broken and hide the truly broken gears of the machine, which would nonetheless continue to grind away and do more damage. The so-called New Electricity Trading Arrangements (NETA) proposal appears to have succumbed to a romance with a market myth. The proposal enshrines trading and traders as desired ends in themselves, not as mere means. The proposal abandons the singular achievement of the coordinated spot market of the pool and replaces it with reliance on aggregators and middlemen. These intermediaries will be happy to see what should be a sharp increase in transaction costs, which they will be paid to manage. But how is this in the public interest?

In any event, despite claims to the contrary, England and Wales will not avoid the need for coordination through a system operator. This central coordinator is there in the new design. It is buried within the National Grid Company. But rather than fixing the rules to reflect the pricing that would prevail in a competitive market, the new arrangements obscure what is being done through ad hoc and costly balancing mechanisms that are at best opaque and at worst unsustainable. If this reactionary reform goes forward, it will take several steps backward. That would be especially disappointing, given the history of leadership in this pioneering market. Worse yet, it ignores the evidence from the United States by rejecting what works there and embracing the elements of its most glaring failure in the California meltdown.

Perhaps the explanation of the different directions across the Atlantic is found in the old adage about two countries divided by a common language. The documents that purport to explain the proposed reforms in England and Wales seem to ignore or misperceive the practical experience in the United States and its embodiment in the scripture of Order 2000— not to mention the workings of the markets in New Zealand, Norway, and Australia. And the alleged purpose of the reforms, to reduce market power, is not connected to the analysis through any sustained argument that can persuade.

The success of power markets that improved upon the British pool model stands in contrast to the cascading failure of the major market that has so far rejected this approach. At the end of 2000, a power crisis in California was laying bare the dangers of ignoring the fundamentals of how power systems operate while creating a monstrous caricature of a market with a dangerous combination of bad economic theory and worse political economy practice.

The bad economic theory was a full embrace of the objective of creating a market for middlemen, no matter what the cost. In California, the pool approach to a coordinated spot market was explicitly rejected in preference for a complicated trading regime much like the proposed reforms in the British NETA effort. Given the inevitable requirements for coordination, this produced an expanding collection of arcane rules to prevent what was natural by making the coordination process ever harder to use in the interest of supporting separate exchanges and marketers. For example, the California system operator was explicitly precluded from providing a least-cost combination of balancing services. Since the operator still had to provide balancing services, these were required to be inefficient and expensive, to create more business for the middlemen.

The bad political economy appeared in the process that produced the compromise rules for the California market. Key parts of the decentralized theory would have customers face market prices, and the old monopolies would be precluded from anything other than providing distribution services. The political process produced the second rule and precluded old monopolies from participating in the market. But customers were protected from the market price by the imposition of a fixed price for retail sales. In the event, this eliminated the market entry opportunity for marketers by eliminating the need for their principal service (price hedging) and left the old monopolies buying at a variable wholesale market price and selling at a fixed retail price. This would prove to be an explosive combination.

The compounding failures in the market design accumulated from its inception in 1998 until, at the end of 1999, federal regulators pronounced the California design "fundamentally flawed." There then began an intense process to rethink the market design from first principles. The process was made more difficult by the rear-guard action of interests that benefited from or had created the flawed design.

In the event, the redesign effort was blown aside in the summer of 2000 when the explosive combination of variable wholesale prices and fixed retail prices confronted the spark of a suddenly tight market. Bad luck collided with bad policy. There had been little addition to generating capacity for more than a decade. Low water reservoirs behind power dams combined with higher natural gas prices and tighter environmental conditions. An unexpected surge in demand from economic growth hit the inefficient market and produced unprecedented price increases. Soon the old monopolies were selling power retail for a small fraction of what they paid to acquire the power in the spot wholesale market. Bankruptcy loomed and supply could no longer be assured. Even those who predicted problems were surprised at the scope and speed of the policy disaster.

Policymakers responded largely by pointing fingers. Surprised and confused, they took virtually no action, and the problem grew swiftly from a bad outcome to a first-order crisis for California and the western U.S. electricity system. Bad rules produced a catastrophic result, and government could not react fast enough to fix the rules. The full fallout from this explosion was not clear at the end of 2000. At a minimum, every other jurisdiction in the world faced an urgent need to make sure that the policymakers could show how their approach differed from that in California. And those who opposed electricity market reform had a ready argument to bolster their own agenda. The blow may yet be fatal to any reasonable market reform in California. The folly of California's peculiar combination of mistakes left at least a serious wound for power markets everywhere.

Pitfalls on the Road Ahead

Electricity market reform in California illustrates the pathologies in an extreme case. The California design began with the insights from England and Wales but soon succumbed to the argument that real markets do not require coordination in the way of the "pool." The right lesson to learn from California is that the fundamentals matter, and the successful experience in many power markets should be distilled and emulated, not rejected because it was not invented here.

It will not be easy, because a major lesson of the electricity reforms echoes the tale of the difference between Harvard's Business School and its Kennedy School of Government. The more inefficiencies in the market and the more market power you can find, the greater the opportunity to transfer wealth and make profits above the competitive norm. We count on the ingenuity and innovation of the market participants that follow this lure of profits, which they hope will be huge profits protected from competition. And the counterbalancing responsibility of governments is to set up the rules so that the market participants succeed individually in the short run and fail collectively in the long run in avoiding competition, as each innovation leads ultimately to lower costs and better products. Competition should eventually eliminate excess profits, but only if the rules support true competition, not just more competitors.

However, the participants do not really want competitive markets for themselves, just for everyone else. Hence there is constant pressure on both sides. On the suppliers' side there are pressures to change the market rules and impose costs that create protected market niches. On the consumers' side there is the constant pressure for regulators to intervene when scarcity and efficient market responses lead to higher prices.

The regulators, as the only group charged with the public interest, don't have it easy. They face a delicate balancing act, and the increased complexity of the unbundled market does not make it any easier. The regulators who are going to do the job well, who are often new to the task, must quickly learn more details than they ever wanted to know about the electricity grid they regulate. Not only must the regulators ensure that the grid operator does the obvious things to keep the lights on and costs down, but they must do so in a way that uses and maintains a seamless interface with the competitive sectors of the market.

The most important recommendations for regulators:

—Focus on the public interest. If you don't, who will?

—Support competition, not competitors. It is easy to confuse the two.

—Insist on aggressive failure analysis, before you fail. Market design flaws should be identified as soon as possible; never underestimate the ability of market participants to exploit design flaws; never accept a blithe assertion that the market will overcome the design flaws anytime soon.

—Use the market to reinforce operational reliability. Prices and the profit incentive can and should be consistent with the physical reality and the dictates of reliability.

I could go on, but this is enough to make a difference. There has been a revolution in electricity markets, a revolution facilitated by technology but driven by ideas and ideology. The new big idea sharply redefines the boundary between government and business and presents greater challenges for regulators in making a market for power.

Save the Best of the Old Ideas

Finally, there is some urgency to all this, an urgency separate from the high cost of delay. While we dither, we are spending a wasting asset. At the core of the electricity system we typically find a team of engineers with broad experience in running electricity networks. The rules they follow are only partly subject to codification and computer programming. There is still a good deal of judgment involved, and we should be grateful that they are there because, in the end, this is what keeps the lights on.

This engineering corps typically developed its rules and its ethic within the framework of the old monopoly and with reference to the broader engineering profession. The rules were not driven primarily by commercial considerations, not the least because the commercial incentives were so distantly removed. And the engineering ethic to serve the public and keep the system working is worthy of respect and preservation.

However, market reforms are eroding the foundations of this system. Many of the previous functions of the engineers have been unbundled and put in the hands of the decidedly commercial market participants. In the battle over efficient market design, the defeats often appear in the form of restrictions on the operators, to reinforce the profits of the middlemen, rather than to reinforce the reliability ethic of the engineers. If the system operators do not honor a culture that emphasizes the broader public interest, but rather bow to the interests of the most vocal stakeholders, eventually the operators will do not as they know they should, but as they are told or as they are paid.

We have already seen the early signs of this change in behavior in many places in the United States. The most visible evidence is in the pressure to replace the voluntary rules for reliability coordination with a system of mandatory enforcement. But this policing solution pays far too little attention to the force of the new incentives or to the opportunity to design the markets so that the participants have incentives to cooperate with the engineers and support the public interest rather than to work at cross purposes.

We know how to do it. A great deal is at stake here. It is a great opportunity for leadership from the public sector. If we don't do it right, we deserve what we get.

PART II

*Experiments
and Puzzles*

5

PAUL E. PETERSON

Choice and Competition in K–12 Education

HISTORICALLY, MOST SCHOOL boards in the United States assigned students to schools by drawing boundaries that established specific attendance areas. Where one lived determined the school one attended, if one chose to attend a public school. Families did not *seem* to have any choice at all—though the reality, as we shall see, was not quite that simple.

The situation has changed substantially in recent years. Today a wide variety of school choice mechanisms are available to parents and students—vouchers, magnet schools, charter schools, interdistrict choice programs, home-schooling, tax credits and tax deductions for private tuition, and, above all, school choice through residential selection. Responding to the increasing demand by parents for greater choice among schools, states today provide a greater range of choices to parents than ever before. Approximately 63 percent of American families with school-age children are making a choice when sending their child to school. According to a 1993 Department of Education survey, 39 percent of all parents said that where they had chosen to live was influenced by the school their children would attend.[1] Another 11 percent of the population sends their children to private school.[2] And still another 13 percent of families can choose a public magnet school or charter school or participate in an interdistrict or other choice program.[3] Choice programs are rapidly expanding in size and number, and the topic has become a matter of significant public discussion and debate, with most public opinion studies finding increased demand for school choice, especially among citizens from low-income and minority backgrounds.[4]

In this essay I review the growth in the range of choices available in American education and examine in depth the way in which the most market-based of existing choice programs, school vouchers, has worked in practice in the few cities where vouchers have been tried.

Origins of the Choice Concept in Education

The extended and explicit practice of school choice in the United States came of age only in the late 1980s and early 1990s. But choice in education is an ancient concept, dating back to the days when Socrates and his fellow philosophers walked the Athenian agora, teaching for a fee.[5] The earliest forms of choice left education strictly to the private market. It was John Stuart Mill who first made a fully developed argument on behalf of school choice within the context of publicly funded universal education: "Is it not almost a self-evident axiom, that the State should require and compel the education . . . of every human being who is born its citizen?" he asks. He then goes on to point out:

> Were the duty of enforcing universal education once admitted, there would be an end to the difficulties about what the State should teach, and how it should teach, which now convert the subject into a mere battlefield for sects and parties, causing the time and labor which should have been spent in educating, to be wasted in quarrelling about education. . . . It might leave to parents to obtain the education where and how they pleased, and content itself with helping to pay the school fees.[6]

In the United States school choice within a system of publicly funded universal education was first seriously proposed by economist Milton Friedman, who in 1955 argued that a voucher-like arrangement where the government finances the education but families choose the school would lead to a more efficient educational system.[7] The idea gained considerable public currency in the 1970s, when the Office of Economic Opportunity helped fund a school choice experiment in the Alum Rock school district in California. When this experiment encountered strong opposition from teacher organizations and failed to be implemented effectively, enthusiasm for school choice waned for about a decade, except for sporadic use of the magnet school concept as a tool for school desegregation.[8]

Then, in the 1980s and early 1990s, a number of events helped give the school-choice movement new impetus. First, a major study by a research team headed by James Coleman reported that students in Catholic schools outperformed their public school peers. These findings were subsequently supported by a second major study by the Brookings Institution that in addition explained the original results by showing that private schools had more autonomy and, as a result, were organized more effectively than public schools.[9] The authors, John Chubb and Terry Moe, proposed school vouchers as the solution. Although critics questioned both studies, their impact was reinforced by a Department of Education proposal to give compensatory education funds directly to low-income families to be used as vouchers.[10] At the same time, experiments that gave families greater choice of public school began to appear in Minnesota, Massachusetts, Wisconsin, and East Harlem. When test-score gains were reported for East Harlem, public interest in the idea grew rapidly, producing today a wide variety and ever-growing set of school-choice initiatives.[11] What had been a gleam in the eye of a few intellectuals in 1970 had become by the end of the century a major political movement with a wide variety of policies operating in many parts of the United States.

Residential Location and School Choice

Although explicit school-choice programs are quite recent, in fact school choice by selection of one's place of residence is a deeply entrenched part of American education. Self-conscious school choice has long been exercised by many families when they rent or purchase a house in a place where they think the school is good. Because the quality of the school affects a family's residential decisions, housing prices vary with the quality of local schools. As a result, many families pay indirectly for their children's education by purchasing homes that cost more, simply because the home is located in a neighborhood that is perceived to have a higher-quality school.[12]

School choice by residential selection is highly inegalitarian, especially when one considers that the purchase of a home requires a capital investment. As school quality drives up housing prices, access to the neighborhood school is determined by one's capacity to obtain a mortgage. Those with higher earning power and more capital resources are able to command access to the best schools. But school choice by residential selection is becoming more widespread, simply because more families have more choice in selecting a neighborhood in which to live than ever before. A half-century ago, the attractiveness—and thus the average cost (per square foot)—of a residential location was strongly influenced by its proximity to workplaces, which were concentrated in specific parts of a metropolitan area, primarily the central city. But when highways replaced railroads and rapid transit systems as the primary mode of transport in metropolitan areas, employment opportunities diffused throughout the metropolitan area. Once jobs became widely distributed, the dominant factors affecting community housing prices became local amenities, such as the neighborhood school.[13] By 1993, 39 percent of families said they considered the local schools when selecting a place to live.[14]

The amount of school choice by residential selection varies across metropolitan areas. In the Miami metropolitan area, for example, this form of choice is restricted by the fact that one school district is responsible for almost the entire metropolitan area, whereas the Boston metropolitan area is divided into more than one hundred school districts.

The quality of education is higher in metropolitan areas that give parents more choice by virtue of the fact that they have more school districts. Students take more academic courses and spend more time on their homework, classes are more structured and disciplined, parents are more involved with schools, student test scores are higher, and sports programs are given less emphasis.[15]

It is difficult for low-income families to exercise choice through residential selection. Most do not have the earning power or access to financial markets to locate in neighborhoods with schools perceived to be of high quality. On the contrary, they often can afford a home or apartment only because it is located in a neighborhood where schools are perceived to be of low quality, a perception that depresses property values. In short, in a system of residentially determined school choice, such as exists in most metropolitan areas today, low-income families are very likely to be concentrated in areas where schools are thought to be of low quality. Conversely and ironically, once a neighborhood school serving a low-income community improves, local land values rise, making it more difficult for additional poor families to gain access to the school.

It was this link between school and residence that provoked one of the most turbulent periods in American educational history, the school busing controversy. Since school choice by residential selection gave better-off families access to better schools, many felt that racial segregation and inequality could be eliminated only by forcefully breaking the link between school and residence by compelling families to send their children by bus to schools distant from their place of residence.[16]

Magnet Schools

So unpopular was compulsory busing with many Americans that the magnet school, exploiting the choice concept, was developed to replace it. Magnet schools were designed to increase racial and ethnic integration by enticing families to choose integrated schools that offered distinctive and better education programs. The magnet idea was initially broached in the 1960s. But it was not until after 1984 that the magnet school concept, supported by federal funding under the Magnet Schools Assistance program, began to have a national impact: "Between 1984 and 1994, 138 districts nationwide received a total of $955 million" in federal funds to implement this form of school choice.[17] As a consequence, the number of schools with magnet programs doubled between 1982 and 1991, while the number of students tripled.[18] In some school districts, parents can choose a magnet school only if their child's enrollment increases the level of racial integration within the magnet school. In other school districts, magnet school places are offered on a first-come, first-served basis. In still other school districts, schools that are highly magnetic must choose students by means of a lottery. Nationwide, in the early 1990s, over 1.2 million students attended 2,400 magnet schools in over 200 school districts.[19]

Cleveland provides an illustrative example of the way in which school desegregation controversies led to the introduction of magnet schools. In 1981 the federal district court issued an order that explicitly asked the Cleveland school district to establish magnet schools. Gradually, a number of magnet schools were created, and in 1994 the city of Cleveland and the state of Ohio agreed to a plan that would "enlarge the capacity of its magnet schools from 6,800 seats in 1992–93 to approximately 12,800 seats by the 1994–95 school year."[20] In the 1999–2000 school year twenty-three magnet schools were expected to enroll well over 10,000 students in kindergarten through eighth grade.

The magnet school concept, if taken to its logical conclusion, opens all the public schools in a district to all families, allowing them to select their

preferred public school, subject to space constraints. Such programs, generally identified as open-enrollment programs, can be found at the high
school and middle school levels in a few school districts.

Most studies of magnet schools and open-enrollment programs find that
they have positive effects on student learning.[21] Although some of these apparent effects may simply have been a function of the initial ability of the students
selected to attend magnet schools,[22] two studies that carefully addressed this
issue still found positive effects from attendance at a magnet school.[23]

Interdistrict School Choice

Although most magnet school programs limit parental choice to public
schools within a particular school district, in a number of places school
choice also includes access to public institutions outside the local school
district. As early as 1985, Minnesota gave local school boards permission to
allow students from outside their district to attend their school (but the
program was restricted to students who would not adversely affect the
racial integration of participating school districts).[24] By 1997 nearly 20,000
students were participating.[25] In 1966, Massachusetts enacted a program
that allowed minority students to exit the Boston schools and enter participating suburban schools, then in 1991 enacted a more general interdistrict
choice program without regard to a student's ethnicity or a district's racial
composition.[26] By 1995 nearly 7,000 students and more than 300 school
districts were participating in this program. By 1997 similar programs had
been enacted in sixteen states.

Although many of these magnet school programs are too new to enable
researchers to draw conclusions about their long-term effect, preliminary
evidence from Massachusetts indicates that the participating students are
ethnically representative of the student composition of the public schools
more generally. Also, it appears that school districts that lose students to
magnet schools often make significant efforts to upgrade their curriculum
in order to stanch the flow of students to other districts.[27]

Charter Schools

Magnet schools and interdistrict enrollment programs limit parental choice
to schools operated by school boards. Charter schools have enlarged choice

opportunities to include government-financed schools operated by nongovernmental entities. By 1998 thirty-four states and the District of Columbia had enacted charter school legislation, and more than 1,199 charter schools were educating over a quarter million students.[28] At the beginning of the 1999 school year the number of charter schools had increased 40 percent, to 1,684—a notable increment by any criterion.[29] Although the percentage of students in charter schools nationwide is still a small fraction of all students, in some states charter schools are providing the school of choice for a significant fraction of the student population. For example, in 1997, 4.4 percent of the students in Arizona were attending charter schools.[30]

Charter school terminology varies by state, as does the legal framework under which these schools operate. The common characteristics of charter schools are twofold: First, the entity operating the school is ordinarily not a government agency, though it may receive most of its operating revenue from either the state or a local school board. Second, charter schools do not serve students within a specific attendance boundary; instead they recruit students from a large catchment area that may be beyond the attendance boundaries of traditional public schools. As a result, they must persuade parents that their offerings are superior to those provided by traditional public schools in their vicinity.

Studies of charter schools find that, on average and taken as a whole, students attending charter schools are fairly representative of the school population more generally.[31] Most charter schools are popular with parents and substantially oversubscribed, though some have been closed because their safety and education standards were inadequate. Charter schools are better able than traditional public schools to attract teachers who were educated at selective colleges and who have received higher education in mathematics and science.[32] Whether students learn more in charter schools than in traditional public schools has yet to be ascertained by an independent research team.

Tax Deductions or Credits for Private Education

In the late 1990s, two states—Minnesota and Arizona—facilitated parental access to private schools by providing tax deductions or tax credits that can be used to help pay the cost of private education. In Minnesota, families earning less than $33,500 per year can claim a tax credit of up to $1,000 per child ($2,000 per family) for school-related expenses, including costs incurred in attending a private school, such as the purchase of books and other educational materials—although a credit cannot be claimed for private school tuition. Any family can claim a tax deduction for educational expenses of up to $1,625 for students in kindergarten through sixth grade and $2,500 for students in seventh grade through high school. Private school tuition counts toward the deduction.[33] Demonstrating its popularity, 37,951 Minnesotans claimed the tax credit in 1998, averaging $371 per credit. (Information on the deduction is not available at this writing.)[34] In Arizona, any person who contributes to a foundation that provides scholarships to students attending private schools may receive a tax credit of up to $500. Again, this program has proven popular, with 5,100 Arizonans claiming the credit in the first year.[35] If this practice should spread to other states, the number of students attending private school might increase in future years.

Although research on the operations of these programs is not yet available, other information about the place of private schools in the U.S educational system is extensive because private schools offer the oldest form of school choice—dating back to before the Constitution was ratified. At that time, education was privately provided, mainly by schools that had a religious affiliation. Those who wanted to enhance people's educational opportunities sought to do so by means of voucher-like arrangements. For example, when the radical populist Thomas Paine proposed a more egalitarian system of education, he recommended that government provide monies to parents so that they could send their children "to school, to learn reading, writing and common arithmetic; the ministers of every parish, of every denomination to certify . . . that the duty is performed."[36]

State-operated schools were constructed in the United States only many decades later, largely in response to the migration of poor Catholics from Ireland and Germany into the large cities of the Northeast in the 1840s. In 1852 the Boston School Committee urged that "in our schools they [the foreign-born children] must receive moral and religious teaching, powerful enough if possible to keep them in the right path amid the moral darkness which is their daily and domestic walk." Horace Mann, the first secretary of education for the Commonwealth of Massachusetts, explained the need for public schools in the following terms: "How shall the rising generation be brought under purer moral influences" so that "when they become men, they will surpass their predecessors, both in the soundness of their speculations and in the rectitude of their practice?" When Mann established public schools in Massachusetts, the new institutions won praise from the Congregational journal *New Englander*, which excitedly exclaimed in language that anticipated the phrasing (if not quite the sentiments) of the Gettysburg Address: "These schools draw in the children of alien parentage . . . and assimilate them to the native born. . . . So they grow up with the state, of the state, and for the state."[37]

Over the ensuing decades, public schools grew rapidly, and the share of the population attending private schools shrank substantially. In some states—most notably Nebraska and Oregon—the state legislature attempted to consolidate state power over the education of children by closing private schools, but key Supreme Court decisions declared such actions unconstitutional.[38] Nonetheless, the share of the population educated in private schools dropped steadily throughout the late nineteenth and early twentieth century until by 1959 the percentage of students attending private school was but 12.8 percent and by 1969 as low as 9.3 percent.

After reaching this nadir, the place of the private school began to stabilize and edge back upward. By 1980, 11.5 percent of students in kindergarten through twelfth grade were attending private schools, a number that has stayed relatively constant since then.[39] Families who could afford the cost of private education began to conclude that they needed to consider an alternative to what was being provided by the public sector.

The image of private education held by some is of an expensive day school catering to well-to-do families or an exclusive boarding school attended by college-bound "preppies." The reality is quite different. Most private schools have a religious affiliation, modest tuition, and limited facilities. Nationwide, the average private school expenditures per pupil in 1993–94 were estimated at $3,116, considerably less than the public school expenditure per pupil, which was $6,653.[40]

Inasmuch as private schools have fewer fiscal resources, for many years it was generally believed that the education provided by these schools was, on average, inferior to the education provided by public schools. As a result, researchers and policymakers were surprised when a national study, funded by the U.S. Office of Education, undertaken by a research team headed by the respected sociologist James Coleman, found that students attending Catholic schools outperformed public school students.[41] This result was obtained even after Coleman and his colleagues took into account family background characteristics that also affect school performance.

Coleman's findings were so surprising and upsetting that they were subjected to careful scrutiny. Many methodological issues were raised, and numerous similar studies have subsequently been undertaken. Some scholars continue to find that students learn more in Catholic and other private schools; other scholars do not detect any differences.[42] Two conclusions may be drawn from the literature, taken as a whole:

—Students, on average, learn at least as much in Catholic schools.

—Although it is not altogether clear whether middle-class students learn more in Catholic schools, low-income minority students clearly do. For this segment of the population, private schools provide a definite advantage.[43]

Where access to private schools is more readily available, their presence seems to provide desirable competition that spurs a positive response from public schools: The test scores of public school students are higher, the likelihood that public-school students will attend college increases, and the wages they earn later in life are higher.[44]

Home-Schooling

Home-schooling constitutes one of the more rapidly growing segments of the American educational system. Although home-schooling has an enviable historic record—Abraham Lincoln was home-schooled, and so were Theodore and Franklin Delano Roosevelt—as late as 1980 only three states explicitly sanctioned the practice. But between 1982 and 1992, thirty-two states changed their compulsory school attendance rules to allow families, under certain conditions, to educate their children at home.[45] In recent years home-schooling has grown rapidly, though the full size and extent of home-schooling is unknown; estimates of the number of students who are home-schooled vary between a half-million and 1.2 million.[46] Despite the fact that at least one study suggests that home-schooled students are learning more than students in traditional schools, the recent growth in home-schooling has generated a good deal of controversy.[47] When a charter school in California offered its services to home-schooled students over the Internet, the state legislature passed a law limiting the practice to students within the county and adjacent counties.[48] Nonetheless, as the Internet's educational potential is more fully exploited, it is likely to give further impetus to the home-schooling movement.

Voucher Programs

Residential selection, magnet schools, interdistrict enrollment, private schools, and charter schools are mechanisms that provide options to a wide range of groups, but on balance these options, when taken together, tend to give more choice to middle-income than to low-income families. Publicly and privately funded vouchers, as currently designed and operated, serve almost exclusively a low-income population. In this respect, they provide in a few places a significant, egalitarian complement to other choice programs by offering choice opportunities to those who otherwise have none.

Publicly Funded Voucher Programs

The three publicly funded voucher programs are to be found in Cleveland, Milwaukee, and the state of Florida. In Cleveland, students began matriculation in private schools in the fall of 1996; in the fall of 1999 the number of participating students was nearly 4,000. In 1999 students received a scholarship of up to $2,250, substantially less than the amount spent per student by Cleveland public schools or the amount provided to students at community schools.

The Milwaukee program, established in 1990, originally allowed students to attend schools without a religious affiliation. Only a few hundred students participated in the program in its first year. In the 1998–99 school year, the program, after overcoming constitutional objections, was expanded to include religious schools, and the number of participating students in 2000 increased to approximately 12,000. In that year participating students received a scholarship or voucher of up to nearly $5,000.[49] In the fall of 1999 a small number of students became eligible to participate in the Florida program when the legislature said that students attending "failing" schools could apply for vouchers. In that year participating students could receive a scholarship or voucher of up to $3,389.[50] Initially, only two schools met the legislative definition of failing, but many more were expected to fall within this category in subsequent years. But no additional students became eligible in 2000, because the concept of failing was redefined and the performances on statewide tests of students attending potentially failing schools improved. In all three of the publicly funded programs students are selected by means of a lottery if the number of applicants exceeds the number of school spaces available.

Privately Funded Voucher Programs

In the United States, the private sector often plays a major role in social experimentation. Ideas that are initially too untried and controversial for governments to attempt will often be explored by private or nonprofit entities with the sponsorship of tax-exempt private foundations. The Ford Foundation sponsored the "gray areas" program that became the model for the community action program of the War on Poverty established in 1965.[51] Results from evaluations of privately funded preschool programs provided the impetus for Head Start. Privately funded services for disabled students antedated and facilitated the design of the federally funded special education program enacted in 1975.[52] In all cases, privately funded programs provided important information to policymakers about the potential value of a social innovation.

Learning about school vouchers is taking place in much the same way. Several privately funded voucher programs are providing valuable information about how voucher programs operate in practice. These voucher programs differ from traditional scholarship programs in two important ways. First, the offer of the voucher to students is not conditioned on student performance. If more applications are received than can be funded by resources available to the private foundation sponsoring the program, the vouchers are distributed either by means of a lottery or on a first-come, first-served basis. Second, the scholarship is not tied to a particular school or religious denomination. Instead, a family may choose from among a wide variety of participating secular or parochial schools with different religious affiliations. In these ways, the private programs are approximations of what is developing in the public sector.

The privately funded voucher programs that have been studied by independent research teams are located in Dayton, Ohio; the Edgewood school district in San Antonio, Texas; Indianapolis; New York City; and Washington, D.C. The major characteristics of these programs as well as a number of additional scholarship programs are described in table 5-1.

Relationships among School-Choice Programs

One cannot understand the full range of school choices available to families apart from an appreciation of the relationships among the wide variety of programs and policies that have been outlined. In every state, families have some choice of school, even if it is limited to paying for a private education or choosing to live in a neighborhood served by a school the family thinks desirable. In many metropolitan areas, including Cleveland, families can also choose among magnet schools, charter schools (called community schools in Ohio), and a voucher program.

When several programs are located in the same place, they can affect one another in important ways. Schools that once participated in a voucher program may establish themselves as charter schools, perhaps because charter school funding generally exceeds state funding under voucher programs.[53] Parents with students in private schools may decide to save money by enrolling their children in charter schools instead.

All of these choice programs provide traditional public schools an incentive to improve their practices in ways that will maintain their enrollments—and the per pupil state aid that they have previously received. Already there is some evidence that the availability of school vouchers is affecting public school policies and practices. In the Edgewood school district in San Antonio, Texas, for example, the local school board accepted the resignation of its superintendent and, in a reversal of an earlier decision, began requiring students to wear school uniforms.[54] In Florida, the first two schools judged to be failing by the state—and therefore placed immediately in the voucher program—made significant policy changes after receiving their ignominious designation. One school introduced uniforms, a new phonics reading program, and class-size reduction in kindergarten; the other introduced Saturday and after-school tutoring sessions and had school staff visit parents at home to discourage truancy. Both schools have begun to focus on the basics of reading, writing, and math, in part by hiring more full-time reading and writing specialists.[55]

Within a year of the enlargement of the voucher program in Milwaukee, a new school board, elected in a hotly contested race, accepted the resignation of the school superintendent and announced its determination to respond to the challenges provided by the new choice arrangements. In Albany, New York, all the students at a particular elementary school (deemed to have the lowest scores in the city) were offered a voucher by a private individual; the school board responded by changing the principal, the teaching staff, and the curriculum.

More systematic evidence is available from ongoing research on other choice experiments. According to a study of the impact of charter schools on traditional public schools in Arizona, "districts that have lost large numbers of children to charter schools make efforts to win those children back. Sometimes those efforts pay off."[56] Similarly, in Massachusetts, districts losing students to interdistrict programs are making efforts to retain their student body, with some apparent success.[57]

These are only preliminary pieces of information. It is not yet possible to know how this ferment in American education, which is undoubtedly

Table 5-1. *Characteristics of School Choice Programs for Low-Income Families*

City or state	Sponsor	Religious schools included	Grades	First school year	Initial enrollment (number)	Enrollment in 2000–01	Schools in 2000–01 (number)	Maximum payment in 2000–01 (dollars)	Selection method (number)
Charlotte	CSF[a]	Yes	2–8	1999–2000	388	438	52	1,700	Lottery
Cleveland	Ohio	Yes	K–8	1996–97	1,996	3,900	67	2,500	Lottery
Dayton	PACE[b]	Yes	K–12	1998–99	542	680	42	Elementary: 1,785 / High school: 2,300	Lottery
Florida	Florida	Yes	K–12	1999–2000	146	52	2	3,500	Lottery
Indianapolis	ECCT[c]	Yes	K–8	1991–92	746	2,387	82	1,000	First come[d]
Milwaukee	Wisconsin	Yes	Pre-K–12	1990–91	341	9,638	103	5,326	Lottery
Milwaukee	PAVE[e]	Yes	K–12	1992–93	2,089	819	52	Elementary: 1,000 / High school: 1,500	First come
New York City	SCSF[f]	Yes	1–5	1997–98	1,200	1,650	216	1,400	Lottery
San Antonio	CEO[g]	Yes	1–8	1992–93	930	1,319	62	4,000	First come
Washington, D.C.	WSF[h]	Yes	K–12[i]	1993–94	30	1,300	116	Elementary: 2,000 / High school: 3,000	Lottery
National	CSF[a]	Yes	K–12[j]	1997–98	1,000	40,000	7,000	1,700	Lottery

Source: Paul E. Peterson and Jay P. Greene, "Vouchers and Central-City Schools," in Christopher H. Foreman Jr., ed., *The African American Predicament* (Brookings, 1999). Table was revised by Samuel Abrams, Stanford University, 2001.
a. Children's Scholarship Fund. The program originated in Washington, D.C., and was expanded nationally for the 1999–2000 academic year.
b. Parents Advancing Choice in Education.
c. Educational Choice Charitable Trust.
d. Program enrollment in Indianapolis is supplemented with periodic lotteries.
e. Partners Advancing Values in Education.
f. School Choice Scholarships Foundation.
g. Children's Educational Opporunity.
h. Washington Scholarship Fund.
i. Only students in grades K–8 may begin the Washington program.
j. Once awarded a scholarship, a student is guaranteed continued assistance for three additional years. However, the first-year scholarship must be awarded while the student is enrolled in grades K through 8.

giving families greater choice than previously available, will affect education policy and governance in the long run. Nor do we know for certain how school choice will affect students and families in the long run. It is important to continue to try out the full range of school options in a variety of contexts in order to determine which, if any, will benefit students and their families over the long term.

What Happens When Voucher Programs Are Introduced

Fortunately, a substantial amount of information is available about how the most market-based of all choice programs, school vouchers, works in practice. A series of studies provide valuable information about the kinds of students and families who participate in voucher programs; the effects of vouchers on student learning; the school climate at voucher schools, and the impact of vouchers on homework, school-home communications, and parental satisfaction. In the remainder of the essay, I discuss some of the issues that have arisen around these topics and report results from recent evaluations.

Characteristics of Voucher Recipients

Critics say that voucher programs "cream" or "cherry-pick" the public schools, attracting the participation of the most talented students and the higher-income, better-educated families. As a consequence, public schools will be left with an increasingly difficult population to educate and without the support of informed, engaged parents. Defenders of vouchers respond that families have little incentive to move a child from one school to another if the child is already doing well in school.

Considerable information is now available on the types of students and families who participate in means-tested voucher programs. In general, there is little evidence that voucher programs either skim the best and brightest students from public schools or attract only the lowest-performing students. On the contrary, voucher recipients resemble a cross-section of public school students, though in some cases they may come from somewhat more educated families.

In the Edgewood school district in San Antonio, Texas, vouchers were offered to all low-income residents. Those students who used the vouchers had math scores which, upon beginning their new private school, were similar to those of students in public schools. Their reading scores were only modestly higher. Voucher students were no more likely to have been in programs for gifted students, though they were less likely to have been in special education. Household income was similar, as was the percentage of families with two parents in the household. Mothers of voucher recipients had, on average, an additional year of education.[58]

In Cleveland, the parents of students using vouchers had lower incomes and the mothers were more likely to be African American than a random sample of public school parents. Mothers had less than a year of additional education beyond that of the public school mothers, and they were not significantly more likely to be employed full time.[59] And the voucher students were not themselves the "best and the brightest." On the contrary, students with vouchers were less likely to have been in a program for gifted or talented students than were children remaining in public schools. However, students with vouchers were less likely to have a learning disability.[60]

School Quality and Student Learning

Proponents of school vouchers expect that schools will perform better—and students will learn more—if families can choose their children's schools. They also predict that there will be a better match between the students' needs and the schools' characteristics; a stronger identification between family and school; and greater competition among schools, which will spur each to higher levels of performance. Critics of vouchers say that student performance is mainly a function of a child's family background and that little can be gained by giving families a greater choice among alternatives.

Preliminary information about these issues can be obtained by examining both student test scores and the quality of the school experience, including discipline within school, the amount of homework students are doing, the communication between home and school, suspension and school-mobility rates, and the level of parental satisfaction with the school. In general, the information suggests that vouchers enhance students' school experience by giving them a more structured school environment, engaging them in more homework, improving communication between home and school, and raising the level of parental satisfaction with the school.

TEST SCORES. The debate over student achievement is likely to continue for some years to come, not only because it is very difficult to measure how much children are learning in school but also because different groups and individuals have different views about what *should* be learned in school. According to results from three randomized field trials, African American students from low-income families who switch from a public to a private school do considerably better after two years than students who do not receive a voucher opportunity. However, students from other ethnic backgrounds seem to learn after two years as much as but no more than their public school counterparts.[61]

HIGH SCHOOL COMPLETION AND COLLEGE ATTENDANCE. It is too early to know what impact vouchers will have on high school completion rates and college attendance. However, information on the effects of attendance at a Catholic high school are contained in a recent University of Chicago analysis of the National Longitudinal Survey of Youth, conducted by the Department of Education, a survey of over 12,000 young people. Students from all racial and ethnic groups are more likely to go to college if they attended a Catholic school, but the effects are the greatest for urban minorities. The probability of graduating from college rises from 11 to 27 percent for a student who attended a Catholic high school.[62]

The University of Chicago study confirms results from two other analyses that show positive effects for low-income and minority students of attendance at Catholic schools on high school completion and college enrollment.[63] University of Wisconsin professor John Witte has concluded that studies of private schools "indicate a substantial private school advantage in terms of completing high school and enrolling in college, both very important events in predicting future income and well-being. Moreover, . . . the effects were most pronounced for students with achievement test scores in the bottom half of the distribution."[64]

SCHOOL DISCIPLINE. School discipline seems to be more effective in the private schools voucher students attend than in the inner-city public schools of their peers. Parents and students who have received vouchers report less fighting, cheating, property destruction, and other forms of disruption than do the students in public schools and their parents.

In Washington, D.C., students in grades five through eight were asked whether they felt safe at school. Twenty percent of the public school students and only 5 percent of the private school students said they did not feel safe.[65] Nationwide information on public and private schools yields similar information. A survey undertaken by Educational Testing Service found that eighth-grade students encounter more such problems in public than in private schools. Fourteen percent of public school students, but only 2 to 3 percent of private school students, say physical conflicts are a serious or moderate problem. Four percent of public school students report that racial or cultural conflicts are a serious or moderate problem and 5 percent say drug use is, while less than 1 percent of private school students indicate that these are problems. Nine percent of public school students say they feel unsafe in school, but only 4 percent of private school students give the same response.[66]

HOMEWORK. Parents of students in voucher programs report that their children have more homework than do the parents of students in public schools. This finding was consistent across a range of studies. In Cleveland, parents of students in the voucher program were significantly less likely than a cross-section of Cleveland public school parents to report that "teachers do not assign enough homework."[67] In New York City, 55 percent of the parents with students in private schools reported that their children had more than one hour of homework per day, while only 34 percent of a comparable group of parents with children in public schools reported this much homework.[68] Similarly, in the Edgewood school district in San Antonio, half of the parents of students receiving vouchers reported more than one hour of homework, while only 16 percent of parents of students in public schools reported that their children had this much homework.[69]

PARENT-SCHOOL COMMUNICATION. Parents of students in voucher programs report more extensive communication with their school than do parents with children in public schools. In Cleveland, "parents of scholarship students reported participating in significantly more activities than did parents of public school students." A teacher survey also supports this finding.[70] Similarly, in New York City, parents of students in private schools reported that they were more likely to receive grade information from the school, participate in instruction, attend parent nights, and attend regular parent-teacher conferences.[71] In the Edgewood school district in San Antonio, parents of students with vouchers were more likely to report that they had attended a school activity at least once in the past month than were parents of students in public schools. They were also more likely to report that they had attended a parent-teacher conference.[72]

PARENT SATISFACTION. Many economists think that consumer satisfaction is the best measure of school quality, just as it is the best measure of other products. According to this criterion, vouchers are a clear success. All evaluations of vouchers have found higher levels of parent satisfaction among parents receiving vouchers than among comparison groups of parents with students in public schools. In Cleveland, voucher parents were much more satisfied with their school than parents who had applied for but did not use the voucher offered to them. For example, 63 percent of voucher users said they were very satisfied with the academic quality of the school, as compared to 29 percent of those who had not used them. Similar differences in satisfaction levels were observed for school safety, school discipline, parental involvement, and class size.[73]

Some interpreted these findings as showing only that those who had applied for but not received a voucher were particularly unhappy with their public school, not that private school families were particularly satisfied. Those who did not receive a voucher or scholarship might simply be expressing sour grapes. To ascertain whether the "sour grape" hypothesis was correct, the satisfaction levels of voucher parents were compared with the satisfaction levels of a random sample of all of Cleveland's low-income, public school parents. Very little support for the "sour grape" hypothesis could be detected. Voucher parents were considerably more satisfied with the academic program, school safety, school discipline, and other characteristics of the schools their children were attending.[74]

Conclusions

Choice in American education is now widespread and has taken many forms—charters, magnet schools, tax-deduction programs, interdistrict enrollment programs, private schools, choice by residential selection, and school vouchers. Many of these programs give greater choice to middle- and upper-income families than to poor families. In this context, school vouchers, as currently designed, provide an egalitarian supplement to existing choice arrangements. They do so without restricting choices to parents with a specific religious affiliation or without any religious affiliation at all. Given the widespread public interest in finding better ways of educating disadvantaged families, it is particularly important that pilot voucher programs be continued so as to permit an assessment of the effectiveness of school vouchers as tools for achieving greater equity in American education, especially since early evaluations of their effectiveness have yielded promising results. If vouchers do not work, they will be discarded. If vouchers do work, their adoption will gradually spread. But if their exploration is prematurely ended, the country will be denied a valuable tool that could help it consider the best ways of improving its educational system.

Notes

1. U.S. Department of Education, National Center for Education Statistics (NCES), Findings from *The Condition of Education 1997*, "Social Context of Education," publication 97981; and NCES, "Public and Private Schools: How Do They Differ?" publication 97983 (Washington, 1997) (http://nces.ed.gov/pubsearch/).

2. U.S. Department of Education, NCES, Common Core of Data and "Fall Enrollment in Institutions of Higher Education" surveys; Integrated Post-Secondary Education Data System (IPEDS), Higher Education General Information Survey (HEGIS), "Fall Enrollment: Surveys and Projections of Education Statistics to 2007" (Washington, 1997) (http://nces.ed.gov/pubs/digest97/d97t002.html).

3. Lynn Schnaiberg, "More Students Taking Advantage of School Choice, Report Says," *Education Week*, September 22, 1999, p. 6.

4. Joint Center for Political and Economic Studies, *1997 National Opinion Poll* (Washington, 1997), table 7.

5. Andrew J. Coulson, *Market Education: The Unknown History* (New Brunswick, N.J.: Transaction, 1999), chap. 2.

6. John Stuart Mill, "On Liberty" in George R. La Noue, ed., *Educational Vouchers: Concepts and Controversies* (New York: Teachers College Press, 1972), pp. 3–4.

7. Milton Friedman, "The Role of Government in Education," in Robert Solo, ed., *Economics and the Public Interest* (Rutgers University Press, 1955), p. 127.

8. David K. Cohen and Eleanor Farrar, "Power to the Parents? The Story of Education Vouchers," *Public Interest* (Spring 1977), pp. 72–97.

9. John Chubb and Terry Moe, *Politics, Markets, and America's Schools* (Brookings, 1990).

10. Paul E. Peterson, "The New Politics of Choice," in Diane Ravitch and Maris A. Vinovskis, eds., *Learning from the Past* (Johns Hopkins University Press, 1995).

11. Joseph P. Viteritti, *Choosing Equality: School Choice, the Constitution, and Civil Society* (Brookings, 1999), pp. 60–62; Bruce Fuller and others, *School Choice* (Policy Analysis for California Education; University of California, Berkeley; and Stanford University, 1999).

12. H. S. Rosen and D. J. Fullerton, "A Note on Local Tax Rates, Public Benefit Levels, and Property Values," *Journal of Political Economy*, vol. 85, no. 2 (1977), pp. 433–40; G. R. Meadows, "Taxes, Spending, and Property Values: A Comment and Further Results," *Journal of Political Economy*, vol. 84, no. 4, pt. 1 (1976), pp. 869–80; M. Edel and E. Sclar, "Taxes, Spending, and Property Values: Supply Adjustment in a Tiebout-Oates Model," *Journal of Political Economy*, vol. 82, no. 5 (1974), pp. 941–54.

13. Paul E. Peterson, "Introduction: Technology, Race, and Urban Policy," in Paul E. Peterson, ed., *The New Urban Reality* (Brookings, 1985), pp. 1–29.

14. U.S. Department of Education, NCES, Findings from *The Condition of Education 1997*; and NCES, "Public and Private Schools."

15. Caroline Minter Hoxby, "The Effects of School Choice on Curriculum and Atmosphere," in Susan B. Mayer and Paul E. Peterson, eds., *Earning and Learning: How Schools Matter* (Brookings, 1999), pp. 281–316; Caroline M. Hoxby, "Does Competition among Schools Benefit Students and Taxpayers?" *American Economic Review*, vol. 90, no. 5 (2000), pp. 1209–38; Caroline M. Hoxby, "Analyzing School Choice Reforms That Use America's Traditional Forms of Parental Choice," in Paul E. Peterson and Bryan C. Hassel, eds., *Learning from School Choice* (Brookings, 1998), pp. 133–51.

16. Gary Orfield, *Must We Bus? Segregated Schools and National Policy* (Brookings, 1978).

17. Fuller and others, *School Choice*, p. 26.

18. Lauri Steel and Roger Levine, "Educational Innovation in Multicultural Contexts: The Growth of Magnet Schools in American Education" (Palo Alto, Calif.: American Institutes for Research, 1996).

19. Denis P. Doyle and Marsha Levine, "Magnet Schools: Choice and Quality in Public Education," *Phi Delta Kappan*, vol. 66, no. 4 (1984), pp. 265–70; Rolf K. Blank, Roger E. Levine, and Lauri Steel, "After 15 Years: Magnet Schools in Urban Education," in Bruce Fuller, Richard Elmore, and Gary Orfield, eds., *Who Chooses? Who Loses? Culture, Institutions and the Unequal Effects of School Choice* (New York: Teachers College Press, 1996), pp. 154–72.

20. *Reed* v. *Rhodes*, 934 F.Supp. 1533, 1575 (N.D. Ohio 1996).

21. R. Kenneth Godwin, Frank R. Kemerer, and Valerie J. Martinez, "Comparing Public Choice and Private Voucher Programs in San Antonio," in Peterson and Hassel, *Learning from School Choice*, pp. 275–306; Corrie M. Yu and William L. Talor, "Difficult Choices: Do Magnet Schools Serve Children in Need?" (Washington: Citizens' Commission on Civil Rights, 1997).

22. California Department of Education, as cited in Fuller and others, *School Choice*, pp. 30, 38–39; Carnegie Foundation for the Advancement of Teaching, *School Choice: A Special Report* (Princeton, N.J., 1992).

23. Adam Gamoran, "Student Achievement in Public Magnet, Public Comprehensive, and Private City High Schools," *Educational Evaluation and Policy Analysis*, vol. 18, no. 1 (1996), pp. 1–18; Robert L. Crain, Amy Heebner, and Yiu-Pong Si, "The Effectiveness of New York City's Career Magnet Schools: An Evaluation of Ninth-Grade Performance Using an Experimental Design" (Berkeley, Calif.: National Center for Research in Vocational Education, 1992).

24. Viteritti, *Choosing Equality*, pp. 62–63.

25. Fuller and others, *School Choice*, p. 33.

26. David J. Armor and Brett M. Peiser, "Inter-District Choice in Massachusetts," in Peterson and Hassel, *Learning from School Choice*, pp. 157–86; David J. Armor and Brett M. Peiser, *Competition in Education: A Case Study in Inter-District Choice* (Boston: Pioneer Institute for Public Policy Research, 1997).

27. Armor and Peiser, *Competition in Education*.

28. Bryan C. Hassel, *The Charter School Challenge* (Brookings, 1999), p. 1.

29. "Operating Charter Schools, Fall 1999–2000," Memorandum prepared by the Fordham Foundation, Washington, D.C., October 1999.

30. Robert Maranto, Scott Milliman, Frederick Hess, and April Gresham, "Real World School Choice: Arizona Charter Schools," in Robert Maranto, Scott Milliman, Frederick Hess, and April Gresham, eds., *School Choice in the Real World: Lessons from Arizona Charter Schools* (Boulder, Colo.: Westview, 1999), p. 7.

31. U.S. Department of Education, Office of Educational Research and Improvement, *A Study of Charter Schools: First-Year Report* (Washington, 1997); Gregg Vanourek, Bruno V. Mann, Chester E. Finn Jr., and Louann A. Bierlein, "Charter Schools as Seen by Students, Teachers, and Parents," in Peterson and Hassel, *Learning from School Choice*, pp. 187–212.

32. Caroline Minter Hoxby, "The Effects of Charter Schools on Teachers," Department of Economics, Harvard University, September 1999.

33. Minnesota Department of Children, Families, and Learning, "Take Credit for Learning," 1997 (http://www.children.state.mn.us/tax/credits.html).

34. John Haugen, Legal Services Division, Minnesota Department of Revenue, telephone interview, October 21, 1999.

35. Rob Robinson, senior tax analyst, Arizona Department of Revenue, telephone interview, October 21, 1999.

36. Thomas Paine, *Rights of Man* (1792), 1:245, as quoted in David Kirkpatrick, *Choice in Schooling: A Case for Tuition Vouchers* (Chicago: Loyola University Press, 1990), p. 34.

37. Charles L. Glenn Jr., *The Myth of the Common School* (University of Massachusetts Press, 1987), pp. 83–84.

38. *Meyers* v. *Nebraska*, 401 U.S. 399 (1923); *Pierce* v. *Society of Sisters*, 268 U.S. 528 (1925).

39. U.S. Department of Education, NCES, Common Core of Data and "Fall Enrollment in Institutions of Higher Education" surveys; Integrated Post-Secondary Education Data System (IPEDS), Higher Education General Information Survey (HEGIS), "Fall Enrollment: Surveys and Projections of Education Statistics to 2007" (Washington, 1997) (http://nces.ed.gov/pubs/digest97/d97t002.html).

40. Coulson, *Market Education*, p. 277.

41. James S. Coleman, Thomas Hoffer, and Sally Kilgore, *High School Achievement* (Basic Books, 1982).

42. Major studies that have found positive educational benefits from attending private schools include Chubb and Moe, *Politics, Markets*; Derek Neal, "The Effects of Catholic Secondary Schooling on Educational Achievement" (University of Chicago, Harris School of Public Policy; National Bureau of Economic Research, 1996). Critiques of Coleman's findings and other studies have been offered by Arthur S. Goldberger and Glen G. Cain, "The Causal Analysis of Cognitive Outcomes in the Coleman, Hoffer, and Kilgore Report," *Sociology of Education*, vol. 55 (April–July 1982), pp. 103–22; and Douglas J. Wilms, "Catholic School Effects on Academic Achievement: New Evidence from the High School and Beyond Follow-up Study," *Sociology of Education*, vol. 58, no. 2 (1985), pp. 98–114.

43. John F. Witte, "School Choice and Student Performance," in Helen F. Ladd, ed., *Holding Schools Accountable: Performance-Based Reform in Education* (Brookings, 1996), p. 167.

44. Caroline Minter Hoxby, "The Effects of Private School Vouchers on Schools and Students," in Ladd, *Holding Schools Accountable*, pp. 177–208; Caroline Minter Hoxby,

"Do Private Schools Provide Competition for Public Schools?" Working Paper 4978 (Cambridge, Mass.: National Bureau of Economic Research, 1994).

45. Christopher J. Klicka and Gregg Harris, *The Right Choice* (Gresham, Ore.: Noble Publishing Associates, 1992), pp. 356–57, as cited in Coulson, *Market Education*, pp. 120–21.

46. Patricia Lines, "Home Schools: Estimating Numbers and Growth" U.S. Department of Education Technical Paper, 1998; U.S. Bureau of the Census, *Current Population Reports. Population Characteristics: School Enrollment—Social and Economic Characteristics of Students: October 1995* (GPO). Paul Hill, University of Washington, provided me with this information.

47. The study is based on a group of families who agreed to participate, making it difficult to generalize to all home-schooled students. Lawrence M. Rudner, "Scholastic Achievement and Demographic Characteristics of Home School Students in 1998," *Education Policy Analysis Archives*, vol. 7, no. 13 (1999). For a commentary on this article, see Kariane Mari Welner and Kevin G. Welner, "Contextualizing Home-Schooling Data: A Response to Rudner," *Education Policy Analysis Archives*, vol. 7, no. 13 (1999).

48. Jessica L. Sandham, "Calif. Rules Hitting Home for Charter Schools," *Education Week*, September 8, 1999.

49. Paul E. Peterson and Jay P. Greene, "Vouchers and Central-City Schools," in Christopher H. Foreman Jr., ed., *The African American Predicament* (Brookings, 1999), p. 85.

50. "Florida Begins Voucher Plan for Education," *New York Times*, August 17, 1999, p. A15.

51. J. David Greenstone and Paul E. Peterson, *Race and Authority in Urban Politics: Community Participation and the War on Poverty* (Russell Sage Foundation, 1973).

52. Paul E. Peterson, *Making the Grade* (Twentieth Century Fund, 1983), chaps. 4–5.

53. Jeff Archer, "Two Cleveland Schools Plan Rebirth with Charter Status," *Education Week*, July 14, 1999.

54. Anastasia Cisneros-Lunsford, "Munoz Leaving District, Edgewood Chief Gains New Position," *San Antonio Express-News*, September 10, 1999; Anastasia Cisneros-Lunsford, "Edgewood Oks Uniforms for Youngsters," *San Antonio Express-News*, April 28, 1999.

55. Jessica L. Sandham, "Schools Hit by Vouchers Fight Back," *Education Week*, September 15, 1999.

56. Robert Maranto, Scott Milliman, Frederick Hess, and April Gresham, "Lessons from a Contested Frontier," in Maranto, Milliman, Hess, and Gresham, *School Choice in the Real World*, p. 237.

57. Susan L. Aud, "Competition in Education: 1999 Update of School Choice in Massachusetts" (Boston: Pioneer Institute for Public Policy Research, September 1999), p. 36.

58. Paul E. Peterson, David Myers, and William G. Howell, "An Evaluation of the Horizon Scholarship Program in the Edgewood Independent School District, San Antonio, Texas: The First Year," Occasional Paper, Program on Education Policy and Governance (Cambridge, Mass.: Kennedy School of Government, Harvard University, September 1999), tables 2, 3, pp. 41–42. Available from www.ksg.harvard.edu/pepg.

59. Paul E. Peterson, William G. Howell, and Jay P. Greene, "An Evaluation of the Cleveland Voucher Program after Two Years," Occasional Paper, Program on Education Policy and Governance (Cambridge, Mass.: Kennedy School of Government, Harvard University, June 1999), table 1, pp. 16–17. Available from www.ksg.harvard.edu/pepg.

60. Ibid., table 2, p. 18.

61. William G. Howell, Patrick J. Wolf, Paul E. Peterson, and David E. Campbell, "Test-Score Effects of School Vouchers in Dayton, Ohio, New York City, and Washington, D.C.: Evidence from Randomized Field Trials," Paper presented at the annual meetings of the American Political Science Association, 2000. Available from Program on Education Policy and Governance, Kennedy School of Government, Harvard University, 2000 and at (http://data.fas.harvard.edu/pepg/).

62. Derek Neal, "The Effects of Catholic Secondary Schooling on Educational Achievement" (Harris School of Public Policy, University of Chicago and National Bureau for Economic Research, 1996), p. 26.

63. William N. Evans and Robert M. Schwab, "Who Benefits from Private Education? Evidence from Quantile Regressions" (Department of Economics, University of Maryland, 1993); David Siglio and Joe Stone, "School Choice and Student Performance: Are Private Schools Really Better?" (Institute for Research on Poverty, University of Wisconsin, 1977).

64. John F. Witte, "School Choice and Student Performance," in Ladd, *Holding Schools Accountable*, p. 167. Professor Witte's criticisms of voucher programs can be found in John F. Witte, "The Milwaukee Voucher Experiment: The Good, the Bad, and the Ugly," *Phi Delta Kappan*, vol. 81, no. 1 (1999), pp. 59–64.

65. Paul E. Peterson, Jay P. Greene, William G. Howell, and William McCready, "Initial Findings from an Evaluation of School Choice Programs in Washington, D.C.," Occasional Paper, Program on Education Policy and Governance (Cambridge, Mass.: Kennedy School of Government, Harvard University, September 1998), table 9A, p. 53. Available from www.ksg.harvard.edu/pepe. This finding remains statistically significant after adjustments are made for family background characteristics.

66. Information in this paragraph is from Paul E. Barton, Richard J. Coley, and Harold Wenglinsky, *Order in the Classroom: Violence, Discipline and Student Achievement* (Princeton, N.J.: Policy Information Center, Research Division, Educational Testing Service, 1998), pp. 21, 23, 25, 27, and 29.

67. Peterson, Howell, and Greene, "An Evaluation of the Cleveland Voucher Program," table 5, p. 23.

68. P. E. Peterson, D. E. Myers, W. G. Howell, and D. P. Mayer, "The Effects of School Choice in New York City," in S. E. Mayer and P. E. Peterson, eds., *Earning and Learning: How Schools Matter* (Washington and New York: Brookings and Russell Sage Foundation, 1999), table 12-2, p. 328.

69. Peterson, Myers, and Howell, "An Evaluation of the Horizon Scholarship Program," table 1.13, p. 52. Similar results were obtained when school effects were estimated controlling for family background characteristics. See table 2.4, p. 63.

70. Kim Metcalf, "Evaluation of the Cleveland Scholarship and Tutoring Program, 1996–1999," Working Paper, Indiana Center for Evaluation (Indiana University, September 1999), pp. 18–19.

71. Peterson, Myers, Howell, and Mayer, "The Effects of School Choice in New York City," table 12-3, p. 329.

72. Peterson, Myers, and Howell, "An Evaluation of the Horizon Scholarship Program," table 1.14, p. 53.

73. Greene, Howell, and Peterson, "Lessons from the Cleveland Scholarship Program," table 1.8, p. 56.

74. Peterson, Howell, and Greene, "An Evaluation of the Cleveland Voucher Program," table 3c, p. 21.

6

L. JEAN CAMP

The Shape
of the Network

What we are promulgating is a set of social norms for which the various licenses are actually just proxies.

TIM O'REILLY, personal communication,
November 2000

MARKETIZATION REFERS TO the unleashing of a market in a previously government-provided service. What is happening with government on the Internet and with information products takes marketization even further. In the rich tradition of creating nouns in the policy disciplines, I refer to this as *propertization*.[1] Marketization is about the utilization of market forces to distribute artifacts (such as a kilowatt-hour or a pound of postconsumer glass) already identifiable as subject to trade. Propertization is the creation or re-creation of property from intangibles.

The creation of information property, or information, is a necessary enabler in the network economy. However, there is nothing predetermined

This work was funded in part by NSF Career Grant #9985433. I would like to acknowledge the participants in the Visions of Governance program for their assistance. I would particularly like to acknowledge R. Zeckhauser.

about the market parameters defined by propertization. Thus there is nothing predetermined about the network shaped by the resulting market. The types of property rights created and how those rights are balanced with other rights (such as speech and privacy) and values (innovation and equity) are determinations being made now. The information market will be bigger, but it may or may not be better, or even competitive, depending on the parameters chosen now.

It is my purpose here to examine how property and the property-rights bundle are being defined. I classify the expansion of property rights into three categories: information property, code as a distinct class of information property, and information transport networks. I refer to these as content, code, and conduit. I discuss regulatory threads in the creation and expansion of intellectual property around both words and code, and changes in the regulation of transport networks. Together these trends threaten the characteristics of the Internet that have enabled an inchoate academic network to grow into an engine driving global prosperity.

The creation of an information market requires the creation of a bundle of rights that together create a tradable property. In the network society, the information revolution, or information economy (or whatever nomenclature is finally adopted), the size, duration, and reach of the bundles of rights that are property are increasing monotonically.

The creation of a market also requires the creation of a set of rules for transactions that involve the newly defined property. With physical property, the fundamental right has been the right of exclusion—the ability to prevent another from accessing or using one's property. The ability to exclude others creates the greatest incentive to invest in physical property and is thus the ideal outcome for society and for the individual.

With respect to intellectual property, the law has a fundamentally different orientation: the goal is to create more property and ensure the most fruitful possible use of that property. The goal of permanent exclusion of others is antithetical to the fundamental goals of intellectual property protection. Copyright, trademark, and patent have all been modeled in order to maximize the total amount of information in circulation. The total amount of information in circulation—that is, the size of the marketplace of ideas—is optimized by a short term of exclusion that creates an incentive to create. There is no comparable motivation with physical property. No owner of physical property is expected to return the property to the commons after some defined period. Limits on the rights of physical property owners would not expand the physical property marketplace. A physical property owner's exclusive right to ownership does not prevent others from creating additional property. However ill-suited, the linear model of property (that is, that more protection yields more production) is replacing the broader traditions of intellectual property.

Simultaneously with the change in the conceptualization of intellectual property, the ancient concept of the common carrier is being replaced by vertical integration. Common-carrier regulations date from Roman times, when the owners of ships were forced to have nondiscriminatory pricing policies for those who would transport goods.[2] There was an understanding that an infinite number of ships could not exist and that trade was thus optimized by limiting the property rights of the owners of the transport infrastructure. That basic concept of common carriers held sway as private investment built bridges in early modern Europe and as telegraph carriers laid lines across the United States. When the basic concept of common-carrier transport regulation has been forgotten, the result has often been economic disaster leading to yet more regulations in the long term. In America the resulting regulation of the railroads and the extensive broadcast regulation of what were open wireless networks are examples from the last great economic alteration. It is not coincidental that the physical layer as provided by the owners of local infrastructure is fundamentally connected with the transport layer. This lesson is being forgotten, and the result risks the closing of a network, the closing of the carrier layer on which our information commons critically depends. (The lesson has been forgotten, in the case of public Network Access Points [NAPs], yet this is not my focus.)[3]

The construction of the Internet required available content, common-carriage conduit, and open code. I argue that the policy definitions of code, content, and conduit will alter the fundamental assumptions of the Internet and that the principles currently embodied in the network are the result of a particular set of assumptions and require certain regulatory realities. Those assumptions can be altered and will be shaped by the definition of the information property that crosses the networks and the regulation (or lack of regulation) of the wires on which the signals run.

Some may argue that the innate nature of the Internet will prevent it from being altered by definitions of property. John Gilmore's concept that "the net treats censorship as damage and routes around it" is a widely believed myth.[4] Yet the governmental takeover of B-52 in Serbia illustrates that without virtual people real censorship is quite possible. Such a myth should not guide policy. A similar error can be seen in the famous cartoon by Peter Steiner that carries the caption, "On the Internet nobody knows you're a dog." Such a widespread assumption of anonymity reflects the ability to project false identity but does not negate concerns about privacy.

In short, the "innate nature" of the Internet is neither. Of course, the Internet has no "nature." It is entirely constructed. It is constructed on protocols and networks that today have fundamental characteristics that appear, in practice, to support democratic pluralism: content neutrality and bidirectional information flow. All three of these—code, content, and conduit—result from the design and implementation of the underlying system. There was no natural outcome in the choices made by protocol designers. The choices were made in a particular social environment. The design of the protocols underlying the Internet resulted not only from stated design goals (such as survivability) but also from certain social assumptions (such as equality of users). The assumption that technology has innate characteristics that will not be changed is referred to as technological determinism and has been widely discredited; technology and society form each other in a complex dance of a thousand steps.[5]

The design characteristics of the Internet that have consistently been said to support democratic pluralism are content neutrality, consumer voice, and synchronous information flow. Together these add up to the ability to create as well as consume content. At the technical level these result from the "end-to-end" argument—a reference to the ability to innovate. All two people need is compatible software on each of their machines; the network will connect them regardless of how innovative or radical the software is (radically good or radically bad).

Content neutrality refers to the idea that information is transmitted through the network regardless of the contents of the packet. This means that owners of specific content could not, traditionally, cause their content to be preferred over the content of others. Think of bits as water and the information flow as water flow. There are a few ways to make sure that water is transmitted to a particular location. One is to build very fat pipes and send as much as can possibly be desired. This so-called fat-pipe strategy was the Internet practice up to the late 1990s. A second way is to put meters on the water and decrease demand. This is the strategy of the various quality-of-service proposals.[6] A third is to have a slow normal flow and allow privileged areas to build tanks. This is the approach used by Akamai, an Internet content distributor. Note that the need for content distributors is in part a result of the failure of the governments or any self-governance mechanism to create functional interconnection agreements.

The ability to speak as well as listen is critical to maintaining the oft-heralded democratic implications of the Internet. But the ability to be heard is being undermined in at least two ways. First, the creation of a bundle of property rights for content producers prevents derivative works or criticism. The Internet Corporation for Assigned Names and Numbers (ICANN) and the expansion of trademark and copyright interests by Congress are effective legal mechanisms for silencing criticism.[7] In particular, the Digital Millennium Copyright Act (DMCA) is undermining innovation by prohibiting individuals from reverse-engineering software.

The second force undermining content neutrality is the marketization of information flow. The Internet creates an affordable mechanism for distributing content by depending on best-effort transport and network mechanisms. This means, using the analogy above, that no water can be targeted or delivered more quickly than any other water because they all use the same pipes. While this may be true of water pipes, it is not necessarily true of bits, because bits can be self-identifying. The network can be engineered so that widespread distribution of content requires contracts with the holders of selected caches and discovery requires payment for selected search engines. Engineering the network in this manner would remove the advantage of cheap distribution and create a closed network.

Bidirectional information flow is the assumption that people speak as well as listen. Synchronous information flow means that my machine can send as much as it receives in a standard connection to the Internet: 56.6k means 56.6k either way, uploading or downloading. Next-generation broadband technologies are altering that assumption. Next-generation broadband networks presume that home users are always clients and never servers—for example, that people mostly listen, and speak only when given permission by the owner of a server. Next-generation networks can be built so that independent Internet service providers (ISPs) must jump additional hurdles to reach clients and wireless users receive only information selected by the marketer of connectivity, so that content is determined by conduit. Further, with closed code such decisions cannot even be seen by the customer.

In this discussion I touch on namespaces, markets, and governments, with the common thread being how the construction of social and technical standards can create, negate, enable, or handicap civil society. The issues I bring to light are often referred to in engineering as the "law of unintended consequences"—meaning that the unintended consequences of a widely adopted technology will overwhelm the design goals in the long term. I argue that these consequences, though unintended, can nonetheless be predicted in the case of the policies and technologies being considered now. This offers the promise that such consequences can be avoided. Policy is very much like engineering in that at its best what is built is an infrastructure that enables individuals and societies to pursue their goals with efficient grace. They are also alike in that both policy and engineering are invisible when successful and gracefully designed, and dramatically visible when they fail.

Code

Is code a machine or speech? Should code be patented like a machine or subject to copyright like text? Previous work has focused on the ethical implications of code, a specific regulatory approach, industry practices, or potential regulatory regimes for intellectual property as a whole.[8]

Code comes in several forms. First, there is source (or high-level) code. Second is assembly code. And third is executable or binary code, which can be disassembled or reverse-engineered into source code; but this is a difficult, tedious, and uncertain process. High-level source code is readable by humans:

```
#include <stdio.h
main()
{
int a,b;
a = 1;
b = 2;
printf("%i\n", a + b);
}
```

With some examination one can see that the code adds two numbers (a + b) and prints out the result.

Code may be translated to an interim form, which is called assembly. Assembly is a low-level language, in contrast to high-level languages. Assembly code consists of human-readable commands in the order in which they are implemented: for example, move a previously stored number from one register to another so that the number can be loaded into the arithmetic logic unit to be added. Grace Hopper's invention of compilers freed humans from writing in binary (see list below).[9]

Alternatively, high-level code may be interpreted into a lower-level form and then executed on a virtual machine. Interpreted code is compiled every time it is run. LISP and Java are interpreted languages. In this discussion, interpreted code can be considered equivalent to compiled code. Scripting languages such as Javascript are interpreted every time they are run and inherently distributed in source form. Similarly, HTML is simply a mark-up language and the distribution is inherently open.

The following is annotated assembler pseudo-code for adding two numbers:

ORG 0	The program begins at location 0
LDA A	First number is at location A
ADD B	Add number from location B
STA C	Store the result in location C
HLT	Stop computer
DEC 01	First number is 1 in base ten (e.g., decimal)
DEC 02	First number is 2 in base ten (e.g., decimal)
DEC 0	Sum stored in location C
END	End of program

Machines read binary code. Machine code is specific to a particular hardware and operating system. Interpreted code is specific to a particular virtual machine, which can theoretically be run on any hardware with any operating system.

In licensed, proprietary software, users receive binary code, which cannot be read by humans. This part of the binary code is for a particular machine and a particular compiler, which does part of the work of adding two numbers.

```
0010 0000 0000 0100
0001 0000 0000 0101
0011 0000 0000 0110
0111 0000 0000 0001
0000 0000 0101 0011
1111 1111 1110 1001
0000 0000 0000 0000
```

Currently the protection of the various levels of code is complex. Code can be subject to copyright, as with the Gnu General Public License (GPL).[10]

Code can be the subject of trade secrets, and code can be patented. Because it can be treated as a service, it can also be licensed. In particular, the Uniform Computer Information Transactions Act (UCITA) would allow the producers of software to share the same very low levels of liability with custom professional services customers, negating traditional consumer protection.

Code is subject to trade secret. Microsoft is using a combination of contract law and trade secret claims to prevent the publication of its implementation of Kerberos. Kerberos is an open standard or protocol. A protocol is a definition of the syntax and order of messages. Kerberos is used to manage resources (such as websites, databases, or particular digital services) that are protected by passwords. When you receive a response to your submission of a password, you have usually interacted with Kerberos. Microsoft's implementation of Kerberos changes the protocol so that it no longer works with traditional implementation.

To understand the importance of viewing code, a note on Microsoft business practices is in order. Microsoft has a business practice called "embrace and extend," which is commonly referred to as "embrace, extend, and extinguish" by those who have been so embraced. Microsoft "embraces" a standard by implementing it and ensuring its compatibility with Windows. Microsoft then "extends" the standard so that it is not compatible with any but Microsoft products. With Linux, a Microsoft competitor, making headway in the server market, making a cornerstone of network security inoperable with Linux would leverage Microsoft's monopoly on the desktop to extend the hold to the server.

In other words, in Microsoft's view, Kerberos would be an ideal standard to embrace, extend, and extinguish. The current Microsoft policy is to allow individuals to look at source code on the web on the condition that the user view and accept a contract prohibiting discussion or any public exposure of the code. This could in practice prohibit open-code proponents from making implementations interoperable with the new "extended" Kerberos.

A reader of Slashdot.org, a community of open-code developers and proponents, crafted a small program that allows anyone using it to view the Microsoft Kerberos code without agreeing to the license provisions. By clicking on the link provided on Slashdot to this small program, anyone could see the Microsoft Kerberos code and never see the license. Using this license bypass, another reader of Slashdot posted the Kerberos code. Microsoft sued Slashdot on the basis that Slashdot was exposing a trade secret.

Code can also be subject to patent. In particular, the algorithms used to write the code can be patented. Algorithms are widely seen as ideas in the scientific environment, even among those who own or are pursuing patents. It is seen as a necessary practice required by bad law and worse business practice. Software patents have been the subject of much derision because they do not cover the implementation of a particular idea; that is, they do not cover the particular coding of an idea but rather the concept itself. This claim is in opposition to the written law of patents but is widely shared among scholars.[11]

Patents and propertization have expanded the rights of patent holders over innovators and consumers. Proprietary software and patents have trumped consumers' right to choose and know what they purchase, entrepreneurs' desire to add value, and scientists' right to investigate.

In addition, the legal definition of code is confusing and has no clear underlying principle. Where clearly applicable principles exist in the law, such as in the assignment of liability, those principles are not being applied to code. The creation of code in its varying forms of property offers an irrational distribution of liability; expands the rights of those who market the code at the expense of consumer and citizen rights; and allows an excessive fencing off of the commons through patents.

Content

Imagine that a builder could own all the papers taken into any building he or she built, and that extracting the papers from the building is extremely expensive, requiring a specialist with specific tools. Now imagine that that building is your home or your office. Even detecting the surveillance equipment and learning what information about you has been compiled and resold would require special tools. But the law prohibits the use of those tools. Who owns your ideas and who owns your business? Who owns your identity? How much autonomy do you have?

Welcome to the world of the Digital Millennium Copyright Act. The DMCA, which prohibits reverse-engineering, has enabled Microsoft to sue programmers for speaking about the Microsoft implementation of a public standard. The DMCA has enabled the prosecution of an innovative programmer who unbundled Microsoft's operating system (Windows) and movie player (DVD content scrambling system). Because the programmer's software allowed users to view movies on operating systems not made by Microsoft, and because the software enabled this unbundling by decrypting the weak security of the Content Scrambling System (CSS), this act of innovation is illegal. While the Department of Justice tries to prevent the bundling of browsers with one hand, it requires the bundling of video players with the other.[12]

You have just entered the office and the home of the future, according to U.S. government policy. Imagine that your papers are digital and your words are written in an application. You have no rights over the file format. If the files were written in a secure (encrypted) manner, or even encrypted with something as trivial as pig latin, any reverse-engineering to create a compatible product would be prohibited.

Trademark

The old forms of property were defined as trade secrets, patents, and copyrights. Intellectual property law is almost as varied and confused as real property law, yet there are a few clear issues. The primary threads of intellectual property law are trademark, patent, copyright, and trade secrets. Trademark law was originally established to allow businesses to distinguish themselves and prevent customer confusion.[13] Trademark law was applicable when one company presented itself in such a way as to be confused with another. Trademark law has not been actionable in cases where businesses with similar names were separated by lines of business or geography.

The rights of trademark holders are being radically expanded on the Internet with applications of trademark law not only to businesses but also to geographic regions, union organizing drives (Historic Williamsburg), artistic endeavors (etoys), and political speech (gwbush). Trademark holders are being given rights over speech that criticizes their commercial practices. In the case of Colonial Williamsburg, the Hotel and Restaurant Employees Local 25 had a site both to unionize the employees in the area hotels and to inform potential area visitors of the practices of the hospitality businesses with respect to workers. The members of the union had been working without a contract, while the employers were seeking federal permission to import workers. On the basis that such a site harmed the identity of the businesses that had invested in the regional name Colonial Williamsburg, the union was required to cease using the domain name "colonial-williamsburg.com." The court so ruled despite the fact that

Colonial Williamsburg is the name of a region, not of a particular business. The union changed its domain name to "cwunions.com."

The result was to take away what was an effective bully pulpit for the workers. Because some of the original site's content was clearly political and social speech, it was moved on the basis that the recipient of the criticism had property rights, which trumped the speech and organization rights of the union. Judge Rebecca Smith issued the injunction against the union and for the hotels without union counsel present, stating, trademark violations "can happen very quickly, potentially in minutes, hours and certainly days."[14]

In another case, etoys.com sued etoys.org on the basis of trademark violation. etoys.org was the site for a performance art group whose speech was entirely artistic. etoys.org preceded etoys.com on the Internet by several years, but etoys.org had no legal recourse.[15] There is no place in the current domain name resolution policy or trademark law as it is being applied to domain names for artistic, political, or critical speech. The only defense available to etoys.org was public outrage. etoys.org maintained its domain name only through an effective consumer boycott, yet there was no change in legal doctrine despite the clear citizen outrage at the ability of etoys.com to remove etoys.org's domain name.[16]

A trademark is a valuable piece of intellectual property. Before the battles over domain names, trademarks existed for the purpose of differentiating products. Now propertization has expanded the property rights of trademark holders by redefining the balance between trademark rights and speech rights.

Copyright

The radical changes in copyright law, intended to bring copyright to the digital age, are evidenced in the Digital Millennium Copyright Act. Recall that the objectives of copyright are to encourage and protect innovation and to create a marketplace with the greatest amount of innovation.

The best-known case being brought under the new copyright law is known as the DeCSS case. The Content Scrambling System was not a technical masterpiece. Its primary purpose was to create in code a protection of the business practices of the Motion Picture Association of America (MPAA). Currently movies are released in different places around the world. The Content Scrambling System controls when, how, and where movies are watched. It marks copies of otherwise identical movies with location markers so that a movie meant to be sold in one region cannot be resold in another (for example, through eBay). Purchased and rented videos are watermarked to prevent consumers from making copies. (Unfortunately this watermarking often prevents the digital tracking mechanisms on video players from working, so that consumers get worthless goods, but that would be the subject of another paper.) CSS was intended to control the legal viewing of movies, yet CSS was included in a typical pirate copy and the pirate copy would fit well with the CSS-enabled player.

The factual core of the case is as follows. A young man in northern Europe wanted to watch movies in France while on vacation. He had a DVD player at home, with the television. He also had a portable computer, which he took on vacation. His portable computer used the Linux operating system, which did not allow him to watch movies protected with the Content Scrambling System. In fact, even if his machine had had the CSS, the machine would have been useless in France because the rentals would play only on players identified with the region.

Only machines with Microsoft or Apple operating systems can legally use DVD players to play movies protected with the Content Scrambling System. So this young man subverted the Content Scrambling System in order to be able to rent videos and watch them while on vacation. He then posted the code so that others could use it. In no case or court has it been proposed that this young man, Jon Johansen, intended to copy movies in order to avoid having to purchase them. He wanted only to be able to watch movies he had already purchased or rented.

Johansen and his father were arrested and brought to the United States for trial. In addition to prosecuting this teenager and his father, the MPAA has filed suit against every website that posts the DeCSS code or links to the DeCSS code. Judge Lewis A. Kaplan issued a preliminary injunction on January 21 ordering the 2600.com website and its ISP to cease posting or in any other way "trafficking" in DeCSS. The fact that the posting at 2600 was in part to discuss the technical and legal merits of the DMCA case was not held to be justification to allow posting or linking.

So, in short, an information innovation that allows consumers who buy or purchase movies to watch them on the operating system and in the location of their choice is a felony. It is a felony even to discuss this debate at the source code level. In other words, it is prohibited by law to take a movie from New York and watch it in Amsterdam if the MPAA would like such an action to be prohibited and can implement this prohibition in computer code.

The findings in the DeCSS case will have tremendous implications. Removing the option to innovate cripples the open-source and free software communities. The bindings created by weak technical protections in bad code can be sufficiently strengthened by criminal law to cripple the open-code movement. Without free code there would have been no Internet. The destruction of open code through the redefinition of patents and copyright will prevent the evolution of an Internet that maintains democratic principles in design. Modern copyright law is radically extending the amount of control copyright holders have over content and users of content. This is not happening only in entertainment but also in education.

Richard Stallman, founder of the Free Software Foundation, claimed in 1984 that password-protected, single-user, code-controlled textbooks and reference books would eventually be introduced. At the time he was widely seen as paranoid. From today's vantage point it remains clear that having medical reference books that become unavailable after the semester in which they are used is over is not socially optimal. Yet Vital Source Technologies is providing time-limited and user-specific digital medical textbooks to universities to sell to students. Should a medical emergency, or even a question, arise after the textbook's life has expired, the student would no longer have access to the text. These are exactly the controls enabled by the Digital Millennium Copyright Act. Should the student who becomes a doctor break the encryption that protects the content in order to review the information, that doctor would technically be a felon, subject to a $500,000 fine and five years in jail. Or, should a medical student lend another student his or her textbook, both the lender and the borrower could face similar penalties. The Copyright Office recently released the acceptable reasons for circumventing encryption technology, and protecting fair use for education is not among the exceptions. (Only computer security research and breaking filtering software are allowable.)

The Digital Millennium Copyright Act is radical legislation, judging by its results. Intended only to protect modern business models, it has instead negated fair use and limited speech rights. Although the income of the movie studios is insignificant in comparison with that of the software industry, some argue that movie production creates soft power for the United States.[17] Yet that soft power is most important in areas where the DMCA and CSS would prevent users from watching the content. Soviet citizens could not have watched American movies with the CSS in place.

Similarly, today any person under a regime opposed to the United States could be prevented from watching a movie protected with DeCSS because the MPAA would never have released the content in that region. Smugglers and sellers of information would have to be hackers as well as traders.

In short, the DMCA harms American strategic interests, economic interests, and the marketplace of ideas. The DMCA was seen as merely enabling a market. Instead, it altered the right of content producers from the right to sell their product to the right to control who uses the product, in what locations, under what terms, and on what equipment. In addition to this increase in control, DVD players that are network enabled also have an "ET feature"—that is, the software phones home to the MPAA and reports what material was watched, when, and under what conditions. Breaking this surveillance software would make the user seeking privacy a felon. The expansion of property rights under copyright is so extreme as to undermine the original and fundamental tenets of copyright.

Trespass to Chattel

Thus is it clear that, increasingly, intellectual property rights triumph over speech rights. A second significant area where property law is trumping speech law is in the noble service of prohibiting spam. Under the doctrine of trespass to chattel, narrowcast or broadcast e-mail can be prohibited on the basis of content. In one case, a former Intel employee obtained an employee e-mail list through public sources.[18] He then sent his thoughts about Intel, intended to be scathing, to Intel employees. Intel was able to legally prohibit the ex-employee from sending his opinions to Intel employees. The construction of the spam law is such that firms, including ISPs, can object to mail entirely on the basis of its content. Given the concentration of the backbone and high-speed routing in the hands of very few firms (in many regions and nations just *one* firm), the ability to limit distribution of speech offers a very real concentration of power.[19] Badly written definitions of spam have defined as chattel the networks of those who connect to the Internet. Such a definition allows network owners to reject content; the effect is propertization that overpowers listeners' right to hear. This practice has already been widely used in the America Online (AOL) network. AOL users are not allowed to come together to discuss topics of which AOL management disapproves. In particular, users are not allowed to organize to discuss AOL rates. Certainly the company will not consider any filtering or surveillance that AOL and Time Warner choose to implement to be worthy topics of conversation. Current definitions of spam allow the network provider to censor information that the user may want to hear. Combined with the lack of open-access requirements, this means that AOL and Time Warner will be able to determine the information available to homes in their service area by deciding which e-mail, television channels, discussion groups, and web content are acceptable. Spam laws will provide the force of law to AOL should users attempt to make anti-AOL speech widely heard.

A Proposal for Code and Content

Given the critical comments I have made in this chapter, it is only fair for me to offer alternative ideas of my own design for consideration. My own perspective on how the different types of code should be regulated is summarized in the following list.[20]

<table>
<tr><td colspan="2" align="center">Models of protection</td></tr>
<tr><td align="center">Code type</td><td align="center">Application</td></tr>
<tr><td>Code as a product or functional invention</td><td>Patents (limited to specific implementations)
Object code (a functional invention)</td></tr>
<tr><td>Code as a professional service</td><td>Custom code (code written once for a specific customer)</td></tr>
<tr><td>Code as embodied speech</td><td>Source code</td></tr>
<tr><td>Ungoverned code</td><td>Code in the public domain</td></tr>
</table>

This is a coherent and cohesive proposal on at least three levels. First, it treats executable code as if it were a machine. Code that is sold in executable form is expected to work, as any other machine would work. Patents would be granted for the particular design and implementation of an idea, not for the algorithm or concept underlying the idea. Reverse-engineering would be allowed for interoperability, as in the DeCSS case. These are the principles of machines, engineering, and innovation in the machine age.

Code as a professional service would allow open-code creators to prosper. Open code is frequently used to create custom designs for specific consumers. In contrast, UCITA would provide the lowest level of protection and consumer expectation for widely used source code. UCITA would subject custom code to the highest reliability constraints and mass-marketed code to no constraints. This is clearly an irrational distribution of liability.

Treating source code as embodied speech is not ideal because it is possible to write code that functions but cannot be read. The code-as-speech analogy fails on this one point. In order to be functional and useful, speech must be readable by humans, but the same is not true of code. Open code can be made difficult to read, and it is possible that spaghetti code would proliferate under such a regime, in order to avoid the liability associated with the manufacture of machines.[21] Yet badly written code proliferates now, so even the worst-order effect would produce nothing worse than the status quo.

My proposal would leave open the question of the extent of copying allowable under fair use. Yet it would solve the problems of excessive protection of code and content and irrational assignments of liability; and it would not undermine open code. This framing fits well with what can be said about the open-code agenda. This agenda is based on "funding for basic research, avoidance of excessive intellectual property protection, and enforcement of open-source licenses—or the policies can be direct—government funding for open-source developers and government promotion of open-source standards."[22] Other members of the community also seek to create economic mechanisms that can support younger hackers trying to build reputations.[23] This objective is at least not harmed by these proposals, and the rational application of patents would allow young innovators to innovate.

Another alternative is a strict limit of five years on copyright.[24] The argument against this is that such a change would destroy the free software and open-source communities that depend on copyright. Furthermore, code, unlike prose, is not readable just because it is open. Obtuse, compressed, and unreadable code can provide almost as little information as closed code, as an annual competition held by Carnegie Mellon University to write unreadable code clearly illustrates. Another alternative is to retain copyright and limit its use. This requires rejecting the Digital Millennium Copyright Act and protecting fair use. Recalling the forgotten wisdom of the importance of common carriage and the value to consumers in trademarks is critical. Yet any and all of these proposals would require a government that sees itself rightfully as the creator, not the handmaiden, of markets.

Conduit

Conduit has been used in telecommunications to refer to the medium of transmission. The word itself reflects that the transmission medium is simply that: a conduit for something else rather than intrinsically valuable in and of itself. Yet it also reflects the reality of telecommunications that it is not the wire or cable that is valuable, but its placement. The most expensive element is the labor of putting the cable in place—making the wire into conduit.

The Internet was enabled by interconnection. The ability to connect modems to telephone systems was hotly contested by the telephone systems. AT&T sought to prohibit connections as benign as a small plastic cup on the receiver to improve the clarity of the speaker's voice (the Hush-A-Phone), and if the courts had upheld this claim to network purity the Internet would have remained exclusively an academic pursuit.

The interconnection of networks requires open standards, open protocols, and open implementations of the code that implements these standards and protocols. A protocol is a description of an ordered set of messages to implement a specific task. A standard may be an implementation of a protocol for a particular environment (for example, the Internet protocol [IP] over coaxial cable) or a description of the goals that should be met by a protocol (see various International Standards Organization [ISO] standards).[25] Code is the implementation of a protocol as described in a standard. In this section I discuss how the rules governing conduit are changing and how the technologies being built in this time of transition are in opposition to the practices of common carriage and interconnection.

The dominant high-bandwidth technologies in the home are digital subscriber line, cable Ethernet, and wireless. Each of these involves conduits and regulations that enable a one-way system, with the result being that there is emerging an oligopoly in content control based on ownership of the wires.[26] Consider for a moment the developments that have driven cable Ethernet and high-speed phone line (xDSL) services. Initially there was stasis, with no line of business threatening another. Packet-switched technologies enabled convergence as early as 1980, but there was no driving business logic pushing companies to abandon their cash cows. The rush for broadband to the home arrived with the creation of direct broadcast satellite and threatened the income flow of the owners of the cable infrastructure. Competition with direct broadcast satellite companies forced cable companies to upgrade their services and networks. When cable companies with upgraded networks began to offer high-speed network connections, they could compete directly with the small-office and home-office markets that were purchasing T1 and T3 frame relay services at ten times the cost from local telephony providers. Before this competition existed there was no reason for the phone companies, cable companies, or wireless companies to roll out services that would require massive investment in the network and gutting the companies' profit margins in their core markets (data, pay TV, and mobile voice, respectively). Thus competition is without question the critical driver in the marketplace. And competition and common carriage are not only complementary; competition in service provision *requires* common carriage.

Phone Lines

Phone lines are being moved to the next generation with asynchronous digital subscriber line technologies, known as xDSL.[27] DSL is of interest for several reasons. Phone lines consist of sets of wires, each individually clad with insulating material and then twisted together and clad a second time. Thus discussions of phone wires often refer to a twisted pair, even though modern phone lines have more than two wires.

Phone company rollouts of DSL are closely correlated with rollouts of cable modems. Cable modems are closely associated with the availability of direct broadcast satellite services. In fact, ISPs could provide DSL-equivalent technology by using the clean copper provided for alarm circuits. When the purchase of alarm circuits for cheap data transmission was noted by the phone companies, phone companies responded by refusing to offer new alarm circuits. Thus even when there is money to be made, companies will prevent innovation when it is a radical departure from their way of doing business and cannibalizes far more profitable offerings. Phone companies were content to have data lines remain forever segregated into modem lines and expensive frame relay lines. The principle of interconnection, if applied to alarm circuits, would have allowed a far earlier rollout of DSL. Thus the arguments against open access—arguments that say monopoly returns the best investment in infrastructure—have been proven wrong in the case of telephony.

Digital subscriber line (DSL) technologies enable broadband speeds over telephone wires. DSL technologies are much slower than cable technologies for a single subscriber's link because the two telephone wires are a twisted pair of wires. Thus while telephone technologies may continue to increase data transmission rates, the coaxial cable has a fundamental physical advantage in terms of the interaction of the currents in the two wires, so cable will always be able to provide higher throughput than a twisted pair. However, just as with cable companies, phone companies are slowly pulling fiber closer to the home. Thus any analysis of hybrid fiber coaxial cable should compare it with a hybrid fiber twisted pair, not with a twisted pair.

Cable provides more bandwidth on a single line, yet DSL may provide more bandwidth for a single subscriber. DSL provides each subscriber with his or her own line up to the switch. Thus the higher bandwidth provided over cable is shared by multiple households for the last mile. The lower overall bandwidth provided by DSL may be higher than the cable bandwidth to a particular home depending on the intensity of the use of Internet services on the street or in the neighborhood.

Recall that the first point of interest is that competition increases rollout. The second point is that DSL technologies are often asynchronous. DSL technologies may expect the user to listen rather than speak. DSL services, however, can support home servers. DSL offers in the Boston area often include fixed domain names, with the purpose of enabling servers. Of course this is in part because the DSL market targeted by the phone companies is the small-office and home-office (SOHO) market. DSL contracts do not prevent the user from setting up his or her own server. DSL offers open access and is not bundled with content.[28]

DSL technologies enable users to speak as well as listen. When possible, DSL technologies were delayed by phone companies, even when the companies were offering their own ISP services. A stronger requirement for interconnection and service guarantees could have provided DSL services far earlier. However, some believe that allowing phone companies to offer the service with only the phone companies' ISP would have encouraged faster rollout. Yet even with the increased income from ISP subscriber fees, the phone companies would not have had economic justification to cannibalize their frame relay services.

Wireless

Wireless systems may be built in a manner that enables fully synchronous information flows or as a strictly broadcast model where the user is a passive recipient. Consider synchronous networks. Point-to-point microwave networks are an example of this type of architecture, as are some third-generation cellular technologies.

Consider asynchronous technologies. Wireless systems may be built with the assumption that the greater bandwidth is downstream—that is, with the assumption that the user is a listener. This is most common with wireless systems that depend on satellite downlinks because low back-channel bandwidth allows for lower power and cheaper home equipment.

The greatest threat to the end-to-end argument comes from the wireless access protocol (WAP), which is not HTML compliant. WAP interacts with wireless markup language (WML) rather than with HTML. WML addresses the low-bandwidth and limited-screen-space issues with wireless.[29] However, WAP does more than that. WML rewrites simple HTML so even the most basic tags (such as a link or a page break) no longer mean the same thing in WAP that they do in HTML. Thus authors who would speak to the world must write two versions of a web page: an HTML version and a WAP version. The market as currently constructed does appear to be addressing this: there is currently a consumer WAP-backlash.

All intelligence in WAP is built into the gateway rather than the end-point, which means choices are made or delineated at the gateway, not by the user. The relative intelligence required in a machine to support a browser client is more than that available in a handheld device (such as a HandspringVisor or a Palm Pilot) or a modern cellular phone. Moving intelligence to the gateway is a fundamental rewrite of the network protocols, which ends the end-to-end argument. The distinction between obscure protocol elements such as the style of acknowledgments and encryption may seem trivial until one notes that these all require one fundamental design assumption—that the WAP user connects to a predetermined gateway and the gateway defines these services. The services provided at the gateway include content selection and portal provision. Note that concurrent with the development of WAP, the Internet Engineering Task Force (IETF) is developing protocols to enable transactions over wireless networks. However, the IETF assumes some processing capacity in the wireless receiver and the ability to change providers. IETF places a premium on interoperability and flexibility. The IETF proposals and the WAP proposals are not interoperable.

Imagine if you had to buy a new computer to change ISPs or to select a new portal or home page. This is the choice offered the user by WAP. WAP systems connect conduit and content.

Cable Ethernet

The differences between Ethernet and cable Ethernet connection are primarily contractual and regulatory. A core policy difference is the (lack of) open-access requirements. In addition, it is worth mentioning that many providers of cable Ethernet contractually prohibit users from setting up servers. This prohibition is interesting for three reasons. One, it forbids the user from using certain technologies that allow a machine to serve others and be a client itself. Possibly prohibited are highly distributed computing applications, of which the SETI program is the best known. Similarly, this prohibition in theory covers the use of Napster and its many clones and derivatives (such as Gnutella). All peer-to-peer computing is, in theory, prohibited by contract. Again, as with the phone companies and DSL, the cable companies have a specific business model. These companies are uninterested in any innovation that may alter that model.

Most important, the inability of user computers to be servers over cable Ethernet means that the cable Ethernet provider does not support home servers. The expansion of this high-bandwidth network topology to the home should mean that all users could provide simple servers. That is, everyone could be a publisher on the Internet on equal terms, as in the days when Usenet dominated dialogue. Combined with a domain name system that is hostile to small users and free speech, this lack of technical support threatens the potential for democracy on the Internet.

Ethernet as implemented in cable networks is quite capable of supporting multiple providers and supporting servers. However, some of the networks are being built in a manner that prevents open access. Open access is a traditional requirement of owners of conduit so that all may speak on equal terms. The new terms of connection are an example of propertization—that those who own fast conduits own the data and eyeballs of those they connect. The regulation of the transport layer of Ethernet ignores the fundamental reality of common carriage: that transport networks need to be open for all comers to optimize economic growth. In an information economy, the transport networks need to ensure the free flow of information.

With the AOL Time Warner merger the assumption is that users should see what is determined by conduit owners. Furthermore, the AOL-Warner policies and protocols make certain that users are allowed to speak only in limited arenas and on approved topics. AOL, for example, allows only those in positions of authority in the corporation to broadcast e-mail. In addition to preventing subscribers from discussing its rates, it also does not support the creation of e-mail lists by its subscribers. AOL audits and tracks all subscriber use, reserves the right to censor web pages, does not support user-owned domain names, and prevents user innovations. Sadly, AOL will be the only option available to many Americans for high-speed Internet access, which means that many Americans will not have access to the two-way Internet but rather carefully controlled access where offending AOL is not allowed.

Caching

Caching is the storage part of the store-and-forward network. A network cache holds packets while waiting for the call to forward them. As packets and information are routed, temporary copies are made (and cached) in servers across the network. When the network is congested, each router chooses which bits to forward and which bits to discard. (Congestion occurs whenever the demand for network services is greater than the supply.) Similarly, servers choose which bits are kept, in case another copy is needed, and which are deleted. Such decisions have long been made on the basis of technical efficiency using variables such as protocol and file size. For example, it is unlikely that many people will request an e-mail but very likely that many people will request a web page. So e-mail protocol-based messages are not stored for later local use, while web pages are.

There are several levels of storage across the network. There are caches at the point where the local area network and the wide area network connect. There is a cache on each individual hard drive and a cache where the wide area network meets the Internet. Caching choices have traditionally been driven by research on networks. Of course, there is some suggestion that studies of the networks of research institutions may be misleading, because researchers' use of the Internet varies somewhat from the average surfer's.[30] Yet regardless of the efficacy, the practice of caching in the networks of the 1990s has been to minimize transmission and optimize network performance.

The practice of optimizing network performance as driven by user desires for content has been altered with the entrance of ISP provider Akamai into the market. Dave Clark, past head of the Internet Architecture Board and senior network researcher at MIT, is fond of saying, "The Internet routes packets and Akamai figures out how to route the money." Akamai provides caching at strategically chosen network points in order to provide higher-quality network service for those who pay for the space. Thus information provided by rich backers can be provided quickly and made universally available, while speech from random individuals, nonprofits, and NGOs other than corporations can be slowed.

Caching expands property rights by creating technologies that can alter the fundamental assumptions of the network. There has never been regulation of caching, only the social norms that assume that caches are designed to optimize network performance. Thus while this change alters the fundamental assumption of content-neutrality of routing on the Internet, it is likely to be problematic only if transport networks are not open. With open networks, consumers could choose to use a different provider with different caching practices.

Policy-Based Routing

The Gilmore statement about routing around censorship has a foundation in truth, and that foundation is IPv4, the Internet protocol as currently implemented. Traditionally routing has been based entirely on engineering concepts of efficiency (which can be very different from economic concepts of efficiency). Policy-based routing enables the owners of routers to charge differential rates for different customers and to block those who will not pay the acceptable rate. Thus routing is moving from engineering concepts of efficiency to more narrow economic concepts of efficiency. For example, AOL could give priority to all Time Warner and AOL content, thus giving AOL e-mail higher priority than video not owned by Time Warner. The result would be time delay for video content not owned by Time Warner, perhaps so long that such video would be difficult to watch.

The losses in the embrace of policy-based routing are the following: the loss of common carriage, the potential end of price certainty, the end of overprovision, and the ability to remove content critical of the owner of the router.

The first, the loss of common carriage, is covered earlier in this essay. The second, the end of price certainty, would result in far lower adoption rates of Internet services. Every known study of adoption and use of communication technologies illustrates that individuals prefer a flat rate, even when a flat rate is more expensive. Every telecommunications service has adopted an increasingly simple fee structure over time. As fees become more predictable, more users are able to use the service. The variance possible in monthly rates is the dominant driver of disconnection of the poor in telephony.[31]

The end of overprovision would vastly increase the cost of networks over time, and policy-based routing could encourage scarcity. Although traditional economics rarely sees scarcity as an inherently bad thing, those interested in universal access and the ability to innovate with systems requiring greater performance recognize that created scarcity is not ideal in all markets. To return to the metaphor of physical property, a created scarcity of water in an urban environment may make economic sense, but it does not make sense in the policy arena, where death by dehydration and cholera are not feasible options.

The End of End-to-End?

History is rich with battles over property rights and human rights. With the recent battles over environmental laws, physical property rights have been rewritten and balanced with the common good. It is easy to forget that battles over property rights were a part of discussion about the abuse of children (the abuse of animals was prohibited first) and the abomination of slavery, and those same battles underlie environmental debates as well. Just as the definition of physical property is an ongoing process, the definition of intellectual property will be at least as difficult. Yet it will be made less difficult by recalling the lessons learned in the past with respect to common carriage and by addressing the meaningful distinctions between real and virtual property.

In information property the trend toward limiting real property rights to create a functional and balanced market is being reversed. The theory that there are no costs, only benefits, to the expansion of property rights is applied in the extreme, thereby limiting opportunities for the exchange of ideas and innovation.

The issues of intellectual property are not linear. More control by owners does not automatically lead to more innovation or investment. The balance between the commons and the private has been and continues to be a complex question. The issues are no easier in the information realm, and assuming away complexity does only harm. The democratic potential of the Internet requires user-driven content: "On one side of the battle over freedom of information are people who believe that sharing information with other interested people is a good thing even if the information comes from someone who does not want it to be shared. Individuals and companies that would prefer that the information remain proprietary are on the other side of the fight."[32] As Jack Valenti of the MPAA notes, his ideal protection time frame would be "forever minus one day."[33] Even the compromise solution on content suggests that some content would "never be available in digital form," with the canonical example being the movie *The Wizard of Oz*.[34] Valuable information was always meant to become part of the commons, with copyright only a temporary monopoly. Now that trend has been reversed, with information being made forever proprietary if it becomes culturally valuable. This appears to be a global rush to fence in the commons, beyond the point of reasonable economic returns.

The wires as well as the content are being closed. Open access refers to the requirement that owners of transport networks (that is, conduit) must resell the transport at reasonable rates to allow competition, particularly for value-added services. Open access is common carriage. The current regulatory arguments suggest that companies will not invest in bringing high-bandwidth services to the home without the ability to capture users and the right to exclude content. History both near and far argues that the rollout of services, in this case broadband services, is best served by truly competitive forces and not by government-enhanced monopoly. Furthermore, rejecting open-access regulation violates the fundamental tenet of telecommunications and centuries of transport regulation—interconnection and common carriage.

Competition in transport and common-carrier status can be and has been compatible.[35] The defeat of open access allows technology that expands the rights of network holders over the traditional rights of liability-exempt common carriers. In this case it is the regulatory redefinition that allows transport network holders to fence in their users, withholding from them the information commons.

Freedom of ideas, freedom to innovate, and freedom to speak should belong to all citizens, computer users as well as companies. The Internet has enabled all of those things, simply by its construction. Yet the construction of the Internet is not the result of its innate nature. Being entirely constructed, it can be entirely reconstructed, so that the open and free part of the Internet returns to technologists and scientists while the bulk of the population receives the AOL version. IP over everything is a choice, an optimal choice for the information commons but not for the individual income-maximizing players.

Under the banner of progressive "un-regulation" the Federal Communications Commission (FCC) is encouraging the creation of closed broadcast-style networks. The courts are expanding property rights to include the right to prevent speech unwelcome by the property owners, even if the occupants of the virtual property are interested in the speech. Congress has passed legislation (the DMCA) that denies even the most basic rights of speech, evaluation, and full information to citizens, thus redefining us as consumers of narrowly licensed information goods. This act is supported as a simple definition and modernization of contracts for information property, with no examination of the long-term costs or the implications for civil society.

Governments create markets, except in the most primitive barter societies. In the creation of post-convergence markets, governance faces a fork in the road. Many governments believe that their decisions are enabling Internet commerce and thus choose as guides only stakeholders in the private sector. Yet the power of the government is to create the market. Ignoring government power when "enabling" a market does not decrease that power; rather it increases the unintended consequences. By expanding the rights of intellectual property holders in a misguided attempt to motivate production, abandoning past commitments to interconnection in networks, and forgetting principles of democratic leadership by taking the role of mere handmaidens to the market, governments are creating a marketplace in which democratic principles will be subverted. Democratic governments ignore their own strength only at the peril of democracy.

Notes

1. See, for example, Carl Shapiro and Hal Varian, *Information Rules* (Harvard Business School Press, 1999); Chris DiBona, Sam Ockman, and Mark Stone, eds., *Open Sources: Voices from the Open Source Revolution* (Cambridge, Mass.: O'Reilly and Associates, 1999); and Michael Froomkin, "Of Governments and Governance," in *The Legal and Policy Framework for Global Electronic Commerce: A Progress Report* (Berkeley, Calif.: Haas School of Business, University of California).

2. Even today most shipping lines and railroads are common carriers. Shipping lines participate in organizations that set the schedules and usually the rates charged by common carriers on most major ocean routes. Railroads are usually under national regulation.

3. "Fool Me Once Shame on Me, Fool Me Twice Shame on You: What We Can Learn from the Privatizations of the Internet Backbone Networks and the Domain Name System," Law and Economics Working Paper 00-01, University of Illinois College of Law (February 2001).

4. See John Gilmore, "How Publius Thwarts Censorship," *Scientific American*, October 2000, p. 86.

5. Donald Mackenzie, *Inventing Accuracy* (MIT Press, 1990); James R. Beniger, *The Control Revolution: Technological and Economic Origins of the Information Society* (Harvard University Press, 1986); Brian Winston, *Media Technology and Society: A History: From the Telegraph to the Internet* (London: Routledge, 1998); and Susan J. Douglas, *Inventing American Broadcasting 1899–1922* (Johns Hopkins University Press, 1997).

6. D. Clark, "Explicit Allocation for Best Effort Packet Delivery Service," in L. W. Mackie-Mason and J. P. Bailey, *Internet Economics* (MIT Press, 1997); and Shapiro and Varian, *Information Rules*.

7. See Pamela Samuelson, "Intellectual Property and the Digital Economy: Why the Anti-Circumvention Regulations Need to Be Revised," *Berkeley Tech. Law Journal,* vol. 14, no. 2 (1999), p. 519.

8. Rob Kling, ed., *Computerization and Controversy: Value Conflicts and Social Choices* (Academic Press, 1996); Deborah G. Johnson and Helen Nissenbaum, eds., *Computer Ethics and Social Values* (Prentice Hall, 1995); DiBona, Ockman, and Stone, *Open Sources*; Carliss Y. Baldwin and Kim B. Clark, *Design Rules: The Power of Modularity* (MIT Press, 2000); Shapiro and Varian, *Information Rules*; National Academy of Sciences, *The Digital Dilemma: Intellectual Property in the Information Age* (Washington: National Academy Press, 2000).

9. For further explanation of these examples and the interaction of computer hardware and software in general, see M. Morris Mano, *Computer System Architecture*, 3d ed. (Prentice Hall, 1992).

10. Richard M. Stallman, *The GNU Manifesto* (www.fsf.org/gnu/manifesto.html), originally written in 1984.

11. As a patent owner myself, I also oppose software patents. Yet I have no desire to force Carnegie Mellon University, which sought and obtained the patent on my work, to unilaterally disarm. See Tim O'Reilly, "Ask Tim" (www.oreilly.com/ask_tim/amazon_patent.html), last viewed July 5, 2000. See also League for Programming Freedom, "Against Software Patents," *Communications of the ACM*, vol. 35, no. 1 (1992), available at (http://lpf.ai.mit.edu/Patents/against-software-patents.html); Simson L. Garfinkel, "Patently Absurd," *Wired*, July 1994.

12. For a clear discussion of the case, see Wendy Grossman, "DVDs: Cease and DeCSS?" *Scientific American*, May 1999; also available at (www.sciam.com/2000/0500issue/0500cyber.html).

13. Johnson and Nissenbaum, *Computer Ethics and Social Values*.

14. Alison Freehling, Patti Rosenberg, and Deborah Straszheim, "Judge Issues Order against CW Union," *Daily Press*, Hampton, Va., April 21, 2000; also at (www.gilinda.com/clippings/injunction.html).

15. Patricia Jacobus, "eToys Settles Net Name Dispute with etoy," CNET News.com, January 25, 2000, available at http://news.cnet.com/news/0-1007-200-1531854.html?tag=st.ne.1002.bgif.1007-200-1531854.

16. For other cases where the property rights of those criticized or satirized have trumped speech that is clearly satirical or political and other dialogue critical to civil society, see http://208.56.174.5/domainnews.htm. In only one case has a complainant claiming misuse of trademark been unable to show that the use of the trademark was not identical or confusing.

17. Robert Keohane and Joseph Nye, *Power and Interdependence* (Longman, 1989).

18. Jonathan Rabinovitz, "Gadfly Presses His Email Case against Microsoft," *San Jose Mercury News*, July 6, 1999; Maria Alicia Guara, "Email delivered by Horsemail," *San Francisco Chronicle*, p. B2, September 29, 1999; alternatively see www.faceintel.com.

19. Dan Burk, "The Trouble with Trespass," *The Journal of Small and Emerging Business Law*, vol. 4, no. 1 (2000), pp. 27–55.

20. L. Jean Camp and Syrena Syme, "A Coherent Intellectual Property Model of Code as Speech, Embedded Product or Service," *Journal of Information, Law, and Technology*, vol. 2 (July 2001) (http://elj.warwick.ac.uk/jilt/01-2/camp.html [July 2, 2001]).

21. Code must allow the data to flow in a logical line. Yet instead of being laid out like the dividing line on asphalt, this code is rather more like the single noodle in a package of instant Ramen or Bachelor's noodles, entangled so as to be impossible to lay out flat.

22. Lawrence Lessig, Eric S. Raymond, Nathan Newman, Jeff A. Taylor, and Jonathan Band, "Should Public Policy Support Open-Source Software? A Roundtable Discussion in Response to the Technology Issue of *The American Prospect*," *American Prospect*, vol. 11, no. 10 (2000), available at www.prospect.org/controversy/open_space.

23. Stig Hackvan (www.devlinux.org [November 2000]).

24. Jonathan Zittrain, "The Un-Microsoft Un-Remedy: Law Can Prevent the Problem That It Can't Patch Later," *Connecticut Law Review*, vol. 31, no. 4 (1999), p. 1361.

25. For an extended discussion of standards/protocols/code, see L. Jean Camp, *Trust and Risk in Internet Commerce* (MIT Press, 2000).

26. For a detailed discussion of access technologies see the May 2001 issue of *info*, which has a series of articles written for the layperson on access technologies.

27. I use "phone companies" to refer to LECs. Because this is about broadband access, I refer to those providing modem-based services as ISPs, to distinguish them from local exchange carriers. The local exchange carriers (LECs) are either CLEC, meaning new *competitive* phone competitors, or ILEC, meaning old *incumbent* phone competitors. Thus these companies own the network and provide Internet access. I do not address any long-haul networks, such as the five Internet backbone carriers or the long-distance companies, because the local loop is my focus. CLECs are predominantly local exchange bypasses for densely populated areas that have broadband access, or cable-based companies that also offer phone services.

28. Because of flaws in privatization of the network, five major companies can provide fixed IP addresses for SOHO users. While this oligopoly of five may limit competition and hinder small ISPs, the availability of IP addresses to home users enhances the ability of those subscribers to speak.

29. Ruth Cover, "The XML Cover Pages: WAP Wireless Markup Language Specification (WML)" *OASIS*, 2000 (www.oasis-open.org/cover/wap-wml.html).

30. S. Manley and M. Seltzer, "Web Facts and Fantasy," Proceedings of the 1997 USENIX Symposium on Internet Technologies and Systems, Monterey, Calif., December 1997.

31. Milton L. Mueller and Jorge R. Schement, "Universal Service from the Bottom Up: A Study of Telephone Penetration in Camden, New Jersey," *The Information Society*, vol. 12, no. 3 (1996), pp. 273–92.

32. Samuelson, "Intellectual Property and the Digital Economy."

33. E. Eldred, *Battle of the Books: The ebook vs. the Antibook* (Derry, N.H.: Eldred Press, 1998).

34. National Academy of Sciences, *The Digital Dilemma*.

35. The clearest exposition of the reasons for interconnection can be found in the work of the Berkeley Roundtable on the International Economy; see François Bar, Stephen Cohen, Peter Cowhey, Brad DeLong, Michael Kleeman, and John Zysman, "Defending the Internet Revolution in the Broadband Era: Why Open Policy Has Been Essential, Why Reversing That Policy Will Be Risky," BRIE E-conomy Working Paper 12, August 1999 (http://econ161.berkeley.edu/econ_articles/broadband_brie.html).

AKASH DEEP
GUIDO SCHAEFER

Deposit Insurance: An Outmoded Lifeboat in Today's Sea of Liquidity

7

THE PAST FEW DECADES have witnessed tremendous changes in financial markets. The dismantling of fixed exchange rates, rapid growth in securitization, vast creation of mutual funds, and the advent of derivative securities have altered the financial landscape in the United States and around the world. The rapid evolution and expansion of these structures has substantially enhanced the ability of market structures and forces to channel capital to its most productive uses. Yet one major segment of financial activity and regulation—one that touches almost every individual directly—has remained broadly unchanged for almost three generations: the federal insurance of deposits at U.S. commercial banks and savings institutions. This chapter seeks to analyze the utility and efficacy of this large public safety net that has been an integral part of the financial system, that has been credited with "restoring public confidence and stability to the banking system" in the 1930s, and that has also been blamed for causing over $225 billion in losses during the savings and loan crisis in the 1980s.[1]

Despite its shortcomings, the essential structure and spirit of deposit insurance have been retained based on the continuing view that banks

We would like to thank Richard Zeckhauser and participants of the Visions Seminar at Harvard University for their valuable comments and suggestions. Any remaining errors are our own.

167

perform the crucial task of liquidity transformation—accepting short-term, liquid deposits and making longer-term, illiquid loans—thereby directly affecting the successful channeling of savings to productive investment.[2] This aspect of financial intermediation exposes banks to specific liquidity risks, and it is these risks that are sought to be addressed, and mitigated, by the federal provision of deposit insurance. Douglas Diamond and Philip Dybvig provide the classic theoretical model that demonstrates how liquidity transformation makes even sound banks vulnerable to bank runs and explain the role of government provision of deposit insurance in avoiding such runs.[3] Most existing research and policy initiatives have focused on this traditional view of banks. Consequently, they have missed the profound changes that have ensued in liquidity provision and its implications for deposit insurance. In addition, there has been no systematic effort to measure liquidity directly in spite of its central role in financial intermediation. The objective of this chapter is to fill these gaps by exploring changes in the banking sector at both the macro and the micro level amid a rapidly changing financial environment. Our analysis indicates that the relative role of commercial banks as liquidity transformers has contracted significantly. This contraction is confirmed by an analysis of liquidity at the individual bank level using a liquidity measure that we develop. This measure also reveals that the role of deposit insurance in enhancing liquidity is marginal at best. Therefore neither insurance against liquidity risk nor other rationales relating to equity, legitimacy, and stability that we briefly examine withstand closer scrutiny as a valid explanation for the federal provision of deposit insurance.

The laws that govern the U.S. banking sector today were designed over sixty years ago in the aftermath of the Great Depression, when more than 8,800 commercial banks suspended operations within a five-year span from 1929 to 1933. At that time, it was recognized that the liquidity transformation role of banks made them vulnerable to a sudden, self-fulfilling demand for funds that could lead to the collapse of an otherwise sound bank. Because of the crucial role played by commercial banks as financial intermediaries for the entire economy, it was felt that only a federal safety net could prevent bank runs. Federal deposit insurance was instituted as the most important component of such a federal safety net, the other components being the discount lending window and the payment settlement system. Today a multitude of government agencies led by the Federal Deposit Insurance Corporation (FDIC) insure all bank deposits at U.S.-chartered commercial banks, thrifts, and savings institutions up to deposit levels of $100,000. Although federal law does not explicitly require deposit insurance for commercial banks that are not part of the Federal Reserve System, it is a virtual necessity for all depository institutions. Deposit insurance covers 99 percent of deposit accounts and 65 percent of the value of total deposits. The FDIC maintains two centralized deposit insurance funds with a combined current capitalization of $40 billion (or 1.4 percent of insured deposits) to bail out depositors in the event of the failure of commercial banks and savings institutions.

A deposit insurance structure entails various costs.[4] These stem from the nature of moral hazard inherent in all insurance schemes along with agency problems that affect the system's public controllers. Moral hazard encourages banks to assume riskier behavior because any gains from the additional risks are enjoyed by the shareholders, while losses, if large enough to cause the bank to collapse, are borne by the public exchequer. The moral hazard problem is exacerbated by the poor incentives of fully protected depositors to monitor the risk profile of banks and demand commensurate interest rates on deposits. The system is also plagued by excess regulatory forbearance due to delayed remedial action on problem banks by regulators hoping for improvements that might avert collapse and thus hide their prior lack of oversight. Edward Kane identifies the adverse incentives of fixed-rate deposit insurance and belated bank closures as the most important factors in explaining the catastrophic savings and loan crisis of the 1980s that required the closure or bailout of about 2,000 banks and savings and loan associations.[5] Similarly, Asli Demirgüç-Kunt and Enrica Detragiache find international evidence that the existence of an explicit deposit insurance scheme has contributed to banking system fragility.[6]

This extensive theoretical exploration and empirical documentation of the benefits and shortcomings of deposit insurance has resulted in the periodic adjustment of banking regulations to address some of its flaws, with mixed success. Significant among these has been the lifting of restrictions on interstate banking, the removal of rate ceilings on deposit accounts, the imposition of improved capital standards, and most recently, the introduction of risk-based deposit insurance premiums. Risk-based premiums were introduced in the Federal Deposit Insurance Corporation Improvement Act of 1991 (FDICIA) to address the obvious moral hazard–related pitfalls of flat rate deposit insurance, but the FDICIA has led to the perverse outcome that today 93 percent of all banks and thrifts do not pay *any* premium at all. Thus FDIC concludes: "A decade that began with a legislative mandate for risk-based insurance premiums ended with the FDIC providing a free guarantee of almost three trillion dollars in bank and thrift liabilities. As a result, the moral hazard problems FDICIA intended to address . . . may have become more firmly entrenched than ever."[7] Similarly, the adoption of risk-based capital regulation over the past fifteen years has not prevented banks from shifting risk onto the safety net, as has been documented empirically by Armen Hovakimian and Edward Kane.[8] The continued federal provision of deposit insurance therefore suggests that policymakers view the problems of moral hazard and agency as a necessary price to be paid for the support of liquidity transformation performed through the commercial banking sector. This regulatory perspective, as well as much extant theoretical research on deposit insurance, ignores fundamental changes in banking and financial markets that have been documented by John Boyd and Mark Gertler and others.[9] We believe that a prerequisite for any meaningful debate on deposit insurance reform is a reevaluation of the traditional notion of banking as essentially deposit-taking and loan-making.

In the first part of the chapter we focus on the aggregate structure of liquidity provision by the commercial banking sector. Our analysis suggests a significant contraction of banks' role as liquidity transformers and hence a reduction in their susceptibility to the specific risks of liquidity transformation, including systemic runs due to contagious spillovers. But is this reduction substantial enough to recommend a second look at the structure of deposit insurance?

To answer this question, we suggest a direct measurement of the net liquidity of individual banks' portfolios of assets and liabilities and the effect of deposit insurance in enhancing this liquidity. Although liquidity risk has been a major concern for regulators and researchers of banking, little systematic effort has been devoted to precisely defining and measuring the liquidity position of banks. In contrast to other gauges of the financial health of banks, such as capital adequacy, interest rate exposure, and credit risk, the measurement of liquidity has somehow remained on the sidelines. This is all the more startling because the specific liquidity structure of banks plays a key role in theories of financial intermediation and bank regulation. The Diamond-Dybvig model of liquidity transformation, the most enduring theoretical justification for deposit insurance, is based upon the specific liquidity characteristics of banks. In its 2000 report the Basel Committee on Banking Supervision emphasizes the importance of liquidity risk and recommends that "all banks should have the ability to calculate their liquidity positions, on a day to day basis for the shorter time horizons (e.g. out to five days) and over a series of specified time periods thereafter, including for more distant periods, in order to enable them to effectively manage and monitor their net funding requirements."[10]

In the second part of the chapter we attempt to systematically measure the liquidity of banks' portfolios by suggesting liquidity coefficients for each distinct component of their liquid assets, liabilities, and off-balance-sheet elements. Because of the complexity of the problem and the lack of prior research, ours should be seen as only a first, and highly simplified, approach to exploring the major dimensions of the problem and to prepare the ground for future research. We define a *liquidity gap* measure and implement it to estimate the liquidity of U.S. commercial banks. This exercise leads us to the somewhat surprising result that most banks have either excess liquidity or a small liquidity gap.

This gap is small enough that, in the event of a sudden surge in liquidity demand, it can be bridged easily by the temporary collateralization of a fraction of a bank's illiquid assets. Furthermore, the effect of deposit insurance in mitigating the liquidity mismatch is remarkably modest. Thus, together with our results for the banking sector as a whole, our findings suggest a diminished need for deposit insurance as a facilitator of the liquidity transformation process.

The third section of the chapter discusses these findings along with some of the other rationales that have been suggested for the continued provision of deposit insurance, namely the stability and legitimacy of the banking system and the promotion of distributional equity in favor of small depositors. We argue that although these objectives are of great significance, they cannot adequately justify the current structure of deposit insurance.

For our analysis, we use quarterly data from the Reports of Condition and Income (commonly referred to as "call reports") filed by all federally regulated commercial banks. Data from several banks that belong to a top-tier bank holding company have been integrated into one economic unit or "commercial bank" because of their integrated regulatory treatment. As a result we have 7,725 banks in our sample consisting of 7,278 small banks (defined as those with assets below $1 billion at the end of the third quarter of 1999), 359 medium banks (with assets between $1 billion and $10 billion), and 88 large banks. These data are supplemented by annual data from the Flow of Funds Accounts of the United States provided by the Federal Reserve.[11] Our data normally cover the period 1976 to 1999, but in some cases shorter series are presented because data for certain items do not go as far back as 1975 or because the latest data were not available at the time of this analysis.

Trends in the Aggregate Supply and Demand for Liquidity

The historical structure of financial intermediation, in which commercial banks served as the primary liquidity transformers and hence were provided protection through deposit insurance, was based on the following two salient assumptions:

—the supply of liquidity: The banking sector finances itself largely through demand deposits while they hold mainly illiquid loans as assets. Hence banks do not have substantial businesses other than deposit-taking and loan-making and are thus plagued by the risks that liquidity provision creates.

—the demand for liquidity: Depositors rely on their demand deposits to meet immediate liquidity needs while firms obtain long-term financing for illiquid projects largely from banks. Thus other sectors of the economy depend primarily on the commercial banking sector to meet their short-term liquidity and long-term credit needs.

The need for and role of deposit insurance may have changed substantially if the structural transformation of financial markets has altered these basic assumptions. In this section we look at aggregate data to discern these changes.

The Supply of Liquidity

The illiquidity of bank asset portfolios provides a major justification for deposit insurance. The share of loans in bank portfolios has remained steady at about 60 percent over the past twenty-five years (see figure 7-1), and the holding of liquid assets, primarily cash, federal funds, and securities, has declined to about one-third of all assets. Together these might suggest the continued illiquidity of bank portfolios, but evidence identifies some important trends to the contrary.

First, asset securitization as a fraction of total loans and leases has grown tremendously (see figure 7-2).[12] Today between a quarter and a third of all loans originated by banks are securitized despite the fact that commercial banks have not been most active in the securitization market even though they have been the leading originators of commercial, mortgage, and consumer loans. For example, in 1998 banks and thrifts together originated 58 percent of all commercial loans but provided only 13 percent of the commercial loan–backed securities in the market. Similarly, their share of mortgage-backed securities and asset-backed securities was only 15 percent and 13 percent respectively.[13]

The rapid growth in loan securitization in recent years, along with the limited relative participation of commercial banks in securitization, suggests that there is sizable potential for increasing the liquidity of banks' loan portfolio through securitization. Real estate loans, usually considered the easiest asset class to securitize, constitute almost 40 percent of the loan portfolio; in the mid-1970s real estate loans accounted for less than a quarter of loans.

Adding to the liquidity of the loan portfolio is the fact that almost a third of the loans have maturity of less than a year. Further, more than 2 percent of the loans on the balance sheet are "held for sale" and hence may be regarded as fairly liquid. Finally, raising liquidity on short notice against illiquid loans has become substantially easier for solvent banks because of the significant expansion of interbank and repurchase agreement ("repo") markets, along with access to the Federal Reserve's discount lending window.

It is important to keep in mind that these data represent banks' behavior in a regime with deposit insurance that provides meager incentives to develop innovative approaches and structures to reduce the risk, and illiquidity, of bank portfolios. Banks have embraced the technical and financial innovations that have permeated financial markets, but most such activity has been spurred by the desire to increase the return (by increasing risk) of their portfolios rather than to mitigate the liquidity risk that the intermediation role creates. The Basel Committee on Banking Supervision suggests that to the limited extent that banks have undertaken securitization they appear to have been motivated primarily by "regulatory capital arbitrage."[14] It is this feature of the data that leads us to conjecture that the potential for increasing the liquidity of bank portfolios is significantly higher than has been consciously sought by the banks or can be gleaned from the data presented.

Even if a bank's portfolio of assets is illiquid, such illiquidity exposes it to liquidity risk only if these loans are financed primarily through deposits that could be withdrawn on short notice. Whereas deposits accounted for almost 100 percent of banks' liabilities in the 1950s, today they constitute about 60 percent of total liabilities for large banks and about 75 percent for

Figure 7-1. *Banks' Assets, 1976–99*

Percent

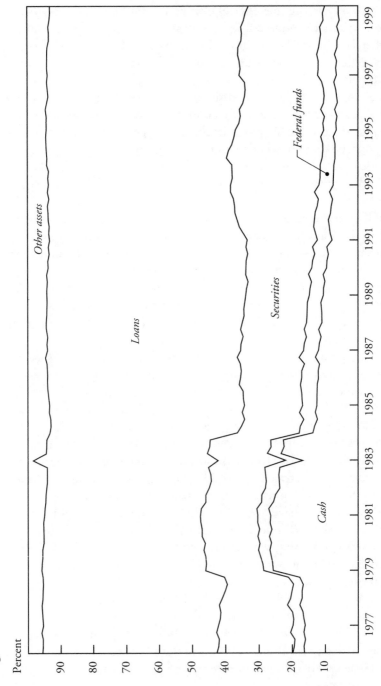

Source: Authors' calculations based on data from: reports of condition and income of individual banks; Board of Governors of the Federal Reserve System, *Flow of Funds Accounts of the United States: Annual Flows and Outstandings* (Washington, 2000).

Figure 7-2. *The Growing Trend of Loan Securitization, 1992–99*

Loans securitized as a percentage of total loans and assets

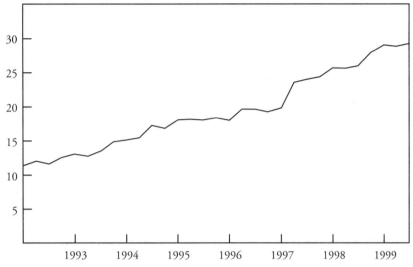

Source: Authors' calculations based on data from: reports of condition and income of individual banks; Board of Governors of the Federal Reserve System, *Flow of Funds Accounts of the United States: Annual Flows and Outstandings* (Washington, 2000).

medium-sized banks.[15] Furthermore, the emergence of money-market deposit accounts (MMDAs) in 1983 and the growing popularity of time and savings accounts that pay competitive interest rates have resulted in a significant decline in the role of demand deposits: from almost 35 percent of total liabilities to less than 10 percent in 1999. Figure 7-3 shows these trends. A combination of features, including minimum account balances, restrictions on the number of withdrawals and transfers, and variable interest rates, makes these accounts less vulnerable to sudden withdrawals than traditional demand deposits. The declining trend in demand deposits has also increased the cost of funds for banks, because they have to pay competitive rates to attract deposits to MMDAs and time and savings deposits. These higher costs have led banks to turn to other funding sources, such as repurchase agreements, commercial paper (issued by the holding company), and federal funds. which now account for a third of the total liabilities of banks. Finally, equity has been consistently on the rise.

Thus although on the asset side progress in reducing proneness to bank runs may be more potential than present, the decline in deposits has been

Figure 7-3. *Banks' Liabilities, 1976–98*

Percent

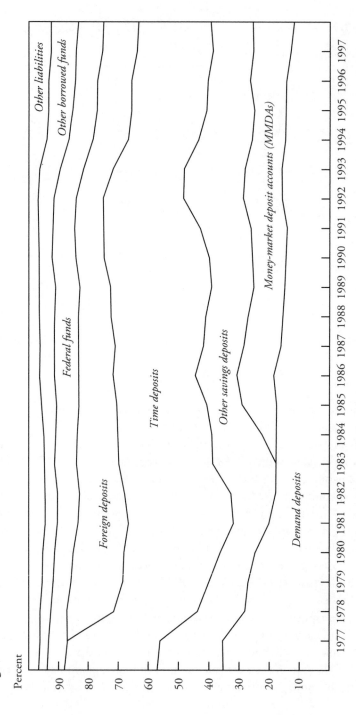

Source: Authors' calculations based on data from: reports of condition and income of individual banks; Board of Governors of the Federal Reserve System, *Flow of Funds Accounts of the United States: Annual Flows and Outstandings* (Washington, 2000).

remarkable and sizable. Together these two trends are leading banks to explore other income sources and thus to rely less on the liquidity intermediation role as the sole source of revenue. These other sources, collectively referred to as noninterest income, include income from fiduciary activities, service charges on accounts, trading gains and losses, fees generated through loan commitments, standby letters of credit, and derivative activities. Even between 1984 and 1999 noninterest income grew from less than 10 percent to almost 30 percent of the aggregate income of the commercial banking industry and will clearly increase further because of the recent dismantling of the Glass-Steagall Act.

For a traditional bank that only takes deposits and makes loans, the danger of an illiquidity crisis may be high enough to provide a sufficient rationale for deposit insurance. However, as banks move away from this old business model, deposit insurance may no longer be needed to facilitate liquidity. It would then increasingly cover losses from activities unrelated to liquidity transformation. The further these structural changes in the banking industry continue, the more urgent it will become to confront this issue both in academic research and in regulatory practice.

The Demand for Liquidity

Traditionally, the liquidity transformation role has been attributed more or less uniquely to commercial banks. Few other institutions or structures in financial markets could provide liquidity at the time that deposit insurance was established. The evolution of capital market instruments such as corporate bonds, commercial paper, mutual funds, money-market funds, and securitized assets has significantly undercut the relative size and scope of the banking sector as liquidity providers. Households and corporations are increasingly relying on capital markets, both for their steady credit and investment needs and to meet short-term positive and negative liquidity shocks. In this section, we document some evidence on the declining investment and credit provision role of commercial banks.

Figure 7-4 shows the trend in household financial assets across major investment classes. The broad choice of very liquid capital market investment opportunities has attracted investors away from all types of bank deposits. A rapid decline in transaction costs has made these opportunities, from taxable and tax-exempt money-market funds to equity and diversified mutual funds, almost as liquid as deposit accounts while providing a much wider span of risk and return. More recently, money-market funds have

Figure 7-4. *Households' Financial Assets, 1976–99*

Percent

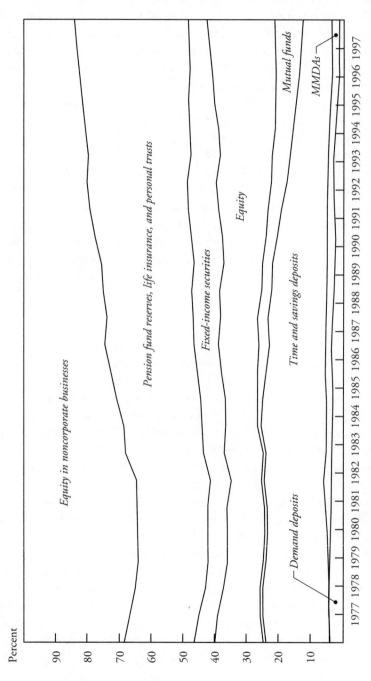

Source: Authors' calculations based on data from: reports of condition and income of individual banks; Board of Governors of the Federal Reserve System, *Flow of Funds Accounts of the United States: Annual Flows and Outstandings* (Washington, 2000).

also started offering all of the services traditionally provided by deposit accounts like check writing, access to funds via automatic teller machines, and electronic bill payments. The result has been a spectacular decline in household assets held in demand deposit accounts, from about 7 percent in 1952 to 1 percent in 1999. Investment in money-market mutual funds alone is now double the amount held in cash and demand deposit accounts.

Even the relatively small fraction of wealth held in demand deposit accounts may not be the primary source of liquidity for households. Figure 7-5 shows that credit card commitments and the holding of money-market mutual funds grew substantially during the 1990s. Together these accounted for over two-thirds of the liquidity available to households, thereby diminishing the exposure of demand and money-market deposits to sudden liquidity shocks.

Commercial borrowers are also increasingly relying on nonbank sources of long-term financing. Figure 7-6 shows the total outstanding nonmortgage debt of nonfinancial businesses. The share of bank loans in total credit market debt has declined from over 35 percent in the mid-1970s to almost 20 percent in recent years.[16] This decline has been caused primarily by an expansion of nonbank loans and advances (primarily from the U.S. government, its agencies, foreign banks, and finance companies), as well as the growth in commercial paper, municipal securities, and contingent credit. The total level of loan commitments grew substantially in the 1990s and now exceeds total loans themselves.

Thus liquidity provision to households and corporations, traditionally provided through demand deposit accounts, is increasingly being met by other sources more closely linked to capital markets. Even the limited amount of liquidity provision being performed by banks appears to be through credit card and loan commitments. Clearly, contingent provision of funds appears more efficient in dealing with liquidity shocks than building up deposits in accounts that pay very low or zero rates of return. A shift away from holding deposits toward contingent borrowing significantly lowers the likelihood of bank runs and hence the need for deposit insurance.

Estimating Liquidity

Deposit insurance is supposed to increase the stability of the banking system. It reduces the likelihood that insured depositors will withdraw their

Figure 7-5. *The Bearers of Potential Liquidity Shocks, 1990–99*

Percent

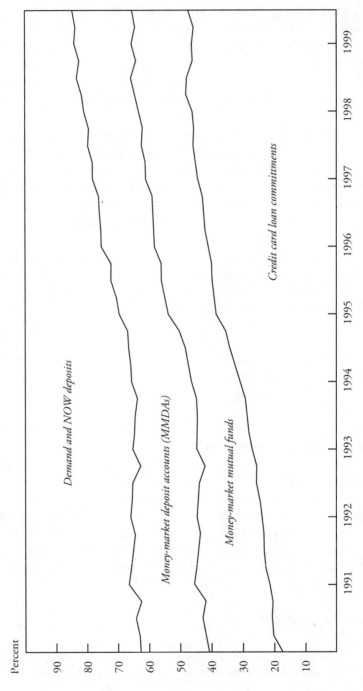

Demand and NOW deposits

Money-market deposit accounts (MMDAs)

Money-market mutual funds

Credit card loan commitments

Source: Authors' calculations based on data from: reports of condition and income of individual banks; Board of Governors of the Federal Reserve System, *Flow of Funds Accounts of the United States: Annual Flows and Outstandings* (Washington, 2000).

Figure 7-6. *Financing for Nonfinancial Firms, 1976–99*

Percent

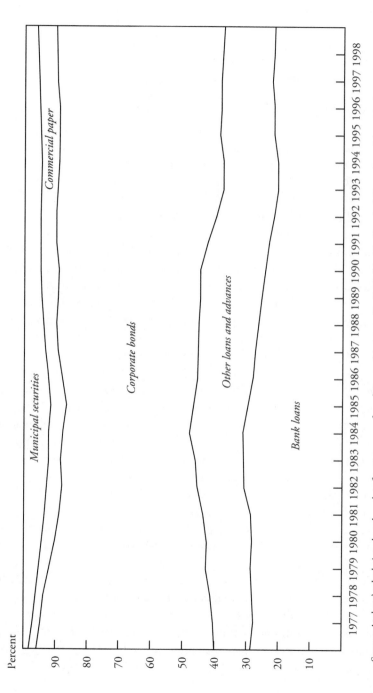

Municipal securities

Commercial paper

Corporate bonds

Other loans and advances

Bank loans

90 80 70 60 50 40 30 20 10

1977 1978 1979 1980 1981 1982 1983 1984 1985 1986 1987 1988 1989 1990 1991 1992 1993 1994 1995 1996 1997 1998

Source: Authors' calculations based on data from: reports of condition and income of individual banks; Board of Governors of the Federal Reserve System, *Flow of Funds Accounts of the United States: Annual Flows and Outstanding* (Washington, 2000).

funds in a liquidity crisis that could result in a collapse of the bank and potentially endanger the entire financial system. As a stabilizing tool, deposit insurance is expected to both reduce the likelihood of a bank run and, were it to occur, contain its adverse impact on the bank. In this section we estimate the liquidity of bank portfolios and use this measure to analyze the stabilizing impact of deposit insurance.

The overall liquidity structure of on- and off-balance-sheet items reveals the extent to which a bank relies on deposit insurance to mitigate a liquidity crisis. Using this information we define a measure, which we call the *liquidity gap*, that captures the liquidity position of a bank facing a sudden withdrawal of funds by depositors. Our objective is to calculate the liquidity shortfall that would remain if a bank tried to cover such a liquidity demand using its liquid assets only (primarily cash and securities). Such a measure of the liquidity gap of a bank tells us the extent to which an institution would have to raise additional liquidity by collateralizing or selling its illiquid assets (primarily loans) to meet the sudden outflow of liquidity.

We calculate the liquidity gap for two opposite scenarios. In one scenario, deposit insurance is assumed to fully curtail withdrawals by insured depositors. In the other, deposit insurance is assumed to be entirely ineffective: insured depositors withdraw their funds as if they were uninsured. By comparing the liquidity gaps in these two scenarios, we can estimate the effect of deposit insurance. If the liquidity gap is found to be small or negative in the scenario with ineffective deposit insurance, a solvent bank could deal with sudden surges of liquidity demand relatively easily without having to rely on the stabilizing power of deposit insurance. Vulnerability to a bank run would be minimal for such banks. For banks with positive liquidity gaps, the difference in the liquidity gaps between the two scenarios provides a direct measure of the efficacy of deposit insurance in curbing a liquidity-based run on the bank. It reveals the extent to which deposit insurance can reduce the liquidity drain in a crisis.

To calculate the liquidity gap, we first assign *liquidity coefficients*, which lie between zero and one, to the on- and off-balance-sheet items of a bank. The liquidity coefficient of asset items reflects the maximum amount of funds that could be raised within three weeks by liquidating all highly liquid assets of the bank. The liquidity coefficients of liabilities represent the fraction of funds that depositors, having lost confidence in the bank, may be expected to withdraw within a period of three weeks. The more liquid an individual item is, the higher its liquidity coefficient. For the scenario in which deposit insurance is effective, we apply the appropriate liquidity coefficients for each deposit category to the uninsured portion of deposits only, whereas when deposit insurance is ineffective, all deposits, regardless of insurance status, are considered. Therefore liquidity coefficients are the same in both scenarios; only the amount of deposits varies, depending upon the assumption made about the effectiveness of insurance. A similar reasoning underlies the assignment of liquidity coefficients to off-balance-sheet items, which are also classified as assets or liabilities.[17]

The product of the dollar magnitude of an item and its liquidity coefficient yields the *liquidity equivalent* of that item. For example, if the magnitude of time deposits is $200 million and its liquidity coefficient is 0.1, then the liquidity equivalent of time deposits is $200 million $\times$ 0.1 = $20 million. Thus $20 million may be interpreted as the direct dollar exposure to liquidity risk that the bank faces over a three-week horizon due to its $200 million liability in time deposits. If the liquidity coefficient were 0.3 instead, the liquidity equivalent would have been $200 million $\times$ 0.3 = $60 million.

We can now define the *liquidity gap* measure. The liquidity gap is the sum of the liquidity equivalents of all liabilities less the sum of liquidity equivalents of all *liquid* assets, divided by total assets. Therefore this measure represents the *net* liquidity gap of the bank as a fraction of total assets. Let a_i be the magnitude of (on- or off-balance sheet) asset i, w_i be the liquidity coefficient for item i, l_j be the magnitude of (on- or off-balance sheet) liability j, w_j be the liquidity coefficient for item j, and A be the magnitude of total assets. Then, for any individual bank, the liquidity gap may be estimated as:

$$Liquidity\ gap \ \equiv \ \frac{\Sigma_j w_j l_j - \Sigma_i w_i a_i}{A},$$

where I and J represent the set of assets and liabilities (including off-balance sheet items).

It is important to note that this measure considers only highly liquid assets in the bank's portfolio. Significant portions of banks' assets are illiquid, and normally these would have to be employed, through partial collateralization or sale, to meet an unexpected surge in liquidity demand. Thus a liquidity gap measure of 0.2 would indicate that the bank could meet its liquid obligations by liquidating all its highly liquid assets and borrowing an *additional* amount equal to 20 percent of assets against the illiquid part of its portfolio. If such illiquid assets constitute 80 percent of total assets (highly liquid assets therefore being 20 percent of total assets), the bank would need to borrow twenty-five cents against every dollar of illiquid assets to bridge the liquidity gap. A bank with a zero or negative liquidity gap would be able to meet the entire liquidity demand through its highly liquid assets without borrowing against illiquid assets. A positive gap does not necessarily mean that a bank faces a liquidity crisis. It only indicates that proceeds from the sale of liquid assets do not satisfy the entire liquidity demand and that additional liquidity has to be raised, either by borrowing against less liquid assets or by selling some of them. Banks with a high-quality loan portfolio or other valuable illiquid assets should be able to raise liquidity by borrowing as long as the liquidity gap is not too high.[18]

Distinction between the scenarios with and without effective deposit insurance is achieved by considering the amount of deposits for which the bank would be liable in the event of a liquidity shock. If deposit insurance is ineffective, the *full* amounts of deposits, *insured and uninsured*, are multiplied by the appropriate liquidity coefficients to obtain the liquidity equivalents. The rationale is that without the protection of effective deposit insurance, all depositors will be tempted to withdraw funds regardless of their insurance status. For the case where deposit insurance is fully effective, insured depositors would not make any withdrawals at all. Therefore we calculate the liquidity gap in this scenario by multiplying liquidity coefficients in each deposit category by the *uninsured* portion of deposits only.[19]

We can estimate the effectiveness of deposit insurance in mitigating a liquidity crisis by calculating the mathematical difference between the liquidity gaps in these two scenarios. This difference reveals the extent to which deposit insurance enhances the liquidity of banks' portfolios and thus acts as a stabilizer during a bank run. It is important to note that we have set up the scenarios such that ineffective deposit insurance appears somewhat weaker and effective insurance somewhat stronger than would be the case in reality. Even effective insurance cannot prevent withdrawal by insured depositors entirely, just as ineffective insurance will not lead to withdrawal by each and every depositor. Thus the difference in the liquidity gap measures in the two scenarios overstates the effectiveness of deposit insurance.[20]

A key issue for measuring liquidity is the determination of an appropriate set of liquidity coefficients that adequately captures the liquidity position of different asset and liability items. Ideally, a liquidity "ladder" should be designed to reflect the increasing liquidity, and hence liquidity coefficients, of different items over multiple maturities, ranging from a day to a few years. This would facilitate a measurement of the liquidity gap over various intervals of time as recommended by the Basel Committee on Banking Supervision and Graeme Chaplin, Alison Emblow, and Ian Michael.[21] Our singular choice of a three-week horizon is simply an intermediate one to capture the relevant time frame for a bank run and to introduce the concept. The suggested liquidity coefficients are based on background research about the nature and degree of liquidity of the various on- and off-balance-sheet items, but clearly a more detailed analysis is required for the precise determination of these coefficients. In cases where there is substantial indeterminacy about the coefficients, we make a conservative choice (more liquid for liabilities and less liquid for assets) in order to arrive at a lower bound for liquidity.

The details of the liquidity coefficients are provided in the appendix. Along with the coefficients, we have also provided the magnitude of each item for the third quarter of 1999, the latest quarter for which call report data were available at the time of this analysis, to convey some sense of the relative importance of each item in the final liquidity gap calculation. Because banks' balance sheets change only very gradually between quarters, our results are not just specific to the quarter we consider.

On the asset side, cash and balances due from depository institutions, securities, federal funds, and loans held for sale are supposed to be fully liquid and therefore receive a liquidity coefficient of one. A bank should be able to turn these items easily into liquidity on short notice, either by sale or, in the case of federal funds and government securities (which constitute over 70 percent of all securities), by borrowing against them using repurchase agreements. All other asset items have a lower degree of liquidity and therefore have been assigned a liquidity coefficient of zero. By far the largest item with a coefficient of zero is "loans," which comprises all loans that are not made to other banks or held for sale. Very short-term loans and some securitized assets are also contained in this category even though they are highly liquid and constitute a significant fraction of the loan portfolio for many banks.[22] Therefore liquidity should be understated on the asset side of the bank, making the liquidity gap seem bigger.

On the liability side, time deposits with a maturity of less than one year and MMDAs are the largest items. Because banks can restrict withdrawals from these accounts to some degree during the three-week period we consider, and because it is unlikely that all depositors would withdraw their funds, we choose a liquidity coefficient of 0.5 for both. This means that 50 percent of these deposits are liable to be withdrawn. Private demand deposits, private NOW accounts, and foreign deposits are supposed to be fully liquid and have therefore been assigned a liquidity coefficient of one. Time deposits with maturity exceeding one year are fairly illiquid and hence have a coefficient of 0.05. Nondepository items such as federal funds purchased, trading liabilities, certified checks, and other liabilities are considered to be fully liquid.

Liquidity coefficients for off-balance-sheet items are harder to assess because of their contingent nature. We suggest that loan commitments and standby letters of credit cause a liquidity drain of 10 percent of the total amount. This is a reflection of the fact that only a small fraction of loan commitments are called upon; and perhaps more important, in most cases banks can postpone or withdraw their commitment in the event of a liquidity shortfall. Positions in exchange-traded derivatives and securities lent and borrowed are assigned a coefficient of one, because they are highly liquid.

Empirical Findings on the Liquidity Gaps of U.S. Commercial Banks

Liquidity gap measures are calculated for the entire banking industry as well as for three subgroups based on asset size in the two scenarios we consider.[23] We add up individual balance-sheet items across all banks in the respective size categories and calculate the liquidity gap for the "aggregate bank." The two scenarios with effective and ineffective deposit insurance differ with respect to the treatment of insured deposits as described above.[24] The results are presented in table 7-1.

In both scenarios, *all banks hold very sizable amounts of liquidity*. For the total industry the liquidity gap without insurance is 17 percent of total assets; that is, banks would have to raise additional liquidity on the order of 17 percent of total assets. To put this number into perspective, table 7-2 shows that banks would have to borrow 30 percent of the value of their loan portfolio ("loans") to make the liquidity gap zero. Because more than 42 percent of loans are secured by real estate and 11 percent have a remaining maturity or repricing frequency of three months or less, it appears that a sound bank should be able to raise this volume of liquidity without much difficulty. Note further that the collateralization of even non–real estate loans should provide substantial revenue because these assets would be collateralized or liquidated, not because of a threat to their underlying cash flows, but simply because of a liquidity crunch at the lending bank.[25] Hence it seems that a liquidity gap of 17 percent can easily be bridged by the collateralization of a fraction of the loan portfolio. In the opposite scenario,

Table 7-1. *Aggregate Liquidity Gaps with Effective and Ineffective Deposit Insurance*

	Total industry	Large banks	Medium-sized banks	Small banks
Liquidity gap with effective insurance	0.04	0.09	−0.10	−0.17
Liquidity gap with ineffective insurance	0.17	0.20	0.09	0.07
Differential impact of deposit insurance (percent of total assets)	13	11	19	24

with fully effective insurance, the liquidity gap for the total industry equals 4 percent of total assets.

In contrast, a hypothetical bank devoted purely to liquidity transformation in the traditional sense by transforming fully liquid deposits into fully illiquid loans, would have a liquidity gap of 0.9 (assuming that the bank has 10 percent of equity in total assets). Although this number ignores any liquidity holdings of banks for day-to-day liquidity management, it provides a point of reference which shows that in both scenarios banks perform a lot less liquidity transformation than would be expected by the traditional notion of a bank for which deposit insurance was mainly designed.

Comparing the liquidity gaps for the two scenarios shows that the differential impact of deposit insurance is to reduce the liquidity gap by at most 13 percent of total assets. Because we derive an upper boundary on the differential impact of deposit insurance, it is quite likely that the actual

Table 7-2. *Liquidity Needs, Real Estate Loans, and Short-Term Loans*
Percent of total loans

	Total industry	Large banks	Medium-sized banks	Small banks
Liquidity needs	30	34	15	12
Real estate loans	42	36	60	63
Loans with a remaining maturity or repricing frequency of less than three months	11	7	25	28

differential impact is substantially smaller. Therefore we arrive at the result that the stabilizing impact of deposit insurance on the banking industry is to reduce the liquidity gap of banks by less than 13 percentage points of total assets. Clearly, the overall impact of deposit insurance appears to be very modest and calls into question its importance in providing stability to the banking industry.

The overall liquidity gap for the industry is dominated by the largest banks because they hold over three-quarters of the assets in the commercial banking industry. The group of large banks has a liquidity gap of 20 percent of total assets if deposit insurance is ineffective and 9 percent if it is effective. Thus they would have to borrow 34 percent of loans to cover the gap, which appears quite reasonable given that 36 percent of their loan portfolio is collateralized by real estate and 7 percent of loans have remaining maturity or repricing frequency of less than three months. The impact of deposit insurance on enhancing liquidity for large banks is strikingly low, at just 11 percent of total assets.

Deposit insurance is more important for medium-sized and small banks. According to our calculations, it reduces the liquidity gap for small banks by 24 percentage points of total assets and for medium banks by 19 percentage points of total assets. However, these two groups of banks have substantially smaller liquidity needs than large banks. Not only do they have a significantly smaller liquidity gap than large banks, they also hold portfolios that can be borrowed against more easily. Thus, even in the case of completely ineffective deposit insurance, small banks would have to borrow a mere 7 percent of total assets (12 percent of total loans) in order to cover their liquidity gaps. This looks easily achievable with their relatively liquid loan portfolio, 28 percent of which has a remaining maturity or repricing frequency of three months or less, and 63 percent is collateralized by real estate. Medium-sized banks would have to borrow 9 percent of total assets (15 percent of total loans) to close their liquidity gaps. They could borrow against a loan portfolio consisting of 60 percent of real estate loans but could also raise liquidity against short-term loans that constitute 25 percent of total loans. Therefore, although large banks may have better access to financial markets to bridge any existing liquidity gaps, the liquidity needs of medium-sized and small banks are smaller and their relatively high share of secured loans and short-term loans should make it easy to raise funds.

Finally, figure 7-7 represents the distribution of liquidity gaps for individual banks for the third quarter of 1999 in the scenario of ineffective

Figure 7-7. *Liquidity Gap Histogram, 3d Quarter 1999*

Number of banks

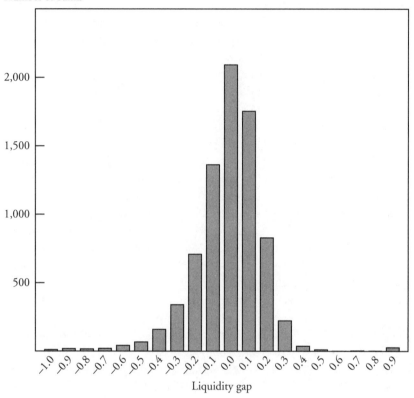

Liquidity gap

Source: Authors' calculations based on data from: reports of condition and income of individual banks; Board of Governors of the Federal Reserve System, *Flow of Funds Accounts of the United States: Annual Flows and Outstandings* (Washington, 2000).

deposit insurance. Even in this situation over 35 percent of the banks have negative liquidity gaps, indicating excess liquidity. Further, only 1 percent of the banks have liquidity gaps greater than 0.4. Thus in spite of the conservative assumptions behind our liquidity calculations, we find that banks manage liquidity such that a sound bank is highly likely to cover liquidity needs stemming from a sudden withdrawal of deposits, even without deposit insurance. Furthermore, it is indeed remarkable to note the extent to which the high liquidity of bank portfolios has lowered the marginal impact of deposit insurance.

The Effectiveness of Deposit Insurance

In this section we briefly assess deposit insurance not only in achieving the efficient provision of liquidity but also in realizing other economic and social goals that have been attributed to it. We analyze whether deposit insurance is effective in protecting individual banks, stabilizing the banking industry as a whole, promoting equity, and encouraging community investment. Our discussion does not question the normative justification of these goals, but solely appraises the ability of deposit insurance to achieve these goals effectively.

Our analysis puts a big question mark behind the overall effectiveness of deposit insurance to protect banks. According to our calculations, deposit insurance reduces the liquidity needs of the banking industry in a liquidity crisis by less than 13 percentage points of total assets. We also argued that sound banks could bridge the relatively small liquidity gap by raising liquidity from their sizable portfolio of short-term loans, real estate loans, and other loans. These results should not be very surprising when viewed through the lens of structural changes in liquidity transformation documented earlier in the chapter. Today, deposit categories that made banks prone to runs in the past constitute only a moderate share of total liabilities. As the share of these types of deposits has dwindled over time, so has the potential of deposit insurance to enhance the financial stability of banks.

The effectiveness of deposit insurance appears even less significant when one brings the notorious "too-big-to-fail" phenomenon into the picture. This refers to the understanding that regulators can provide full protection to all depositors and creditors, not just insured ones, when they determine that a failing bank is too big to fail—that is, that its failure could have a substantial adverse impact on the banking industry and the overall economy.[26] The eighty-eight largest banks, each with over $10 billion in assets (as of the third quarter of 1999), together hold 78 percent of total assets in the banking industry but have a mere 24 percent of these assets in the form of insured deposits. Many of them would presumably be considered too big to fail. Because this implicit support of regulators is well understood by the financial markets, and because it encompasses not only insured deposits but *all* liabilities of a bank, the too-big-to-fail doctrine is probably the key stabilizing factor for big banks. Thus we conclude that, for the largest banks, deposit insurance has minimal effect in providing protection against risks stemming from liquidity transformation.

As the trend toward consolidation in the banking industry continues, fewer big banks will capture an even larger share of the market, and the effects analyzed above will become more pronounced. Fortunately, market developments enhance not just the rising scope of the too-big-to-fail doctrine but also the ability of banks to manage liquidity. The too-big-to-fail doctrine is a vague regulatory policy that can easily be abused and may lead to worse moral hazard problems than deposit insurance. However, even though deposit insurance is losing importance in relative terms for the banking industry, it still constitutes a huge potential liability for the government that may eventually have to be borne by taxpayers.

Deposit insurance is supposed to protect not just individual banks but the entire financial system, thereby preventing the widespread disruption of financial activity. The primary factor that makes banks vulnerable to a crisis is the illiquidity inherent in their financial intermediation activities. It is feared that a run on one of these banks, due to either a perceived deterioration in its fundamentals or merely a temporary surge in demand deposit withdrawals, could set forth an irrational, panic-driven, contagious run on other "healthy" banks in the region, or the entire nation, and thereby cause a systemic liquidity crisis. In fact, the FDIC asserts that not only did deposit insurance "put an end to the devastating bank runs" of the 1930s but "for the next three generations, the system served its purpose by helping prevent banking problems from becoming banking panics."[27] However a large body of empirical and theoretical research casts doubts on the vulnerability of the U.S. financial system to a self-fulfilling run on the banking sector, and perhaps more importantly, were such a crisis to occur, on the ability of deposit insurance to stem it. Reviewing empirical research based on the experience of recent bank failures in the United States and abroad, Furfine concludes: "modern bank runs can be interpreted as a rational market response to new information rather than a contagion effect caused by either direct or interbank linkages or interbank panic."[28] Even the conventional wisdom that the banking crisis that accompanied the Great Depression was essentially a systemic liquidity crisis is rejected in a recent paper by Charles Calomiris and Joseph Mason based on a comprehensive econometric analysis of bank data from the 1930s.[29] International evidence presented by Demirgüç-Kunt and Detragiache covering banking crises in sixty-one countries from 1980 to 1997 also shows that deposit insurance tends to increase, rather than lower, the likelihood of banking crises.[30]

A comparison of the United States deposit insurance system with those of other developed countries in the European Union and G-10 provides an additional perspective on the failure of the deposit insurance to induce stability and confidence in the banking system. Figure 7-8 plots deposit insurance coverage, as a fraction of per capita gross domestic product (GDP), against financial market sophistication, as reported by the World Economic Forum. Coverage in the United States, at over three times GDP, is higher than in any other country except Italy, even though it has the most sophisticated financial system.[31] It is tempting to conclude that high deposit insurance coverage gives rise to a sound banking system, which, in turn, helps create sophisticated financial markets. However, the same survey also measured the perceived soundness of the banking system in these countries. These numbers, plotted against deposit insurance coverage in figure 7-9, suggest that, paradoxically, greater coverage leads to less-sound banks.

Another policy goal attributed to deposit insurance is the protection of small depositors who are not well equipped to evaluate the soundness of a bank before placing their savings in its custody. Deposit insurance, it is argued, is a net benefit to small depositors and therefore promotes greater equity. However, if equity were the sole surviving objective of the provision of deposit insurance, coverage similar to the level of savings typical of low- and moderate-income families (that is, those with annual family income below $50,000) ought to suffice. Table 7-3 shows the median level of bank account holdings of families classified by annual income for the year 1998. Median bank holdings for low- and moderate-income families are in the range of $7,500 to less than $22,000. In contrast, deposit insurance coverage currently stands at a whopping $100,000 at *each* bank *per* account beneficiary. Hence coverage can be increased almost limitlessly by opening bank accounts at different FDIC-insured institutions or by declaring additional beneficiaries to the account.

It is therefore not surprising to find that, of the aggregate amount insured through federal deposit insurance, only 25 percent belongs to low- and moderate-income families. Further, deposit insurance is a benefit to only those who *do* have a bank account; 25 percent of low- and moderate-income families do not (compared with only 3 percent for those with higher income). Thus it is hard to justify deposit insurance at its current coverage levels on the basis of equity for small depositors alone. The justification appears particularly puzzling in light of recent proposals under discussion to raise the coverage to $200,000.

Figure 7-8. *Deposit Insurance Coverage and Financial Market Sophistication*

Deposit insurance coverage as a percentage of GDP per capita

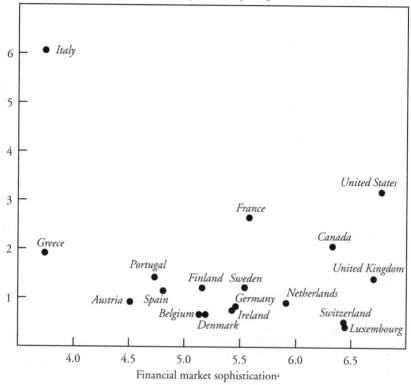

Source: World Economic Forum, *The Global Competitiveness Report* (Oxford University Press, 1999).

a. On this scale, 7 is most sophisticated.

Another equity-related argument portrays deposit insurance as a quid pro quo for the imposition of the Community Reinvestment Act of 1977 (CRA) on commercial banks. CRA is a federal law that is intended "to encourage banks and thrifts to help meet the credit needs of their entire communities, including low- and moderate-income neighborhoods, consistent with safe and sound lending practices" (Regulations 12 CFR parts 25, 228, 345, and 563e). By most accounts CRA has been successful in promoting investment in low- and moderate-income neighborhoods by drawing the attention of commercial banks to lending opportunities in

Figure 7-9. *Deposit Insurance Coverage and the Soundness of Banks*

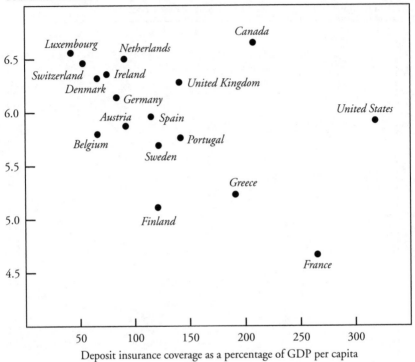

Source: See figure 7-8.
a. On this scale, 7 is most sound.

Table 7-3. *Median Value of Bank Account Holdings, 1998*
Dollars

Family income	Transaction accounts	Certificates of deposit	Total
Less than 10,000	500	7,000	7,500
10,000–24,999	1,300	20,000	21,300
25,000–50,000	2,500	14,500	17,000
50,000–99,999	6,000	13,300	19,300
100,000 or more	19,000	22,000	41,000

Source: Arthur B. Kennickell, Martha Starr-McCluer, and Brian J. Surette, "Recent Changes in U.S. Family Finances: Results from the 1998 Survey of Consumer Finances," *Federal Reserve Bulletin* (January 2000), p. 11.

their own communities.[32] But the view that CRA-related lending is an otherwise unprofitable service provided by commercial banks that might vanish if the benefit of underpriced deposit insurance is withdrawn or diluted appears puzzling. It is important to note that CRA does not require banks to make unprofitable loans to meet the provisions of the act. A recent study by the Board of Governors of the Federal Reserve indicates that commercial banks consider over 90 percent of their CRA-related lending as "profitable," 8 percent as "marginally profitable," and another 1 percent "break even."[33] If less than 1 percent of CRA-related lending is "marginally unprofitable" or "unprofitable, it is unclear why deposit insurance is required to subsidize it. Furthermore, deposit insurance would be a poorly targeted way of subsidizing community banking because a majority of its expenses are incurred on items unrelated to the actual purpose of the subsidy.

The presence of deposit insurance within the U.S. commercial banking system in its current form is certainly psychologically comforting and politically appealing. But competitive disintermediation has diminished this role substantially, and this economic shift calls for corresponding regulatory modernization. Our analysis suggests that both the economic efficiency and the equity of deposit insurance have declined in recent years and are likely to diminish further in the future. Unfortunately, the protracted political and institutional wrangling that preceded the passage of the FDIC Improvement Act of 1991, in spite of its relatively moderate changes, makes it clear that any serious effort to overhaul this system will not be easy.[34]

Conclusion

Deposit insurance was established as part of the Banking Act legislation in 1933. Another significant part of the same legislation was the Glass-Steagall Act, which separated commercial banking from the securities underwriting business. Both provisions were enacted to address the fragility of the banking system that was believed to have been one of the root causes of the Great Depression. In March 2000, restrictions imposed by the Glass-Steagall Act for over six decades were lifted pursuant to the implementation of the Gramm-Leach-Bliley Act. This repeal, preceded by incremental doses of dilution over the prior two decades, was a delayed but inevitable acceptance of the changing role of commercial banks amid bigger, better financial markets. In this chapter, we have tried to extend that same recognition to the federal provision of deposit insurance.

Using aggregate banking data from the past twenty-five years, we have shown that the relative importance of commercial banking in liquidity intermediation, both for depositors and for borrowers, has declined significantly and been largely overtaken by other market structures and institutions. We have suggested a simple methodology to measure the liquidity of bank portfolios. The liquidity gap measure that we calculate reveals that individual bank portfolios are surprisingly liquid and hence may not need the support that deposit insurance provides. This measure also reveals the marginal effect of deposit insurance in the event of a bank run. In addition, we do not find much support for this extensive federal safety net for reasons related to equity or stability in the financial services system. These findings cast the shortcomings of the federal provision of deposit insurance, arising from moral hazard and agency problems, in a sharper light and make a compelling case for the overhaul of this system.

Many proposals seek to reform the U.S. banking system and mitigate the severe incentive problems inherent in the public provision of deposit insurance. George Hanc provides a comprehensive overview of the current state of the debate.[35] One strand suggests scaling back the coverage of deposit insurance and relying on larger, better-informed depositors to monitor banks through introduction of coinsurance or fractional insurance. A different approach taps market forces to do the same through measures like the mandatory issuance of subordinate debt and privatization of deposit insurance or reinsurance. Finally, a third strand suggests the restriction of deposit insurance to "traditional banks," which would be involved purely in liquidity transformation, or to "narrow banks," which would operate essentially like money-market funds by investing proceeds from deposits in only liquid, risk-free assets. Reform initiatives that seek greater reliance on market instruments and private institutions must also be mindful of the differential ability of large and small banks to utilize these structures effectively.[36]

We have not made specific policy recommendations but only identified key factors that they should conform to. Whatever reforms they make, policymakers in the most sophisticated financial market in the world must become more cognizant of the abilities of that market. The appropriate set of reforms will continue to seek the adequate provision of public liquidity through the right private incentives, as it will ensure equal access to financial intermediation services and a stable financial system. What we have established is that in today's financial markets deposit insurance plays a modest and rapidly diminishing role in the achievement of these objectives.

Notes

1. See Federal Deposit Insurance Corporation, *A Brief History of Deposit Insurance in the United States* (Washington, 1998) for a brief history of deposit insurance; and David H. Pyle, "The U.S. Savings and Loan Crisis," in R. Jarrow and others, eds., *Finance: Handbooks in Operations Research and Management Science,* Vol. 9 (Amsterdam: Elsevier, 1995) for an analysis of the savings and loan crisis.

2. Douglas W. Diamond and Raghuram Rajan, "Liquidity Risk, Liquidity Creation and Financial Fragility: A Theory of Banking," *Journal of Political Economy,* vol. 109, no. 2 (2001), pp. 287–327; Anil K. Kashyap, Raghuram Rajan, and Jeremy C. Stein, "Banks as Liquidity Providers: An Explanation for the Co-Existence of Lending and Deposit-Taking," *Journal of Finance,* forthcoming.

3. Douglas W. Diamond and Philip H. Dybvig, "Bank Runs, Deposit Insurance, and Liquidity," *Journal of Political Economy,* vol. 91, no. 3 (1983), pp. 401–19.

4. See Sudipto Bhattacharya, Arnoud W. A. Boot, and Anjan V. Thakor, "The Economics of Bank Regulation," *Journal of Money, Credit, and Banking,* vol. 30, no. 4 (1998), pp. 745–70, for a comprehensive survey.

5. Edward Kane, *The S & L Insurance Mess: How Did It Happen?* (Washington: Urban Institute Press, 1989).

6. Asli Demirgüç-Kunt and Enrica Detragiache, "The Determinants of Banking Crises in Developed and Developing Countries," IMF Staff Papers 45 (Washington: International Monetary Fund, 1989), pp. 81–109.

7. Federal Deposit Insurance Corporation, "Options Paper" (Washington, 2000).

8. Armen Hovakimian and Edward J. Kane, "Effectiveness of Capital Regulation at U.S. Commercial Banks, 1985 to 1994," *Journal of Finance,* vol. 55, no. 1 (2000), pp. 451–68.

9. John H. Boyd and Mark Gertler, "U.S. Commercial Banking: Trends, Cycles, and Policy," *NBER Macroeconomics Annual 1993,* vol. 8, pp. 319–67; John H. Boyd and Mark Gertler, "Are Banks Dead? Or Are the Reports Greatly Exaggerated?" *Federal Reserve Bank of Minneapolis Quarterly Review,* vol. 18, no. 3 (1994), pp. 2–23; Allen N. Berger, Anil K. Kashyap, and Joseph M. Scalise, "The Transformation of the U.S. Banking Industry: What a Long Strange Trip It's Been," *Brookings Papers on Economic Activity* 2: 1995, pp. 55–217; Franklin R. Edwards and Frederic S. Mishkin, "The Decline of Traditional Banking: Implications for Financial Stability and Regulatory Policy," *Economic Policy Review,* vol. 1, no. 2 (1995), pp. 27–45; Robert E. Litan and Jonathan Rauch, *American Finance for the 21st Century* (Brookings, 1998).

10. See Basel Committee on Banking Supervision, "Sound Practices for Managing Liquidity in Banking Organizations," February 2000. However the report does not provide specific techniques for measuring these risks.

11. Board of Governors of the Federal Reserve System, *Flow of Funds Accounts of the United States: Annual Flows and Outstandings* (Washington, 2000).

12. We use the category "loans serviced to others" in call reports as a measure of securitization.

13. Peter J. Elmer, "Conduits: Their Structure and Risk," *FDIC Banking Review*, vol. 12, no. 3 (1999), pp. 27–40.

14. See Basel Committee on Banking Supervision, "Capital Requirements and Bank Behaviour: The Impact of the Basle Accord," Working Paper 1 (April 1999). This is achieved by securitizing higher-credit-quality (lower-yield) loans, thus removing them from the balance sheet and replacing them with lower-credit-quality (higher-yield) loans. The removal of low-yielding loans is essential because capital adequacy regulations limit the ratio of maximum assets to capital.

15. It is also important to note that more than 10 percent of deposits are held by federal, state, and local governments.

16. Note that we are not including corporate equities and mutual fund shares in the total credit market. In 1999 the market value of corporate equities and mutual fund shares outstanding was almost four times the size of the total credit market.

17. Where the classification is ambiguous, as in "other assets and liabilities," we assume it to be a liability in accordance with our overall conservative approach.

18. Note that we are focusing on solvent banks because we wish to measure vulnerability to self-fulfilling bank runs that occur because of coordination failures or panic among depositors. This is distinct from a "fundamental run" in which a bank's ability to borrow against illiquid assets may be impaired by its own insolvency.

19. Because banks do not report the exact amount of insured deposits for each of the deposit categories that we consider, we assume that the ratio of insured deposits and total deposits for each deposit category is the same as the ratio of total insured deposits to total domestic deposits. Foreign deposits are unaffected by this procedure because they are not legally covered by insurance.

20. Note further that our data come from a system in which deposit insurance is believed to be effective. Hence calculation of the liquidity gap with ineffective or nonexistent deposit insurance does not incorporate the more prudent portfolio and liquidity choices (such as holding fewer uninsured deposits) that banks would adopt if deposit insurance were not effective. This introduces an additional upward bias in our estimate of the efficacy of deposit insurance.

21. See Basel Committee on Banking Supervision, "Sound Practices"; and Graeme Chaplin, Alison Emblow, and Ian Michael, "Banking System Liquidity: Developments and Issues," *Financial Stability Review*, issue 9 (December 2000), pp. 93–112.

22. Because of data limitations we cannot identify the exact amounts of these liquid items.

23. Large banks held 78 percent of total assets in the commercial banking industry in the third quarter of 1999; medium-sized and small banks held about 11 percent each.

24. Note that none of the banks for which we have data is actually affected by a bank run. Therefore our calculations of liquidity measures relate to the situation of a hypothetical liquidity crisis occurring right after the reporting date.

25. In a study of the sale of the illiquid assets of 412 failed banks by the FDIC between 1985 and mid-1988, Christopher James found that loans that were not classified under the category "loss" or "substandard" fetched an average of 87 cents per dollar of value. Furthermore, individual banks have much stronger incentives to seek out the highest pay-

ing buyer than the FDIC. See Christopher James, "The Losses Realized in Bank Failures," *Journal of Finance,* vol. 46, no. 4 (1991), pp. 1223–42.

26. There are no explicit guidelines on which banks qualify for this status. See Ron Feldman and Arthur Rolnick, "Fixing FDICIA: A Plan to Address the Too-Big-to-Fail Problem," *The Region,* March 1998, for a detailed discussion of this provision.

27. FDIC, "Options Paper."

28. Craig Furfine, "Interbank Exposures: Quantifying the Risk of Exposures," Conference on Bank Structure and Competition 1999: Global Financial Crisis: Implications for Banking and Regulation, pp. 313–28.

29. Charles W. Calomiris and Joseph R. Mason, "Causes of U.S. Bank Distress during the Depression," Working Paper W7919 (Cambridge, Mass.: National Bureau of Economic Research, 2000).

30. Asli Demirgüç-Kunt and Enrica Detragiache, "Does Deposit Insurance Increase Banking System Stability?" Working paper (Washington: World Bank, 2000).

31. Even with their limited coverage, deposit insurance systems in most other developed countries rely on significant participation by the private sector in monitoring and administration.

32. The National Community Reinvestment Coalition estimates that CRA has encouraged formal commitments of some $1 trillion in low- and moderate-income neighborhoods since it was enacted.

33. Board of Governors of the Federal Reserve System, "The Performance and Profitability of CRA-Related Lending," Report submitted to the Congress pursuant to section 713 of the Gramm-Leach-Bliley Act of 1999 (2000).

34. See Randall S. Kroszner and Philip E. Strahan, "Obstacles to Optimal Policy: The Interplay of Economics and Politics in Shaping Banking Supervision and Regulation Reform," in Frederic S. Mishkin, ed., *Bank Supervision: What Works and What Doesn't* (Cambridge, Mass.: National Bureau of Economic Research, forthcoming) for an analysis of interest groups within the industry and the role of political and institutional factors affecting this legislation.

35. George Hanc, "Deposit Insurance Reform: State of the Debate," *FDIC Banking Review,* vol. 12, no. 3 (1999).

36. The U.S. payment system is an excellent example of a hybrid arrangement. For an overview, see William R. Emmons, "Recent Developments in Wholesale Payment Systems," *Review* (Federal Reserve Bank of St. Louis), vol. 79, no. 6 (1997), pp. 23–43.

8

FREDERICK SCHAUER

The Market for Truth

How should a society's resources be produced, deployed, allocated, and regulated? This question is at the heart of most of the contemporary debates about "marketization," for the marketization debates are largely about the extent to which, if at all, government or another central authority should make these decisions, and the extent to which, if at all, the operation of market forces should make these decisions.

The locution "marketization" presupposes not only a nonmarket alternative but also a nonmarket baseline. Only because so much of the world was so comfortable with nonmarket solutions to the issues of production and allocation of resources for so long do we have a debate about marketization at all. If markets were the norm, we would not talk about marketization, just as we only talk about vegetarianism because meat-eating is the norm, and we only talk about globalization because state-based governance is the norm. Just as the signs on the Massachusetts Turnpike warning drivers not to back up on a limited-access highway tell us much about the proclivities of Massachusetts drivers (such signs are rarely seen elsewhere), so too does a debate about marketization exist only because nonmarket solutions to resource allocation and resource production questions have been so

I gratefully acknowledge research support from the Joan Shorenstein Center on the Press, Politics and Public Policy.

dominant in the post–New Deal United States and in the post-1919 social-ist world.[1]

As we think about market-based approaches against the background of a nonmarket baseline, however, we have available an instructive model. "The marketplace of ideas" has long been thought to encapsulate one of the most powerful arguments for a strong free-speech principle. But that principle itself presupposes a baseline of regulation, and we would not be talking about free speech as a distinct principle at all were it not for the way in which a principle of free speech exists against a background of the per-missibility of greater regulation of non–speech behavior than most liberal democracies permit for speaking, writing, and printing. Free speech itself presupposes nonfree, or at least less free, conduct, and thus the marketplace of ideas as an argument for this differential treatment of speech and non–speech conduct is an argument that exists against the baseline of speech as a traditionally regulated activity, or at least as an activity as sub-ject to regulation as any other form of behavior.

My goal in this essay, therefore, is to make explicit some of the connec-tions between debates about the marketplace of ideas and debates about marketization. What we have learned from observing the marketplace of ideas in operation may be instructive in thinking about which social processes to marketize and which not to; and what we have learned from recent marketization debates may be equally instructive as we continue to explore the foundations and limits of a distinct principle of freedom of speech.

The Marketplace of Ideas as a Market

The notion of the marketplace of ideas exists as the oldest and most often-repeated of the arguments for special protection of freedom of speech and freedom of the press.[2] Against the baseline of an assumption that the deter-mination of truth was for the state or other official authority (especially the church), those who argued for truth to be determined in the marketplace of ideas maintained that an unregulated marketplace in ideas was the best way, and far better than the state or the church, of determining which ideas were sound and which were not. In the most famous and perhaps earliest use of the marketplace-of-ideas metaphor, Justice Oliver Wendell Holmes Jr. opined that "the best test of truth is the power of the thought to get itself accepted in the competition of the market."[3] Reflecting what thinkers as early as John Milton had argued in *Areopagitica*, Holmes captured the idea that a marketized process of determining truth was superior to one that was based on nonmarket official determination.[4]

My purpose here is not to determine whether this or any of the other justifications (self-expression and self-realization, personal autonomy, democratic deliberation, distrust of government, and the like) for a distinct free-speech principle are sound or sufficient. That is for another day.[5] What is important in this context is less the marketplace of ideas as an argument or a justification as it is a state of affairs. So although I examine some dimensions of the marketplace-of-ideas argument, I am even more concerned here with the marketplace of ideas as a description of a state of affairs, especially in the United States and to a (significantly) lesser extent in most other liberal democracies, in which the determination of truth and the acquisition and propagation of knowledge are left largely to noncentral and nongovernmental mechanisms. To the extent that this is the case, then freedom of speech and freedom of the press, again especially in the United States, can be seen as an eighty-year experiment in marketization, an experiment whose lessons may be relevant as we think about marketization in other domains.[6] What, then, can we learn from what may have been a uniquely American experiment in creating a market for truth, and in leaving much of the production and evaluation of knowledge to a marketized process?

Competing Conceptions of Truth

Consider again Holmes's statement that "the best test of truth is the power of the thought to get itself accepted in the competition of the market." There is an instructive ambiguity about the word "test" here. In one reading, the one I examine initially, "test" here means criterion, such that truth is *defined* as that which survives in the competition of the market. Let all of the ideas do battle, Holmes might be understood as saying, and see which wins. The one that wins is the one that is true, he argued, and that is so by definition, because that is just what "truth" *means*.

As both a pragmatist and a skeptic, it is not implausible to suppose that this was the meaning that Holmes intended.[7] He had little patience for abstract concepts, and even less for universal statements. Consequently, it is not at all unreasonable to think that Holmes was comfortable with the view that truth would be defined in much the same way that most economists would define "value." Just as most economists would resist the idea that a product or service had a value that was other than that placed on it by a well-functioning market, so did Holmes probably resist the idea that a proposition had a truth value other than that placed on it by a well-functioning marketplace of ideas.

Holmes's view is not without difficulty. As the criterion for truth (as opposed to the question of participation), it is not clear why winning in the marketplace is superior to any other criterion. Holmes announces that prevailing in the marketplace of ideas is the criterion of truth, but he does not, and perhaps could not, explain why this criterion is superior to, say, proclamation of truth by the elders of the community. Moreover, if truth is defined as the product of an open exchange of ideas, then it is hard to see what kind of arguments people would use in debating the merits of various ideas. If truth exists only as the end point of a deliberation, then the participants in a deliberation cannot make reference to truth to support their claims, and they are left with little more in their argumentative arsenal than the raw assertion of personal preference.[8]

More fundamentally, however, Holmes's view is hard to square with the fact that in many areas of inquiry there appear to be criteria of truth other than market outputs. Take astrology. In the United States there are no legal restrictions on what can be said, printed, or broadcast about astrology. People can and do freely express the view that astrology provides a reliable guide both to people and to the future, and that knowing a person's astrological sign provides significant information about that person's character. And people can and do freely express the view that astrology is bunk. Yet although it is not implausible to believe that the former view is prevailing in the marketplace of ideas, the view that appears to prevail in this open marketplace is nevertheless untrue. Astrology *is* bunk. And we know that because of scientific experimentation, logical reasoning, empirical observation, and a panoply of ways of determining truth other than that of defining truth in terms of a market output.

That astrology is subject to market-independent criteria of truth does not entail that everything is. Holmes was likely thinking not so much of factual or scientific propositions as of propositions of political theory and social policy. Indeed, the most significant of those for him was the debate between those who advocated a pure laissez-faire approach to economic organization and those who favored more extensive regulation in the service of social welfare, as by regulating wages, hours, and the employment of women and children.[9] With this as one of the primary topics of public debate at the time, it would have been understandable for Holmes to have believed that truth was more elusive than it was for the propositions of science or logic, and that relying on the competition of the market was less peculiar for this question of political philosophy than it was for the question of whether, say, the earth was round or flat.

Moreover, questions like the question of whether the country should operate under a regime of paternalism or under a regime of laissez-faire are questions as to which it is not clear that the "true" view should determine social policy even were we confident of a market-independent criterion for the truth of one or the other. As long as democracy represents an independent value, or a goal that is independent of and at times in tension with the goals of discovering truth, then the values of democracy may militate in favor of consumer sovereignty with respect to ideas of social policy even if the ideas selected are wrong as measured by some democracy-independent standard. If democracy is in part a right of the people to be wrong, then one way of understanding Holmes's view is as arguing that the criterion of *political* truth is winning the competition of the market. If this is so, then, at least in the area of policy, the Holmesian view might be explained in terms of defending the view that when the issue is policy the claims of democracy and the claims of epistemology converge, even if on other issues they may at times diverge.

The Marketplace of Ideas as Register of Preferences

Is there anything that this first understanding of the Holmesian view about the marketplace of ideas can tell us about markets more generally? Initially, it suggests that markets may be especially appropriate as social decision-making mechanisms when questions of truth or value are unsettled or unavailable. This is not to say that markets may not often be appropriate mechanisms for identifying truth, antecedently conceived, and I will address this in the following section. But where there are no antecedent understandings about value, or truth, or sound policy, the desirability of markets will be less dependent on contingent empirical assessments. So if there is a preference-independent conception of, say, good health care, or prudent investment for one's retirement, then the Holmesian skeptical argument for markets may be a weak one. But if there is no fact of the matter, if there is no preference-independent conception of right and wrong, true or false, valuable or valueless, sound or unsound, then the argument for market-based solutions may be stronger precisely because of the way in which market-based solutions can be seen as preference-registering in areas in which preferences are all there is.

Intriguingly, this distinction between topics about which there is a preference-independent fact of the matter and topics about which there is not is embedded in the free-speech principles of even the United States.[10] When the questions are ones of policy, of theory, of religion, of politics, and of value, it is axiomatic in American free-speech doctrine that "under the First Amendment there is no such thing as a false idea."[11] The determination of truth, as far as the law is concerned, must be for the marketplace of ideas and not for official authority. But when the question is a question of hard fact, whether scientific or not, the doctrine is different. In some circumstances, factual falsity is regulable under libel law, commercial advertising may be regulated when its factual representations are false or misleading, and arguments that the First Amendment in some way prevents the Federal Trade Commission, the Food and Drug Administration, and the Securities and Exchange Commission from being in the business of determining truth and penalizing falsity have gotten nowhere.[12] If one lesson from Holmes is that markets are good ways of determining truth when there are no antecedent conceptions of truth, the subsequent lesson from American free-speech doctrine is that markets may not be entitled to the same deference when there is.

Related to this is the close connection between market-based decision-making and democracy. If using the marketplace of ideas is the appropriate way of determining political truth, then this is largely because one of the demands of democracy is that the determination of political truth be a relatively broad-based affair.[13] The converse of this, however, is that a decision to rely on a market-based mechanism for making allocation decisions is, under counterfactual conditions of wealth equality, similarly broad-based and similarly democratic. Once the constraint of wealth equality is relaxed, of course, then the "one person, one vote" presuppositions of democracy would fail to exist for a market-based decisionmaking structure, even assuming that the consumers had the same preferences and the same utility curves. Nevertheless, the connection between the marketplace of ideas for the determination of political truth and the consumer-sovereignty dimensions of any market is a useful reminder of the democratic underpinnings of markets under conditions of small disparities of wealth.

The Marketplace of Ideas as Location of Truth

Although a view that the marketplace of ideas supplies the definition or criterion of truth may be a moderately close fit with Holmes's own philosophical outlook, it is not the only interpretation of the argument from the marketplace of ideas. Alternatively, we may accept, in all, many, or some domains, that there are speech-independent, discourse-independent, and deliberation-independent understandings of truth. The earth was round even when everyone believed it flat; the claims of astrology would be false even were 99 percent of the population to believe them true; and slavery was as wrong in 1843 South Carolina as Aryanism was in 1937 Germany, the beliefs of the majority of the contemporaneous populations of South Carolina and Germany notwithstanding.

Yet even if there are speech-independent truths of fact and even of value, it remains a task for any society and for any decisionmaking process to identify and embrace those truths and to identify and reject falsehoods. One way to do this would be official identification of truth and falsity, but another understanding of the marketplace of ideas posits that the marketplace of ideas is instrumentally a superior method of accepting truth and rejecting falsehood, even when truth and falsehood are defined independently of the process of identifying them.[14] In this conception of the marketplace of ideas, therefore, there are indeed truths out there to be found, but allowing an unrestricted marketplace of ideas is the most reliable method for finding them.

This understanding of the marketplace of ideas may not be Holmes's, but it can be linked to Holmes's aphorism if we take "test" not as a criterion but in its more literal sense as a method of identifying some property defined independent of the testing procedure. So "the best test of truth is the power of an idea to get itself accepted in the competition of the market" now can be taken to claim that succeeding in the market is a more reliable *indicator* of truth than any other testing procedure. And understood in this way, the claims for the marketplace of ideas hook into an even older free-speech tradition. When John Milton asked in the *Areopagitica*, "Who ever knew truth put to the worse, in a fair fight with falsehood," and indeed even when the Bible claimed that "the truth is mighty and shall prevail," what was offered was a view that truth, defined independently of any process for locating it, would through a process of open encounter with falsehood make itself known.[15] Similar claims dominate the argument for liberty of speech and discussion in chapter 2 of John Stuart Mill's *On*

Liberty, explain Justice Brandeis's view that "sunlight is the best disinfectant," and undergird the standard American Civil Liberties Union view that the best remedy for false speech is more speech.[16] In all of these variations, letting truth confront its adversaries will, as an empirical proposition, produce greater awareness of truth than would exist under any alternative truth-identifying or truth-determining procedure.

A more modern way of understanding the claim would be to posit that the truth or falsity of a proposition has more explanatory power in determining which propositions will be accepted and which will be rejected than does any other variable. And if the causal powers of truth on belief consequently offer the greatest ability to cause the acceptance of true propositions and the rejection of false ones, then all we need do is allow all propositions to flourish, so the argument goes, and the intrinsic power of the truth will take care of the rest.

Yet because this version of the marketplace-of-ideas claim rests on an empirical proposition about the relationship between truth and acceptance, we must remain open to the possibility that the empirical underpinnings of marketplace theory, however venerable their lineage, are false. Does truth in fact have more explanatory power than other variables in determining what people will believe and what they will not believe? Or is there a role for prejudice, self-interest, superstition, charisma, manipulation, deception, the structure of discourse, authority, and numerous other truth-independent variables, and might it sometimes or usually be the case that those variables explain more about persuasion and belief-acceptance than does truth? In *Twelve Angry Men*, Henry Fonda, initially the lone holdout on a jury, persuades the other eleven of his point of view, and it also turns out that he is right.[17] But suppose that the eleven were right, and that Henry Fonda, using his charm, authority, stubbornness, and passion, had persuaded the eleven to abandon what was in fact the correct view in favor of the incorrect one. Implicit in traditional marketplace theory is that truth is the most powerful weapon to have in the process of persuasion. Yet implicit in modern marketing theory is that catchy music, clever dialogue, and Michael Jordan as an endorser may be far more important than the truth of a proposition in getting the public to accept it. If this is the case, then the fundamental rationalist underpinnings of the marketplace concept are substantially weakened.

These are empirical questions, and it is no compliment to the American free-speech culture to note that, at least in the context of anything looking like the free-speech literature, there has been essentially no attempt to test any of them.[18] Yet once we see that the relationship between a market mechanism and the ability to identify the truth is contingent, empirical, and possibly less reliable than has often been assumed, we should entertain the same possibility with regard to market mechanisms and other social goods. If markets are perceived not as defining value, or defining the good, but rather as instrumentally effective ways of locating independently defined social goods, then their ability to do so is a hypothesis to be tested and not a conclusion to be accepted as axiomatic. It may be that markets, for ideas or for anything else, are effective, but it may be that they are ineffective. And it may be that, even if ineffective, they are, as Winston Churchill said of democracy itself, more effective than any of the other ineffective alternatives. Yet the lesson of astrology, for example, remains. If left to their own devices people will sometimes or often prefer falsity to truth, this has important implications for taking the empirical claims of marketplace-of-ideas theory as sufficient to justify allowing harmfully false propositions to flourish.[19] And if the fragile empirical underpinnings of the marketplace-of-ideas argument might lead to hesitation, then the possibility is open that the same hesitation may apply to markets in general.

Conclusion: The Marketplace of Ideas as a Market

The concept of the marketplace of ideas has traditionally been taken as a metaphor, and only that, but in important respects the marketplace of ideas should be seen more as descriptive and less as metaphorical. Initially, most of the sources of market failure in markets for goods and services may also be relevant to the marketplace of ideas. According to the rationalist understandings that first generated marketplace-of-ideas theory, most sources of market failure were irrelevant. For example, if a producer of one proposition had ten times the resources that the producer of another proposition had, the Enlightenment rationalist would have been unconcerned, because the truth of even an outnumbered and outspent proposition would ensure its ultimate acceptance by the population.

In the context of modern developments in communications and information technology, however, market failure in the marketplace of ideas becomes especially important. If disparities of resources on the part of those who offer propositions are relevant, and disparities in perception or information on the part of recipients of propositions are relevant as well, then the marketplace of ideas is no longer best thought of as a metaphor, but rather as just another market, a market in which the relevant trade is not in widgets, and not in services, but in ideas, in knowledge, and in propositions. The more we reject the rationalist assumptions of the Enlightenment, then the more we accept that truth-independent factors will determine what propositions people accept, what truths they believe, and what knowledge they have. And the more we accept that truth-independent factors will determine success and failure of propositions in the marketplace of ideas, then the more the marketplace of ideas ought to be thought of as a market in the nonmetaphorical sense. This may mean, as it has for many people, that we ought not suspend what we believe and know about markets when we are thinking about the marketplace of ideas, and that the same concerns for market failure, resource disparity, and capture, for example, that pervade our thinking about markets should increasingly pervade our thinking about the marketplace of ideas.[20] Alternatively, it may mean, as it has meant for others, that the same libertarian assumptions that we have traditionally applied to the marketplace of ideas ought also to be applied to the market for goods and services.[21]

In some sense, these two approaches may look different, for one has strong regulatory tendencies and the other has just the opposite. Yet in a more important sense they are the same, because they both urge rejection of what may be an increasingly unsupportable line between propositions, on the one hand, and the other sorts of things that may be offered by purveyors and evaluated by consumers, on the other. This attack on the line between prevailing norms about speech regulation and prevailing norms about goods and services regulation may in turn reflect the fragility of the speech-action line on which almost any version of free-speech theory must rest, but in the present context it may reflect something else as well.[22] It may reflect the fact that in a modern society knowledge, information, and truths are as much the subject of trade as any other goods and services. Microsoft, after all, was found to have attempted to monopolize illegally largely in the context of a language and a system, and it may be no accident that free speech is often the rallying cry of the open-source/open-code proponents in contemporary debates about control of information technology. For many people, as this last example suggests, eighty years of modern American free-speech theory provide the touchstone for questions of how, if at all, to regulate the world of information technology. But for many others, the increasing commodification of knowledge and information, and the increasing dependence of knowledge on tangible resources, may suggest that it is also time to reconsider the past eighty years of American free speech doctrine and to reconsider the lessons of the marketplace of ideas.

Notes

1. John Searle, *Speech Acts: An Essay in the Philosophy of Language* (Cambridge University Press, 1969), pp. 141–46. The point in the paragraph is an application of John Searle's important insight about "no remark without remarkableness." Assertions presuppose the empirical plausibility of their negation (few of us would be pleased if our sobriety were pointed out at a public gathering), and thus an argument for marketization presupposes a nonmarket baseline that would have been far less conceivable a century ago.

2. For a useful (and critical) history, see Stanley Ingber, "The Marketplace of Ideas: A Legitimizing Myth," *Duke Law Journal*, vol. 1, no. 1 (1984), pp. 1–91.

3. *Abrams* v. *United States*, 250 U.S. 616, 630 (1919) (Holmes, J., dissenting).

4. John Milton, *Areopagitica:* A Speech of Mr. John Milton for the Liberty of Unlicensed Printing, to the Parliament of England, London, 1644.

5. Actually, that day was roughly twenty years ago. See Frederick Schauer, *Free Speech: A Philosophical Enquiry* (Cambridge University Press, 1982).

6. Although free-speech rhetoric dates from the seventeenth century, and although the First Amendment was adopted at the end of the eighteenth century, strong free-speech protection in the United States dates only from an era starting in approximately 1919. Before that, little in American law or American practice (and even less outside of the United States) treated freedom of speech as being different from any other activity, and thus writing and printing were subject to regulation whenever official authority believed them to be harmful. See David M. Rabban, "The IWW Free Speech Fights and Popular Conceptions of Free Expression before World War I," *Virginia Law Review*, vol. 80, no. 5 (1994), pp. 1055 ff.

7. See Yosal Rogat and James O'Fallon, "Mr. Justice Holmes: A Dissenting Opinion— The Speech Cases," *Stanford Law Review,* vol. 36, no. 6 (1984), pp. 1349 ff.; and Vincent Blasi, "Reading Holmes through the Lens of Schauer: The *Abrams* Dissent," *Notre Dame Law Review*, vol. 72, no. 4 (1997), pp. 1343–60.

8. In more modern times, the failure to attend to the question of the purchase for argument during a deliberation or discursive process is common criticism of Habermas, and of any other view that defines truth in terms of the outcome of that discursive or deliberative process. See Frederick Schauer, "Discourse and Its Discontents," *Notre Dame Law Review*, vol. 72, no. 4 (1997), pp. 1309–42.

9. See, most famously, Holmes's dissenting opinion in *Lochner* v. *New York*, 198 U.S. 45 (1905), in which he claimed that the decision between paternalism (extensive regulation) and "Mr. Herbert Spencer's Social Statics" was not a matter of "fundamental principles," but was instead to be decided by the "natural outcome of a dominant opinion."

10. I say "even" because the free-speech principles of the United States are speech-protective outliers even by the standards of industrialized liberal democracies. On issues of, for example, protection of factually false libel of public officials and public figures, *New York Times Co.* v. *Sullivan* 376 U.S. 254 (1964); publication of information illegally obtained, *New York Times Co.* v. *United States*, 403 U.S. 713 (1971); and the incitement to racial

hatred and other forms of hate speech, *Brandenburg* v. *Ohio*, 395 U.S. 444 (1969), the United States offers a degree of protection for the speaker (and a degree of nonredress for the victims) unknown elsewhere in the world.

11. *Gertz* v. *Robert Welch, Inc.*, 418 U.S. 323 (1974).

12. *Dun & Bradstreet, Inc.* v. *Greenmoss Builders*, 472 U.S. 749 (1985); *Friedman* v. *Rogers*, 440 U.S. 1 (1979); *Virginia Board of Pharmacy* v. *Virginia Citizens Consumer Council, Inc.*, 425 U.S. 748 (1976).

13. The same might well apply to those institutional facts that are socially constructed rather than antecedent to society. For those factual assertions that are dependent on socially constructed institutions (law, language, contract bridge, the Brooklyn bridge, and others), there are important concerns about the array of people who participate in the social construction, and the democratic underpinnings of marketplace theory might be as applicable here as they are to questions of political theory and social policy.

14. Consider in this regard the Truth and Reconciliation Commissions in South Africa, Chile, and several other transitional societies. Although the theory of the marketplace of ideas is premised on the marketplace as the primary determinant of truth, it is worth remembering that the official identification of truth and the suppression of opposing views are analytically distinct, for there could be officially announced truth even in a society that freely allowed views opposed to that truth to be expressed.

15. Third Book of Esdras.

16. John Stuart Mill, *On Liberty* (London: Longman, Roberts, and Green, 1869).

17. *Twelve Angry Men*, directed by Sidney Lumet, Metro Golden Mayer, 1957.

18. See Frederick Schauer, "The First Amendment as Ideology," *William and Mary Law Review*, vol. 33, no. 3 (1992), pp. 853–69.

19. The problem with the marketplace of ideas might be that truth is a classic public good, and that society as a whole has a greater need for truth than the individual preferences of individual consumers of propositions would support. If this is right, then marketplace-of-ideas theory may get things exactly backward.

20. See, for example, Catharine MacKinnon, *Only Words* (Harvard University Press, 1993); Catharine MacKinnon, *Feminism Unmodified: Discourses on Life and Law* (Harvard University Press, 1987), pp. 155–58; C. Edwin Baker, "Advertising and a Democratic Press," *University of Pennsylvania Law Review*, vol. 140, no. 7 (1992), pp. 2097–2204; and Owen Fiss, "Why the State?" *Harvard Law Review*, vol. 100, no. 2 (1987), pp. 781–99.

21. See R. H. Coase, "The Market for Goods and the Market for Ideas," *American Economic Review*, vol. 64, no. 2 (1974), pp. 384–90 ("It is hard to believe that the general public is in a better position to evaluate competing views on economic and social policy than to choose between different kinds of food. Yet there is support for regulation in the [latter] case but not in the [former]." [p. 389]); Aaron Director, "The Parity of the Economic Marketplace," *Journal of Law and Economics*, vol. 7, no. 1 (1964), pp. 1–14.

22. I have explored this theme elsewhere. See Frederick Schauer, "The Phenomenology of Speech and Harm," *Ethics*, vol. 103, no. 4 (1993), pp. 635–53; and Frederick Schauer, "The Ontology of Censorship," in Robert Post, ed., *Censorship and Silencing: Practices of Cultural Regulation* (Santa Monica, Calif.: Getty Research Institute for the History of Art, 1997), pp. 203–22.

9

ANNA GREENBERG

The Marketization of American Politics?

IN MANY RESPECTS, politics in democratic systems resembles a market. Charles E. Lindblom makes this comparison explicit by arguing that both markets and democracies are systems of popular control over "public decisions."[1] Both systems he argues, are tied to individual preferences (either votes or dollars) that actors strive to shape or capture, leading to competition among groups for market share. As he sees it, any political system that requires parties and candidates to attract voters in order to win elections or public support in order to govern effectively will exhibit at least some elements of a market model: "[Polyarchies] are . . . political systems that are . . . like markets. They practice decentralization, diffusion of influence and power, and mutual adjustment so that individuals and small groups rather than national collectivities can strive for whatever they wish."[2]

In the United States, since the expansion of the franchise in the mid-1800s, groups have vied for votes and public support; only the "currency of politics" has changed.[3] In the nineteenth century, party machines distributed patronage and employed the partisan press to shore up their partisan base. In the Progressive era, reformers distributed pamphlets and literature to directly educate the voters about pressing social issues and garner political support for government reform. In the early twenty-first century, parties, candidates, and interest groups struggle to gain power by selling their political agenda (product) to voters (consumers) through the media, the mailbox, the telephone, and increasingly, the Internet. In contemporary times, party organizations narrowly slice the electorate to target the "swing voter," while interest groups mobilize grassroots politics from the top down to influence elections and policymaking.

Since the mid-nineteenth century, the American political system has undergone a series of changes that have heightened the market character of U.S. politics. This transformation is rooted in a series of political reforms and innovations that increased the size and breadth of the electorate as well as the volume of electoral activity. These changes occurred simultaneously with the rise of interest groups as actors in American politics, the infusion of money into the political system, and changes in technology that generated the need for expertise to master the new campaign and communication technologies. Scholars characterize the shift created by these changes as the move from popular politics to "merchandised politics" to "advertised politics."[4] Margaret Scammell calls the current model "political marketing," or a consumer-oriented approach to politics, where politics is defined as "what the market (electorate) wants and what it will bear."[5]

The rise of modern political marketing coincides with the development of a professional political class where the selling of expertise in the political marketplace is a billion-dollar business.[6] Political consultants, media advisers, public relations specialists, and pollsters use mass marketing techniques to attract political support for parties, candidates, issues, ballot initiatives, and referendums. Recalling Max Weber, these professionals either live "for" or live "off" politics; as he describes their role in political parties:

> The modern forms are the children of democracy, of mass franchise, of the necessity to woo and organize the masses, and develop the utmost unity of direction and the strictest discipline. . . . "Professional" politicians outside the parliaments take the organizations in hand. They do so either as "entrepreneurs"—the American boss and the English election agent are, in fact, such entrepreneurs—or as officials with a fixed salary.[7]

Increasingly, though, the professional class appears to live "off" politics, as consulting becomes divorced from political ideology and parties and political consultants take on an increasing number of corporate clients. The future of such an industry appears limitless as Internet and global markets open up new frontiers for the importation of political expertise and technology.

What are the normative consequences of a political system based so heavily on the employment of political marketing techniques by political professionals? There is an impulse to hearken back to the days of popular politics when local interests, grassroots organizers, and mass participation prevailed. But American politics has always exhibited market characteristics, so it is difficult to bemoan the current state of affairs on these grounds. Romanticizing the nineteenth century, moreover, is misspent energy because it ignores the ways elite, patrician politics systematically disenfranchised blacks, women, and men without property. Even the Progressive efforts to "educate" voters to undercut the "popular" party machine included support for municipal disenfranchisement. Mass appeals may be an inevitable result of expansion of the electorate and may even empower voters, as political elites are required to communicate with a wider array of voters and citizens.[8]

On the other hand, the marketing techniques of modern American politics may be complicit in creating the distance between political leaders and mass public represented by the increase in distrust and cynicism about politics and the decline of political participation.[9] Just as Robert Putnam sees the rise of television as fundamental to creating disconnection from civic life, similarly, political marketing may weaken the tenuous ties between citizens and government.[10] The fact that the political use of the Internet, which has been hailed as an equalizer and a stimulator of political engagement, exhibits the same marketing and advertising characteristics as other communication media, which does not bode well for people seeking to "reconnect people to politics."[11]

Innovation in Political Marketing

Since the rise of universal white male suffrage in the early 1800s, parties and candidates have organized politics around attracting voters with a combination of mass appeals and distribution of material benefits.[12] Jacksonian reforms such as "white manhood suffrage, the paper ballot, small polling districts, direct election of governors, presidential electors, head of state executive departments and local government officials" moved American politics away from elite politics to popular politics characterized by high voter turnout and intense partisanship.[13] In the mid-century, northern electoral politics revolved around highly organized, cross-class torchlight parades, mass rallies, campaign clubs, marching companies, and importantly, the partisan press. Later in the century, parties and their machines relied on the distribution of material benefits—jobs or services— to shore up partisan loyalties.[14]

The expansion of the electorate and the advent of direct elections, as well as the demands of party organizing, required both a local and a national professional political class.[15] First, popular politics was a local affair with party committees acting as small, decentralized units.[16] Second, the expansion of office subject to popular elections meant that elected officials were relatively dependent upon party professionals, especially because few candidates in this period publicly campaigned. Finally, party machines, while the beneficiaries of federal patronage, largely relied on ties with municipal governments for jobs and services to distribute to the party faithful. As Martin Shefter describes the situation, it seems remarkably similar to the professional class of today:

> These developments made it possible for such men-on-the-make to live off politics by serving as agents for private interests in their dealings with government (the Jacksonian period saw the rise of the lobby), by moving into and out of public office, and by making personal contacts and obtaining public contracts (e.g., printing contracts) that were useful in their private careers. The Jacksonian reforms, then, placed at the very center of the political system a group of middle-class professional or semiprofessional politicians.[17]

The rise of liberal or reform politics initiated the demise of party machines and weakened political parties but did not spell the end of political marketing or the role of political professionals. Popular politics gave way to "education politics," where party reformers promoted "objective" and "intelligent" communication with the voters particularly through pamphlets and brochures.[18] The reform goal was to communicate directly with the voters or "respond directly to the voice of the people" rather than through local party organizations or the partisan press.[19] Education politics also strengthened the national party committees at the expense of local party organizations as their "literary bureaus" bypassed party machines. Education politics, however, did not prevent the rise of candidate-centered campaigns, what Perloff calls "merchandised politics." President McKinley's campaign manager, Mark Hanna, was the early master of "packaging" candidates. He urged McKinley to respond to William Jennings Bryan's mass appeals and oratory by offering interested parties railroad passes to travel to McKinley's front porch to listen to his well-rehearsed stump speech.[20] Campaigns started placing advertisements in newspapers and magazines, mimicking the practices of the emerging advertising industry. In the 1912 presidential campaign, all three major candidates had "publicity bureaus." By 1920,

> the transformation of political style was complete. The belief that reasoned appeals should persuade thinking voters—the hallmark of an educational campaign—had disappeared, lost among the billboards decrying "wiggle and wobble." Abandoning education, the political advertisers would manipulate the voter, seize the "psychological moment" to shape his perceptions, and sell him a product.[21]

In this same period, Progressive activists promoted reforms that increased the number of elections people participated in and the number of people who participated in politics. Because direct primaries, the direct election of U.S. senators, and the rise of ballot initiatives required direct appeals to the public, the opportunities grew for extra-party groups to wield political influence. Progressive reformers and voluntary associations such as supporters of prohibition and temperance took an active part in promoting referendums and ballot initiatives.[22] South Dakota held the nation's first referendum in 1898, and ballot initiatives were employed frequently during the Progressive era between 1910 and 1930. Direct democracy declined during the Depression and World War II, though it expanded in the 1970s; one of the most far-reaching referendums approved by voters was California's Proposition 13, which in 1978 limited the state legislature's ability to raise property taxes.[23] Between 1898 and 1992, 1,700 initiatives appeared on ballots, mainly in Oregon, California, North Dakota, Colorado, and Arizona.[24] Currently twenty-four states permit direct democracy in some incarnation.[25]

Modern Political Marketing

Over time the American electorate expanded in size and breadth while the political system exhibited increasing electoral activity, and extra-party groups entered the political fray. The requirement that voters be property owners was eliminated by the mid-1800s, and women received the right to vote in 1920. By the mid-1960s, federal legislation had eliminated the legal barriers to blacks' political participation. Also in the 1960s the increase in government activity and regulation created more need and opportunity for interest groups to influence policy outcomes.[26] In this environment, changes in technology, particularly communication media, and campaign finance meant the political sphere embraced political marketing on a different scale than in the nineteenth century.

Technological Changes

Various technological innovations altered the manner in which politicians, parties, and interest groups communicated with the public and expanded the toolkit these actors used to persuade voters and influence public opinion. In the nineteenth century, though politics was largely a local affair, politicians and parties communicated to the public and their partisans via newspapers, pamphlets, and handbills. The explosion in mass communication through the introduction of the telephone, the radio, and the television, however, altered strategies of political communication and persuasion. Political groups, politicians, and parties acquired an ability to reach an audience unimaginable in the past. Once introduced, both radio and television expanded rather rapidly (in comparison with telephones, which took longer to reach 93 percent of households).[27] For example, it took only a decade, from 1950 to 1959, for 90 percent of American homes to own televisions.[28]

Radio and television created national audiences for political candidates; Franklin D. Roosevelt's fireside chats, which reached 60 million listeners, are an often-cited early example.[29] These communication media enabled candidates to communicate with the mass public, a development that Larry Sabato associates with the shift from "retail" politics to "wholesale" politics. Dwight Eisenhower was the first presidential candidate to make extensive use of communication technology; he hired agencies from the advertising world to produce forty-nine television spots and twenty-nine radio spots and spent an estimated $1.5 million on the "first media blitz."[30] Campaigns began to rely heavily on television advertising, as well as the broadcasting of the debates and conventions, to reach win voters. By 1996 the candidates for president, the House of Representatives, and the Senate spent an estimated $400 million on advertising and television, which remains the dominant mode of political communication to the general public.[31]

Polls and surveys used by candidates, parties, and interest groups to gauge their success with the mass public stemmed from the scientific techniques developed by the market research industry. Polling legends George Gallup, Elmo Roper, and Archibald Crossley, all of whom got their start in market research, successfully predicted the outcome of the 1936 presidential race, attracting the interest of an audience already attentive to newspaper-sponsored straw polls.[32] Despite being beset by various polling disasters (remember "Dewey Defeats Truman"), the political polling industry grew rapidly. Presidents as early as Franklin D. Roosevelt paid attention to public opinion surveys, especially the polls sponsored and published by *Fortune* and *Literary Digest* magazines.[33]

Advances in the application of sampling theory and use of telephones, rather than face-to-face interviews, spurred the development of the industry. The nearly universal penetration of the telephone and the advent of random digit dialing (RDD) meant wide access to cheap and accurate surveys and polls. Soon consultants adopted other innovations from market research, such as focus groups and dial meter testing (in which groups of voters register their opinions of video on dial meters), to test the effectiveness of the massive volume of television ads produced by media consultants. Microcomputers with the capacity to process data quickly and other innovations such as computer-assisted telephone interviewing (CATI), which permits complicated branching and randomization in surveys as well as simultaneous data entry, can make data available the moment a survey ends. Thus during the 1992 Democratic convention, the Clinton campaign could conduct national sample surveys every evening, testing the impact of each night of the convention, and produce "banner books," or complete survey results, by 4 A.M. the next day.

Technology has also sped up the process of producing political advertising. Media firms now have the ability to produce ads in a matter of days or hours in response to campaign events. Campaign ads can be tested with "dial groups" and introduced into the advertising rotation the following day.

Money

The massive infusion of money into the American political system is one of the most well documented and bemoaned innovations in modern politics. Although money has long been a feature of our nation's political landscape, in recent years candidate and party spending and campaign costs have far outpaced inflation.[34] The rising costs of campaigns are linked to the requirements of television advertising and campaign technology—certainly not to any increased competitiveness for seats in the houses of Congress (98 percent of incumbents were reelected in 1998). Money is raised by parties and campaigns, from individuals, and by political action committees (PACs) representing interest groups, corporations, and unions. Money is spent during and between election cycles by parties and candidates, as well as by interest groups and PACs on independent campaigns on behalf of parties, candidates, and ballot initiatives.[35]

Current campaign finance law limits individual contributions to $2,000, and PACs can contribute a total of $10,000 during the primaries and general elections. In 1998 federal candidates and national parties raised approximately $1.5 billion (including soft money) from individuals and PACs.[36] Large individual donors contributed a plurality of the funds, though small donors and PACs chipped in a significant amount as well. In fact, over time, PACs have contributed an increasing proportion of campaign funding; in 1972, PACs gave $12.5 million; and in 1998 their contributions reached $269.2 million. In comparison, in 1974 nearly 80 percent of donations came from individuals, but in 1998 individual donations constituted only 58 percent of campaign donations.[37]

Although there are limits on contributions to candidates and PACs, individuals and PACs can give unlimited money to campaign committees.[38] This so-called soft money is an unintended consequence of the current campaign finance system.[39] In the 1990s the party committees set new records for raising soft money during each election cycle. For instance, the Democrats raised $84.4 million in soft money between January 1997 and November 1998, 82 percent more than in the 1993–94 period. The Republicans raised $111.3 million in soft money in the same period, an increase of 112 percent over 1997–98.[40] In the 1999–2000 election cycle, the Democratic Party and its committees raised $372 million (46 percent in soft money), and the Republican Party and its committees raised $506 million (52 percent in soft money).[41]

Campaign spending has vastly outpaced inflation. Sandy Maisel finds that the mean expenditure of an incumbent in a House race increased 785 percent, from $53,384 in 1974 to $472,000 in 1998.[42] In 2000 the mean expenditure for a House race was $645,090.[43] The mean expenditure of an incumbent Senate candidate increased 697 percent, from $437,482 in 1974 to $3,484,927 in 1998. In 2000 the mean expenditure for a Senate race was $5,545,737. Some individual races reached new heights in campaign spending. In the New York Senate race between First Lady Hillary Clinton and Representative Rick Lazio, for example, collectively the candidates and groups spent $93 million. Overall, House and Senate candidates spent $963 million during the 1999–2000 election cycle, a significant increase over both the 1993–94 and 1995–96 campaigns. In the presidential race, George W. Bush spent $183 million and Al Gore spent slightly less, $118 million.[44]

Campaign spending is not limited to parties and candidates; according to a report released by the Annenberg Public Policy Center, the major advocacy groups spent between $130 and $150 million on "issue" advertising during the 1996 campaign.[45] The AFL-CIO, for instance, spent $35 million in the 1996 presidential advertising against freshman GOP members of Congress.[46] In the 2000 election, labor spent $56 million and business groups spent $841 million in support of Republican and Democratic candidates.[47]

The Modern Professional Political Class

These changes—the expansion of the franchise and campaigns, the greater number of political actors, the advances in campaign and communication technology, and the infusion of money—create a set of conditions amenable to the development of a modern professional political class. It is estimated that the number of political consultants tripled in the 1990s.[48] Consultants have myriad and numerous opportunities to work for parties, candidates, and interest groups at the local, state, federal, and increasingly, international levels. It is estimated that candidates and parties spent roughly $3 billion on campaigns in 2000, which kept busy the estimated 3,000 consulting businesses in the United States.[49] Consultants will sell their expertise in general strategy, polling, media and communication, direct mail, fund-raising, and website development. They work in many capacities—as strategists (consulting, campaign management, polling, media, direct mail), specialists (research, telemarketing, fund-raising, media buying, speech writing), and vendors (of website development, printing services, voter files, campaign software).[50] Moreover, there is ample money to fund the retention of expertise, which does not appear to be diminishing in the absence of campaign finance reform.

Modern political consulting emerged from advertising, public relations, and journalism. The first paid modern political professionals were Clem Whitaker, a journalist, and Leone Smith Baxter, a public relations specialist, who were hired to help defeat a ballot initiative championed by Pacific Gas and Electric (PG&E) in 1933.[51] They went on to work on over seventy-five campaigns with a 90 percent success rate through a combination of "public relations with candidate and referendum campaign consulting."[52]

Political consulting exploded in the 1960s and 1970s. For example, witness the transformation of market research tools into the development of political polling. President Kennedy relied on pollster Louis Harris, and President Johnson employed Oliver Quayle, but President Nixon institutionalized the use of survey data in the White House, commissioning 233 private polls between 1969 and 1972 during both the campaign and the administration. Nixon developed a specialized staff and distribution system for gauging public opinion, which guided policy development and media relations.[53] Later presidents employed high profile pollsters such as Pat Cadell (President Carter), Richard Wirthlin (President Reagan), Fred Steeper (President George Bush), and Stanley Greenberg (President Clinton; he later also used Dick Morris, Mark Penn, and Doug Schoen). These consultants do the work of what Sidney Blumenthal cynically calls the "permanent campaign," or the transformation of governance into "an instrument designed to sustain an elected official's public popularity."[54]

As the polling industry exploded and survey research became more affordable, polls trickled down from the presidential level. By 1966 most Senate candidates used surveys in their campaigns, as did roughly half of the House candidates.[55] In 1992 nearly two-thirds of the candidates for the House of Representatives (and 75 percent of the incumbents) hired consultants.[56] Today the party committees employ pollsters and often make in-kind contributions in the form of polling data to House and Senate candidates or subsidize presidential polling. At the state level, using a party's preferred consultant is often a prerequisite for receiving party funding.[57]

Of course, interest groups hire political consultants both during and between election cycles as well. The interest group universe is made up of a variety of groups—membership organizations, business associations, trade associations, labor unions, farm groups, professional associations, citizens' groups and advocacy groups, civil rights and social welfare organizations, corporations, and public interest law firms—all concerned with affecting policy outcomes on behalf of their membership, constituency, or industry.[58] In fact, increasingly, political consulting firms are shifting to issue and corporate work, in part to avoid the financial instability inherent in a client base available only during the election cycle.[59]

The health care debate in 1993–94 is an instructive example of both the permanent campaign and interest group use of consulting to affect public policymaking. In its early days, the Clinton administration commissioned a substantial number of surveys to gauge the level of public support for health care reform and, after the release of the blueprint, to present the reform plan to the public.[60] President Clinton's consultants played a central role in framing the health care reform plan, along with administration officials. At the same time, the Health Insurance Association of America (HIAA) and the National Federation of Independent Business (NFIB) launched their own offensive against the proposed health care plan. The HIAA hired Republican pollster Bill McInturff who, along with consultants Ben Goodard and Rick Claussen, created the infamous "Harry and Louise" advertising campaign that helped undercut public support for the reform.[61] The HIAA spent $14 million on the Harry and Louise ads as part of the estimated $100 million spent by organizations in favor of and opposed to the health care plan.[62] The public relations battle over health care, while tapping real concerns in the general public about the state of the nation's health care system, was defined by the battle between interest groups and the Clinton administration to control how people thought about reform.

The resurgence of ballot initiatives has fueled the consulting industry as well, particularly because working on initiative campaigns is often more lucrative for consultants than working for candidates.[63] For example, in the 2000 season, wealthy backers poured millions into funding the signature and advertising campaigns for school voucher ballot initiatives in California and Michigan.[64] Most ballot initiatives require the signatures of between 2 and 15 percent of a state's population, often with limits imposed on the amount of time for gathering signatures.[65] For example, under California law, organizers have 150 days to get 433,000 valid signatures of registered voters. Signature-gathering firms charge a fee for each signature, and costs increase as the organizers near the time deadline. In the 1990s, signature gatherers were paid 25–35 cents per signature, crew chiefs were paid 5–10 cents per signature, and the companies charge the client an additional percentage on top.[66] The half-dozen signature-gathering firms in

California and Nevada can charge between $700,000 and $1 million for a single ballot initiative.[67]

As the ballot initiative example suggests, political consulting is lucrative. Twenty percent of political consultants earn more than $200,000 a year, though their incomes differ widely.[68] Media consulting is the most profitable sector. First, in response to the rise of television politics, campaigns spend an enormous amount of their budgets on paid media rather than get-out-the-vote or direct mail. Media expenditures (advertising and consulting) generally consume at least half of a candidate's budget.[69] Second, media consultants receive a percentage of the "media buys" they place on behalf of their campaigns. In statewide or national races, this cut of the media budget can mean millions of dollars for consulting firms.

The Next Frontier: The Internet

According to many scholars and commentators, the Internet promised to expand political participation and civic engagement as it equalized access to political information and provided expanded opportunities for political interaction.[70] Most studies show, however, that the politically engaged and interested, not the disenfranchised, go online for political information and news.[71] In the current period, the real political promise of the Internet rests on how groups—parties and candidates, interest groups and grassroots organizations—use it as an organizing tool and for political communication.[72] Not surprisingly, campaign professionals and others are attempting to make the Internet the next frontier in political marketing.

Presidential candidates and parties began thinking about the power of the Internet to reach voters, recruit volunteers, and raise money in 1996, but the 2000 presidential primaries truly raised its political profile when it was reported that John McCain had raised $3.7 million online through February 10, 2000.[73] This fund-raising success represents a significant increase over prior election cycles: in 1997–98 candidates raised only $100,000 over the Internet, or one-tenth of 1 percent of all campaign funds.[74] Consultants and firms, however, are busy figuring out how to use the Internet to raise money for political candidates and groups. For example, Campaign Solutions, the web consultants to the McCain campaign, earned a percentage of each dollar contributed on the McCain website.[75] Firms, moreover, have successfully lobbied the Federal Election

Commission to accept innovations in Internet fund-raising. For instance, Campaign Advantage, an Internet campaign consulting firm, successfully sought approval for the use of "e-checks" instead of credit cards, and the FEC ruled in June 1999 that credit card contributions are eligible for federal matching funds.[76]

Candidates and party committees are developing strategic partnerships with websites in order to increase their pool of campaign contributors. For example, Voter.com joined with eContributor.com to create "strategic partnerships with web 'portals,' which will spend millions of dollars on advertising this political season in hopes of becoming the most heavily trafficked site for political information. Campaigns that sign up with Voter.com can then raise money—using eContributor.com's system—from all the visitors lured there by ads."[77] Although online fund-raising does not rival conventional methods, of the estimated $3 billion spent during the election candidates raised $50 million over the Internet.[78]

Political consultants use "cookies" to track the online profile of potential contributors and voters to generate targeted fund-raising and political appeals.[79] Companies hope to use this information to reach particular voters and contributors efficiently. For example, Aristotle Publishing, an established campaign technology firm, and America Online will use information about online users to target banner ads to specific voters (at a cost of 1 to 7 cents an ad). They will define their audience by "congressional district, legislative district, party affiliation, vote history and other political information."[80] Others are developing software to create online political profiles of users or "collaborative filtering" to "slice and dice the electorate into preference groups [for example, soccer moms] so that they can be targeted with more precise and effective messages."[81]

Political sites are often for-profit ventures that lack an analog in the "real" world.[82] Many of the highest profile "grassroots" sites received venture capital from prestigious firms such as Charles River Ventures and have awarded stock options to their famous political board members such as former White House press secretary Mike McCurry and former White House chief of staff John Sununu at Grassroots.com and former representative Tom Downey at SpeakOut.com.[83] Sites that promote civic engagement and the dissemination of "neutral" political information such as SpeakOut.com, Grassroots.com, Votenet.com, and Voter.com are all for-profit ventures that collect data about their registered users, which they hope to provide to political clients.[84] SpeakOut.com, for example, uses its database of registered users as a pool for focus groups and public opinion information. Sarah Schafer of the *Washington Post* reported, "[Ron] Howard [founder of SpeakOut.com] hopes to make more than $5 million in revenue this year by selling polling data to special interest groups and others."[85] In fact, SpeakOut.com calls itself an "opinion research company"; it compiles the views of its registered users for its strategic partners and conducts surveys among the user base, who are rewarded with frequent-flier miles and other incentives for participating.[86] After the 2000 election, Grassroots.com formed a partnership with a public affairs firm to create lobbying software for their clients such as Amnesty International and Verizon, a telecommunications company.[87]

Voter.com, which raised $15 million in its first round of financing, hoped to generate revenue by selling web server space to political groups for $50 a month.[88] (Voter.com, however, went out of business in 2000.) Grassroots.com will sell "Web hosting and Web site services to candidates, politicians, interest groups . . . online advertising and online capabilities such as email distribution, online polling and surveys."[89] Even the political parties are getting on board. In 2000 the Republican National Committee launched a for-profit subsidiary—GOPnet.com—that sells dial-up services with "contacts, volunteering opportunities, chat rooms, news, and humor for Republican activists."[90]

The Internet even hosts profit-making ventures in areas that were formerly the purview of government. In the 2000 primary season the state of Arizona experimented with online voting with the aim of increasing voter turnout. The state hired Election.com to conduct the online election, which previously worked for groups such as trade associations and labor unions. The founder of the company sees limitless possibilities: "There are 512,000 public elections annually, as well as elections held by 1.7 million private organizations."[91] Votation.com is behind the ballot initiative Campaign for Digital Democracy, which seeks to legalize online voting in California.[92] Its loosely associated advocacy arm, Votesite.com, aims to submit electronically signed petitions to the Registrar of Voters as it builds its Internet Initiative System (IIS), a system to collect digitally signed initiative petitions.[93]

Finally, polling and survey research have migrated to the Internet. Because more and more people are using caller identification and call blocking to block phone marketing calls to their homes, telephone response rates have declined. In response, polling firms are attempting to conduct survey research over the Internet, which promises to be an affordable way to contact people and to employ sophisticated multimedia with large samples. Online polling faces many challenges, most significantly generating a representative random sample.[94] Currently, most web polling ventures rely on volunteer-based Internet panels recruited by banner advertisements. Web panels are used most widely in market and commercial research because survey researchers generally are skeptical about the existing sampling procedures. Firms, however, are attempting to attract political clients. Harris Interactive (formerly Louis Harris and Associates), a well-known public opinion firm, has invested a significant amount of its own capital in an Internet panel with millions of participants worldwide devoted to market, political, and opinion research. Harris Interactive entered into a partnership with Excite.com, which hosted "Harris Interactive Election 2000" surveys throughout the election season.[95] Harris's first forays into political prediction have not been entirely successful, and great skepticism remains in the survey research community about its sampling and weighting procedures.[96]

Conclusion

As we moved from nineteenth-century populist politics to the mass politics of the twentieth century, political marketing remained a constant feature of the American political landscape. As we begin the twenty-first century, the Internet does not appear to have fundamentally altered the transactional relationship among parties, candidates, consultants, interest groups, and voters. Moreover, the relative failure of efforts to introduce campaign finance reforms, the exponential increase in ballot initiatives, and the increasingly lucrative nature of political consulting do not bode well for critics of political marketing. All of these forces conspire to sustain mass marketing as a way to organize American politics.

Given that the use of marketing techniques to reach voters is likely to endure, we need to consider the impact of mass marketing on our democracy. In the aggregate, one could argue that mass marketing is an effective and efficient way to target information in large democratic systems. In a nation of this size, it is difficult to imagine town meetings, caucuses, or direct democracy as a way of communicating our preferences to political leaders. Moreover, these idealized forms of democratic participation are often biased in unacceptable ways, because the most ideologically and politically engaged tend to participate and drown out marginal voices.

But from the perspective of distributive equity, there are ways that political marketing undermines the democratic reach of our political system. Marketing places a premium on targeting citizens who are likely to vote or hold strong partisan views. The political effort to "slice and dice" the electorate to reach the "swing voter" is not an exercise in mobilizing new participants to join the political debate. The infusion of big money into electoral politics, ballot initiatives, and lobbying means that the barriers to entry for the average citizen are high. Moreover, the transformation of grassroots lobbying into a highly professional enterprise means that mobilization occurs from the top down rather than from the bottom up. Ultimately, modern political marketing remains a one-sided transaction between elites and citizens, a circumstance that probably limits the diversity of voices in our political debate and inhibits greater citizen engagement in electoral politics and public policymaking.

Notes

1. Charles E. Lindblom, *Politics and Markets: The World's Political Economy Systems* (Basic Books, 1977), p. 163. The crux of Lindblom's argument is that polyarchy and markets are linked because they both emerge out of constitutional liberalism: "If we understand that polyarchy is a component of a highly developed form of constitutional liberalism and that constitutional liberalism in turn is a set of institutions assuring individuals of their liberty to enter into trade in order to develop their own life opportunities, we would not expect a polyarchy without a market." Also see Anthony Downs, *An Economic Theory of Democracy* (Harper Collins, 1957). Downs built his "median voter theorem" on the assumption that parties position themselves ideologically in the political "marketplace" to attract voters.

2. Lindblom, *Politics and Markets*, p. 165.

3. My thanks to Archon Fung, assistant professor of public policy in the John F. Kennedy School of Government, Harvard University, for this formulation.

4. Richard M. Perloff, "Elite, Popular and Merchandised Politics," in B. I. Newman, ed., *Handbook of Political Marketing* (Thousand Oaks, Calif.: Sage, 1999).

5. Margaret Scammell, *Designer Politics: How Elections Are Won* (St. Martin's, 1995), p. 8.

6. Dennis W. Johnson, "The Business for Political Consulting," in J. A. Thurber and C. J. Nelson, eds., *Campaign Warriors* (Brookings, 2000).

7. Max Weber, "Politics as a Vocation," in H. H. Gerth and C. W. Mills, eds., *From Max Weber* (Oxford University Press, 1946), p. 102.

8. Scammell, *Designer Politics*.

9. Joseph S. Nye Jr., Philip D. Zelikow, and David C. King, eds., *Why People Don't Trust Government* (Harvard University Press, 1997).

10. Robert D. Putnam, *Bowling Alone: The Collapse and Revival of American Community* (Simon and Schuster, 2000).

11. Margaret Weir and Marshall Ganz, "Reconnecting People and Politics," in S. B. Greenberg and T. Skocpol, eds., *The New Majority: Toward a Popular Progressive Politics* (Yale University Press, 1997).

12. Property requirements were eliminated comprehensively in 1850. See L. Sandy Maisel, *Parties and Elections in America* (Lanham, Md.: Rowman and Littlefield, 1999).

13. Martin Shefter, *Political Parties and the State* (Princeton University Press, 1994), p. 67.

14. Ibid.; Michael E. McGerr, *The Decline of Popular Politics* (Oxford University Press, 1986); and Steven P. Erie, *Rainbow's End: Irish-Americans and the Dilemmas of Urban Machine Politics, 1840–1985* (University of California Press, 1988). Keep in mind, as McGerr notes, that in the South parties effectively disenfranchised black voters and were uninterested in forging cross-class alliances. Note in addition that in 1850, 95 percent of newspapers claimed some partisan loyalty.

15. See Theda Skocpol, *Protecting Soldiers and Mothers: The Political Origins of Social Policy in the United States* (Belknap Press of Harvard University Press, 1992).

16. Maisel, *Parties and Elections in America.*

17. Shefter, *Political Parties and the State*, p. 69.

18. Perloff, *Handbook of Political Marketing.*

19. Shefter, *Political Parties and the State.*

20. Kathleen Hall Jamieson, *Packaging the Presidency: A History and Criticism of Presidential Campaign Advertising*, 2d ed. (Oxford University Press, 1992); and McGerr, *The Decline of Popular Politics.*

21. McGerr, *The Decline of Popular Politics*, p. 171.

22. See Thomas E. Cronin, *Direct Democracy: The Politics of Initiatives, Referendum, and Recall* (Harvard University Press, 1989). Throughout the 1900s, especially in the later part of the century, voluntary associations grew in size and scope. As Theda Skocpol documents, women's associations and veterans' groups successfully lobbied for the institution of welfare state programs such as widows and mothers pensions and civil war benefits. Given that women legally could not participate in party politics, lobbying through voluntary organizations such as the Women's Christian Temperance Union or the women's club movement represented an alternative way for women to influence decisionmakers. See Theda Skocpol, *Protecting Soldiers and Mothers: The Political Origins of Social Policy in the United States* (Harvard University Press, 1992). Also see Elisabeth S. Clemens, "Organizational Repertoires and Institutional Change: Women's Groups and the Transformation of American Politics, 1890–1920," in T. Skocpol and M. P. Fiorina, eds., *Civic Engagement in American Democracy* (Brookings, 1999).

23. David B. Magleby, *Direct Legislation: Voting on Ballot Propositions in the United States* (Johns Hopkins University Press, 1984).

24. Todd Donovan and Shaun Bowler, "An Overview of Direct Democracy in the American States," in S. Bowler, T. Donovan, and C. J. Tolbert, eds., *Citizens as Legislators: Direct Democracy in the United States* (Ohio State University Press, 1998). In fact, ballot initiatives and referendums are seen in greater frequency in the West than any in other part of the country.

25. Peter Schrag, "Rule by Referendum," *American Prospect*, vol. 11, no. 16 (2000), pp. 38–40.

26. See Jeffrey M. Berry, *Interest Group Society* (Boston: Little, Brown and Company, 1984).

27. Pippa Norris, *Digital Divide?* (Cambridge University Press, 2001).

28. Putnam, *Bowling Alone*.

29. Jamieson, *Packaging the Presidency*.

30. Larry Sabato, *The Rise of Political Consultants* (Basic Books, 1981).

31. Deborah Beck, Paul Taylor, Jeffrey Stanger, and Douglas Rivlin, *Issue Advocacy Advertising during the 1996 Campaign* (Philadelphia: Annenberg Public Policy Center, 1997).

32. Jean Converse, *Survey Research in the United States: Roots and Emergence, 1890–1960* (University of California Press, 1987).

33. Lawrence R. Jacobs and Robert Y. Shapiro, "The Rise of Presidential Polling," *Public Opinion Quarterly*, vol. 59, no. 2 (1995), pp. 163–95.

34. See David B. Magleby and Candice J. Nelson, *The Money Chase* (Brookings, 1990).

35. Campaign fund-raising is governed by the Federal Elections Campaign Act of 1971, which limited advertising expenditures and required the disclosure of campaign contributions and a candidate's own contributions to a campaign. But the new restrictions on media spending in primaries and general campaigns did nothing to stop the growth of campaign spending. The Watergate scandals produced the 1974 FEC amendments, which strengthened disclosure laws and instituted contribution limits on individuals and PACs, but lifted the cap on media spending by congressional candidates. See Anthony Corrado, "A History of Federal Campaign Finance Law," in A. Corrado, T. E. Mann, D. Ortiz, T. Potter, and F. Sorauf, eds., *Campaign Finance Reform: A Sourcebook* (Brookings, 1997); and Maisel, *Parties and Elections in America*. In *Buckley* v. *Valeo* (1976), the Supreme Court ruled that PACs could mount independent expenditure campaigns, as long as efforts were not coordinated with a campaign or party. It ruled against spending limits for House and Senate candidates on the grounds that they violated the First Amendment.

36. In some sense, the growth of political marketing has revitalized parties as organizations. Parties and their committees serve essential functions as fund-raisers and providers of technical expertise. See Paul S. Herrnson, "Do Parties Make a Difference? The Role of Party Organizations in Congressional Elections," *Journal of Politics*, vol. 48, no. 3 (1986), pp. 589–615.

37. Maisel, *Parties and Elections in America*.

38. Historically, the Democratic National Committee and the Republican National Committee raised the bulk of party funds. Recently, fundraising by the campaign committees for the House (Democratic Congressional Campaign Committee, National Republican Congressional Committee) and the Senate (Democratic Senatorial Campaign Committee, National Republican Senatorial Committee) has outpaced that of the national committees.

39. See Magleby and Nelson, *The Money Chase*; and Maisel, *Parties and Elections in America*.

40. David Magleby and Marianne Holt, "The Long Shadow of Soft Money and Issue Advocacy Ads," *Campaigns and Elections*, vol. 20, no. 4 (1999), p. 22.

41. Center for Responsive Politics, "2000 Presidential Race: Total Raised and Spent," (http://www.opensecrets.org/2000elect/index/AllCands.htm [December 18, 2000]).

42. Maisel, *Parties and Elections in America*.

43. Center for Responsive Politics, "2000 Presidential Race."

44. Ibid.

45. Beck and others, *Issue Advocacy Advertising during the 1996 Campaign.*

46. Magleby and Holt, "The Long Shadow of Soft Money."

47. Center for Responsive Politics, "2000 Presidential Race."

48. Leslie Wayne, "Political Consultants Thrive in the Cash-Rich New Politics," *New York Times*, October 24, 2000, p. A1.

49. Susan B. Glasser, "Hired Guns Fuel Fundraising Race," *Washington Post*, April 30, 2000, p. A01.

50. Johnson, "The Business of Political Consulting."

51. Sabato, *The Rise of Political Consultants.*

52. David B. Magleby and Kelly D. Patterson, "Campaign Consultants and Direct Democracy: Politics of Citizen Control," in Thurber and Nelson, *Campaign Warriors.*

53. Jacobs and Shapiro, "The Rise of Presidential Polling."

54. Sidney Blumenthal, *The Permanent Campaign: Inside the World of Elite Political Operatives* (Boston: Beacon Press, 1980), p. 7.

55. Sabato, *The Rise of Political Consultants.*

56. James A. Thurber, "The Study of Campaign Consultants: A Subfield in Search of a Theory," *PS: Political Science and Politics,* vol. 31, no. 2 (1998), pp. 145–49.

57. Robin Kolodny, "Electoral Partnerships: Political Consultants and Political Parties," in J. A. Thurber and C. J. Nelson, eds., *Campaign Warriors* (Brookings, 2000).

58. Kay Lehman Schlozman and John T. Tierney, *Organized Interests and American Democracy* (Harper and Row, 1986).

59. Johnson, "The Business of Political Consulting."

60. Lawrence Jacobs and Robert Y. Shapiro, *Politicians Don't Pander* (University of Chicago Press, 2000).

61. Haynes Johnson and David S. Broder, *The System: The American Way of Politics at the Breaking Point* (Boston: Little, Brown, 1997).

62. Darrell M. West and Richard Francis, "Electronic Advocacy: Interest Groups and Public Policy Making," *PS: Political Science and Politics*, vol. 24, no. 1 (1996), pp. 25–29.

63. Magleby and Patterson, "Campaign Consultants and Direct Democracy." According to Magleby and Patterson, only 11 percent of their clients are grassroots organizations. Instead ballot initiative firms usually work with special interest groups (33 percent) or political candidates with an interest in a particular outcome (28 percent).

64. In California, Tim Draper contributed $27 million; in Michigan, Dick DeVos gave $20 million. See Jodi Wilgoren, "School Vouchers: A Rose by Other Name?" *New York Times*, December 20, 2000, p. A1.

65. William C. Binning, Larry E. Esterly, and Paul A. Sracic, *Encyclopedia of American Parties, Campaigns, and Elections* (Westport, Conn.: Greenwood, 1999).

66. David McCuan, Shaun Bowler, Todd Donovan, and Ken Fernandez, "California's Political Warriors: Campaign Professionals and the Initiative Process," in Bowler, Donovan, and Tolbert, *Citizens as Legislators.*

67. John L. Moore, *Elections A to Z* (Washington: Congressional Quarterly, 1999); Magleby, *Direct Legislation.*

68. Yankelovich Partners, Inc., *Are Political Consultants Helping or Hurting Democracy?* (Washington: Center for Congressional and Presidential Studies, 1999).

69. Wayne, "Political Consultants Thrive."

70. Ownership of personal computers and the use of the Internet have increased at a rapid pace. In a national sample survey conducted by the Pew Research Center for the People and the Press (April 2000), 68 percent of respondents reported using a personal computer at work or at home. Fifty-four percent of those users reported going online, up from 14 percent in June 1995. Of course, fewer people have access at home.

71. See Pippa Norris, "Who Surfs? New Technology, Older Voters, and Virtual Democracy," in E. C. Kamarck and J. S. Nye, eds., *democracy.com? Governance in a Networked World* (Hollis, Mass.: Hollis Publishing 1999).

72. Anna Greenberg, "Reply to Pippa Norris's 'Who Surfs?'" in ibid.; see also Norris, *Digital Divide?*

73. Elizabeth Shogren, "Campaign 2000: Candidates' Efforts Clicking on the Net," *Los Angeles Times*, February 10, 2000, p. A20.

74. John Phillips, "Fast Changes to Campaign Software," *Campaigns and Elections Magazine*, vol. 20, no. 3 (1999), pp. 54–55.

75. Susan B. Glasser, "Consultants Pursue Promising Web of New Business," *Washington Post*, May 3, 2000, p. A01.

76. Derek Willis and Anne Perra, "The Future of Fundraising," *CQ Weekly*, January 1, 2000, pp. 28–30.

77. Glasser, "Consultants Pursue Promising Web of New Business."

78. Aaron Pressman, "Lessons for Campaign 2004," *The Industry Standard* (www. thestandard.com/article/display/0,1151,20131,00.hmtl [December 18, 2000]).

79. A cookie is a small text file that resides on a user's computer that allows a Web host to track the user's activity on its website. See Willis and Perra, "The Future of Fundraising."

80. Tom Hockaday and Martin Edlund, "Banner Advertising as Voter Outreach Tool," *Campaigns and Elections*, vol. 20, no. 4 (1999), pp. 13–14.

81. Chris Sullentrop, "Net Election: Hiding behind the Web," *Slate* (2000) (www. thestandard.com/news/special/display/0,2129,m16435,00.html [December 18, 2000]).

82. Like most Web ventures, political sites have yet to show a profit. See John Greenwald, "Can Dotcoms Really Make Politics Pay?" *Time*, August 14, 2000, p. 54.

83. See Glasser, "Consultants Pursue Promising Web of New Business"; and Elizabeth Wasserman, "Net Election: Old Pols Join the Online Party," *The Industry Standard*, January 20, 2000.

84. Lakshmi Chaudhry, "Voter Ed for Online Profit," *Wired* (1999) (www.wired.com/ news/pring/0,1294,326500,00.html [May 31, 2000]).

85. See Sarah Schafer, "To Politically Connected, and Profitability Collect; Ron Howard's Web Site Wants to Get People Involved—and to Sell the Results of Its Internet Polls; The Question: Will It Work?" *Washington Post*, December 13, 1999, p. F10. Dick Morris, founder of Vote.com, also hopes to sell information about public opinion collected on his site. After Alan Keyes won the Republican Party straw poll on his site, however, his data may not have a lot of credibility. It should be noted that information collected about registered users is not public opinion data as most researchers would understand it. These data are not generated from probability sampling, the foundation of survey research, but rather are straw polls of volunteer participants.

86. Piper Fogg, "Tight Squeeze in the Political Portal," *National Journal*, vol. 32, no. 43 (2000), pp. 3344–45.

87. Rebecca Airley Raney, "With the Polls Closed, Political Sites Seek a New Focus," *New York Times*, November 27, 2000, p. C4.

88. Matthew A. DeBellis, "Voter.com Raises $50 million to Campaign for Voters' Eyeballs," *Red Herring* (www.redherring.com/insider/2000/0115/vc-voter.html [July 15, 2000]).

89. Ken Yamada, "Politicos Dream of IPO," *Red Herring* (www.redherring.com/0120/news-grassroots012000.html [cited May 31, 2000]).

90. Neil Munro, "The New Wired Politics," *National Journal*, April 22, 2000, pp. 1260–63.

91. Stewart Ain, "L.I. Company in Forefront of Voting by Internet," *New York Times*, March 12, 2000, 14LI, p. 6.

92. Jodi Kantor, "Obstacles to E-Voting," *Slate* (www.slate.msn.com/netelection/entries/99-11-02_44394.asp [July 6, 2000]).

93. See www.votesite.com/about.html [July 6, 2000]).

94. To generate a statistically valid sample, everyone in the population must have a known, nonzero probability of being selected into the sample. But because not everyone has access to the Internet, there are people with a zero probability of selection. Moreover, there are systematic biases in access; most notably poorer, rural, and minority members of the population are unlikely to have wide access to the Web. Volunteer samples, moreover, are not random, and there are biases in the kinds of people who volunteer to participate in Web surveys (for example, more men than women volunteer; and volunteers are more politically interested and older than typical Web users). Even if everyone had access to the Internet, it is not clear how to generate a sampling frame. There is no equivalent of random digit dialing on the Internet or an e-mail address directory, so sampling problems will continue to plague Internet polling.

95. "Harris Interactive's Election 2000 Program Provides Comprehensive Polling to Excite@Home's New Elections Site," *Business Wire*, April 25, 2000.

96. G. Evans Witt, "Into the Pool," *American Demographics*, February 1, 2000. In the interest of full disclosure, note that the author has consulted for one of Harris Interactive's main competitors in this area, Knowledge Networks, an Internet polling firm based in Menlo Park, California.

PART III

Governing Well
When Markets Rule

10

DAVID M. HART

New Economy, Old Politics: High-Technology Industry and the Influence Game

POLITICALLY ATTENTIVE AMERICANS have surely noticed something new in the coverage of elections and policymaking: an explosion of stories about high-technology companies and issues.[1] Led by the legal travails of Microsoft, the high-tech policy agenda encompasses concerns about privacy, the effect of the Internet on China, taxation of e-commerce, and much more. Presidential candidates and congressional leaders are regularly photographed hobnobbing with computer executives at fund-raisers and media events. Suddenly, it seems, there is a whole "new politics" that parallels the so-called new economy.

The journalists are undoubtedly right that there are new players on the Washington scene whose interests derive in one way or another from the deployment of new information technologies in society. Firms such as Microsoft, Cisco, and America Online (AOL) took an interest in public policy only in the second half of the 1990s and seem to have made a big impression on elected officials and policy outcomes during that period.[2] Their involvement is an important development in American politics, with consequences that can only dimly be foreseen. The media buzz, however,

The author thanks the participants in the Visions of Governance in the 21st Century Project (particularly Graham Allison) and the members of the Harvard American Politics workshop (particularly John Gerring and Burt Johnson) for their helpful comments.

exaggerates the novelty of high-tech's presence in Washington. The attention paid to a few prominent newcomers leads readers, viewers, and surfers to overlook the many high-tech firms and associations that have established themselves in the nation's capital over the past quarter-century or more. There is a larger and longer political learning process in progress within this industry, and the late 1990s represent but the latest stage of it.

Moreover, viewed in the broadest context, the "new politics" represented by the high-tech industry is as old as the marriage of capitalism and democracy that has distinguished the United States since its founding.[3] Market economies like ours must continually generate and diffuse innovations in production and distribution to remain healthy. Efforts to innovate inevitably generate tensions that find expression in our pluralistic politics. Although the specific forms and outcomes of innovation-related political conflicts are historically contingent, the presence of a new economy and a new politics in contention with the old ones is, paradoxically, not new at all.

In this chapter, I attempt to put the political development of the contemporary high-tech industry in perspective in the ways sketched above. I provide a typology of generic processes that draw technologically innovative industries into American politics. I illustrate this typology with examples drawn from the contemporary high-tech industry. I then make a more systematic empirical reconnaissance of this industry, showing that its political development does not follow the contours that a casual reading of the press would lead one to expect. I conclude with some speculations about the political future of this industry and others like it that will surely emerge in the coming century.

Premises: Pluralism, Instrumentalism, and Bounded Rationality

Before turning to the meat of my analysis, I want to make some of its key premises explicit. These premises situate my views with respect to several major debates in the study of American politics and frame my data collection and interpretation. One premise is that political power in the United States is divided in significant ways among a variety of institutions and actors. Elected officials, bureaucrats, and interest groups of various sorts, including businesses, jostle for control of governmental authority and resources. Any emerging industry takes its place on an already crowded stage, rather than being invited to join a power elite (as some theorists of American politics would have it) or securing official representation in decisionmaking processes (as might be the case in a corporatist system). That is not to say that power is divided equally or fairly; one needs resources to participate. But there are many kinds of resources, including some that cannot be held by any business (such as the right to vote in an election or on the floor of Congress).[4]

Another premise is that influence in Washington is exercised, at least in important part, overtly. People meet, presentations and appeals are made, pressure is mobilized, contributions are given. To get their way on issues that they care about, high-tech businesses have to do the things that other interest groups do, which means that they must invest in specialized organizational capabilities. They cannot simply assume that they are so important that governmental actors will look out for their interests (as a structural power perspective would suggest) or rely entirely on their symbolic authority to overcome any resistance to their wishes (as theorists of cultural hegemony might claim). Some of these investments in politics and public policy can be observed, such as when a firm opens a Washington office or makes campaign contributions, and so can some of their immediate results, like invitations to appear before congressional committees. That is not to say that the system is perfectly transparent; much goes on behind the scenes. But such observations, I assume, can serve as the basis for making inferences about the overall process of an industry's political development.

In addition to pluralism and instrumentalism (as I would characterize my first two premises), I also take bounded rationality as a premise; it applies to all of the actors in the policy process, including high-tech firms. Attention is a scarce commodity, and the capacity to collect, process, and act on relevant information is limited. Uncertainty is common with regard to likely outcomes of policy debates and implementation, others' intentions and actions, and even one's own (or one's organization's) best interests. (Indeed, if some recent accounts of interest group politics in the United States are to be believed, uncertainty in such matters has become pervasive.)[5] Institutionalized relationships resolve uncertainty by shaping beliefs and thereby drive action.[6] Of course, change is nonetheless possible. But for change to occur, something (like a threat to a critical resource) has to get the attention of those in control, and their reactions may not lead to outcomes that correspond to their intentions.

The policy-related activities of high-tech firms are particularly subject to these constraints. Washington is usually peripheral to the main objectives of these firms; senior managers tend to worry more about customers and suppliers than about members of Congress. Indeed, if they lack a dedicated government affairs function, these managers may receive very little information about public policy at all. Moreover, they may not have the knowledge and skills to react effectively when they begin to pay attention. On top of these internal difficulties in addressing public policy issues, high-tech firms face the collective action costs that all unorganized groups face without much in the way of an institutional infrastructure that might reduce those costs.[7]

The first two premises, pluralism and instrumentalism, lead me in the next section to define two processes of political engagement that characterize innovative industries. The third, bounded rationality, helps me then to explain why these processes have played out the way they have in high-tech industry.

The Politics of "Creative Destruction"

The motivations for firms in innovative industries to get involved in electoral politics and public policymaking flow from their role in the larger process of economic growth that Joseph A. Schumpeter famously characterized as "creative destruction." The motor of the economy, in Schumpeter's view, is entrepreneurship based on innovation, particularly the development of new products and services. Entrepreneurial creativity is stimulated by the possibility of windfall profits, reaped by a fortunate few. The destruction the fortunate few wreak is on those whose livelihoods are tied to the existing ways of doing things. Henry Ford's automobiles, for instance, crippled the railroad industry; corporate empires evaporated and whole occupations virtually disappeared. Schumpeter's ideas have attained a new respectability in the past couple of decades, but their political implications have yet to be explored in the way that those of Adam Smith, Karl Marx, or John Maynard Keynes have been.[8]

In this section, I describe two sets of processes that stimulate the political development of innovative firms and industries. The first derives from entrepreneurial creativity, which is not necessarily restricted to building organizations and products, but may also extend to mobilizing public resources to secure new markets. I label these "offensive processes," because the innovating industry takes the initiative to influence public policy. The second has its roots in the destruction wrought by entrepreneurs, as the "old economy" seeks to deploy governmental authority to strike back at the "new economy." These are "defensive processes," which have been well characterized by the great American political scientist E. E. Schatt-schneider. I illustrate both sets of processes with examples from the high-tech industry, but I believe they are more general phenomena of capitalism and democracy that can and should be explored in the development of other high-tech sectors in other places and at other times.

Offensive Processes

Entrepreneurs assemble and deploy resources, especially money, knowledge, and people.[9] Although we tend to think of them spending their time per-suading venture capitalists, technical experts, and managers to work with them, they may also recruit the state to put its resources behind their efforts. If entrepreneurs are entering areas in which government has an established interest, new enterprises (as in the contemporary biotechnology-pharmaceutical industry) may be "born political." Indeed, for a few firms, such as the telecommunications start-up MCI in the 1960s, political action is an essential component of the entrepreneurial business plan.[10] The entre-preneurs who built the contemporary high-tech industry have occasionally but not systematically relied upon state-supplied or state-subsidized resources.

Public money, for instance, was a key determinant of the fate of early American high-tech entrepreneurs. From the late 1940s until well into the 1960s, U.S. government agencies were the main buyers of computers and the dominant funders of computer-related research and development (R&D). Government support was particularly critical at the cutting edge of technology, where firms honed products and services that were often incorporated later into commercial products. Not surprisingly, some of the oldest high-tech industry public policy offices in Washington, such as IBM's, began as adjuncts to or spinoffs from federal sales divisions. Keeping public money flowing was a vital task. Tax breaks can be as valu-able as direct subsidies, at least for firms with revenues or the near-term prospect of them. High-tech executives have been prominent among those who have made the case in Washington that the market provides inade-quate incentives for private R&D and investment spending and that the public ought to enhance those incentives with tax credits. Hewlett-Packard's public policy program, for example, emerged in the early 1980s in part as a response to this opportunity.

Mobilizing government assistance to secure knowledge for entrepre-neurial gain is a somewhat more subtle process than mobilizing government subsidies. The same market failure that justifies a tax subsidy for R&D, however, justifies intellectual property rights, which invest private knowledge with public protection (as Jean Camp discusses in chapter 6). Entrepreneurs typically employ lawyers to pursue and defend those rights, but occasionally technological innovations pose such a challenge to the established jurisprudence that entrepreneurs seek legislative or other policy actions to buttress their legal positions.[11] Ebay and Amazon.com, for instance, have invested in public policy capabilities with specific intellectual property objectives in mind. Another important source of knowledge for high-tech firms is academia. Publicly supported scientists can contribute ideas to such firms in a variety of ways, including through the granting of licenses to university-held intellectual property. But because the benefits of academic research funding are diffuse and take a long time to materialize, most entrepreneurs have difficulty recognizing and acting on an interest in it. Not surprisingly, the high-tech industry has until recently done relatively little to advocate for public funding of academic R&D. This reticence stemmed in part from the fact that the defense establishment has been intensely interested in computer science and related disciplines and served as a surrogate advocate for the industry. With the end of the Cold War, though, industrial interest in nondefense academic R&D has grown to the point that the issue engages high-tech executives who in an earlier era would have had little or nothing to do with Washington.

Academic R&D also produces well-trained and creative people, a third important resource for high-tech entrepreneurs. Because the U.S. university system draws talent from around the world, often subsidized by foreign governments, the American high-tech industry has been able to recruit a multinational work force rather easily. In recent years, this recruitment has been so intense that the industry has bumped up against limits on immigration of highly trained workers, and this restriction has prompted a collective political response by the industry. Immigration and, to a lesser extent, improvement of American education are now high-priority agenda items for such organizations as the Information Technology Association of America (ITAA).

Defensive Processes

Schumpeterian entrepreneurs seize opportunities, but in doing so they may pose threats to established interests. Such threats prompt a characteristic response, which was described by Schattschneider, albeit in a different context.[12] A fight is never over, Schattschneider argues, until the entire audience has been drawn in. An interest imperiled by a technological innovation, Schattschneider leads us to believe, is likely to try to expand the scope of conflict, to capture the attention and support of previously unengaged parties. What would otherwise be lost as a result of market competition may be salvaged through political appeals. Such appeals provoke a countervailing response, drawing high-tech companies into a political arms race. Several sorts of arms races can be observed in high-tech's political history.

The most obvious pit older industries against newer ones. As new technologies bite into existing businesses, those businesses, which are typically experienced in Washington politics, may fight back by seeking to impose barriers to entry or to raise their new opponents' costs. The long-running skirmish between the computer and telephone industries illustrates the point. In the 1960s and 1970s, AT&T sought to classify as much computer equipment as possible as communications equipment so that it would be subject to Federal Communications Commission oversight, an arena in which it held a substantial advantage. IBM (among others) objected vehemently, and the success of the deregulatory coalition of which IBM was a part contributed substantially to the conditions that allowed the Internet to grow so rapidly in the 1990s. More recently, Internet applications have sparked a new round of conflict over the boundaries of communications regulation, such as the debate over open access by Internet service providers to cable television and telephone networks. Indeed, the commercialization of the Internet has substantially broadened the scope of interindustry conflict in Washington. Broadcasters, for instance, have come into conflict with the high-technology sector in the debate over high-definition television. Electronic commerce threatens distributors of many types of goods; the recent effort to limit interstate wine sales over the Internet reveals the political power of one such distribution network. Some of these conflicts will undoubtedly be resolved in the marketplace (the AOL–Time Warner merger, for instance, brings together Internet and broadcasting interests), but just as certainly, others will play out on the political stage.

Creative destruction occurs both within and across industry boundaries, and so do efforts to expand the scope of conflict. In IBM's heyday, for instance, its competitors lobbied to make it hard for government agencies to buy IBM products, and they egged on the antitrust suit that the Department of Justice filed against IBM in 1969. Sun and Netscape (among others) are said to have played similar roles in the antitrust cases filed against

Microsoft in the 1990s.[13] U.S. semiconductor firms engaged the U.S. government in their struggle with Japanese competitors in the 1980s (competitors, it should be noted, which had access to important Japanese government resources that their U.S. competitors lacked, but which also had made important technological innovations that threatened U.S. firms). Ironically, the 1986 U.S.-Japan Semiconductor Trade Arrangement (STA), which granted a measure of protection to the U.S. semiconductor industry, provoked a defensive domestic reaction of its own. U.S. computer manufacturers, who faced higher prices in the STA's aftermath, established the Computer Systems Policy Project (CSPP) to counter the Semiconductor Industry Association (SIA), and CSPP lobbied to remove the most objectionable conditions when the agreement was renewed in 1991. Intra-industry conflicts like these may make it difficult for the industry to work together to fight interindustry conflicts or broader social conflicts.

Such broader social conflicts may ensue when technological change threatens economic interests, such as those of workers who might be displaced, and when noneconomic values are challenged as well. Interestingly, the high-tech industry has been relatively immune through much of its history from the most powerful opponents of business in American society, such as labor unions and environmental and consumer activists. As early as 1974, for instance, IBM CEO Frank Cary feared that a Nader-like movement would emerge around privacy concerns, but the rumblings tailed off. This immunity seems to have eroded in recent years; again, privacy provides an indicator. A number of new advocacy groups have joined the venerable American Civil Liberties Union to build public interest in and political support for privacy protection legislation. Privacy advocates are particularly well equipped to take advantage of the general lowering of the transaction costs of aggregating diffuse societal interests caused by the Internet. Hence Intel, for instance, faced a massive and nearly instantaneous backlash in 1999 when critics revealed that one of its chips made it much easier to identify and monitor individuals in cyberspace. Whether this issue or another (such as investor protection) will trigger a full-scale political arms race remains to be seen.

The issue of privacy also illustrates a fourth defensive dynamic, one in which the threatened interest is an element of the state, rather than of society. In a pluralistic system, state agencies have to mobilize support, much as private interests do. Entrepreneurial firms may undermine the established capabilities of state agencies or even their reason for being, and the agencies may fight back, as national security, intelligence, and law enforcement agencies have done in the case of encryption software. These agencies are among the most powerful in the United States, and they have provoked a more vigorous arms race response from the high-tech sector than any nonbusiness societal interest. Some firms and industry associations have attempted to mediate the dispute, with little success. Others have done their best to strike down controls that restrict exports of encryption software and to head off domestic encryption regulations. A similar snarl has pitted the high-tech industry against state and local governments over the applicability of sales taxes to e-commerce purchases.

From Typology to History: An Empirical Reconnaissance of High-Tech Politics

To this point, I have established that innovative industries in general, and the high-tech industry in particular, have been drawn into politics and policymaking for two broad sets of reasons. In the offensive mode of action, they seek to use the state to help them assemble the resources they need to be successful entrepreneurs, including money, knowledge, and people. In the defensive mode of action, they get involved in order to fend off efforts by market competitors and critics in society and government to use the state to hamstring them. This typology does not necessarily lead to predictions about what might happen in any particular case of the political development of an innovative industry. One might think, for instance, that offensive motivations would dominate the early political development of an innovative industry and that defensive processes would kick in later. However, in a period in which entrepreneurial resources are plentiful and the dominant ideology among entrepreneurs denigrates state intervention, the sequence might be reversed, particularly if the opponents of the industry were successful in their policy advocacy.

Indeed, my guess (which is all that I can offer in the absence of a larger set of case histories) is that no simple pattern can describe the political development of innovative industries. Whether entrepreneurs in any particular circumstance recognize political opportunities (as they must, in order to act in the offensive mode) or political threats (which can only trigger the defensive mode if recognized) depends on their capacities for gathering and processing policy-relevant information. These capacities, are presumed to be bounded, sometimes severely so. Although I cannot claim to have identified all the factors that determine the boundaries of rationality in high-tech politics, I can point to three important factors suggested by the literature in this area and by my empirical research to date.

One factor is the focusing event, to use the term of political scientist John Kingdon.[14] Such an event breaks through the routines and pressures of daily life that dominate the attention of corporate executives. The Department of Justice, for instance, got the attention of IBM's top brass with its antitrust lawsuit in 1969 and did the same with Microsoft in 1998; both of these events were turning points in the political histories of these firms. A second factor is leadership. AOL, for example, is based near Washington, D.C., in northern Virginia and is run by a person with a strong interest in public policy, Steve Case. AOL was therefore quick to recognize the threat posed by the Communications Decency Act in 1995 (which might have made the firm liable for content that passed over its network), even though it was still a relatively small firm at the time.[15] A third factor is policy-related organizational investment. The formation of a trade association, for instance, can lower the costs and increase the benefits of policy involvement. The Semiconductor Industry Association (SIA), for example, changed the mind-set of leading high-tech entrepreneurs in the late 1970s and facilitated their effective engagement in the trade policy debates of the 1980s.

In the rest of this section, I use these ideas to help interpret a suggestive set of time series data. These data describe the policy involvement of a universe of 120 firms that at one time or another have been included in the Fortune 1000 in a computer or information-related category. (The firms are listed in appendix 10-A.) Although this list does not encompass the entire high-tech industry and one might quibble with some of the inclusions, it provides an excellent starting point for systematically analyzing the industry.[16]

Corporate Representation in Washington

Perhaps the most commonly used indicator of interest in and capacity to influence public policy is Washington representation. Some firms open offices in Washington to manage their affairs there; others retain a Washington law or lobbying firm to do the job. Some do both. Figure 10-1 displays the number of high-tech firms found in *Washington Representatives* (*WR*), a standard reference on the subject. The 1980s edition listed seventeen high-tech firms with a public policy office and twenty-three that had hired outside counsel to represent them on policy issues (see figure 10-1). (Only 58 of the 120 firms were in business in that year.) By 1988 the num-

Figure 10-1. *Washington Representatives of High-Tech Firms*

Number of firms

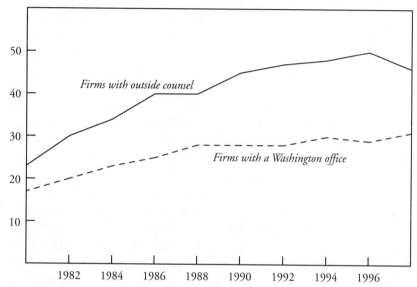

Source: *The Washington Representatives,* various years (Washington: Columbia Books).

ber of offices had reached twenty-eight, which is roughly where it stayed through 1998 (out of a total of just over 100 firms). (The total number of professional staff members in those offices seems to have followed a roughly similar trend.) The number of firms that retained outside counsel in the capital leveled off at forty between 1986 and 1988, but then rose slowly to fifty in 1996 before dropping off slightly in 1998.

This measure has its weaknesses. *WR*'s coverage of Washington is imperfect. More important, it does not capture government affairs investments made at the headquarters office, where some high-tech firms choose to locate much or all of this function. Nonetheless, the picture is worth studying. The aggregate high-tech investment in Washington appears to have leveled off after the mid-1980s, or at the very least grown considerably more slowly. However, these figures conceal a certain amount of churning. Between 1980 and 1982, for instance, although the net change in the number of Washington offices was three, six high-tech firms opened offices, and three closed them. That cycle marked the peak of turnover until the two most recent cycles. Between 1994 and 1996, five offices

opened and six closed, for a net loss of one; in the next two years, ten
opened and eight closed, for a net gain of two. Casual observers may mistake that increasing volatility for an increased presence.

To get some purchase on the motivations that led high-tech firms to
invest in a Washington office, I have gathered additional quantitative data,
conducted interviews, and collected press coverage. (The reader should be
aware, however, that these sources do not provide systematic information
on all 120 firms.) The list of high-tech firms already entrenched in
Washington in 1980, as one might expect, was dominated by defense contractors; 11 of the 17 firms with their own offices there appeared on the list
of the top 100 contractors used by the Department of Defense (DOD).[17]
This offensive motivation waned as the civilian market grew ever more
important; one might say that the end of the Cold War was an event that
focused high-tech attention away from Washington. By 1989 fewer than
half of the high-tech firms with Washington offices appeared on the DOD
list. Moreover, of the original eleven, four relied on DOD for less than
10 percent of their total sales. Among these was IBM (for which the DOD
share of sales was less than 2 percent); it opened its government programs
office in Washington in 1975 primarily for defensive reasons, such as opposition to the union-inspired Hartke-Burke bill, which would have imposed
a large additional tax on the company's foreign operations.[18]

Defensive concerns also brought Intel to Washington in September
1985, AOL in February 1995, and Microsoft in May 1995. Intel's main
objective was to bring U.S. government pressure to bear on the Japanese
chip industry, which it succeeded in doing. To "finish the job" once a managed trade regime had been imposed, the company turned to the offensive
task of winning federal funding for Sematech, an industrywide R&D con-
sortium. Its involvement in this task was facilitated by the existence of the
SIA and the historically close links among Silicon Valley firms, which made
it relatively easy for semiconductor firms to put forward a united front.
AOL's public policy office was established to fight the Communications
Decency Act (CDA), which aimed to limit Internet access to content
deemed offensive; AOL feared the CDA would slow its growth. Steve
Case's leadership seems to have been an essential element in AOL's recognition of the threat. Microsoft provides a different sort of example with
regard to the importance of leadership. From 1995, when it first opened,
until 1998, Microsoft's Washington policy office contained only two professional staff and was co-located with its federal sales group. "I'm sorry we
have to have a Washington presence," Microsoft CEO Bill Gates told the

Washington Post in 1995.[19] Not until a series of antitrust actions crested in the suit currently being contested (and Gates brought himself to testify for the first time before a congressional committee) did Microsoft expand this office and move it to a separate site. A very powerful focusing event had to occur before public policy issues got Gates's full attention.

Industry Associations

Industry associations provide another mechanism through which firms may attempt to influence the policy process. Participation in such associations represents the most significant policy-related investment of nearly all small firms and many large ones as well. Politically sophisticated large firms are less dependent upon associations and use them more strategically, in conjunction with narrower corporate and broader coalition efforts, but associations nonetheless play an essential part in their policy and political strategies.

"High-tech industry association" is inevitably a fuzzy category. I have identified about twenty permanent public policy-oriented organizations that draw corporate members from the computer hardware, software, and networking industries (see table 10-1). The number of such associations has grown steadily.[20] The number of professional staff of these associations, as listed in *WR*, has also increased, although more slowly in the 1990s than in the 1980s. They constitute about half the total number of staff working in the corporate offices described earlier.

The dates and names in table 10-1 suggest the variety of pathways into the high-tech industry and the industry's increasing complexity. The two oldest associations trace their roots to the office machine and radio industries of the 1910s and 1920s. The youngest one was formed in 1999 and included Internet giants AOL, Amazon.com, and Yahoo! In between, one sees the emergence of software, computer components, and information services as distinct interests, particularly after IBM unbundled these products (which it originally sold almost entirely in packages) in the late 1960s. The associations vary in breadth, from umbrella groups representing the entire high-tech "food chain" to one-person shops that embrace narrow slices of it.

A more detailed history of some of these organizations illustrates the forces that brought them into being. The West Coast Electronics Manufacturers Association (WEMA) was founded in 1943 for the offensive purpose of securing more defense contracts for California-based firms. The

Table 10-1. *High-Tech Industry Associations*

Original name and year established	Name changed to and year	Name changed to and year	Name changed to and year
National Association of Office Appliance Manufacturers, 1916	Business Equipment Manufacturers Association, 1960	Computer and Business Equipment Manufacturers Association (CBEMA), 1973	Information Technology Industry Council, 1994
Radio Manufacturers Association, 1924	Radio and Television Manufacturers Association, 1950	Radio, Electronics, and Television Manufacturers Association; Electronics Industry Association, 1957	
West Coast Electronics Manufacturers Association, 1943	Western Electronics Manufacturers Association (WEMA), 1959	American Electronics Association, 1978	
Association of Data Processing Services Organizations, 1960	Computer Software and Services Industry Association, 1986	Information Technology Association of America, 1991	
Information Industry Association (IIA), 1968	Software and Information Industry Association (merger of IIA and SPA), 1999		
Semiconductor Equipment and Materials Institute, 1970	Semiconductor Equipment and Materials International, 1989		
Computer Industry Association (CIA), 1972	Computer and Communications Industry Association (CCIA), 1976		

Semiconductor Industry Association, 1977

Interactive Services Association, 1981

Electronic Messaging Association (EMA), 1983

Software Publishers Association (SPA), 1984

Business Software Association, 1988

Computer Systems Policy Project, 1989

Association of Interactive Media, 1993

Interactive Digital Software Association, 1994

Electronic Commerce Association, 1998

TechNet, 1998

Netcoalition.com, 1999

Internet Alliance, 1998

EMA—The E-Business Forum, 1999

Software and Information Industry Association (merger of SPA and IIA), 1999

Business Software Alliance, 1990

Source: Association documents and personal communications.

western tail of the industry eventually wagged the eastern dog, and WEMA became the American Electronics Association. IBM's opponents banded together to form the Computer Industry Association (CIA) in 1972, which helped to broaden the scope of conflict within the high-tech industry by supporting antitrust litigation. Adding "Communications" to its name in 1976, the new CCIA sided with IBM in the industry's defensive conflict with AT&T. Both the antitrust litigation and the so-called "Bell bill" served as focusing events for the CCIA's founders and members. (Interestingly, the CCIA's historical focus on antitrust issues has left enough of a legacy that it is a prominent public opponent of Microsoft today.) The CCIA's 1970s antagonist, the Computer and Business Equipment Manufacturers Association (CBEMA), was widely perceived as an IBM front group and ultimately changed its name in 1994 to reposition itself in the eyes of potential members and interlocutors in government.

TechNet, which has received an inordinate amount of media coverage, is the most prominent new entrant to this organizational field. In this case, the focusing event was a 1996 California state ballot initiative (Proposition 211) that would have made it easier for high-tech companies to be sued by disgruntled investors. John Doerr, a venture capitalist with Kleiner Perkins Caufield and Byers, who later forged close links with Vice President Al Gore, is usually given the lion's share of the credit for leading this effort. The hastily assembled group Taxpayers against Frivolous Lawsuits handily defeated Proposition 211, raising and spending some $35 million to do so. The organizational infrastructure constructed during the fight against Prop 211 became the basis for TechNet, which was founded in 1997 at the instigation of Doerr and his Republican colleague Floyd Kvamme. Although its mission and structure are evolving, TechNet to date has served mainly as a sponsor of fund-raising visits by prominent politicians, at which high-tech CEOs could "educate" their visitors about the industry while making individual contributions to their campaigns.

Campaign Contributions

The TechNet story provides an entry point for consideration of the relationship of the high-tech industry to political parties and candidates. The main quantitative indicators that I rely on are campaign contributions. Ideally, one would like to know about in-kind support (including site visits), endorsements, advisory relationships, and even the backgrounds of candidates themselves, but these are difficult data to assemble. Like the

Figure 10-2. *High-Tech PAC Contributions to Congressional Candidates,*
1978–98

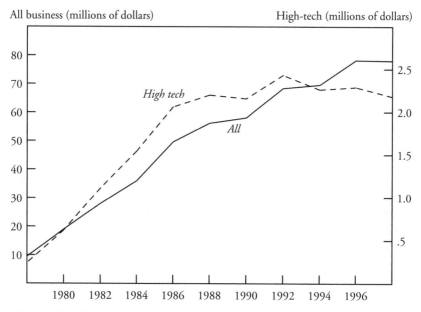

Source: Federal Election Commission.

other indicators, campaign contribution figures should be seen as noisy
measures of corporate interest and effort.

Figure 10-2 shows the total contributions to congressional candidates
made by political action committees (PACs) sponsored by high-tech firms.
These contributions rose from about a quarter-million dollars in the
1977–78 election cycle to about $2.2 million in 1987–88 and stayed
around that level for the following decade. (Only a quarter to a third of the
firms in my sample maintain PACs, a fraction that has risen only slightly
over time.) Surprisingly, given the overall growth in campaign contributions and the dramatic growth of high-tech firms' resources, the high-tech
line in figure 10-2 resembles figure 10-1, leveling off over a decade ago.

Figure 10-3 traces "soft money" contributions made by high-tech firms
to the major political parties.[21] Adding these contributions (which have
only been disclosed in recent cycles) to those of high-tech PACs brings us
closer to the popular notion of a burst of high-tech interest in Washington.
From about $350,000 in 1991–92, the high-tech soft money total rose to

Figure 10-3. *Soft Money Campaign Contributions by Business, 1992–98*

All business (millions of dollars)   High-tech (millions of dollars)

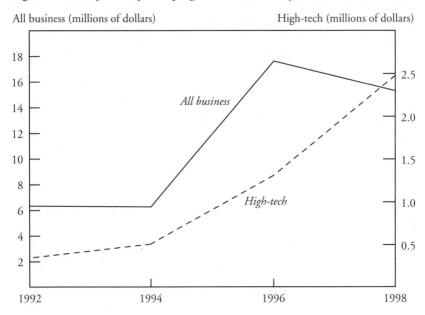

Source: Author's calculation based on Center for Responsive Politics database (www. opensecrets.org).

surpass the PAC total in the 1997–98 cycle. Nonetheless, these figures taken together still seem modest in comparison with those from other industries, reflecting the overall growth of the campaign finance system but not the rapid growth of the high-tech industry relative to the rest of the economy.

High-tech PAC and soft money contributions, like the contributions of most firms, tend to go to Republicans and incumbents. Although the Democrats narrowed the gap between 1986 and 1994, the Republican takeover of Congress in 1994 boosted the GOP share of high-tech contributions back over 70 percent. Nearly 90 percent of high-tech PAC contributions accrued to incumbents in 1998, a figure that has increased steadily since 1980, when support provided to challengers and contestants for open seats exceeded that given to incumbents. High-tech business as a whole seems to have learned what the rest of American business has learned as the modern campaign finance system has matured over the past quarter-century: contributions mainly provide access to like-minded incumbents. The old politics trumps anything new on this dimension of political "participation." High tech's relatively small role in the system to date may reflect a distaste for or lack of interest in electoral politics. It may also reflect high tech's cultural cachet; the industry does not necessarily need to contribute as much as other industries to get access to influential policymakers.

The aggregate picture belies "the conventional wisdom that Silicon Valley is Democratic" (as *Fortune* put it in 1998).[22] The perception that the high-tech industry is Democratic goes back to Tom Watson Sr., the founder of IBM (who was a supporter of Franklin D. Roosevelt) and his namesake and successor, Tom Jr. (who was close to John F. Kennedy). (Dick Watson, Tom Watson Jr.'s brother and a high-ranking IBM executive in his own right, however, was a prominent Republican.) The Watsons' imprint on the firm demonstrates the importance of leadership in this context. Larry Ellison, the CEO of Oracle and the chief challenger to Bill Gates for the title of world's richest person, also illustrates this phenomenon. It may be that Oracle's large soft money contributions to the Democratic Party are a product of Ellison's fierce personal competition with Gates, whose own firm increased its contributions to the GOP between 1996 and 2000.[23]

The Democrats have made a concerted bid for high-tech support since the mid-1980s, when some Democratic members of Congress and presidential candidates strongly backed "competitiveness" policies (particularly those aimed at Japanese competitors) that were rejected by the Reagan administration. Hewlett-Packard CEO John Young, for instance, led the formation of the Council on Competitiveness in 1986 to push this agenda. Young's activism led candidate Bill Clinton to seek his support (and that of other high-tech CEOs) in 1992, while then President George Bush's campaign ignored the high-tech industry. President Clinton's 1995 veto of the federal equivalent of "frivolous lawsuits" legislation angered many of his high-tech backers, opening the door for the administration's opponents to make inroads into the high-tech community. Thus, in the 2000 campaign, George W. Bush (and other candidates) paid close attention to high-tech issues, companies, and people. The Republican members of TechNet, for instance, worked hard to counter the perception that the high-tech sector was in Al Gore's pocket; as early as April 1999, they placed an advertisement in the *San Jose Mercury News* urging George W. Bush to run for the presidency.[24]

Figure 10-4. *Congressional Testimony by Executives of High-Tech Firms, 1969–98*

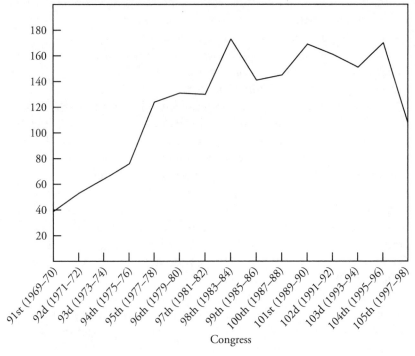

Number of executives providing testimony

Congress

Source: Congressional Information Service.

Congressional Testimony

Congressional testimony is best seen as an intermediate output of investment in corporate public policy capacity. In other words, an invitation to testify is the result of a firm's taking the effort to make its interest in a policy issue known, but the invitation does not necessarily mean that its policy objectives have been achieved.[25] Figure 10-4 shows the number of appearances before congressional committees by witnesses from the high-tech sector over the past thirty years, 1,861 in all. In the 91st Congress (1969–70), for instance, about forty witnesses from the high-tech sector (much of which, of course, did not yet exist) gave congressional testimony. By the 98th Congress (1983–84), the total had risen to a peak of

173, and it stayed near that figure through the 104th Congress (1995–96), before dropping in the most recent sessions for which complete data are available.[26]

Figure 10-4 provides only a very rough measure of the success of high-tech firms in getting their voices heard in Washington. These appearances relate exclusively to legislative matters, depend on the initiative of members of Congress (and of firms), and are subject to the whims of personality and timing. Nonetheless, like the other figures, they suggest that the high-tech presence in Washington grew steadily in the 1970s, leveled off in the 1980s, and stayed stable through 1998. High-tech firms as a group were not strangers to politics; indeed, they seem to have matured politically some time ago, or at least reached a sort of equilibrium, especially after the high-tech trade conflict with Japan.

In order to get an idea of the content of these appearances, I drew a random sample of one hundred of them. Combining what I know about the firm represented, the timing of the hearing, and its title, I classify (again, in a very rough fashion) the thirty-eight appearances in my sample from the 1990s as offensive, defensive, or other (see list). Offensive issues, such as appropriations and intellectual property, account for just over half of the appearances, while defensive issues, like export controls and high-definition television, make up a fifth of the sample. Another quarter relate to general business issues, including health care reform. The data are not displayed here, but the full 100 appearances suggest that the offensive share has risen slightly over time. Clearly, though, one should not make too much of this trend, given the weaknesses of the underlying classification process.

100 Randomly Selected High-Tech Congressional Testimonies in the 1990s

Topic	Year
Offensive	
Increasing Disclosure to Benefit Investors	1999
National Summit on High Technology: Day Three—Advance, Part III	1999
Year 2000 (Y2K) Computer Problem:	
Are Small Businesses Ready for the Turn of the Century?	1998
Technology and Education: Working Together for the Future	1998
Simplifying and Streamlining the Federal Procurement Process	1995
Heading on Education Standards	1995

(continued on next page)

100 Randomly Selected High-Tech Congressional Testimonies in the 1990s (Continued)

Topic	Year
Space Shuttle Program in Transition: Keeping Safety Paramount	1995
VA/HUD/Independent Agencies Appropriations, FY96, Part 2	1995
Educational Technology in the Twenty-First Century	1995
Trade Agreements Resulting from the Uruguay Round of Multilateral Trade Negotiations	1994
Health Care Reform and Possible Effects on Innovative Therapies: Cancer as a Case Study	1994
Copyright Reform Act of 1993	1993
Technology for Education Act of 1993	1993
National Communications Infrastructure	1993
Information Technology and Government Efficiency	1993
Telecommunications Network Security	1993
Land Remote Sensing Policy Act of 1992	1992
Biotechnology and Technology Transfer	1991
Earth Observing System Engineering Review	1991
VA/HUD/Independent Agencies Appropriations for 1992, Part 6	1991
Defensive	
U.S. Trade Policy	1996
U.S.-China Trade Relations and Renewal of China's Most-Favored-Nation Status	1995
International Standards and U.S. Exports: The Key to Competitiveness or Barriers to Trade	1994
High-Definition Television	1993
Need to Reform Export Controls	1993
Export Control Reform in High Technology	1993
Comprehensive Occupational Safety and Health Reform Act, Vol. 1	1991
Super 301: Effectiveness in Opening Foreign Markets	1990
Other	
Assessing Health Care Quality	1998
Hearing on Health Care Reform	1995
Employment Eligibility Verification System	1994
Malcolm Baldrige Quality Award: Has It Made a Difference?	1993
NAFTA and Related Side Agreements	1993
Export-Import Bank Charter Renewal	1992
Health Insurance Options: Health Insurance Costs of Large Corporations	1991
Fair Credit Reporting Act	1991
Certain Pension Access and Simplification Issues	1991
Health Insurance Options: Reform of Private Health Insurance	1991

New Economy + Old Politics = New Policies?

The empirical reconnaissance of the preceding section suggests that there are no offensive and defensive phases in the politics of creative destruction, but rather that the two intersect and intermingle. Entrepreneurial policy offensives, as one might have expected, figured prominently in the early political history of the high-tech industry, but they have not disappeared as it has matured. If high-tech pressure for public money has abated somewhat in recent years, the industry's demands for a government role in the provision of knowledge and people have grown somewhat stronger. Defensive conflicts naturally came to the fore later in its development, since only the most far-sighted opponents recognized the high-tech industry (or particular firms in it) as threats before the danger actually materialized. These conflicts have been sporadic to date, and I suspect that the most contested phases of high-tech's political development still lie in front of it. As information technology transforms more and more production processes and experiences of daily life, it seems likely that more and more aggrieved parties will appeal to the government for protection.

The political mobilization of the high-tech industry, whether for offensive or defensive purposes, does not occur automatically; someone in the industry has to recognize an opportunity or threat and develop the capabilities to act on it. Focusing events play an important role in this process. These events were generally threatening, including the "Bell bill" of 1976, the Japanese semiconductor "invasion" of the late 1970s, the Communications Decency Act of 1994, and Proposition 211 in 1996, all bookended by the IBM and Microsoft antitrust suits of 1969 and 1998. Some firms and segments of the industry perceived the importance of policy-related events and trends more quickly than others. The qualities of leadership seem to be important determinants in this regard. The now well-worn contrast between AOL's Steve Case and Microsoft's Bill Gates provides the clearest example of this factor. Organizational factors also shape the pattern of development. For all its vaunted distance from Washington, for instance, Silicon Valley proved quick to perceive threats and mobilize to counter them, whether in the heyday of Japanese competition or in the battle against Prop 211. A key reason is that the existing networks of relationships in the Valley allowed firms there to coordinate expectations and activities at relatively low cost. The personal computer manufacturing industry, by contrast, which was spread more widely across the country and lacked such dense networks, was relatively slow to find its voice.

My primary research focuses on understanding and explaining the high-tech industry's interest in and efforts to influence Washington. Whether these efforts have been the key causes of changes in policy outcomes is a different and more difficult question to answer. On most issues, there are so many forces at play in so many policymaking venues that attributing causal significance to any one factor is a tricky business. A convincing analysis would need to get beyond the instant assignment of credit and blame that passes for news; it would also need to overcome the bias of sources anxious to take credit for any outcome that redounds to their benefit and to avoid discussion of those that do not. Not having made such a study, I can only offer impressions that require further research to be substantiated.

I believe that spokespeople for the industry are correct in asserting that it has won more of the fights it has engaged in than it has lost (putting aside, of course, intra-industry fights). On relatively narrow issues, such as semiconductor trade policy in the mid-1980s and shareholder suits in the mid-1990s, its influence has been substantial. It should be noted, though, that few of these victories have been entirely straightforward. Semiconductor users later mobilized against the trade policy, for instance. Similarly, even though the high-tech industry handily defeated Prop 211 governing shareholder suits in California, it was stunned by the president's veto of favorable legislation at the federal level the year before. On broader issues, such as the deregulation of the telephone industry in the late 1970s, the passage of R&D tax credits in the early 1980s, and the major trade bills of the 1990s (culminating in the establishment of permanent normal trade relations with China), the industry has usually been on the winning side as well, although whether it was the difference-maker in any of these massive battles is debatable.

The win-loss record is not unblemished. On encryption and export controls, for example, the industry's opponents have given ground grudgingly and have mounted occasional counterattacks. The gradual loosening of restrictions over time may have more to do with the relentless pace of technological innovation at home and abroad than with the campaign for policy change mounted by high tech. One observes a similar tug and pull on such issues as R&D tax credits, which have lapsed a number of times over the past two decades, and on taxation of e-commerce by states and localities, which remains unresolved. Even the industry's most celebrated victory of the 106th Congress, the expansion of the number of visas to be granted to highly skilled workers, probably owed as much to the easing of opposition from minority and labor groups benefiting from the strong labor market as it did to the industry's efforts.

As my theme of old politics suggests, these victories have generally advanced a vision of the industry's interest that is narrowly conceived, much like that of any other industry. The leaders of the high-tech sector have usually been either unable or unwilling to take longer-term, broader perspective, or simply uninterested in doing so. Considering its reliance on knowledge and trained people, for instance, the high-tech industry (with important exceptions) has not been particularly active on issues related to research and education. There is an unfortunate, if understandable, tendency to opt for the quick fix in advancing policies related to knowledge and people. However, it should be said that the industry's pursuit of narrow self-interest has paid substantial dividends, most notably in the development of a booming market, which now provides a third or more of aggregate economic growth. Its aggressive support for free trade in the 1990s, for example, was an important factor enabling growth.

As the boom subsides, the industry is likely to face substantial new political challenges. Any perception that it is somehow "new" and therefore speaks in the common interest is likely to be a passing phenomenon. Indeed, if the economy goes into a stock market–led tailspin, the backlash could be rapid and intense. In pursuing self-interest narrowly conceived, some high-tech firms are pushing the boundaries of public values. Perhaps, for instance, Doubleclick has awakened the sleeping giant of public concern about privacy through its now-abandoned plan to merge data about consumers gathered offline with that gathered online. The next phase of high-tech's political development, like phases in the development of other cutting-edge industries that have gone before it, from railroads to automobiles to chemicals, may well be troubled.

The politics of creative destruction, like the process of technological innovation itself, is messy, not linear. As long as entrepreneurs are creatively destroying anything that stands between them and a fortune, democracy is likely to force them to learn something about politics. The ultimate balance, so to speak, between creativity and destruction in any particular case is a matter of historical contingency, depending on imperfect and idiosyncratic decisionmakers. As markets grow bigger and, one hopes, better, the politics of creative destruction will loom larger on the policymaking landscape.

Epilogue: The 2000 Campaign and the Transition

Media interest in the role of the high-technology sector in American politics did not abate during the 2000 campaign. And, at first glance, the available figures for the sector's "participation" suggest that this attention was warranted. High-tech PAC contributions jumped by 40 percent between 1997–98 and 1999–2000, and soft money contributions rose about 55 percent. The growth in the industry's PAC contributions stands in stark contrast to the surprising 18 percent decline in such contributions from all businesses. On the other hand, soft money contributions from all businesses grew by 50 percent, and high tech was only slightly ahead of this pace. Given the extraordinary growth in the sector's revenue and market capitalization during 1999–2000 (though much of the latter was given up during the campaign itself) and the rising importance of soft money relative to PACs in the campaign finance system, a strong case can be made that the high-tech sector's political development still lags well behind its economic development.[27]

Despite this apparent lag (or perhaps because of it), the high-technology industry has been courted intensely by the George W. Bush administration. On January 4, 2001, the president-elect met exclusively with a group of seventeen high-tech CEOs, a lobbying opportunity offered to no other economic interest. According to the *Wall Street Journal*, Mr. Bush "endorsed the high-tech industry's political agenda," while its representatives, in turn, endorsed the president-elect's agenda, including his tax cut proposal. The president-elect was also said to be pondering a White House position to oversee policy development on issues of interest to the high-tech industry, even as the new administration's allies called upon the industry to defend the nomination of former Missouri senator John Ashcroft for attorney general.[28]

It is, of course, too soon to tell whether these signals are of long-term significance. However, the development of a widespread perception that the high-tech industry is a core constituency of the new administration would have profound consequences for the industry's political development. If such a perception took hold, Democrats might move to represent the industry's opponents more vehemently than in the past, stimulating a more aggressive arms race response. Republicans might call upon the industry to range far beyond the policy territory with which it has been comfortable in the past. A firm coalition between the purported libertarians of the high-tech industry and the cultural conservatives who anchor the

Republican right wing would be an impressive political achievement for the new Bush administration.

Notes

1. In this chapter I generally use the terms "high technology" and "high-tech" industry to mean computer hardware, software, and networking. This usage is colloquial and admittedly imprecise. Below, I supply a more precise definition, which was used to assemble statistics. Economists often use "high technology" to mean a firm or industry with a high ratio of R&D spending to sales. This definition lumps together industries with very different policy interests and political histories, such as pharmaceuticals, aircraft, and "high technology" as I have defined it. Others include media and communication firms along with my "high-technology" firms under the rubric "information industries." Again, such a definition lumps together firms and sectors with very different historical relationships to government. For purposes of political analysis, I believe these industries are most usefully treated separately. Occasionally in this chapter I use the term "innovative industry" to denote "high technology" in a more generic sense—that is, an industry offering important technological innovations at any time in history.

2. Bear in mind that these firms, particularly AOL (founded in 1989) and Cisco (founded in 1984), were relatively small before the second half of the 1990s. Microsoft was founded in 1975, but even it remained in the shadow of IBM until the early 1990s.

3. The reader should note here that I am opining about only one of many hypotheses that might link a "new politics" to the "new economy." This chapter does not touch on, for instance, the rise of mass shareholding, the emergence of a putatively libertarian high-technology work force, or new modes of political communication.

4. Virginia Gray and David Lowery, "A Neopluralist Perspective on Research on Organized Interests," paper presented to the Midwestern Political Science Association Annual Meeting, Chicago, April 27, 2000.

5. John P. Heinz and others, *The Hollow Core: Private Interests in National Policy Making* (Harvard University Press, 1993); Rogan Kersh, "Washington Lobbyists as (Semi)-Autonomous Actors," paper presented to the Midwestern Political Science Association Annual Meeting, Chicago, April 27, 2000.

6. Cathie Jo Martin, "Nature or Nurture? Sources of Firm Preferences for National Health Reform," *American Political Science Review*, vol. 89, no. 4 (1995), pp. 898–913; Douglas A. Schuler, "Corporate Political Action: Rethinking the Economic and Organizational Influences," *Business and Politics*, vol. 1, no. 1 (1999), pp. 83–97.

7. Mancur Olson, *The Logic of Collective Action* (Harvard University Press, 1965).

8. Joseph A. Schumpeter himself attempted to work through some of the issues in *Capitalism, Socialism, and Democracy* (Harper and Bros., 1942) but (viewed with more than a half-century's hindsight) got it all wrong.

9. Nicolai J. Foss, ed., *Resources, Firms, and Strategies* (Oxford University Press, 1997).

10. David B. Yoffie and Sigrid Bergenstein, "Creating Political Advantage: The Rise of the Corporate Political Entrepreneur," *California Management Review*, vol. 28, no. 1 (1985), pp. 124–39.

11. I distinguish here between legal and policy processes, although admittedly the boundaries are fuzzy.

12. E. E. Schattschneider, *The Semi-Sovereign People* (Holt, Rinehart and Winston, 1960).

13. John Heilemann, "The Truth, the Whole Truth, and Nothing but the Truth," *Wired*, November 2000, pp. 261–311.

14. John W. Kingdon, *Agendas, Alternatives, and Public Policy*, 2d ed. (HarperCollins, 1995), p. 94.

15. "I've met a lot of the Silicon Valley boys," U.S. Representative Billy Tauzin stated in 1999. "They're fascinating people, but they are not Washington-savvy. Case is ahead of them." Neil Munro, "Building a Case," *National Journal*, vol. 31, no. 31 (1999), p. 2218.

16. Of course, diversification, technological innovation, mergers, and acquisitions limit the validity of any classification scheme of this type, particularly over a long stretch of time. A particular weakness of this selection method is that it excludes firms that never became large. (In the late 1990s, a firm needed approximately $1 billion in sales to make the Fortune 1000.) However, this threshold does not seem too high; firm size has such a strong effect on Washington involvement that casting a broader net would be unlikely to capture many additional corporate high-tech policy players. Moreover, the data include firms that were small for part of the period but grew rapidly enough to make the Fortune 1000 later. These data cannot be directly compared to those generated by the Center for Responsive Politics, which tracks campaign contributions and lobbying expenditures by industry. Its list of firms in the computer industry is broader than the one I use here. In addition, their figures for total contributions by firm include contributions by employees; mine do not.

17. In fact, the only firm in the high-tech group that appeared on the DOD list that did not have a Washington office in 1980 was ITT, which was involved in a major corruption scandal during the Nixon administration.

18. Although the antitrust suits brought by the Department of Justice and IBM's competitors in the late 1960s and early 1970s focused the attention of the firm's senior management on Washington, it decided that the legal battle could only be won in court. A rigid separation was therefore imposed between IBM's Washington office and the legal staff contesting these cases.

19. "Mind behind the Microsoft Miracle; Gates Reflects on the Future of Software, Money and the World of Washington," *Washington Post*, December 3, 1995, p. H1.

20. My universe of high-tech associations has not been compiled systematically; this research is in progress. I have attempted to exclude temporary *ad hoc* coalitions (although many of these survive for a long time) and think-tanks or public policy research organizations (even though many of these receive support from high-tech corporations and engage in advocacy).

21. My definition of "soft money" includes contributions to either major party's national committee, senatorial campaign committee, or congressional campaign committee. These contributions can be made directly from corporate funds; in contrast, PACs must raise the money that they contribute from individual managers and shareholders. Soft money made its first appearance in the 1991–92 election cycle, whereas PACs were first established widely by firms in 1975–76.

22. Jeffrey H. Birnbaum, "Yeah, Silicon Valley Is Full of Geniuses, They Have a Lot to Learn about Politics," *Fortune*, September 7, 1998, p. 110.

23. See also John Markoff and Matt Richtel, "Oracle Hired a Detective Agency to Investigate Microsoft's Allies," *New York Times*, June 28, 2000, p. A1; Ted Bridis, Glenn Simpson, and Mylene Mangalindan, "Search Engine: How Piles of Trash Became Latest Focus in Bitter Software Feud," *Wall Street Journal*, June 29, 2000, p. A1.

24. Ceci Connelly, "High-Tech Outreach to Bush," *Washington Post*, April 4, 1999, p. A5.

25. Other intermediate outputs might include meetings with legislators and attention paid by staff to written communication, but information about these is difficult to gather.

26. One problem with these data is that the *Fortune* list goes back only to 1979; firms that were important in the computer industry but whose fortunes had fallen dramatically by the time *Fortune* compiled its first 500 are not included. Thus the numbers for the 1970s may be understated.

27. I am using the same definition of the high-tech industry in the epilogue that I used in the body of the text. These figures do not represent the final accounting for the cycle, but only disclosures through October 1, 2000. One important weakness is that new entrants to the Fortune 1000 list during the 1999–2000 cycle have not been added because the list had not been published when this chapter was completed. The figures for all business are drawn from the Center for Responsive Politics website (http://www.opensecrets.org/pubs/bigpicture2000/bli/index.ihtml) (1997–98) and (http://www.opensecrets.org/2000elect/storysofar/blio.asp) (1999–2000). These figures are published in CRP's biannual report, *The Big Picture*. This source differs from that used for figures 10-2 and 10-3. The conclusion drawn in the text is necessarily tentative, because the campaign finance indicators are only partially complete for the most recent cycle and the other indicators have not yet been compiled.

28. Jim VandeHei, "Bush Backs Agenda of Tech Executives, Reassures Investors," *Wall Street Journal*, January 5, 2001, p. A12; Lisa Bowman, "Tech Lobby Supports Bush's Pick for Top Cop," CNET news.com, January 4, 2001 (www.news.cnet.com/news/0-1005-201-4376193-0.htm). Ten of the seventeen at the meeting with the president-elect were CEOs of companies in my data set.

Appendix 10A. Companies in Data Set

1. 3COM Corp.
2. A. C. Nielsen Corp.
3. ADC Telecommunications
4. Advanced Micro Devices
5. Affiliated Computer Services
6. Amdahl
7. America Online Inc.
8. AMP Inc.
9. Analog Devices
10. Apollo Computers
11. Apple Computer Inc.
12. Applied Materials Inc.
13. Ascend Communications Inc.
14. AST Research
15. Atari
16. Atmel Corp.
17. Automatic Data Processing
18. Bay Networks Inc.
19. BDM International
20. Bell and Howell
21. Cabletron Systems
22. Cadence Design Systems Inc.

23. Ceridian Corp.
24. CHS Electronics Inc.
25. Cirrus Logic Inc.
26. Cisco Systems Inc.
27. Cognizant Tech Solutions
28. Comdisco Inc.
29. Compaq Computer
30. Computer Associates
    International Inc.
31. Computer Sciences Corp.
32. Control Data Corp.
33. Cooper Industries Inc.
34. Cray Research Inc.
35. Data General Corp.
36. Datapoint Corp.
37. Dell Computer Corp.
38. Digital Equipment Corp.
39. DR Holdings
40. DSC Communications Corp.
41. Dun and Bradstreet Corp.
42. E-Systems
43. Eaton Corp.
44. Electronic Data Systems
    Corp.
45. EMC Corp.
46. Equifax Inc.
47. First Data Corp.
48. First Financial Management
49. Fiserv Inc.
50. Future Now
51. Galileo International Inc.
52. Gateway 2000 Inc.
53. General Instrument Corp.
54. General Signal Corp.
55. Gould Inc.
56. Harris Corp.
57. HBO and Co.
58. Hewlett-Packard Co.
59. Hubbell Inc.
60. Imation Corp.
61. IMS Health Inc.
62. Intel Corp.
63. Intergraph Corp.
64. International Business
    Machines Corp.
65. Iomega Corp.
66. ITT
67. Jabil Circuit Inc.
68. Lexmark International
    Group Inc.
69. Lotus Development
70. LSI Logic Corp.
71. Lucent Technologies Inc.
72. Magnetek Inc.
73. Maxtor Corp.
74. Memorex Telex
75. Micro Warehouse Inc.
76. Micron Technology Inc.
77. Microsoft Corp.
78. Miniscribe
79. Molex Inc.
80. Motorola Inc.
81. National Semiconductor
    Corp.
82. NCR Corp.
83. Novell Inc.
84. Oak Industries Inc.
85. Oracle Corp.
86. Peoplesoft Inc.
87. Pitney Bowes Inc.
88. Qualcomm Inc.
89. Quantum Corp.
90. Raychem Corp.
91. Read-Rite Corp.
92. Rockwell International Corp.
93. Sanders Associates

94. SCI Systems Inc.
95. Science Applications
    International
96. Scientific-Atlanta Inc.
97. Seagate Technology
98. Sensormatic Electronics
99. Silicon Graphics Inc.
100. Solectron Corp.
101. Sperry
102. Storage Technology Corp.
103. Sun Microsystems Inc.
104. Sungard Data Systems Inc.
105. Sybase Inc.
106. Tandem Computers

107. Telex
108. Tellabs Inc.
109. Texas Instruments Inc.
110. Thomas and Betts Corp.
111. UCAR International Inc.
112. Unisys Corp.
113. US Robotics
114. Varian Associates Inc.
115. Vishay Intertechnology
116. Wang Labs Inc.
117. Western Digital Corp.
118. Xerox Corp.
119. Xidex
120. Zenith Electronics Corp.

11

VIKTOR MAYER-SCHÖNBERGER

Information Law amid Bigger, Better Markets

THE IMMINENT ADVENT of the information society was predicted for two decades. At the beginning of the millennium it has finally arrived. Based on global digital and convergent information and communication networks, and epitomized by the Internet, the information society is fueled by a rapidly growing "information economy." Lawyers, economists, and policy experts alike ask how this "new economy" may affect the governance of market transactions. In this chapter I identify three such effects, analyze the resulting challenges for the governance system, and suggest possible responses.

Markets, Trust, and Law

When market participants contract with each other, each needs to trust that the other will fulfill his or her contractual obligation. Thus every mar-

I would like to thank Kate Foster and Gernot Brodnig, as well as my faculty colleagues Jack Donahue, Dorothy Zinberg, Jean Camp, Jerry Grossman, Richard Zeckhauser, David Lazer, John Gage, and Akash Deep, for their valuable comments on earlier drafts of this chapter.

ket transaction entails some risk that the other side may not perform. Market actors have many different means to establish trust, from frequent personal interactions to reliance on third-party rating systems. The online auction site eBay.com, for example, permits auction participants to rate the reliability and trustworthiness of the other parties in the auction. Over time, reliable buyers and sellers establish a strong positive rating, on which potential business partners rely.[1] They may also just find an appropriate substitute to trust in. This can be another human being, like a guarantor, or an institution that enforces societal contracts and resolves conflicts. The latter we usually call the law.[2]

The law permits buyers and sellers to contract without having to establish complete trust in each other's willingness to execute. Instead they rely on the law and its enforcement power to, if necessary, coerce the other side to perform (or at least to pay the damages caused by its nonperformance).

This system works well as long as both parties are members of the same society and hence subject to the same legal framework. However, if the contract's provisions cross jurisdictional borders, multiple and possibly contradictory legal rules may apply. To overcome this difficulty meta-rules have been created.[3] They determine which jurisdiction and thus which set of rules applies to a given case. Similar meta-rules exist for deciding the correct legal venue in which to bring the case and enforce a judgment.

Today nobody assumes that an American super-tanker registered in Liberia and transporting oil from Saudi Arabia to a refinery in the Netherlands operates in a lawless vacuum. It may take some thinking and research to resolve all the legal issues arising from such traditional cross-jurisdictional transactions, but with the involvement of capable international jurists such boundary-crossing poses no fundamental legal problems.

In principle, then, the "legal system" is well prepared for the typical transaction in the information economy: a transaction between parties who have never met, likely live in different jurisdictions, and rely on the law to minimize their transactional risks. And at least in this respect the governance of the rapidly increasing information markets should pose no fundamental challenge.

The Transactional Challenge

Unfortunately, however, meta-rules were designed for cross-border transactions in the "old economy." In the information economy the volume of cross-jurisdictional transactions increases dramatically; at the same time the average value of each such transactions is shrinking. For example, during an average week in November 2000 more than 4.5 million individual e-commerce transactions took place with a total value of $584 million.[4] The average value of each transaction was slightly more than $100. Similarly, online book retailer Amazon.com announced that it had received more than 31 million individual orders in the eight-week period between November 2 and December 23, 2000, and that it had fulfilled more than 99 percent of them by December 25, 2000.[5]

These changes in transaction quantity and value offset the existing economic equation of solving cross-jurisdictional issues. Having lawyers on both sides refine draft after draft of a contract to cover all possible contingencies may be economical for a transaction involving a super-tanker full of crude oil, but it is certainly not for an order of three paperback books from Amazon.com.

Forty years ago, Nobel laureate Ronald Coase pointed out the importance of transaction costs.[6] In general the legal system ensures a smooth resolution of possible conflicts and thus lowers transaction costs. But if using the legal system turns out to be more costly than what the parties involved may gain from it, they will either act regardless of any rules (as has been exemplified by the Napster phenomenon) or look for other methods of enforcement and conflict resolution. If this happens on a large scale the primacy of the legal system as the conflict resolution system of choice will be challenged. Law firms will lose clients and citizens their trust in the law. Ultimately the legal system may be replaced at least partially by something else, perhaps an international for-profit mediation regime, to cite one possibility. Indeed one could argue that global credit card companies already provide substantial parts of such a global regime.[7] They not only process commercial transactions and transfer funds, but effectively insure their customers against the risk of fraud and misuse. They also guarantee enforcement as long as a few formal requirements have been met.[8] And they are used to the high-volume, low-value transactions typical for the information economy. For example, credit card company Visa manages more than a billion credit cards.[9] In 1999 Visa cardholders placed more than 21 billion individual transactions worldwide for an average amount of $74. Visa card transactions alone account for about 8 percent of total global personal consumption expenditures.[10] Similarly ICANN's Uniform Dispute Resolution Policy (UDRP) has instituted a system of mandatory arbitration for domain name conflicts outside of formal legal procedures.[11] Given its potential impact on law as an institution, it is little wonder that this transactional issue has preoccupied much of the legal debate on e-commerce and the information economy.

Potential Responses to the Transactional Challenge

Many have suggested the obvious solution: to lower the transaction costs the parties incur by using the legal system, especially in cross-jurisdictional cases. Doing this may rebalance the cost-benefit structure by making illegal conduct more costly than legal conduct. It may also help the law regain its competitive edge in comparison with other extra-legal conflict resolution structures.

Harmonization of legal rules across jurisdictions provides one possible strategy for achieving this cost-cutting. The directives of the European Union in the area of intellectual property rights,[12] distance selling,[13] e-commerce services,[14] privacy,[15] and digital signatures[16] have attempted to do just that, as have the efforts of the World Intellectual Property Organization (WIPO).[17] But harmonization of national laws has its limits. Few nations are willing to give up their national legal rules, which are based on deeply rooted societal values.[18]

Another strategy for nations may be to increase the transaction costs of illegal actions by, for example, toughening punishment or stepping up enforcement of existing legal rules[19] and possibly even extending them to include transactions outside the national territory.[20] Enforcement may not be perfect, but it does not need to be. Only the total "cost" incurred as a function of the risk of enforcement and the severity of punishment must be higher than the cost incurred by contractual/lawful behavior. For example, when speeding on the highway we are used to weighing the potential punishment for speeding against the likelihood of detection.

Despite these solutions there is no magic potion to quickly end this challenge in favor of the legal system, even though transaction costs may decrease over time. For the foreseeable future the established national legal systems and the international private law counterpart of meta-rules on jurisdictional conflicts will continue to face a double competition, having to battle both illegal behavior and potentially "cheaper" alternative conflict resolution systems.

The Structural Challenge

Lawrence Lessig has eloquently argued for a different challenge to the law (and thus governance).[21] Instead of asking the transactional question of whose rules should apply and pointing to the issue of transaction costs in e-commerce's high transaction volume, he asks who makes the rules. For him the rules of the information economy are not made exclusively by legislators anymore, and not by the market either. Instead, he sees the providers of the technological artifacts we use to participate in the information economy as the new true rule-makers. When AOL's Instant Messenger excludes users of Microsoft's messaging service,[22] when Intel's chips contain a remote accessible unique identifier code,[23] or when Microsoft's Hotmail service automatically filters out e-mail messages Microsoft thinks are junk,[24] software code quite directly limits our communication. By creating the specific shape of cyberspace we interact in, these technological tool providers wield substantial power over how we may behave and interact online.

Lessig's argument is not just that technological tools incorporate implicit rules. This would be simplistic. Frederick Schauer has pointed out that even everyday tools like cars—from the East German Trabant to Daimler's Smart—have built-in restrictions, such as not going faster than seventy miles per hour, though no legal expert would refer to a carmaker as a disguised lawmaker.[25] Rather Lessig's argument hinges upon an important difference between cars and information technologies. As Wilhelm Steinmüller has shown, software code is very flexible.[26] It can be designed almost any way one likes, while cars are restricted by many external rules, most of which—like the laws of physics—cannot be overcome. If the "new laws" shaping cyberspace are nothing but software code, as Lessig suggests, then there is an almost endless variability in how this can be done. Take for example the way web browsers interact with small pieces of personal information called "cookies." There is no law of physics that mandates or prohibits the software from asking the user for permission when web servers gain access to these cookies. Some browsers are designed to ask for the user's consent; others do not bother. Whether a web browser "protects" the personal information collected from an unsuspecting user depends on the programmer's choice, which is not transparent to the consumer.[27] Consequently, Lessig's question is not why code is law, but why we do not have a public debate on how cyberspace is shaped through code.

"Code is law" is the sound bite of a structural challenge to the traditional system of governance in times of an evolving global information economy.[28] It does not compete directly with the transactional challenge of applying law in a high-transaction-volume information economy. And contrary to vulgarized versions, it is not a battle cry against a particular company or against software monopolies. Lessig wants us to focus our public discourse not so much on who designs the rules but on how we can instill a sense of societal legitimacy into these new rule-making processes.

Possible Responses to the Structural Challenge

The open-code community has championed a particular model of software development, whereby the actual rules embedded in the software become accessible to (and changeable by) everyone.[29] The operating system Linux is often called the prime example. Netscape has "opened up" the source code to its web browser Navigator, Sun the code to its application program suite StarOffice, and Apple to the core of its upcoming new operating system Mac OS X.[30] The open-code advocates contend that this transparency of rules will restore legitimacy and thus (re-)democratize cyberspace.[31]

Much can be said in favor of this approach, but it is not without its own difficulties. For one, the open-code community itself divides into rival camps who differ over what kind of "rule transparency" and "changeability" is best. "Opening up" the code sounds easy, but sorting out the minute details may be much harder than some think.

Even if rules are totally "open," the understanding of what actual rules are embedded in the code may be limited to a handful of software experts both knowledgeable and industrious enough to venture into understanding many millions of lines of code. In the end one might not have created democratic transparency, but an odd form of information access for competitors and the ones already in the know. Moreover, the democratic legitimacy of rule-making may be more complex than and different from simple, formal transparency. It may require the release of meta-information about how to read and interpret the rules, guarantees of due process in rule-making, counter-majoritarian protection, and fundamentally, some form of democratic mandate.[32]

Two debates—one transactional and one structural—crystallize the central challenges in maintaining our societal conflict resolution system. They differ, among other things, in how timely they are. Now we are facing the transactional challenge—as the millions of small value e-commerce transactions attest. Online retailer Amazon.com alone claims more than 25 million regular customers. [33] Online auction house eBay.com runs more than 5 million consecutive auctions.[34] For these players in the fast, huge, and efficient markets of the information economy, transactions costs are real, and so is their demand for contract enforcement and conflict resolution. If the legal system does not provide a functioning solution very soon, alternatives will be sought. Lessig's structural challenge is longer term. It may not bite us now, but it will haunt us in a few years. The trouble with this structural challenge is that once we realize societal rule-making has moved away from legislators, it may be very difficult and costly to change.

The legal community has debated at length the former, and Lessig's arguments have confronted it with the latter.[35] These discussions are as important as they are timely. But so far they have been too restricted to the legal community. Broadening the debates by involving public policy experts and economists may not only be useful in realizing important additional methodological insights, but may also be necessary given the far-reaching implications of structural challenges.

The Third Challenge: Substantive

The information economy poses a third challenge for governance, a substantive one. It, too, has the potential to shape directly and permanently the information economy. But unlike the other two it has been largely overlooked by the public debates. The following is my humble contribution to remedying this situation.

A few years ago, Judge Frank Easterbrook argued that the new markets of the information economy posed no fundamental challenge to the legal system. He quipped that new information markets necessitate the creation of a special cyberlaw about as much as horse races and horseback riding necessitate the advent of a "law of the horse."[36] He made but one exception to this claim. Law, he argued, will have to tackle one substantive issue, namely the (re)construction of rules of control over information.[37] This substantive challenge is commonly overlooked, despite its potential importance.

On the markets of the "new economy," primarily information, not physical goods, is traded. This is an important shift from the traditional economy, in which information is mostly a signaling device for supply and demand that fosters and enables market transactions. In the information economy information retains this role but also becomes the central object of market transactions.

To be sure, information has always been valuable. But the information economy creates many new markets for the exchange of information. More markets entail more opportunities for information to be traded and to be valued. "Price-less" information turns into valuable assets. However, this process of valuation and marketization of information depends on the ability of market participants to control access to information and exclude others from using it. Market power is not derived from "having" information, but only from controlling access to it.[38]

Access control is fairly straightforward in the world of traditional physical goods. If one takes somebody else's good, it is quite obvious: an object has been taken away. Through "property" we have extended a societal guarantee to the "controller" of a physical good to use it as he or she sees fit (within the rules set forth by society through law and other norms) and to exclude others from using it. This is the core of "ownership." Without such property rights and related rules, the distribution of goods in our society would be quite different. The legal system in its protection of exclusive control, through ownership and property rights, has shaped considerably the economic landscape and influenced behavior.

Take, for example, the Roman law rules of treasure hunting.[39] If a rule permits a treasure hunter to keep the treasure he finds, and he does not have to pay the owner of the land on which he found it, many others will go treasure hunting, but few landowners will permit them to do so on their land. The opposite system, in which the treasure hunter receives nothing and the landowner gets all, would create a world of consenting landowners but no willing hunters. Obviously, as the Roman jurists discovered, the solution must be somewhere in between. But however the balance is struck and whatever rules the legal system establishes, some people will be relatively enriched and others impoverished.[40]

In a society based in no small part on private property as the exclusive control of land and goods, the rules relating to ownership embedded in our legal system have impact on the distribution of power and wealth. To be sure, there is nothing wrong with that per se, because at least in principle the legal system is the result of a democratic process of societal rule-making. It is important, though, to recognize this implicit power of the law in shaping markets and economic transactions. One may argue then that establishing rules of control or "ownership" of information in cyberspace will have a similar impact on how information is produced, valued, distributed, and transferred.

Some commentators have doubted this and pointed to the dissimilarity of physical goods and information. Information, unlike physical objects, has a few peculiar qualities. It expands as it is used and can be easily and instantaneously transported. It is intangible and nonexclusive. Information is shared, not exchanged. Taken together these qualities make it possible that unlike a physical object, one piece of information may be used by many different people at once at locations far apart, without necessarily diminishing its value to anyone.

Such qualities are usually associated with what is called a "public good." The lighthouse, which signals for everyone, not just for particular ships, is the classic example. In essence, lighthouses are information providers. Because the information lighthouses provide reaches everyone in their range without exclusion, lighthouses benefit everyone. No sensible business will offer such services if free riders cannot be excluded. In such a situation no markets will be created.[41]

Information markets, it is said, suffer from a similar structural flaw—the public-good character of information.[42] And critics point to a further complication due to the digitization of modern information and communication networks. Digitization is the transfer of all kinds of information into a single, unified, binary code. A piece of digital information can be copied, and the copy will be as perfect and genuine as the original. This makes continued control over information very difficult. It is completely different from losing temporary control over a physical object. Suppose one temporarily loses control over a piece of information. Upon regaining control over this information it is difficult to ascertain that the information "returned" is the "original" piece of information and that no other new "originals" have been produced.

This unique quality, it is argued, will make impossible an enforceable and thus effective system of exclusion rights for information similar to traditional property rights for physical goods. Implying that individuals are creative solely because they hope to reap financial benefits, these critics understand information as a public good and believe that government should ensure its provision.[43] Others argue that the public-good character of information puts pressure on the legal system to monopolize the control over information. For them, the public-good character of information is prescriptive, not descriptive. Consequently, they call for a fundamental change in the intellectual property setup toward the public-good goal, for strengthening the open-code community and public funding for creative work.[44]

It is possible, though, that both the descriptive and the prescriptive skeptics of the legal system's ability to maintain an effective system of control over information access have it wrong. Their joint skepticism hinges upon the practical inability to exclude others from information once it is outside of one's immediate control.

But modern information and communication technologies may actually provide technical solutions for selectively denying people access to information. In essence, technology may offer the very tools to draw borders and to exclude others. Digital watermarks, encryption, electronic transaction, and access control and related technologies may actually function as fences, as obvious signaling devices delineating control over information. Lawrence Lessig has made the persuasive argument that intellectual property protection on the Internet may not be getting progressively harder, but easier and more likely to be successful as every information transaction, every move we make on the Net, is recorded and can be scrutinized.[45] With technological control over human interactions in cyberspace increasing, information may become less of a public good. The legal system may have an important role to play in assigning and maintaining individual rights of information control and together with technologies may help information markets to mature by providing the foundation for a finer-grained system of access and usage rights.

Lessig is basically correct. Technology does offer ways not only to overcome the public-good character of information but also to create an access control system that is much more advanced than we may imagine. A modified legal system based on individual claims of control over bits of information provides the foundation for even bigger and more efficient information markets, thus eventually also saving its own existence.

However, this leads to another challenge to norms and governance in the information economy. With the technological tools at hand we now must take a second look at the existing exclusion rights for information.

A Modified Substantive Challenge and Possible Responses

Intellectual property laws give the individual creator an exclusive right of control over his or her work, a right that can be transferred and traded like any other property right. In this sense copyright is like property. Privacy

laws give individuals the right to prevent others from using personal information, but unlike copyright, this individual liberty is not "tradable." This
heterogeneity of the structure of rights controlling access to and use of
information may have been pragmatic in a pre-digital-networks age. But its
maintenance in a digital world is infeasible when it is recognized that both
of these domains confer a very similar ability of exclusive control over
information to certain individuals.

Some commentators have argued for a more homogeneous view of legal
claims on information control, for example by creating a "privacy property"
right.[46] Although this would not create markets for personal information
(those markets already exist), they argue it would empower individuals
themselves to trade their personal information, not just businesses that
have somehow gained access to people's personal data.[47] Some even draw
comparisons to the right to publicity and its quasi-property quality.[48]

Others have criticized such "propertization" as impinging upon the freedom of speech, as well as empowering the individuals only in the most formal sense while actual negotiation and bargaining positions between individuals and businesses remain unbalanced.[49]

The most stinging critique, however, comes from an analysis of the
nature of individual claims to information.[50] Unlike property, information
is not only an object over which an individual wields control. It also reflects
on the individual, revealing a particular side of his or her individuality.
Possession of physical objects, too, may reveal some information about
their owners, but in general a chair I own conveys less information about
me than a book I have written, a picture I have painted, or a song I have
composed. Physical possession also reveals less than personal data about my
health, philosophy, religion, political ideology, or economic status. In this
sense the monodimensional—or better, the monodirectional (from the
subject to the object)—"property" paradigm might be as wrong for privacy
rights as for claims on creative works. Instead one may want to think of
rights over information as being bidirectional, less like property and more
like a right of informational self-determination, to shape one's participation
in the information society through co-decision.

Space does not permit me to expand on such a bidirectional approach.[51]
But it is important to understand the importance of this debate. Together
with the appropriate technological tools, the legal framework may—up to
a point—shape the information economy by setting the rules of information control and use. However, this shaping will work only if we can overcome the current system's contradictions and its uneven treatment of types

of information. What may be needed is not a new "information law" but rather a set of general principles or meta-norms to harmonize the existing information rules, which would create similarly structured rights for how we attribute and link information to an individual and permit him or her to control access to and use of it.

Conclusions

Information markets create transactional and structural challenges for law and governance. These transactional challenges are not new, but technological advances in how we interact have made them much more present and pressing. Our response is primarily to retool the legal system with the help of technological means. The structural challenges pose a more novel but less immediate challenge. Structurally we tend to do the reverse: to respond by changing the technological structures with the help of legal means.

Although these are important, we must not overlook a third challenge, the "substantive" one. This one focuses squarely on the unequal rules of information access and use and demands our riposte simultaneously on both the legal and the technical level. Creating a coherent set of principles to address this challenge may turn out to be a centrally important means to facilitate information transactions and to empower the individuals amid bigger, better markets.

Notes

1. See Paul Resnick and Richard Zeckhauser, "Trust among Strangers: Auction Sales on the Internet," University of Michigan, 2001; it is also important to keep in mind that establishing trust is a process that varies from culture to culture.

2. This does not imply that the law is the only such institution or that it is nothing but a societal contract enforcement and conflict resolution institution.

3. In American law this area is called conflicts of law and includes both substantive meta-rules (meta-rules to which jurisdictional rules apply) and procedural meta-rules (rules about which legal venue is competent to hear the case); see Eugene F. Scoles and others, *Conflict of Law,* 2d ed. (St. Paul, Minn.: West, 1992); Arthur Taylor von Mehren and Donald Theodore Trautman, *The Law of Multistate Problems* (Little, Brown, 1965); Robert A. Leflar, *American Conflicts Law* (Indianapolis: Bobbs-Merrill, 1968).

4. According to *The Industry Standard* and *BizRate.com*, "Online Shopping Volume Statistics," the volume of transactions climbed to 12 million transactions worth $1.326 billion

in the week ending December 12 (www.thestandard.com/research/metrics/indicators_shopping).

5. (www.iredge.com/IREdge/site/002239/custom/12.27.00.htm.).

6. Ronald H. Coase, "The Problem of Social Cost," *Journal of Law and Economics,* vol. 2 (1960), p. 1.

7. One must not forget, however, that legal norms helped fuel the acceptance of credit cards, at least in the United States, by (among other things) limiting the liability of credit card holders.

8. Credit card companies continue to rely on national laws to enforce their claims against any contract-violating customers, but they also insulate their contract-abiding customers from many transactional risks.

9. www.visa.com/av/thanksabillion.html.

10. www.visa.com/av/press_center/digital/statistics.html.

11. ICANN is the Internet Corporation for Assigned Names and Numbers (www.icann.org/udrp/udrp-policy-24oct99.htm); see also Luke A. Walker, "Berkeley Technology Law Journal Annual Review of Law and Technology I. Intellectual Property; C. Trademark ICANN's Uniform Domain Name Dispute Resolution Policy," *Berkeley Tech. Law Journal,* vol. 15 (2000), p. 289.

12. Directive 96/9/EC of the European Parliament and of the Council of March 11, 1996, on the legal protection of databases, *Official Journal* L 077 of March 3, 1996; Council Directive 92/100/EEC of November 19, 1992, on rental right and lending right and on certain rights related to copyright in the field of intellectual property, *Official Journal* L 346 of November 27, 1992; Council Directive 91/250/EEC of May 14, 1991 on the legal protection of computer programs, *Official Journal* L 122 of May 17, 1991.

13. Directive 97/7/EC of the European Parliament and of the Council of May 20, 1997, on the Protection of Consumers in respect of Distance Contracts, *Official Journal* L 144 of June 4, 1997.

14. Directive 2000/31/EC of the European Parliament and of the Council of June 8, 2000, on certain legal aspects of information society services, in particular electronic commerce, in the Internal Market ("Directive on Electronic Commerce"), *Official Journal* L 178 of July 17, 2000.

15. Directive 95/46/EC of the European Parliament and of the Council of October 24, 1995, on the protection of individuals with regard to the processing of personal data and on the free movement of such data, *Official Journal* L 281 of November 23, 1995; Directive 97/66/EC of the European Parliament and of the Council of December 15, 1997, concerning the processing of personal data and the protection of privacy in the telecommunications sector, *Official Journal* L 024 of January 20, 1998.

16. Directive 1999/93/EC of the European Parliament and of the Council of December 13, 1999, on a Community framework for electronic signatures, *Official Journal* L 013 of January 19, 2000.

17. WIPO Copyright Treaty and Agreed Statements Concerning the WIPO Copyright Treaty (adopted in Geneva on December 20, 1996), WIPO publication No. 226 (E); Berne Convention for the Protection of Literary and Artistic Works of September 9, 1886, as last revised by the Paris Act of July 24, 1971, and amended on September 28, 1979 (Revised Berne Convention), WIPO Publication no. 287 (E).

18. This is particularly true with rules regulating communication; see Deborah Hurley and Viktor Mayer-Schönberger, "Information Policy and Governance," in Joseph S. Nye Jr. and John D. Donahue, eds., *Governance in a Globalizing World* (Brookings, 2000), p. 330.

19. This arguably is one of the aims of the Digital Millennium Copyright Act, as well as the recent steps taken by the World Intellectual Property Organization (WIPO); see Pamela Samuelson, "The Digital Agenda of the World Intellectual Property Organization: The U.S. Digital Agenda at WIPO," *Virginia Journal of International Law*, vol. 37 (1997), p. 369.

20. See, for example, James H. Aiken, "The Jurisprudence of Trademark and Copyright Infringement on the Internet," *Mercer Law Review*, vol. 48 (1997), p. 1331; Lea Hall, "The Evolving Law of Personal Jurisdiction for Trademark Infringement on the Internet," *Mississippi Law Journal*, vol. 66 (1996), p. 457.

21. Lawrence Lessig, *Code: And Other Laws of Cyberspace* (Basic Books, 1999).

22. "Trying to Connect You," *Economist*, June 22, 2000.

23. George M. Dery and James R. Fox, "Chipping Away at the Boundaries of Privacy: Intel's Pentium III Processor Serial Number and the Erosion of Fourth Amendment Privacy Expectations," *Georgia State University Law Review*, vol. 17 (2000), p. 331.

24. Brian McWilliams, "Groups Clash over Hotmail Spam Filters," internet.com, January 19, 2001 (www.internetnews.com/isp-news/article/0,,8_565491,00.html).

25. Fred Schauer, presenting at SubTech 2000, the Sixth International Conference on Substantive Technology in Legal Education, July 6–8, 2000, Harvard University; a video clip is available at www.subtech2000.harvard.edu.

26. Wilhelm Steinmüller, *Riskante Netze: Informations- und Kommunikationstechnik zwischen Technologie-Abschatzung und Technik-Gestaltung* (Vienna: R. Oldenbourg, 1990).

27. See Viktor Mayer-Schönberger, "Cookies for a Treat?" *Computer Law and Securities Report*, vol. 14, no. 3 (1998), p. 166; see also www.wvu.edu/~wvjolt/Arch/Mayer/Mayer.htm.

28. See William J. Mitchell, *City of Bits: Space, Place, and the Infobahn* (MIT Press, 1995). Rohan Samaraijiva advanced similar theories in a presentation at the University of Salzburg Department of Communication in June 1994; Joel R. Reidenberg, "Lex Informatica: The Formulation of Information Policy Rules through Technology," *Texas Law Review*, vol. 76 (1998), p. 553; and Viktor Mayer-Schönberger, *Das Recht am Info-Highway* (Vienna: Orac, 1997), p. 40.

29. See Chris DiBona, Sam Ockman, and Mark Stone, eds., *Open Sources—Voices from the Open Source Revolution* (Beijing: O'Reilly, 1999); Eric S. Raymond, *The Cathedral and the Bazaar: Musings on Linux and Open Source by an Accidental Revolutionary* (Beijing: O'Reilly, 1999).

30. See www.mozilla.org; www.openoffice.org; and www.darwin.org, respectively.

31. Opening the source code may not be necessary, as John Gage has informed me. Free access to the application program interfaces (APIs) may be all that is needed. Open-code advocates may reply that exposing the API is all that is needed to break into existing de facto software monopolies, but not to change the underlying rules. To which Gage may reply that opening the API may provide opportunities for competitors to enter the market and thus provide rule pluralism.

32. One option may be to change corporate governance by broadening it from including stockholders to including stakeholders (like end-users) in the decisionmaking processes.

33. www.iredge.com/IREdge/IREdge.asp?c=002239&f=2005&fn =Q39__242.htm.

34. www.eBay.com.

35. See, for example, Henry Perritt, "Jurisdiction in Cyberspace," *Villanova Law Review*, vol. 41 (1996), p. 1; Allan Stein, "The Unexceptional Problem of Jurisdiction in Cyberspace," *International Lawyer*, vol. 31 (1998), p. 1167; Jack L. Goldsmith, "The Internet and the Abiding Significance of Territorial Sovereignty," *Indiana Journal of Global Legal Studies*, vol. 5 (1998), p. 475; Timothy S. Wu, "Cyberspace Sovereignty? The Internet and the International System," *Harvard Journal of Law and Technology*, vol. 10 (1997), p. 647.

36. Frank H. Easterbrook, "Cyberspace and the Law of the Horse," *University of Chicago Legal Forum* (1996), p. 207; for a related argument see Jack Goldsmith, "Against Cyberanarchy," *University of Chicago Law Review*, vol. 65 (1998), p. 1199.

37. Easterbrook, "Cyberspace," p. 208.

38. Robert O. Keohane and Joseph S. Nye, "Power and Interdependence in the Information Age," *Foreign Affairs* (September–October 1998), pp. 81, 84–87.

39. Inst. 2, 1, 39; Tryph. D. 41, 1, 63; Paulus D. 41, 1, 31, 1.

40. See also Ejan Mackaay, "An Economic View of Information Law," in Willem F. Korthals Altes, Egbert J. Dommering, P. Bernt Hugenholtz, and Jan J. C. Kabel, *Information Law towards the 21st Century* (Boston: Kluwer), pp. 43, 57.

41. Ibid., p. 48.

42. See, for example, Hal Varian, "The Information Economy," *Scientific American*, September 1995, pp. 200–201; Oz Shy, *The Economics of Network Industries* (Cambridge University Press, 2001), p. 163; Deborah Spar, "The Public Face of Cyberspace: The Internet as a Public Good," in Inge Kaul, Isabelle Grunberg, and Marc A. Stern, eds., *Global Public Goods: International Cooperation in the 21st Century* (Oxford University Press, 1999).

43. This is in itself a debatable assumption.

44. See the chapter by L. Jean Camp in this volume.

45. Lessig, *Code*.

46. See, for example, Kenneth Laudon, "Markets and Privacy," *Communications of the ACM*, vol. 9 (1996), p. 92.

47. Simon G. Davies, "Re-Engineering the Right to Privacy: How Privacy Has Been Transformed from a Right to a Commodity," in Philip Agre and Marc Rotenberg, eds., *Technology and Privacy: The New Landscape* (MIT Press, 1997), p. 160; also see Simson Garfinkel, *Database Nation: The Death of Privacy in the 21st Century* (Beijing: O'Reilly, 2000).

48. Bruno Seemann, *Prominenz als Eigentum* (Baden-Baden: Noos, 1996); Horst-Peter Götting, *Persönlichkeitsrechte als Vermögensrechte* (Tübingen: Mohr, 1995); Andreas Freitag, *Die Kommerzialisierung von Darbietung und Persönlichkeit des ausübenden Künstlers* (Baden-Baden: Nomos, 1993); Michael Lehmann, "Das wirtschaftliche Persönlichkeitsrecht von Anbieter und Nachfrager," in Hans Forkel and Alfons Kraft, eds., *FS Hubmann* (Frankfurt/Main: Metzner, 1985), pp. 255, 257.

49. Jessica Litman, "Information Privacy/Information Property," *Stanford Law Review*, vol. 52 (2000), pp. 1283, 1294–1301; Anne W. Branscomb, *Who Owns Information? From Privacy to Public Access* (Basic Books, 1994), pp. 177–86; Wendy J. Gordon, "On Owning

Information: Intellectual Property and the Restitutionary Impulse," *Virginia Law Review,* vol. 78 (1992), pp. 149, 153–63; J. H. Reichman, and Pamela Samuelson, "Intellectual Property Rights in Data?" *Vanderbilt Law Review,* vol. 51 (1997), pp. 63–72.

50. Litman, "Information Privacy/Information Property," pp. 1295–1301.

51. However, I have recently attempted that elsewhere; see Viktor Mayer-Schönberger, *Information und Recht* (Vienna: Springer, 2001).

12

JOHN D. DONAHUE
RICHARD J. ZECKHAUSER

Government's Role
When Markets Rule

The legitimate object of government is to do for a community of people whatever they need to have done, but cannot do in their separate and individual capacities.

—A. LINCOLN, 1854

T̲HE MARKET DEFINES our times.[1] In all but a few isolated corners of the world—and especially in the United States—market institutions, market mechanisms, and market players occupy important or dominant places in the mechanics of most people's lives and most people's sense of how the world works (and *should* work). If FDR and G.I. Joe were emblems of ascendant government in the middle of the twentieth century, Lou Gerstner of IBM and Steve Case of AOL symbolize the edgy energy of private enterprise today. Yet just as business retained indispensable roles even at the public sector's high-water mark—the government did not build many weapons for World War II, produce the concrete for Hoover Dam, or (in peacetime) ever employ much more than one-fifth of America's work force[2]—government retains essential functions amid ascendant markets. Doesn't it?

Few would deny the proposition at this pitch of generality; we wouldn't. But government's role in the economic realm is largely defined by reference to the market—making good the market's defects, curbing the market's excesses. As extragovernmental devices for orchestrating collective endeavors improve, a "community of people" (in Lincoln's terms) is able to engineer larger-scale, broader-based, more complex, and less tested forms of cooperation. And as citizens become equipped to amplify their "separate and individual capacities" through growingly sophisticated private arrangements, old questions reopen about the "legitimate object of government."

Beyond their unaccustomed scope and scale, contemporary markets seem prone to mutate at an exceptional pace. Intervening in fast-changing markets is akin to air-brushing a moving picture or editing an unfinished story. How can the agents of governance lower the odds of failure—of acting needlessly, or acting clumsily, or standing idly by while untrammeled markets wreak preventable damage—in such a setting? This essay gropes for some guidelines. Some illustrative examples of bigger, better markets:

—Auto insurance has presented a palpably imperfect market, and regulation has long seemed warranted. Because signals of a driver's risk are either few (city of residence, age, history of accidents and traffic violations) or ruled out of bounds (race, gender), rate-setting is riddled with unfairness and inefficiency. But newly developed sensors and positioning devices make it possible to fine-tune insurance rates to actual driving behavior. Drivers can be charged for risk coverage much as they are charged for telephone service, based on use—the duration, time of day, location, and conditions of driving. Early experience suggests average savings of about 25 percent.[3] As the technology improves, the urban youth who only drives to church will save on insurance, and the elderly drag-racer will have to pay much more.

—Ever since the lead-up to the Great Depression demonstrated banks' vulnerability, the federal government has provided (and required) deposit insurance. In the past decade or so, as Akash Deep and Guido Schaefer relate in this volume, progressive growth in the completeness and efficiency of derivative securities markets allows banks to hedge nearly all of their interest-rate risk through swap contracts.[4] These new financial tools may undercut the case for old-style deposit insurance—while requiring government either to develop the capacity to test the soundness of intricate risk-hedging strategies or to count on depositors (or their private sector agents) to do it themselves.

—Online commerce expands consumers' options and reduces their vulnerability (even in the boondocks) to retail market power. For example, the ease of comparison shopping on the Internet appears to explain a good part of the drop in prices for term life insurance during the 1990s.[5] Meanwhile, e-commerce raises a tangle of new issues, including the legitimacy of differential pricing based on data-powered guesses about customers' price sensitivity; the urgency and feasibility of privacy protection; and the best way of calibrating and allocating the value of information about consumer choices.

Let's not kid ourselves. For many decades America has featured a mixed economy or (as one of us has put it) a "mongrel economy, with public and private efforts jumbled together."[6] The mix of market and public authority depends in small part on analysis and ideology and in larger part on history, politics, and popular judgments. The age of the mongrel is by no means over, and we do not anticipate a purebred market (even less, purebred government) to claim as its exclusive turf any important segment of the American economy. But the new-generation mongrel economy manifests less of the governmental sheepdog and more of the market terrier than even its recent ancestors.

Why Markets Rule

You don't need a weatherman to know which way the wind blows.

—R. A. ZIMMERMAN, 1965[7]

Why has our mongrel economy evolved to favor the price mechanism over government policy as an organizing force? What happened to trigger the market's ascendancy? (Our options at this point are either multiple volumes or a quick once-over. We opt for the latter.)

Technology happened, of course, especially information technology. As the twentieth century neared its end, long-gestating innovations burst from the laboratories and flooded the mainstream economy. Especially in the United States, where flexible workers could readily assimilate and adapt to technological change, these advances have both created a "new economy" and (less vividly but more importantly) transformed much of the "old economy."[8] This phenomenon is no secret to anyone and is discussed elsewhere in this volume. So we simply add our voices to those affirming its overwhelming importance.

Globalization happened, too. International transport and communication costs plummeted, cross-border information flows proliferated, and trade (in goods and services) and transnational investment (both portfolio and direct) exploded.[9] National borders became flimsier barriers to opportunity and competition. At the same time, the intertwining of national economies through stepped-up trade and investment frustrated many conventional tactics for steering or constraining market forces.

Finance evolved. As top talent (especially in the English-speaking world) gravitated to the financial industries, new and improved financing mechanisms proliferated. Sophisticated devices for supporting innovation, diffusing risk, and allocating rewards that in mid-century had been either unimagined or restricted to the parlor games of theorists have become routine workplace tools.

And politics changed. The collapse of communism, the shattering of the Soviet empire, and the Thatcher and Reagan governments were only the most visible examples of a broader and deeper trend. A generally diminishing ardor for intervention is partly explained by, and partly explains, the shrinking role of fiscal policy and the strictures international capital markets impose on national politics. (Developments in macroeconomics, while not our focus here, powerfully shape the context for the trends we discuss.)

But why did these categorical transformations—particularly the last three, globalization, financial evolution, and the political turn from collectivism—occur when they did, and more or less together, instead of fifty years earlier, or fifty years later, or separated by decades of history? Part of the explanation is that the trends are mutually reinforcing. But we suspect there may be a subtler syndrome behind the rise of markets in the late twentieth century.

Market ascendancy may have much to do with a period of stability that is long enough and sufficiently widespread to allow market-based instruments of collective action to be tested, refined, and incorporated into the fabric of society. Most of the West (again, especially the United States) has lived without any truly major social disruption for over half a century. This extraordinarily long period of stability, coupled with the (mostly exogenous, presumably) technological vibrancy of the same period allowed new market mechanisms to take root, thrive, and bear fruit. By another metaphor, markets are like crystals that grow by their own immanent structure. But the pace and extent of their growth are determined by the richness of the solution from which they precipitate (the intensity of technological development), the shape and structure of their container (the cultural and political context), and the length of time that passes without disruptive shaking or shocks.

Markets depend on a measure of trust, validated by experience, both between individual transactors (to make specific markets possible) and among the populace at large (to shore up the legitimacy of market arrangements). Large-scale traumas—wars, invasions, economic crises—can shatter the cultural and institutional underpinnings of trust and inspire a retreat to blunter but less brittle bureaucratic alternatives. Mancur Olson argued brilliantly for a seemingly opposite dynamic: trauma serves to break up encumbering encrustations of special interests, thus clearing space for markets to emerge.[10] But America's recent economic history suggests that the relationship between stability and market orientation may follow a more complex and contingent trajectory.

Diagnosis before Therapy

You better think.

—A. FRANKLIN, 1968[11]

Although the details are endlessly debated, economists have developed a set of coherent justifications—public goods; positive or negative externalities; market power; information asymmetries—for governmental efforts to alter the outcomes markets would produce on their own. This assemblage of theory and data is a marvel of sophistication, but a strikingly unhelpful guide to why and when governments actually intervene. Neither the largest budget item at the federal level (Social Security) nor the largest budget item at the state and local levels (primary and secondary education), for example, is premised on a cut-and-dried case of market failure.

Glaring discrepancies between theoretical justifications for intervention and observed patterns of intervention inspire mutual charges of obtuseness between academic economists and government practitioners. But there are both good reasons and bad reasons for these discrepancies. Governments can nudge or veto market outcomes for reasons that command popular legitimacy but have little to do with market failure. Governments can also commit simple errors in market governance, intervening (or doing so clumsily, or failing to intervene where they should) for no compelling economic *or* noneconomic rationale. We will not discuss the valid reasons for violating economists' criteria for efficient intervention—in part for reasons of space, in part because consensus is elusive (even between coauthors), but mostly because the bad reasons present, on their own, a large and important topic.[12] Market governance in a democracy may never be a science, but it can be a more, or a less, careful craft.

The best way to improve market governance is to avoid making mistakes. This is not the simple tautology it may seem to be. In some domains—science, sports, business—mistakes are inevitable, acceptable, even a healthy by-product of appropriate risk-taking. This is generally not the case when it comes to governmental intervention in markets. Mistakes tend to stick. More subtly, and more commonly, once-sensible interventions tend to endure as the conditions that justified their creation change or fade into history. If the Department of Agriculture, or the Mine Safety and Health Administration, or the Tennessee Valley Authority did not exist, it would not be necessary to invent them—at least not at their present scale and in their present form. Rent control, tax preferences for ethanol production, taxi medallions, and mohair subsidies are examples of interventions that have outlasted most of their disinterested defenders.

There are many reasons for this inertia, most of them eminently familiar. Constituencies of beneficiaries tend to coalesce around any intervention, more motivated by their concentrated and manifest gains to defend the status quo than the diffuse public is to alter it. Activists, sponsoring legislators, and civil servants entrusted with the mission tend to resist change. And citizens, businesses, and other units of government come to depend, in ways large and small, on consistency in governmental policies and processes. The worker looking toward retirement, the investor structuring a real-estate deal to capitalize on tax benefits, the automaker designing the safety features for cars to be marketed five years hence, and the mayor planning a waste-treatment plant all anticipate and rely upon continuity in government policy. Widespread reliance narrows the range of change the government can contemplate without doing damage to (or undergoing intricate negotiations with) those who had accommodated themselves to the status quo.[13] Other factors are at work as well. Behavioral economists have found evidence of a bias toward the status quo even in private choice, and inertia is amplified by the characteristic complexity of collective decisionmaking.[14] The fact that original justifications for intervention tend to be multidimensional—mixing market-failure arguments with noneconomic rationales—means that once an intervention is embodied in policy it can be difficult to dislodge even conceptually, let alone politically.

Hence our watchword for governance amid rapidly changing markets is "diagnosis before therapy." By this we mean that an interval of assessment and analysis, before intervention, is more apt to improve policy today than in earlier eras when markets were less fluid, policy problems were more stable, and correct solutions had a longer shelf life. We offer this not as an iron law, but as a rule of thumb that is broadly sound despite some categorical exceptions (on which more shortly) but often at odds with political reflexes in a democracy. Deferring intervention until the conflict between market outcomes and the public good can be diagnosed requires unnatural humility on the part of elected and appointed officials and an equally unnatural patience on the part of citizens. Premature prescription—commencing therapy in advance of diagnosis—is a common cause of errors, both of commission and omission. Some examples:

—In the mid-1980s many observers—impressed by the apparent success of the Ministry of International Trade and Industry in orchestrating Japan's economy—called for federal measures in the United States to set standards in emerging industries, including semiconductors and high-definition television. Such a strategy, in retrospect, likely would have shackled technological evolution and undercut the vibrancy that blossomed through much of the American economy a decade later.

—The fraction of Americans working in something other than a traditional employment relationship began creeping up in the late 1980s and early 1990s. Alarmed at the prospect that the rise of "contingent workers" would erode employment stability and work place–based benefits, the Clinton administration launched a task force to examine ways to curb the trend. The initiative became controversial within the administration because the broad category of contingent workers included low-paid temporary workers, voluntary part-timers, erstwhile employees pushed into unwelcome "contractor" status, and highly skilled consultants. The policy development effort stalled as participants debated the size of each subcategory and the appropriate policy response, and it was curtailed once the 1994 elections made favorable legislation unlikely. Half a decade later, happily footloose free agents rather than downtrodden temps emerged as the emblems of the contingent work force.[15] And the trend toward contingent work reversed itself later in the 1990s, despite the absence of any intervention.[16]

—In the mid-1990s, as the commercial implications of the Internet were first emerging, Congress enacted and the president signed a tax moratorium on electronic commerce. It is true that e-commerce is new and important. It may be that the temporary tax preference is a reasonable way to nurture the trend. The case for a permanent differential between the tax treatment of electronic and bricks-and-mortar retail establishments, however, is far weaker. Yet once this preference was set in place it became the status quo, and constituencies organized to defend it. There are no signs that the temporary moratorium will end soon, if ever, and the rush to prescribe tax advantages for Internet sales is likely to prove both expensive to other taxpayers and unfair to other retailers, as well as economically inefficient.

In these and many other cases where new problems (or more important, new classes of problems) arise, the identification of a market governance challenge is followed—often honestly and intelligently, let us grant, but prematurely—by the impulse to prescribe a plausible remedy. Premature prescription is not a risk restricted to government. The risk of overly hasty market governance is by no means a twenty-first-century development.[17] But rapidly changing markets strengthen the case for diagnosis before therapy in two ways, both by tending to raise the payoff to incremental evidence and analysis, and (less obviously) by tending to reduce the cost of delay for diagnosis.

Why Is Diagnosis More Valuable?

As change accelerates, fresh evidence is worth more than it would be in a more static context. The signals of stepped-up economic change are reasonably persuasive, if still short of conclusive. One simple measure of marketplace turmoil is the annual turnover in the Fortune 500. Figure 12-1 tracks the one-year change in the 1960, 1970, 1980, 1990, and 2000 lists of companies ranked by revenue. Close to twice as many companies were replaced between 1998 and 1999 as were between 1958 and 1959. This is a coarse measure, to be sure, and may understate the current pace of change; a firm can plow along with high levels of sales long after changing trends have dimmed its future. It may take years, conversely, for even the most glittering new company to register large-scale revenues.

A better measure than revenue rankings may be relative market capitalization—the market's best guess of a firm's worth, aggregating investors' judgments about its future prospects. The more turmoil there is within the hierarchy of top corporations, by the metric of market capitalization, the more persuasive is our generalization about accelerating change. Stable rankings suggest a placid economic environment (at least at the top) while instability suggests a sportier setting. Figure 12-2 summarizes a preliminary attempt to assess the rate of churning over time using this measure.[18] The starting point for analysis is Center for Research on Security Prices data on market capitalization—that is, the number of shares outstanding times the

Figure 12-1. *Annual Turnover in Fortune 500*

Number of companies

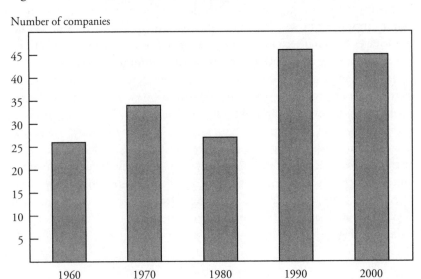

Source: *Fortune,* various annual issues.

end-of-year price per share. For each year-to-year comparison, the list of the 100 publicly traded U.S. firms with the highest market capitalization was determined for the base year, then compared with the *next* year's list for those same 100 firms. (New arrivals were not considered.). A simple measure of market turmoil is the correlation between one year's rankings and the next year's rankings. In a perfectly static economy—the top firm in 1970 is also the top firm in 1971 and in 2000, with equal stability down through the list to the hundredth-most-valuable firm—this correlation would be a steady 1.0. If there is some turbulence in the relative scale of companies' market capitalization, the correlation will be lower than 1.0. And if this turbulence increases, the correlation coefficient will decline. Figure 12-2 traces the correlation of year-to-year rankings from 1970 through the end of the century. (That is, the final data point is the correlation between rankings at the end of 1999 and the end of 2000.) It shows that the year-to-year correlation oscillated around the range of 0.9, then nosed downward toward the end of the period (though only the most recent one or two years suggest a statistically significant departure).[19]

These data are suggestive, not conclusive. They show that increased turmoil is a matter of degree, rather than a sharp discontinuity between a static past and a roiling present. Economic change has always shuffled the deck of policy challenges and rendered evidence and analysis valuable (if often undervalued) inputs into policymaking. Public officials in 1960 knew more about market power in the steel industry, or the potential for jet passenger service, or consolidation among meat processors than had their counterparts in 1955. If legislators and regulators in 1955 had possessed perfect knowledge of the future five years out, they would surely have made better decisions about market governance. But the increment of understanding during that five-year interval was smaller, we suggest, than the news revealed about the Internet or health maintenance organizations between 1991 and 2000, and probably smaller than the news to come about cloning or electronic retailing between now and 2010. As governance challenges become less familiar and more complex, the payoff from patient diagnosis tends to rise. The backdrop of rapidly evolving and unpredictable technology increases the probability that premature prescriptions will turn out to be misdirected. Just as important, but less obvious, it increases the damage done by policy errors as underanalyzed interventions warp the trajectory of technological development and hobble future policy.

Why Has Delay for Diagnosis Become Less Costly?

It may seem paradoxical that rapid change can *lower* the cost of diagnosis. Intuition suggests that fast-changing markets require fast-changing policy. Many of our hair-trigger decisions to commence, avoid, or alter interventions may turn out to be wrong, but so what? Isn't that just life in the new millennium, for government as it is for business? But there are several reasons to believe that the costs of delaying intervention, in the name of better understanding, have diminished.

First, the expected value of public benefits surrendered during the interval of delayed policy response is smaller in a changing and poorly understood setting. This forgone benefit can be expressed as the probability of getting the policy right without careful diagnosis, multiplied by the length of time this serendipitously sound approach would have been correct, multiplied by the annual benefit of the lucky-guess policy. The first two factors, we believe, tend to be shrinking—not in every case or every sector, but for

Figure 12-2. *Correlation in Year-to-Next Ranking of Top 100 Firms by Market Capitalization*

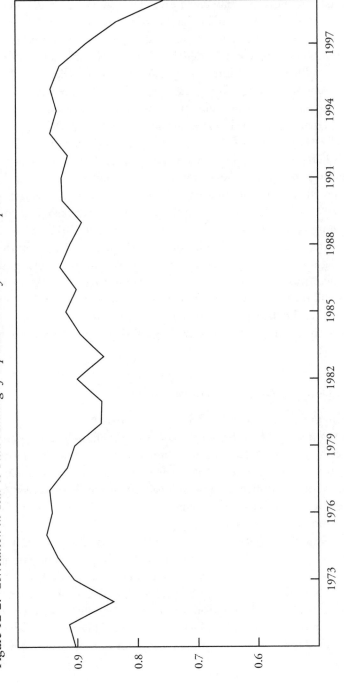

Source: Center for Research on Securities Prices data tapes.

the economy as a whole. If we tried to set the policy this month, we would not be very likely to choose the right response to employers' genetic screening of potential employees. Cherished values and stark consequences are at stake, and any policy—including laissez-faire—has significant potential drawbacks. If we happened, by good luck or good intuition, to develop a response that made sense for 2001, it would be even less likely that the policy would still be correct in 2005.

Second, technological and organizational fluidity lowers the expected costs of business and consumer "reliance" on an interim government policy pending finer diagnosis. In the mid-1970s there were more than 2 million American farmers, most of them basing investment and planting decisions on federal price support and production control policies.[20] It may have been appealing, from the government's perspective, to leave the issue up in the air for a while until the scale and impact of Soviet grain purchases became clear. But the reliance costs of putting policy decisions on hold—inspiring investments not easily undone and locking up resources not easily unfrozen—made more sustained diagnosis unworkable, however desirable it would have been in retrospect. Today a broader swath of the economy is more accustomed to uncertainty, better equipped with instruments for gauging and hedging against risks, and less dependent on specific governmental actions.

Third, greater economic and political fluidity lowers the odds that a potent political constituency will coalesce around some aspect of the status quo, rendering diagnosis moot by entrenching a flawed intervention (or nonintervention). When economic interests are well defined, concentrated, and self-aware, the option to intervene may bear a "use it or lose it" label. Government must move with dispatch to counter a perceived clash between market dynamics and the public interest, even if the perception is murky, lest delay for diagnosis give special pleaders time to dominate the political terrain. Today's political environment—with respect to many areas of market governance—tends to be more complex, fragmented, and unstable. A turbulent market, meanwhile, retards the emergence of dominant firms with fixed political agendas rooted in stable strategic positions and goals.

What evidence is there that business coalitions are becoming more fluid and less likely to entrench regrettable policy regimes? The ideal test of this assertion would require defining some comprehensive metric of political activity by business interests (incorporating campaign contributions, lobbying activities, and other tactics); coding by corporation and industry;

and tracking trends in concentration over a suitably long period. Like our earlier foray into gauging market turmoil, this is a dissertation-scale enterprise; we offer merely some suggestive bits of evidence.

In the late 1970s there were fewer than 1,000 corporate political action committees (PACs); today there are more than 1,500, hinting at a growing diversity of voices in the corporate choir.[21] This is not a particularly satisfying metric, however, because PACs are but one route by which firms can exercise political influence, and because a growing number of PACs is at best a murky measure of political fragmentation. A somewhat better (though still flawed) indicator is the concentration of political contributions of all kinds. The Center for Responsive Politics (using primarily Federal Election Committee data) has tracked major contributors, organized by industry group, since 1990. The center identifies the industry group of PAC contributions with a high degree of precision; soft money contributions by firms and individual contributions coordinated with corporate agendas are coded with somewhat less precision. Table 12-1 summarizes some relevant patterns for seven industry groups during the six election cycles from 1990 through 2000.

Two industry groups—defense and transportation—display relative stability among the top contributors. In defense, only about one-fifth of the top twenty donors changed, on average, between one election cycle and the next, and in transportation the average turnover was only about one-tenth. Defense and transportation had relatively low levels of total political spending and (more to the point) may also feature relatively well-defined political terrain. (Defense, in particular, may be sui generis, given its near-total reliance on government.) For the remaining seven industry groups, at least one-quarter of the twenty top contributors changed, on average, between election cycles.[22]

In most of the industry groups—the exceptions being defense and, this time, energy and natural resources—the share of industry political contributions accounted for by the top five donors dropped between 1990 and 2000. The three industry groups making the heaviest investments in political influence—health; electronics and communications; and finance, insurance, and real estate—warrant particular attention. In these industries the concentration of political spending at the top declined markedly. The identity of the leading corporate spenders also changed. In communications and electronics, two of the biggest spenders in 2000 (Microsoft and Seagram's) had not even ranked in the top twenty just ten years earlier, and only AT&T made the top-five contributor list in both 1990 and 2000.[23] It is also noteworthy that in only two industry groups, defense and transportation, did the top five contributors account for 20 percent or more of the industry's political spending in 2000.

Perhaps the most suggestive pattern, from the perspective of our claim that stepped-up market change erodes old business coalitions and slows the entrenchment of new ones, is the shift from *associations* to *firms* as major contributors. Industry associations, we conjecture, thrive in stable markets. A sufficient degree of continuity in market shares and consensus on policy agendas, for a sufficiently long period, allows firms to overcome collective-action problems and coordinate their political activities through associations. Conversely, when market segments blur, hierarchies topple, and interests splinter, the emphasis tips toward "every firm for itself." In 1990 the top five contributors in the health care and finance, insurance, and real-estate industry groups were multi-firm organizations such as the American Medical Association and the American Bankers' Association. In 2000 only one of these quasi-corporatist associations survived in the top five of each industry, with the rest replaced by individual firms.

These preliminary data are broadly consistent with our suggestion that the old monolithic ice sheets of business influence in politics are fragmenting into shifting floes of company-specific agendas as corporate interests become more heterogeneous. Efforts to forge public policies—if adequately nimble and astutely steered—may be better able to navigate around the obstacles to reach sound results. By this conjecture (in an odd corollary to Olson's argument about institutional turmoil promoting economic growth), market instability preserves room for well-considered government. We find the Microsoft case a comforting data point on this front—not so much for its outcome as for the fact that it occurred. Consider that the federal government and a phalanx of state governments engineered a potentially lethal strike against a well-regarded and hugely valuable industry leader, whose products are used and whose stock is owned by a significant fraction of American voters.[24] Many political analysts, if granted a glimpse at a crystal ball in, say, 1990, would have predicted that a behemoth with Microsoft's reach would prove strongly resistant to governance and would have counseled taming it before it grew too powerful. It could be, of course, that there were peculiarities specific to Microsoft to explain subsequent events.[25] But we suspect it illustrates a broader phenomenon. Government gains breathing room for well-thought-through

Table 12-1. *Shifts in Top Political Donors, by Industry*

Industry group	Total political spending (PACs, soft money, and individual gifts in 2000 election cycle) (millions of dollars)	Average turnover between election cycles among top 20 donors, 1990–2000	Top 5 donors in 1990 election cycle (share of industry total)	Top 5 donors in 2000 election cycle (share of industry total)
Defense	10.8	4	McDonnell-Douglas, Lockheed, Northrop, Textron, Rockwell International (32%)	Lockheed-Martin, General Dynamics, Raytheon, United Technologies, Northrop Grumman (43.5%)
Transportation	38.5	2.2	National Auto Dealers Association, Federal Express, United Parcel Service, Auto Dealers and Drivers for Free Trade, Union Pacific (29.4%)	United Parcel Service, Federal Express, National Auto Dealers Association, Union Pacific, American Airlines (23.5%)
Agribusiness	40	5	Associated Milk Producers, RJR Nabisco, Philip Morris, Mid-America Dairymen, American Crystal Sugar Corporation (15.5%)	Philip Morris, U.S. Tobacco, Brown & Williamson, RJ Reynolds, Archer Daniels Midland (15.5%)

Energy/Natural Resources	46.3	6.8	Rural Electric Cooperative Association, Waste Management, Amoco, Chevron, Atlantic Richfield (13.2%)	Enron, Southern Company, BP Amoco, Dominion Resources, Exxon Mobil (13.4%)
Health	56.4	6.8	American Medical Association, American Academy of Ophthalmology, American Dental Association, American Hospital Association, American Optometric Association (26.4%)	Pfizer, Bristol-Myers Squibb, American Medical Association, Slim-Fast Foods, Eli Lilly (11.6%)
Communications/ Electronics	84.3	5	AT&T, BellSouth, National Cable Television Association, GTE, U.S. West (23.4%)	Microsoft, AT&T, Verizon, SBC, Joseph E. Seagram & Sons (16.4%)
Finance/ Insurance/ Real Estate	195	6.2	National Association of Realtors, National Association of Life Underwriters, American Bankers Association, American Institute of CPAs, American Council of Life Insurance (15.9%)	Goldman Sachs, National Association of Realtors, Citigroup, Ernst & Young, MBNA America Bank (5.8%)

Source: Based on online data assembled by the Center for Responsive Politics (www.opensecrets.org/industries/index.asp [October–November 2000]).

intervention choices when unpredictable change retards the coalescence of stable business interests.

Fourth, and relatedly, even where one or a few firms dominate an *industry*, this dominance may be more fleeting than in earlier eras. "Industries" are seemingly becoming more arbitrary and transitory categories than heretofore. Particular economic *capabilities*—the capability to rapidly and reliably process very large numbers of transactions, for example, or to orchestrate alliances and partnerships, or to organize and motivate creative personnel—are coming to matter more. It is generally harder to dominate such capabilities than it is to dominate a well-defined industry. The old business-school cliché—"You thought you were in the *railroad* industry, but you're in the *transportation* industry!"—hints at what is becoming the general case.[26] As long as both the relative importance and comparative endowments of significant economic capabilities remain in flux, a healthy turmoil can slow the accumulation and erode the security of market power. Such a situation not only undermines the *political* power wielded by dominant firms. It also increases the odds that a disjuncture between market reality and the public interest will turn out to be temporary. This is not to suggest that in the era of bigger, better markets all flaws will be self-correcting. Sometimes they will get worse, and sometimes they will stay bad but in a different way. But it does caution against pursuing the chimera of once-and-for-all fixes, calls into question proven solutions from the past, and highlights the wisdom of looking before leaping.[27]

A fifth factor making diagnosis less costly—obvious, perhaps minor, but certainly not trivial—is that new technologies directly lower the cost of gathering and processing information. A single analyst at the Food and Drug Administration, the Federal Trade Commission, or the Justice Department's Antitrust Division, equipped with web access, Lexis-Nexis, and an off-the-shelf spreadsheet program, can do herself in a few days what would have taken a team of analysts weeks to accomplish twenty years ago.

When Should Therapy Come First?

"Diagnosis before therapy" is a rule of thumb, we noted, not a universal maxim. In certain medical circumstances, therapy rightly precedes diagnosis—when conditions are clearly life-threatening, for example, or when symptoms can be treated with some confidence independent of the underlying cause. Researchers have recently determined that high blood levels of homocysteine (an amino acid) are associated with heart attacks, strokes, miscarriage, and other ailments. But nobody yet knows whether elevated homocysteine is a cause or a side-effect of pathology, and it is unclear whether driving down homocysteine does any real good. Yet physicians are advising some patients to get blood tests anyway and to take steps to reduce high levels of homocysteine. It happens that the therapy for lowering homocysteine—eating less meat and more green vegetables, plus reducing stress—is much more likely to be good for you than bad for you even if homocysteine turns out to be a red herring.[28]

What conditions define analogous cases in the realm of market governance? We suggest three generic categories in which therapy can properly commence in advance of a full diagnosis.

First, and least interesting, are instances in which government has no discretion and diagnosis is superfluous. In some areas—the issuing of patents; certain regulatory arenas where cost-benefit analysis is explicitly proscribed—government is constrained to take action X whenever circumstance Y is encountered.

The second category includes instances in which even a temporary policy lacuna triggers irreversible consequences. These irreversibilities may be *technical* (the default is adoption of a flawed technical standard), *economic* (costly investments made in reliance on current policies), *legal* (formal or informal precedents that give property rights in status quo policy), or *political* (the accretion of constituencies with the motive and the means to resist subsequent efforts at governance).[29]

And the third category—the homocysteine analogue—includes instances in which generically useful therapy can be initiated without precluding its replacement by a more refined, or utterly different, approach following diagnosis. Interventions involving information disclosure— mandating consistent reporting of pension fund adequacy or mutual fund performance, for example—presumably fall into this category.[30] Better education and training may also be a broad-spectrum remedy for a range of ills in the era of bigger, better markets.

We are not suggesting that these three sorts of circumstances are unknown or even uncommon; indeed, with a little reflection most students of policy could cite several plausible examples within each category. What we are claiming is that they are rarer than they used to be, and that in the age of bigger and better markets diagnosis is at once more challenging and tends to matter more.

Concluding Comments

If economists could manage to get themselves thought of as humble, competent people, on a level with dentists, that would be splendid.

—J. M. KEYNES, 1930[31]

The time cannot be far distant when a knowledge of Political Economy will be considered as necessary for legislators as knowledge of Greek.

—J. R. MCCULLOCH, 1823[32]

We could turn out to be wrong. Markets may not be changing any faster, in the aggregate, than they used to; or (more likely) market turbulence may turn out to be a temporary phase—a jagged ridge connecting two placid mesas of relative stability. Alternatively, our arguments about the rising payoff of careful diagnosis could be mistaken. The proper watchword for government's role when markets rule could conceivably be "shoot first and ask questions later," rather than "diagnosis before therapy."

But for the sake of argument, grant (to a first approximation) that our line of thinking is correct. Why might it be *interesting*? What can be more banal and less controversial than a call for more diagnosis in the face of uncertainty? It seems to go without saying. What makes us think it warrants such emphasis? There are three general reasons for our conviction that hasty diagnosis and premature prescription are special perils of governance in an age of bigger, better markets.

First, the game may change more quickly than the players. Most participants in debates about market governance—whether academics, politicians, lobbyists, business leaders, or civil servants—have sunk professional, psychological, and reputational investments into established models of market successes, market failures, and the wisdom of particular interventions. Just as generals chronically prepare to fight the last war, public officials and scholarly kibitzers dispense prescriptions to address the previous decade's problems. This is a minor flaw in a stable world, but a major hazard amid rapid change. Alexander the Great could have stood in for Constantine, in a pinch, more easily than Patton could have replaced Powell. Analysts who cut their teeth on concentration ratios and price leadership may find their instincts outdated when industries cannot be defined, when firms rapidly and repeatedly leap into and out of sharply different areas of endeavor, and when some prices hover near zero.

Second, "diagnosis before therapy" may seem to invite paralysis by analysis, serving as a backdoor counsel of conservatism. But this would miss the point; the guiding phrase is, "laissez faire—pour le moment." It is silent on the nature of the public interest, or on the typical merits or flaws of market outcomes. It merely calls for initial caution and ongoing intellectual diligence when constructing what eventually may turn out to be highly aggressive interventions.[33]

Third, decisionmakers are accustomed to uneven and often shoddy service from diagnosticians. "Diagnosis before therapy" is an unremarkable recommendation in the medical arena, since patients have a well-founded expectation that expert assessment will lead to a better outcome. Academic social science, to a lamentably large degree, is ill-equipped and disinclined to offer practical guidance on emerging problems of market governance. How should Internet sales be taxed? Should new life-forms, gene sequences, or software capabilities be patentable? Even old questions take on new dimensions. In light of the changing nature of work, should overtime laws be abolished or broadened?[34] How should we feel about child labor if a teenager is scribbling software instead of stitching shirts?

Shopping for an accurate diagnosis is a daunting task. Policymakers encounter competing diagnosticians, many who are servants of particular interests or slaves to particular ideologies. But even scrupulously honest investigators tend to be handicapped by overspecialization and disciplinary blinders. Imagine if medical practice were similarly shackled, and one of us suffered, say, a compound fracture of the arm after balancing on the back of a chair to reach a volume on a top-shelf pile. We would call 911, and a bus-sized ambulance would roar up and disgorge a dozen or so white-coated specialists. The orthopedic surgeon would prepare a titanium pin for the broken bone; the plastic surgeon would push him aside to ponder the prettiest way to stitch the ripped skin; one specialist would test a bone chip and warn of inadequate calcium; another would assay the dripping blood and prescribe a crash program to reduce cholesterol. After a few such experiences, it would be understandable if the victim skipped the expert advice, splinted the break with supplies from the corner pharmacy, and hoped for the best. A similar plight sometimes confronts the policymaker seeking guidance on market governance. Diagnosis is too often rigged to justify the treatment an expert has long been peddling, or tuned to fit the dictates of theoretical elegance or disciplinary fashion.

For our academic colleagues, then, we counsel a measure more humility in the face of new classes of market governance problems.[35] We also advise a renewed commitment to *usefulness*—a commendable stance in general, and more so as the stakes of sound assessment rise. Careful diagnosis is an honorable craft, whether or not the candid analyst can offer some ready remedy. Diagnosis and prescription, even when bundled into the same treatise, should be sufficiently separable that those inclined to reject the recommended therapy can still benefit from the assessment.

And for practitioners, we emphasize our central theme: Market fluidity and uncertainty mean that objectionable market outcomes are apt to be imperfectly understood at any one point in time and likely to become less objectionable, or objectionable in different ways. Evidence and analysis are becoming more valuable, as is flexibility in the strategy and tactics of intervention. Substantial and systematic increases in governmental flexibility, however desirable, do not seem probable (at least in the short run). Hence government's role when markets rule, we submit, is likely to involve an unaccustomed, and doubtless uncomfortable, quotient of delay as evidence accumulates, cause and effect become better understood, and the mists of uncertainty dissipate.

Notes

1. Commentary on this broad phenomenon includes Daniel Yergin and Joseph Stanislaw, *The Commanding Heights: The Battle between Government and the Marketplace That Is Remaking the Modern World* (Simon and Schuster, 1998); William Greider, *One World, Ready or Not: The Manic Logic of Global Capitalism* (Simon and Schuster, 1997); Lester Thurow, *The Future of Capitalism: How Today's Economic Forces Shape Tomorrow's World* (William Morrow, 1996); Robert Kuttner, *Everything for Sale: The Virtues and Limits of Markets* (Alfred A. Knopf, 1997); George Gilder, *Telecosm: How Infinite Bandwidth Will Revolutionize Our World* (Free Press, 2000); and Thomas Frank, *One Market under God: Extreme Capitalism, Market Populism and the End of Economic Democracy* (Doubleday, 2000).

2. Government employment—military and civilian, at all levels of government—has ranged between roughly 15 and 20 percent of the work force since the Commerce Department's Bureau of Economic Analysis first compiled the National Income and Product Accounts data in 1948; it peaked at just over 20 percent in the late 1960s and early 1970s.

3. Anne Eisenberg, "Paying for Car Insurance by the Mile," *New York Times*, April 20, 2000, p. E20.

4. See the chapter by Deep and Schaefer in this volume.

5. Jeffrey Brown and Austan Goolsbee, "Does the Internet Make Markets More Competitive? Evidence from the Life Insurance Industry," National Bureau for Economic Research, draft of October 2000.

6. Richard J. Zeckhauser, "The Muddled Responsibilities of Public and Private America," in Richard J. Zeckhauser and Winthrop Knowlton, eds., *American Society: Public and Private Responsibilities* (Cambridge, Mass.: Ballinger, 1986), p. 73.

7. A.k.a. Bob Dylan, "Subterranean Homesick Blues," on *Bringing It All Back Home*, Columbia Records, 1965.

8. In mid-2000, Federal Reserve chairman Alan Greenspan highlighted the interplay between technological progress and flexible labor: "An intriguing aspect of the recent wave of productivity acceleration is that U.S. businesses and workers appear to have benefited more from the recent advances in information technology than their counterparts in Europe or Japan. Those countries, of course, have also participated in this wave of invention and innovation, but they appear to have been slower to exploit it. The relatively inflexible and, hence, more costly labor markets of these economies appear to be a significant part of the explanation." Remarks to the National Governors' Association, College Park, Penn., July 11, 2000.

9. See the chapters by Dani Rodrik and Jeffrey Frankel in *Governance in a Globalizing World*, Joseph S. Nye Jr. and John D. Donahue, eds. (Brookings, 2000).

10. "Countries that have had democratic freedom of organization without upheaval or invasion the longest will suffer the most from growth-repressing organizations and combinations." Mancur Olson, *The Rise and Decline of Nations: Economic Growth, Stagflation, and Social Rigidities* (Yale University Press, 1982), p. 77.

11. Aretha Franklin, "Think," Atlantic Records 2518, 1968.

12. A thoughtful perspective on this theme can be found in Charles Wolf Jr., *Markets or Governments: Choosing between Imperfect Alternatives* (MIT Press, 1988).

13. See John D. Donahue, "Jamming in the Symphony," in Donahue, ed., *Making Washington Work* (Brookings, 1999).

14. See William Samuelson and Richard Zeckhauser, "Status Quo Bias in Decision-Making," *Journal of Risk and Uncertainty*, vol. 1 (March 1988), pp. 7–59, esp. pp. 45–46.

15. The Internet has proven a remarkably effective device for sorting short-term workers into desirable engagements, and the growing number of skilled, and voluntary, contingent workers is almost certainly an important spur to growth and efficiency. It is not that the tales of exploited temps were fictional—they did, and do, exist—but that they turned out to be unrepresentative of a more benign broader trend.

16. We are indebted to Steven Hipple of the Bureau of Labor Statistics for a late-2000 update on the trend. The heterogeneity of nontraditional work is discussed in Anne E. Polivka, Sharon R. Cohany, and Steven Hipple, "Definition, Composition, and Economic Consequences of the Nonstandard Workforce," in Françoise Carré and others, eds., *Non-Standard Work: The Nature and Challenges of Changing Employment Arrangements* (Ithaca, N.Y.: Industrial Relations Research Association, 2000).

17. For some broader commentary on a related theme, see Stephen P. Breyer, *Regulation and Its Reform* (Harvard University Press, 1982).

18. We stress the term "preliminary"; a thorough treatment of this topic would form a nice dissertation chapter, and it may well do so for the graduate student who ran these numbers for us.

19. The sample of thirty correlation coefficients is not large enough to assess normality. If normality is assumed, the correlations for 1998–99 and 1999–2000 are statistically significantly below (at the 0.05 confidence level) those for the rest of the period. Non-parametric kernel estimation yields statistical significance only for 1999–2000. We thank Nikita Piankov for all calculations relating to these correlation coefficients.

20. *Statistical Abstract of the United States 1995*, table 1097: "Farms: Number and Acreage by Tenure of Operator" (GPO, 1995).

21. Data from Federal Election Committee website (www.fec.gov/press/paccnt_grph.html [October 2000]).

22. It would strengthen our case, obviously, if we could say that turnover among top contributors was systematically lower, say, thirty years ago, but comparable data for earlier years are not readily available. We will leave this to some enterprising doctoral student to explore.

23. Illustrating the murkiness of industry boundaries—and complicating comparisons over time—is the fact that although in 1990 Seagram's was not in the communications and electronics industry at all, by the end of 2000 the free-spending entity formerly known as Seagram's had become the global communications giant Vivendi.

24. Nearly 37 percent of U.S. stock funds held Microsoft stock in the second quarter of 2000, and of course a much larger fraction of computer users depend on its products. Aaron Lucchetti, "Is Microsoft Everywhere?" *Wall Street Journal*, July 10, 2000, p. R29.

25. The company's early political ham-handedness is legend, of course. It is probably also significant that the case was brought by relatively apolitical units of governance using existing antitrust authority, rather than requiring new legislation or initiative by elected leaders.

26. Indeed, it appears that in some cases industry boundaries can only be drawn in hindsight.

27. One might object that these points apply only to "new economy" industries and are irrelevant to more settled sectors. Our general theme—diagnosis before therapy—admittedly matters less where problems are far from novel and therapies are tested by time. Yet the border between "old" and "new" economies is shifting and poorly marked as new technologies work their way through the system, making these observations more generally germane.

28. Jane E. Brody, "Taking Action before the Verdict Is In," *New York Times*, June 13, 2000, p. D8.

29. Mergers have conventionally fallen into this category; a merger proposal, once approved or rejected, is not easily revisited.

30. Policies premised on the idea that more and better information is almost always a good thing have been the hallmark of Chairman Arthur Levitt's tenure at the Securities and Exchange Commission, for example.

31. "Economic Possibilities for our Grandchildren," 1930.

32. John Ramsey McCulloch—an early Victorian economist and foil of Charles Dickens—in a letter to George Pryme, May 26, 1823, in *Autobiographic Recollections of George Pryme* (Cambridge: Deighton-Bell, 1870), p. 127.

33. One of us is by instinct a hot Hamiltonian; the other a cool Schumpeterian. The merits of careful diagnosis are pretty much independent of one's appetite for intervention, once the evidence is in.

34. Rules determining coverage by the forty-hour workweek rule are half a century old, and roughly a quarter of workers are now exempt. Cynthia M. Fagnoni, "Fair Labor Standards: White Collar Exemptions Need Adjustment for Today's Workplace," General Accounting Office Report T/HEHS/00/105, May 3, 2000.

35. Altered roles for patents, first-mover advantages, the roles of economic alliances (as distinct from mergers), increasing ambiguity about corporate nationality, privacy, ethical problems raised by biotechnology, and many other practical policy problems may prove resistant to the standard welfare economics models that traditionally inform debates about market governance.

13

MARK H. MOORE

The Market versus
the Forum

A MONG THE CHALLENGES that bigger and better markets pose for governance is the potential impact that the *idea* of markets as a valuable way to organize economic, political, and social life has on *real* capacities to govern. By governance I mean: first, the capacity of some political community to establish a forum within which it can define purposes to be achieved using the power of the state; and second, the community's real ability to achieve the public purposes it defines for itself using both governmental and private capacities to achieve the desired result.

There can be little doubt that market expansion has long influenced real economic conditions throughout the world. The material effect of markets is evident in the growing gross national product of both developing and developed nations, and (to some degree) in declining absolute levels of hunger, illness, and poverty throughout the world. Less happily, market effects are also evident in the ugly and dangerous scars left by the careless use of the environment.

It is equally clear, I think, that the development of active global markets has profoundly shaped prospects for effective governance. The rapid movement of goods, services, capital, and information across governmental boundaries has made it impossible for national and local governments to chart their economic destinies independent of these powerful economic forces. It is these real, material impacts of bigger and better markets—both positive and negative—that are the focus of many of the essays in this book.

Here I want to make an additional argument: namely, that the growth of markets helps to spread a *market ideology*. This effect happens as individuals participate in the market as consumers, employers, entrepreneurs, and investors and have the concrete experience of making independent choices about how they will spend their time, energy, and money. It also occurs as individuals observe the market at work and see its capacity to organize social energy. And it occurs as market actors organize to make increasingly effective political claims on government's power to support the market. Eventually, the market becomes not only a way of organizing the economy of a society but also a way for society's members to think about what they should value as individuals, how they might combine together to produce valuable social results, and how lines ought to be drawn in society between the private and the public, the individual and the collective, and the voluntary and the obligatory.

Of course, the market is not a new phenomenon. As an empirical reality, human beings have long exchanged things in markets without explicit social or political sanction. Moreover, those exchanges have always crossed the boundaries of class, culture, and citizenship and to some degree have unsettled social relationships built on tradition, charismatic authority, and coercive power. What is relatively new in the world, however, is the elevation of markets to the status of a reliable and important social institution for satisfying individuals and achieving social goals. The elevation of the market to this status as a valuable, all-purpose social institution has required the development of a market ideology that legitimates the market in this role—that explains why markets are a good (and fair) way of organizing the productive capacities of society to meet individual needs and wants.

The development of this market ideology has probably been a necessary cultural and political condition for the expansion of real economic markets around the world. Without this ideology to legitimate markets in otherwise hostile social and political environments, the spread of markets might have been slower and less global than it actually has been. It is also true that the success of markets in improving material conditions throughout the world has helped spread commitment to the market ideology. As markets have succeeded in creating wealth, satisfying individual desires and giving individuals a chance to lead their lives more freely than was previously imaginable, the values celebrated by the market ideology have become more powerful.

This would unequivocally be a good thing if market ideology could be confined to offering instructions about how to organize a society's economic life. But market ideology has had a way of extending its reach into social and political as well as economic life:

—The idea that the selfish pursuit of individual material welfare produces efficient economies can affect individuals' ethical views of what they should value as individuals.

—The idea that the market reliably assigns value to individuals' contributions to the productive activities of the society through wages set in competitive labor markets, and that individuals are entitled to keep what they earn from their individual labor, can shape their ideas of what they as individuals are entitled to and what they owe to others.

—The idea that a system in which people own property and make voluntary exchanges with one another produces a kind of global efficiency in the organization of social effort that can shape individuals' social and political views about the importance and location of the boundary between the private (where individuals are free to pursue their own interests) and the public (where individuals decide together on the purposes that are important enough for them to tax and regulate themselves to accomplish).

—The idea that rational individuals can be expected to shy away from making contributions to the general welfare if others can be persuaded to do the work that will benefit all together, and will seek to maximize their own welfare when they act as the fiduciary agents of others, can shape our views about the possible ways in which individuals can combine together to accomplish public purposes and exercise effective control over those whom they rely on to achieve their purposes.

All these ideas together help to support the idea that a wise, good, and effective society would be one that concentrated most of its attention on protecting individual property rights and promoting economic development and much less attention on defining and working toward a common good or an expansive idea of justice.

In all these ways, the market ideology can shape the social and political culture of a society and influence choices about how individual and social life will be conducted in areas far removed from the processes of getting and spending.

I also want to argue that the political and cultural effects of a market ideology are more likely to be negative than positive for the cause of more effective governance. There are, of course, some positive benefits of market ideas for effective governance. But I believe that the main effect of embracing a market ideology is to undermine the sense of collective responsibility for social life that is probably an essential condition for effective governance.

This adverse result derives, in the first instance, from the importance that the market ideology places on satisfying individual *material* desires to live well as individuals over individual *social* and *political* desires to live in a just and good society. In short, the market celebrates *Homo economicus* more than *Homo civicus* or *Homo politicus*. In doing so, the enthusiastic embrace of market ideology may not only discourage the expression of these important aspects of human life; it may also undermine the commitments and capabilities that make an effective social and political life possible.

The adverse effect of market ideology on governance derives, in the second instance, from the undermining of confidence in the capacity of a group of individuals to form and achieve a collective purpose that would be responsive to the political aspirations of the individuals who made up the collective. Economic theory tells us that it is impossible to aggregate individual preferences in a coherent way, that efforts to mobilize individuals to produce "collective goods" will be frustrated by "free-rider problems," that much of what lies beneath the surface of politics is "rent-seeking behavior" by materially self-interested people using phony public interest arguments to camouflage their selfish purposes, and that those whom we used to call public servants are really nothing other than bureaucratic empire builders devoted to maximizing their own power, prestige, and salaries.

In short, the market celebrates the processes of individual voluntary exchange and finds an attractive collective result only in the aggregation of these voluntary exchanges. Alternative forms of aggregating individual preferences and commitments (such as deliberation leading to the recognition of shared purposes and an acknowledgement of shared responsibilities for achieving those goals, which are then pursued as a point of honor and social commitment) are deemed insufficiently reliable, too vulnerable to exploitation, and too threatening to individual liberty to be effective means of achieving desirable social results. In short, civic association and politics—understood as the effort to form a collective will and a collective capacity to act from the commitments of individuals—is viewed as a problem rather than an opportunity. So is having to figure out how to use the asset that democratic theory asserts we all own in common—namely, the power of the state to tax and to regulate us as individuals for the common good.

If market ideology celebrates material interests and voluntary exchange among individuals and views other motivations and methods of aggregating social effort as unreliable; and if governance depends on individuals developing and expressing ideas about the common good and joining together in clumsy democratic processes that commit the citizens of a society to giving up some of their money and freedom to accomplish purposes they decided were important to pursue together, then the wide embrace of market ideology could well undermine the prospects for effective democratic governance.

To make this argument, I explore the elements of market ideology at several different levels. I begin simply by noting some important value commitments that are thought by many to be entailed by a social commitment to market ideology. I do not try to show that these ideas about social organization are necessary logical entailments of market ideals, or that they are, in fact, empirical consequences of the extension of markets. I note only that some individuals and societies react to the emergence of markets as though they sought to enshrine certain kinds of social values, relationships, and commitments that seem dangerous to public life. I then explore market ideas as an explicit guide to societies about how they might organize themselves to ensure that their resources are used most efficiently to satisfy individual desires. In effect, I deal with market ideology as though it were a more or less complete social and political theory. Third, I explore how market ideas can affect social choices about the sizes and character of different social sectors and the ways in which market ideals end up favoring the institutions of civil society over those of politics and government in achieving social results.

Market Ideals as a Social and Political Ideology

I will shortly turn to the formal variants of what I term *market ideology*—welfare economics, and the extension of its core concepts into sociology, political science, and other disciplines. But first it is worth paying some attention to the broader intellectual gestalt from which these more structured concepts have been crystallized analytically in important social science theories. The idea of relying on markets and private enterprise to accomplish important social goals operates at this broader and fuzzier level both for market enthusiasts and for market skeptics.

Although it is hard to be conceptually or empirically rigorous in characterizing the particular values that seem to be celebrated by the market as a form of social organization, it is possible to construct a suggestive list. As a starting point for discussion, we might say that the market ideology is believed by many of its supporters to be a philosophy that emphasizes such values as:

—the right of individuals to form their own views of what is valuable over a collective's right to say what ought to be valued;

—the right of individuals to choose and enter freely into contracts over a collective's right to oblige and impose duties;

—the right of individuals to own their own time and decide how to spend it (including the important decision about how they will divide their lives among efforts at "getting and spending," "kicking back and enjoying life," and accepting the responsibilities of being a member of some kind of collective, such as a good spouse, a good parent, a good neighbor, a good congregant, or a good citizen;

—the right of individuals to accumulate the fruits of their own labor and use their property in ways that they choose;

—the importance of ensuring that society's productive capacity is deployed to meet the material desires of individuals, as a goal that individuals would have for themselves and as a goal that society as a whole would embrace as its ultimate purpose;

—the necessity of relying on disciplines produced by contractual accountability and competition as important ways of motivating individuals to produce, and firms to become efficient, over the naive view that people will do things simply because they are right;

—the justice of being able to own and build up private property as a consequence of one's own talents and efforts; and

—a belief that markets produce an important kind of justice in producing fair payments to individuals for the contribution that comes from their talents and effort in applying them.

Note the different kinds of claims in this list. Some of the claims are instrumental; they point to the effectiveness of the market in achieving particular results. Others are value claims; they take a position on what is just and fair in the ordering of social institutions rather than on what arrangement of social institutions works best to achieve individual and social goals. It is in these ways that the market ideology is a social and political ideology offering a vision of how individuals ought to relate to one another in society as well as an instrumental scheme for organizing the productive energies of society.

The market ideology is believed by many *opponents* to be a philosophy that emphasizes: individualism over any important conception of recognized interdependence or collectivist commitment; materialism and consumption of goods and services over the search for spiritual growth and moral virtue as the path toward the good life; economic life as a more important place to spend one's time and derive happiness than social, or civic, or political life; competition over cooperation as an important spur to productive activity and innovation; pragmatism over idealism as a way of orienting oneself to work and motivating others to participate; short-run consumption over long-run conservation and patient investment.

Now, these views may or may not be logical entailments of a commitment to what could be rightly understood as market ideals. It is also true, I think, that given the past century's experience with both fascism and communism we can all imagine the ways in which political ideologies that emphasize collectivism over individualism in the name of individual and social virtue can be used as devices to destroy individual liberty and waste productive activity.

Still, those who are interested in spreading the market ideology, either as an umbrella under which real markets can continue to expand or as an attractive set of concepts to be used in thinking about the overall organization of society, must contend with the fact that market ideals are perceived and either supported or opposed by many on the grounds described above. Moreover, we must be prepared to confront the fact that, insofar as markets succeed and bring with them these particular ideals, the very success of markets may end up giving moral and social license to the values and conduct described above.

Market Ideals as a Guide to Organizing Economies and Societies

Whatever the fuzzy connotations of the market ideology, there is also a very specific idea about markets and why they are to be preferred in organizing both economic and social life to ensure the "maximum good for the maximum number." Often these institutional arrangements are justified on the apparently neutral ground that they are more "efficient" and "effective" in accomplishing social results. And so they may be.

Efficiency as a Feature of Markets and as a Social Goal

Yet one must keep in mind that there are two quite different ideas of efficiency and effectiveness embedded in this general claim about markets. The most commonly understood idea is that the market will *develop efficient and effective technologies or methods for producing any given desired result*—that is, that the same quantity and quality of output can be produced with less use of scarce materials such as land, labor, and capital. That result is ensured (in the short run) by the existence of *market competition*, which forces firms to find and use efficient technologies for producing goods and services lest they lose customers (and investors) to firms that can offer products and services at a lower cost. It is ensured over the long run by the desire of entrepreneurs to make money and the fact that they can do so if they are allowed to keep the benefits of finding a more efficient technology for producing a given result.

The second, less commonly understood but potentially more important idea is that the market will be efficient because it focuses the attention of producers on *supplying what individuals want*. This idea reflects the importance of *consumer sovereignty*. The market is judged to be efficient not only because it produces goods and services at the lowest possible cost (given today's technologies), but also because it does not waste time, effort, and material on producing things that people do not want. Or, somewhat more precisely, it systematically weeds out those enterprises that are wasting resources on things that individuals do not want and therefore guards against social waste.

It is of no small import, I think, to understand that the market ideology gives enormous weight and standing to *individual* desires, aspirations, and preferences. The fundamental social justification for the market is: (1) that it does very well in satisfying the material desires of individuals as consumers; (2) that accomplishing this goal efficiently should be the most important goal of an economy; and (3) that having an efficient economy (in the sense described above) should at least be a very important goal of society if not, in fact, the only important goal.

The Individualization of Politics: Liberal Political Theory

Note that the importance of satisfying individual desires in *markets* aligns quite closely with the *political* ideals of a liberal democratic state. Both free-market economic theories and liberal political theories start from the premise that the most important arbiter of value is the individual. That is as true in *markets* when people are buying deodorant or art, choosing among colleges, or deciding where to sell their labor as it is in the realm of *civic* life where individuals make voluntary contributions to public purposes, or in *political* forums where individuals cast their votes for particular candidates' visions of a good or just society, or in referendums that decide whether something is or is not a problem that ought to be addressed using the collectively owned powers of government.

Of course, the *kinds* of individual preferences that people express in markets might be quite different from the values they express in civic and political life. In markets, individuals are thought to express their preferences for material goods and the ways in which they decide to participate in the economy as investors, entrepreneurs, workers, and consumers. The values they express in civil society and in politics, in contrast, have less to do with individual consumption and more to do with individually held ethical, social, and political aspirations. In the civic and political sphere, individuals seek to find and express ideas about what constitutes virtue in their own lives, what they think is important to do for others, how they would like to combine with others both for camaraderie and to achieve shared goals, and how they would like to use state power to achieve a just and good society. (By describing these values as "individually held," I am not suggesting that, as an empirical matter, they are constructed by individuals standing alone without the important influences of social norms, traditions, or powerful institutions that mediate between the individual and society such as families, communities, and churches. I accept fully the idea that individuals' beliefs, commitments, and actions are profoundly influenced by the macro and micro social conditions in which they find themselves. I am simply observing that it would be possible to observe the values that individuals hold at the level of the individual and to imagine that the individuals both believe themselves to be and to some degree are independent agents in developing these views and deciding when and how to act on them.)

Methods for Aggregating Individual Preferences: Markets and Forums

The methods for aggregating or combining individual preferences and values also differ significantly between the market on one hand, and civic and political life on the other. In the market, aggregate results emerge willy-nilly as the cumulative results of individual exchanges. In the forums of civic and political life, exchange is hardly absent. Many collective arrangements arise from individual exchanges and negotiations among more or less materially self-interested individuals and groups.

But in civic and political forums we sometimes imagine that aggregate results could be produced by a different, more social, less individualistic process: namely, individuals might build up feelings of reciprocity and commitment such that they would do things for each other even without being sure that the account would be instantly cleared; or they might find that they had commonly shared purposes that could be more easily achieved if they cooperated to produce the mutually valued result rather than struggled to find ways to get another person to do most of the work of producing the result that they both want. The discovery of a common cause and the development of a common commitment to pursue it could occur *ab initio* as each person finds another like-minded and equally honorable person. Or the common cause could be created after some process of deliberation and joint action during which individuals who initially have different views about what would be valuable and feasible, and are uncertain about their ability to act together, develop more concerted views about what is worth doing and more confidence in one another's willingness to share their "fair" burden in achieving the mutually desired result.

Note that there is a very close relationship between our understanding of the preferences individuals have and want to express and our understanding about how social aggregation processes might work. If we imagine that the preferences and values that reliably guide human behavior are largely selfish and material—that each individual will evaluate the results of social engagements largely according to whether it was good for him or her alone rather than for the group or some larger purpose, and will neither identify much with others nor feel solidarity with them, nor cooperate as a matter of duty and honor—then the only way in which individuals can combine to accomplish collective purposes is through negotiation and deal-making in which the only things being exchanged are material goods that the negotiators desire.

If, however, we imagine that the preferences and values that reliably guide human behavior include some desire to maintain right relationships with others, and to accomplish larger social objectives than attaining comfort and sustenance, then new ways of combining become possible. Even if we stay in the world of negotiation, more deals become possible if the negotiators care about the welfare of their negotiating partners and take some satisfaction in the overall value produced by the deal as well as their share of it. And, if we step outside the negotiation framework and give greater weight to individuals' desires to help one another or to maintain a right relationship with others, or to achieve the larger purposes of living in a just as well as prosperous community, then these motivations alone can suffice to create an organization that can extract effort from individuals and transform both material and social conditions in a society.

In sum, if we think individuals care about one another as individuals and about the aggregate material, social, and political conditions in which they live, then the aggregating processes we associate with civic and political forums have more potential to organize society than they would if individual preferences were limited to selfish material desires. In that world, the market would be the only reliable mechanism. This is one of the important ways in which economics might properly be viewed as the "dismal science": it is not only gloomy about the prospects of human development; it is gloomy about human nature and humans' ability to combine together as well.

The fact that market ideology emphasizes the value of voluntary exchange among individuals as the preferred way of aggregating individuals into collective units that can accomplish things (whether that aggregation happens in the use of markets to organize much economic activity, or in the combination of capital and labor to form a firm, or in the negotiations that occur among neighbors about how they might build and care for a playground that both their families could enjoy) has important implications for how those imbued with the market ideology will view the aggregation processes that happen in civic and political forums. To market enthusiasts and liberal political theorists who value individual choice and freedom over social obligation, civic and political forums are potentially dangerous to the social goal of satisfying individual desires. In such settings, the weight of the collective bears down on the individual members of the forum. In that weight lies the stench of social coercion against free individuals. In that weight lies the hypocrisy of individuals and groups who assert that their particular desires should be embraced as a public cause. In that weight lies the potential to grasp the power of the state to advance some interests against the interests of others.

This view of any collective deliberation process as a threat to the interests and rights of individuals poses a real difficulty for theories of democratic governance. By definition, a state enjoys the right to use its authority over its citizens to advance common purposes. In democratic theory, that authority is supposed to be jointly owned by the citizens. It is supposed to be used to protect their rights and to advance whatever common interests they might decide that they have. The fact that the state has power to accomplish things and is jointly owned by citizens means that citizens own something in common: namely, the power of the state. It follows, then, that they must have some way of deciding how they will use the power of the state, and that will be, by definition, a collective process. If this process is unreliable in helping individuals achieve their valued goals, it follows that much about the state will be suspect. It follows as well that a society ought to resist using the state whenever possible, for its use can be only imperfectly guided toward the cause of maximizing individual welfare.

Of course, I am describing here the fundamental tenets of a libertarian political philosophy. There are other "liberal" political philosophies that would view the state as a potentially valuable actor in producing prosperous and just societies, and who think of the processes of guiding the state's actions through democratic politics as a reasonably reliable method of advancing individual and social welfare. I want to emphasize, however, that even though liberal political ideals include some acceptance of the necessity of individuals combining together to provide guidance to a democratic state, most liberal political theorists (to say nothing of most welfare economists) remain profoundly suspicious of the idea that a collective—a "we" that can have desires and the will to accomplish collective purposes—can be reliably formed from individual desires.

Despite the bold claims prominently displayed on American currency, liberals of all stripes have serious doubts about the extent to which a "pluribus" can reliably produce an "unum." In liberal political theory as well as welfare economics, the irreducible element of society is the individual—not the family, not the community, not the polity. These collective enterprises—however small, organic, and intimate or large, socially constructed, and impersonal—exist only as long as they can continue to earn the loyalty and commitment of the individuals who constitute them. To say that they can operate together with a collective will is at best a bad metaphor that obscures the important question of how such collectives form and maintain the commitments of freely choosing individuals to them. The idea of a collective will is, at worst, an idea that paves the way to fascism and totalitarianism.

The Social Preference for Markets and Economies over Forums and Governments

The fact that market ideologues and liberal political theorists have such a profound commitment to individuals as the sole arbiters of (economic, social, and political) value, and such a profound suspicion of the possibility of forging collective decisions from those individual valuations in any real collective choice process, causes these groups to favor the market economy over other sectors of society. The reason is simply that markets allow individual preferences to have the greatest power to be satisfied. This is true even though it may only be *material* desires that can be satisfied through markets. If material choices can be satisfied through markets, and political aspirations cannot be well satisfied either through markets or through politics, it follows that if we want to have individuals satisfied rather than frustrated we should encourage them to concentrate on what can be done within markets rather than through politics. A wise society would emphasize the potential of markets, with the wide freedom of expression they allow and their fantastic capacity to enhance material welfare over the worlds of public action.

Politics in a Society Dominated by Market Ideology

Taking this argument from the economic realm into the political realm, those with strong commitments to a market ideology find that they have strong views about political and civic culture: that is, about how individuals should think and act as citizens of a social and political community. They also have strong views about structuring institutions in society: that is, about how the line should be drawn between private and public institutions and what the proper ends of government should be.

More specifically, those committed to a market ideology often think it would be best if politics—understood as a continuing collective discussion about what we should tax and regulate ourselves to accomplish together— were relegated to the margins of individual life and treated as a necessary evil rather than an important and beneficial part of our lives. Given that there is no obvious way that people with conflicting views about the purposes for which and the ways in which society ought to be organized, it is probably best for individuals to keep their political ideas to themselves. To minimize conflict and avoid frustration, then, politics and public life ought to be minimized in favor of more private living.

To the extent that some kind of politics is necessary to give guidance to the democratic state, those who admire market ideals believe that politics should be structured competitively—like markets. We should have a "free market of ideas" about what society ought to try to achieve and how it ought to go about it. We should have "competitive elections" in which individual candidates compete for the votes of individuals by aligning themselves with individuals' views about how they want to be governed: how they would like to divide the world between public and private and what public purposes are important to achieve. The idea is that such "political markets" will produce "efficiency" in the satisfaction of individuals' social and political aspirations in the same way that "economic markets" will satisfy individual material desires.

Such considerations lead to the "welfare economics" view of how best to organize society both economically and politically, and to the "rational choice" view of politics and government. In this view, the best society is one that is designed to meet the desires of individual consumers in the market realm and the aspirations of individual citizens in the political realm. The consumers are thought to be people who have primarily material desires. To the extent that they have moral or political or religious aspirations, these must be satisfied outside the domain of the market by choices they make for themselves in their personal lives, in their communities of faith, or through the act of voting. To the extent they have political aspirations for the shape of society as a whole, they have to compete with many others' views to elect their candidates or otherwise get the government to adopt their preferred ideas. The best political forums will be those in which individuals simply cast their individual votes for preferred social states, and the state is selected that comes closest to satisfying the political aspirations of the "median voter."

The Role of Politics and the State in a Society Dominated by Market Ideology: Libertarianism and Liberalism

Of course, even libertarians understand that there has to be some role for the state, and therefore some political activity to guide the state's activity. Since the market is so important to the satisfaction of individual material desires, a crucial function of the state is to keep the market running properly. At a minimum, the state must be able to protect private property and enforce contracts. Somewhat more ambitiously, the state must deal with "externalities" (the fact that there are some unowned and unpriced but nonetheless valuable resources that are used in economic production) and provide some "collective goods" (goods that are valuable to produce but that individuals cannot be excluded from enjoying even though they have not paid to do so).

It is also true that both libertarians and liberals have ideas about what individuals are entitled to as a matter of political right, and that a state has to exist in order to enforce the rights that allow individuals to freely express their preferences for how to live outside the market economy. In both liberal and libertarian political philosophies, the state must allow people to own and accumulate property and do what they wish with it. It must allow them to speak and associate as they will, guarantee their right to worship as they please, and so on.

And, because a state must exist at a minimum to allow markets to do their work, and to some degree to correct some predictable defects of the market, we must also construct a process that ensures that the collectively owned assets of the democratic state—the power to tax and to regulate—will be guided by the preferences (both selfish/material and altruistic/political if such exist) of individual citizens in whose name the state acts. This means that we must have authoritative policies governing political activities such as voting, the use of the referendum, legislative processes, administrative processes, and so on. In short, every decision that commits the collectively owned property, money, or authority of the (presumably democratic) state must be made vulnerable to the influence of citizens whose interests and political commitments are affected by the choice.

It is important to understand at this stage that an important contradiction has been introduced into the organization of a society. Having created a state as a necessary institution to support the functioning of markets and to protect individual rights that allow citizens to act freely in the civic and political realm, we have created the potential for politics to arise in which individuals decide not to set their civic and political ambitions aside, but instead to pursue them through collective civic and political action. They can join together to achieve common civic purposes using their own resources. Or they can join with others to lay claim to the powers of the state to achieve social purposes that go well beyond the protection of markets and individual political rights. That is, the institutional means have been created for the development and expression of collective purposes beyond the limited ones of ensuring the smooth functioning of the market and the protection of individual rights. In principle, then, individuals could decide to pursue many different purposes rather than these minimal purposes of the state. If they thought the market was eroding important individual and communal values, they could decide to restrict the inroads of the market into their society. If they thought that justice required significant redistribution of income, they could presumably decide to use state power to accomplish this collectively agreed upon result. The point is that there is nothing that necessarily limits their political aspirations to minimizing the use of the state.

At this stage, however, the market ideology steps in and argues for a libertarian political philosophy as the best idea about how to use the powers of the state, rather than a liberal or communitarian political philosophy. The important libertarian idea is that because collective processes are so unreliable, as much of social life as possible ought to be left to the workings of the private market in which individuals can choose what to consume, how to divide their time between leisure and work, and how to live their lives outside of the marketplace. As little as possible ought to be decided collectively. As little economic life as possible ought to be governed by collective decisions to tax and spend. As little social life as possible ought to be brought under the influence of the collective using the authority of the state. In short, the best state would be the one in which we collectively agreed to minimize the use of the state.

Of course, even if one believes in the importance of markets as a useful device for organizing economies (the places where individuals work to satisfy their material desires for food, shelter, clothing, and other necessities), and in the importance of constructing social arrangements that honor individuals over collectives, one does not have to become a libertarian. One can accept the view, for example, that markets are limited in their ability to satisfy individuals needs efficiently and effectively and that we need governmental power to allow markets to work more efficiently. This includes using governmental power not only to protect property and enforce contracts but also to force economic decisionmakers to pay attention to situations when they are using unpriced assets (such as air) in their economic activities, and to recognize that there is social value attached to these assets even though they are not owned and exchanged in markets. It also includes the power to guard against the emergence of monopoly power, and to prevent firms from cheating or defrauding, or coercing their shareholders, employees, and customers. We can call all of this "economic regulation."

Once a state exists with the power to ensure that markets work to satisfy consumer desires efficiently and effectively and a process that grants individuals in the society rights to argue for the use of state power to advance their own ideas (whether those be their individual material interests or their political aspirations to construct their vision of a good and just society), then it is likely that a kind of politics would form around the important discussion of how to use the state power. Further, it is quite possible that that discussion would leap the boundary from a discussion of how state power should be used to allow markets to work efficiently and focus instead on other goals that could be pursued with the collectively owned assets of the state.

For example, the state, guided by the political aspirations of individual citizens, aggregated through the mechanisms of representative government, might seek to realize ideals of justice linked to the distribution of wealth and income. It could turn out, for example, that a society dominated by economic markets would end up with too much economic and social inequality for individual citizens to feel truly satisfied or comfortable with the state of their society. Those at the top might feel guilty about the relative magnitude of their good fortune. Those at the bottom might feel resentful and unjustly treated. Or, both rich and poor might feel that the inequality they experienced in their society offended a commonly shared idea of a transcendent principle of justice or fairness.

In this situation, society might make an important collective decision that went beyond simply trying to help the market work or to preserve liberty: it might decide that it wanted to deal with inequalities of income and wealth that grew up through the workings of market processes by redistributing wealth and income from rich to poor. Of course, this redistribution could reduce some of the incentives for entrepreneurial activity. And it might offend one idea of justice that treated one's earnings as the just reward for talent and effort (rather than luck or the unjust appropriation of the work of others). But one could argue that a society would be "better off" (either in the sense that it satisfied individual conceptions of a just society more reliably or in the sense that it more closely approximated some transcendent principle of justice) if it were organized to produce economic equity as well as efficiency.

Note that even here, however, economics has an important idea to offer. It says that an efficient way to produce the right amount of equity would be simply to transfer income and wealth to achieve the desired distribution, and allow individuals to continue to have the right to make choices about how to spend their newly equalized income and wealth. In short, we would produce the kind of social equity we wanted by distributing wealth and income and then let the individuals decide how to spend their income.

This, in welfare economics, would be more "efficient" than redistributing wealth by providing specific goods to individuals such as food, medical care, or education. The reason is that it allows individuals to decide how to spend their money rather than force individuals to accept the particular things the collective thought that individuals should want and have. Anything other than this—anything that encouraged the poor to buy health care and education over alcohol and video games, or anything that encouraged young people to save so that they would not become a burden to their family or their society in their later years—would be viewed as paternalistic. It would be the effort to substitute some collective's value over the individual's, and in so doing to deny individuals some of the satisfaction of spending their money unconstrained.

Alternatively, a state with the power to tax and regulate could be used to encourage economic entities to achieve *social* rather than *economic* purposes. It might want to use the economic firms to eliminate racial discrimination in markets both as an end in itself and as a way to reduce economic disparities. It might want to use economic firms to help it accomplish health objectives by ensuring that employees worked under safe and healthy conditions, and that customers were protected from unsafe products. And so on. All this could be placed under the rubric of "social regulation" of economic firms. It can be understood as the state's use of its *authority* to accomplish socially valued results as well as economic efficiency through the regulation of economic actors.

All these ideas are more or less broadly within a *liberal* if not a *libertarian* tradition. In each case, we are still holding to the view that it is individual aspirations and preferences that count, and individual liberty that is to be protected. The differences between libertarianism and liberalism lie in two crucial areas: (1) in the amount of room that is given to the idea that individuals could have social and political ambitions that they would like to see realized in the social conditions in which they find themselves, as well as individual preferences for consumer goods; and (2) in the acceptance of the idea that politics (the way in which we aggregate individual preferences for how society ought to be organized) and the state (the institutions we rely on to produce the conditions that politics said were desirable) could be used to develop and respond to these individually held political aspirations at the risk of intruding on individuals' abilities to develop and lead their own lives. In short, the difference between libertarian and liberal views as described here is that liberals accept the idea that individuals can have political aspirations for the ways that society ought to be organized and can accept as a political outcome the fact that individuals voted to use state power to achieve these goals, while libertarians would to some degree deny the right of individuals to make claims on one another through political aspirations and to use politics and the state to advance purposes that the collective decided were important. Liberals look for a collective life guided by freely choosing, politically motivated individuals; libertarians suspect such a society and would view political motivations as thinly veiled self-interest or idiosyncratic conceptions of the public good that should not be allowed to impinge on their freedom.

An Alternative: The Communitarian View of Politics and the State

What both libertarian and liberal traditions miss or underemphasize, however, is a view that takes collective life—whether that be social, civic, or political—far more seriously as an essential part of what human beings both like and need to do. In this view, collective life is not viewed as a necessary evil that has to exist only long enough to remind us of the hazards of trying to live collectively and to reaffirm our collective commitment to live as privately and individually as possible. It is, instead, viewed as a necessary part of both individual and social well-being. Without participating in the processes of collective life—of deciding what we are and could be together as well as who we are and could be as individuals—we cannot be satisfied as individuals. Nor can we develop ourselves as individuals. In short, human beings need collective life not only as a means of creating the conditions under which they can live well with one another but also as an end in itself.

In this conception of the role of collective life, a society might come to the view that a market-dominated society would end up not only without enough social goods and enough equity *but also without enough opportunity for individuals to satisfy themselves as social, political, and communal beings.* In this conception, collective decisionmaking and the means for achieving collectively defined goals and aspirations are not threats to individual choice or problems to be minimized; they are, instead, desirable human activities to be embraced in the interests of a higher-quality individual and collective life. The need to come together to construct and deploy collective power is not just occasionally necessary to create the institutional structures that can guarantee efficient markets and protect liberty. It is, instead, something more systematically and continuously valuable to individuals as they live and develop themselves as individuals, and as they reach for fairer, more just, and more prosperous societies to live within. Individuals have desires to gather together and commit themselves to accomplishing things together, not just a technical need to do so (in short, humans are *political* as well as *economic* creatures); thus, in order for societies to be fully satisfactory to humans, they must provide a vibrant sector of society in which individuals can and do act socially and politically.

From this perspective, the political/governmental world (and the voluntary third sector of associations and civil action) would be an important complement to the market in providing individuals within a society access to the good life. They would have this access not only as individual consumers and laborers but also as neighbors, congregants, and citizens. These roles would be as important to the good life as the roles of consumer, employee, investor, and entrepreneur.

The Public as the Arbiter of Value; Public Value as the Goal of Government

So far, I have argued that we could adopt the view that a collective life of voluntary association, politics, and governmental action is important to individual satisfaction and to the ability to create just and good societies. I have also argued that it is plausible to imagine that such activities do not simply aggregate individual preferences (whether self-regarding or other-regarding) by adding them up through exchanges and contracts, but instead through argument and deliberation about the kind of people we are and the kind of society we want to inhabit. If both these points are (tentatively) accepted, then we could take one more step and note the extent to which this idea would be consistent with the profoundly illiberal idea that a collective "we" could be established that was capable of willing, choosing, and acting as a collective. Further, we might imagine that that "we" could compete with individuals as an arbiter of value in deciding how society's resources ought to be deployed.

In this conception, it is possible to imagine that a *social* utility function could be constructed and make claims on socially available resources as well as *individual* utility functions; further, that this social utility function would become the proper scorecard to use in judging whether some of society's efforts were successful rather than the summation of individual satisfactions. Or, to put it less technically, we as a society and a collective could decide that there are things we want to produce together as desirable features of society: a first-rate military, a reliable criminal justice system, an accessible court system, a means for guaranteeing the safety and cleanliness of the air we breathe and the water we drink, a health care system that provides a high degree of quality care and accessibility to all regardless of ability to pay. These collectively defined purposes could then make claims on us as individuals. We could be taxed to produce the money required to produce these social results. Or we could be regulated and obliged to act in ways that contributed to these objectives directly. We could be drafted into the army, forced to serve on juries, and prohibited from dumping toxic wastes into the air and water.

One way to think about this is to see that the "public policies" that emerge from the processes of representative government are essentially collective statements about the important public purposes that are to be achieved using the assets of the state—both the public funds that were raised through the power of taxation and the state's authority to force individuals to make contributions to the public good. Insofar as these public policies set out purposes to be achieved with social resources, they define the "public value" that is to be pursued through the use of collectively owned resources. (In more technical terms, we could say that public policies established little social utility functions.) Further, we can imagine that these political commitments to particular conceptions of public rather than private value would trump individual market decisions about whether and how much of these valued purposes society as a whole ought to buy.

Thus, for example, the collective could decide that an educated citizenry is important enough to its economic, social, civic, and political future that it would be willing to use its authority to require kids to go to school and its money to pay for books, teachers, and so on. The *collective*, not the market, has decided how much education will be provided and how it will be distributed. (Or more precisely, it has established some minimum universal conditions; if individuals can meet and exceed them through their own efforts, they are entitled to do.) This is the moment when the public as a political collective stepped in and decided what was valuable to produce with its resources rather than leaving the decision to the market.

Arguably, it is the domain marked out by these collective decisions to try to achieve collectively defined purposes through collectively owned assets that is the domain of the government sector. It is this sector (whatever its size) that is guided by collective choices about what is desirable to do and that uses the collectively owned assets of the state (its property, its money, and its authority) to accomplish these goals rather than individually defined purposes. The existence of this domain competes with and shoves aside the idea that *individual* valuations are the only things that matter in society and allows collective decisionmaking processes to make a claim on both the principle of individual choice and the society's overall resources.

Precisely because the government sector depends on collective agreements to decide what is worth doing and relies on collectively owned assets to accomplish this goal, libertarians and others who think individuals are the only arbiters of value would like to keep this public domain as small as possible. But it is also for this reason that communitarians who think that a wholly individual life is both a lie and dissatisfying to individuals would allow for a much greater influence of collective processes (including but not limited to politics and government) in social life.

Vouchers as Collective Support for Individual Decisionmaking

Note that "vouchers" fit into this scheme in an interesting and complex way. In an important sense, vouchers embody simultaneously a collective decision to finance and subsidize a particular kind of purchase by a particular class of individuals (for example, food stamps represent a social commitment to subsidize food purchases by poor people, Medicaid represents a social commitment to subsidize medical care for the poor, school vouchers represent a decision to subsidize education for the rich and middle class as well as the poor). As such, they represent a nonmarket, collective decision that a particular good is sufficiently important to individuals and to the society that the society wants to make sure that everyone gets enough of it.

At the same time, vouchers seem to enshrine the idea that individuals ought to be able to decide how they will meet their nutritional, health, and education needs. The delegation of this choice (but not the financing) from the society to the individual supports not only the market principle of competition on the *supply* side (with its attractive effects on innovation, adaptation, and cost reduction), but also the principle of individual choice on the *demand* side (individuals can pick the kind of food, health, and education they desire rather than have the collective decide for them). Both things promise greater efficiency both in the sense of finding more efficient ways of producing particular socially desired results and in the sense of producing what individual clients want and value rather than simply what society values.

Yet it remains uncertain whether vouchers have really privatized the decision or left it in the collective's hands. After all, the collective has not given out money with no strings attached. It has said to consumers that this money must be spent on particular things and makes significant efforts to ensure that the voucher's economic power is not spent on things that the voucher is not supposed to cover (such as alcohol rather than cereal for the kids, or faith healing rather than real medicine). Presumably, if individuals began making choices that seemed wrongheaded or improper to the collective, the collective would constrain the individual choices further.

Also uncertain is the extent to which vouchers are understood to be valuable because they guarantee the maximum degree of individual satisfaction (given that the purpose has been somewhat constrained by the collectively defined purpose), or because they are more likely to achieve the socially defined purpose they were designed for in the first place (that is, encouraging effective cooperation of the individuals who receive the vouchers in accomplishing the socially desirable goals). This difference could be revealed in the difference between thinking that educational vouchers are valuable because they increase the likelihood that parents and children will *like* the school they attend, or because the combination of liking the school and the new competitive pressures that result in both significant adaptation and innovation achieve the desired social result, which is *more educated kids*. In the first, satisfaction is treated as an end in itself. In the second, satisfaction is treated as one thing that contributes to the efficient and effective production of what is *really* desired: namely, the socially established goal of producing an educated citizenry.

Summary: Political Rights and Decisionmaking about a Just and Good Society

The point, then, is that if the fundamental idea behind the market ideology is that it is important to empower individual ideas about value over collective ideas of value, then this ideology poses a challenge to governance precisely because it undermines the idea that a collective agrees on what would be valuable to accomplish together. After all, even a libertarian society needs a social agreement that it will be a libertarian society. Further, to keep itself libertarian it needs to find some way to undermine the ambitions of those who would like it to be something else. A truly democratic society not yet committed to libertarianism would need some way to keep checking with citizens that libertarianism was still the form of society they wanted.

It follows, I think, that if there is a legitimate collective capacity to decide that a good society would be a libertarian one, there might also be a legitimate collective capacity to decide on a state that became the agent of a collective will to achieve social results different from those that would result from a libertarian political commitment. To make the claim that there are "core functions" of a state and that the state sector should be limited to these "core functions" is not a *technical* statement that emerges from social science understanding; it is a *political* statement about how much of a society's activities ought to be decided on by the collective. It might be good for economic progress and individual freedom for a state to severely limit its ambitions.

But if a collective wanted to produce values other than economic growth and individual freedom—for example, a fairer distribution of wealth and greater opportunities for community engagement—then the "core functions" of government would end up being quite different. A state could be produced that supported the development of a market economy that produced public goods such as state-supported enforcement of contracts and the protection of private property against theft. Or, a state could be enabled to try to produce a kind of social justice or economic equality that suited the political aspirations of its citizens.

To the extent that individuals have social and political commitments that they would like to have realized in their societies—that is, to the extent that they seek to govern themselves—then they have to depart (at least to some degree) from the important market principle that only individual preferences matter. They have to find a way to reach a collective view about their purposes and the means they will use to construct their collective life together, even if their ambition is to make that collective life as limited and as small as possible.

Once we accept the idea that collective purposes can be established through political processes, and that these purposes can trump individual valuations and claim social resources, we can see one of the ways in which the market ideology might undermine a valuable capacity for governance. It might deny individuals the chance to exercise what Hannah Arendt once described as the only kind of liberty worth having: namely, the right to participate in the process of governing the society of which one is a part. In doing so, it would eliminate something that was valuable to individuals, as well as something that was valuable to a society that wanted to be good and just.

But market principles are not finished yet. They can also make claims on how society might think of the role of the voluntary third sector of society as a vehicle both for the expression of social and political aspirations and for dealing with important public problems or advancing important social goals. It is to these ideas that we next turn.

Market Ideology and the Role of the "Voluntary Third Sector"

The burden of my argument so far has been that it is meaningful to talk of "public purposes" as something other than the maximization of the sum of individual valuations; that there is a way in which the processes of representative government can be relied upon to form collective judgments about what constitutes "public value"; and that these collective judgments about public value can, to some degree and in some domains, trump individual valuations and claim resources from the ordinary processes of individual exchange that constitute a well-functioning market economy. Exactly how a "we" forms from collections of individuals to establish such judgments about public value remains a bit unclear, of course. It is also easy to imagine all the ways in which the processes of forming a "we" that could have social preferences could be corrupted. It is for this reason that, as a political view, one might adopt a political philosophy that kept as much of social life as possible out of the reach of the unreliable "we" to maximize the chance that each of us who makes up the "we" would be able to achieve what each of us wants to achieve for ourselves.

The problem with the strictly libertarian view, however, is not only the technical problem that even a libertarian state requires some collective capacity to establish and maintain itself, but the more fundamental problem that it leaves out the following important ideas: first, that individuals might have social and political aspirations as well as material aspirations; second, that it might be important to individual and social welfare for society to construct institutions that would allow *all* of these preferences to be expressed and achieved; third, that often social aspirations can only be met through concerted social action carried out on a scale larger than the individual. That is, welfare economics and associated libertarian political philosophies leave out the idea that individuals have ambitions for what they would like to do *for and with others in activities that exist outside of the market*, and they *have ideas about the kind of society they would like to live in*. Or, more precisely, it says that *if* people have such ideas they ought to be free to express and pursue them, but to do so on their own, without invoking the powers of the state to make claims on others in realizing their more or less idiosyncratic social ambitions.

Although the idea that individuals might have and want to express desires to be virtuous in their lives, to do for others, and to join together in common cause to achieve social conditions they judge to be desirable is not immediately congenial to those who embrace market ideals; once such an idea is accepted, the welfare economist and libertarian would be forced to think about how such ambitions could be satisfied. One answer, of course, is that such ambitions could be satisfied through politics and the construction of a "we" that defined social purposes to be achieved through the power of the state. That is the perspective that is implicitly embraced above. But from the point of view of those who value market principles that emphasize individual choice, this is a bad answer. It makes politics and the state too important. It makes individuals too vulnerable to state compulsion.

The Third Sector as an Efficient Alternative to Politics and Government as a Way of Achieving Public Purposes

As an alternative, welfare economists and libertarians would fall back to a different position: namely, that such civic and political ambitions might best be satisfied through *voluntary civic action* rather than through politics aimed at commandeering state power to compel all to contribute to some more or less idiosyncratic or corrupt conception of the common good. The reasons that a person who admired market ideals would prefer voluntary civic action over political/governmental policy as a way of allowing individuals to express and achieve their social ambitions should be pretty clear.

For one thing, if society constructed a civic space that allowed individuals to hold and act on individually held social and political ideals, then a kind of expressive freedom would be created for the establishment of social conditions as well as for the consumption of goods and services. Utopians of all stripes ranging from Bronson Alcott to the Branch Davidians would be free to create their own little societies that reflected their social ideals. They would not have to subject their ideas about what is good for humans and what constitutes a good and just society to the bruising tests of majoritarian politics; they would be able to act freely to enact their views. They would not have to bend their ideas to the collective opinion of their fellow citizens. No one else would be much discomfited. This creates the kind of "efficiency" that those who favor markets like: the opportunity for each individual to express his or her own views, and (to the extent that their means make possible) for their individual views to be satisfied (even when those views refer to social conditions rather than individual consumption).

For another, establishing a voluntary civil sector would allow society to achieve some public purposes without having to rely on the coercive power of government. If the definition of the voluntary third sector is based on the idea that individuals voluntarily contribute resources—money, time, sometimes even pieces of their body—to others and to public purposes, then this represents an alternative to taxation and regulation to accomplish social purposes. Instead of having to go through the laborious political process of forming a collective agreement strong enough to command the power of the state, and then living with the pain associated with using state powers to accomplish public purposes, a vibrant voluntary sector would allow society to accomplish social purposes simply by stepping back and graciously accepting the contributions that socially and politically motivated individuals would make to the welfare of others and to society. This would relieve government of a burden that it otherwise might have to bear and would simultaneously protect freedom and minimize the use of the coercive powers of the state.

"Governmental Failure" as an Explanation and Rationalization for the Existence of the Voluntary Sector

These are the ideas that lie behind the hypothesis that a kind of "governmental failure" inevitably stimulates the development of a voluntary civil society (at least in societies that do not actively suppress such activity). In this theory, it is assumed that individuals have social and political aspirations they would like to have satisfied, as well as individual consumer desires. The difficulty is that, at any given moment, society can be only one thing. As Charles Taylor has observed, the social conditions in which we live together are an irreducibly shared experience. As a result, at any given moment, the state can satisfy only some individual political aspirations. A libertarian living in a liberal or communal society feels less satisfied than if he lived in a libertarian society.

Because many individuals will necessarily be dissatisfied with the political regime they inhabit, they will feel motivated to act. That social energy will eventually expresses itself either in individual acts or in the creation of voluntary associations that seek to bring about the social conditions that dissatisfied individuals want to see realized. Sometimes the action takes the form of direct *voluntary* action in which the dissatisfied citizens use their own resources to accomplish their goals. They form a volunteer fire department or band together to create an after-school mentoring program for

teenagers. Other times the actions is *political* in the sense that the dissatisfied individuals organize to achieve the kind of political power and leverage they would need to grasp the instruments of the state to help them
achieve their purposes. Whatever form it takes, some portion of society's
resources and activity will be devoted to the articulation and pursuit of
social and political preferences that are not satisfied by the current social
and political conditions; it is this energy that creates the voluntary civic sector and bleeds into the political sector.

Reasons for the Increased Prominence of the Civic Sector

The idea that individuals have social and political aspirations, and that
those can be expressed and achieved through voluntary action in a civic
sector of society, helps us understand at least some of the reasons why this
voluntary third sector is becoming important in contemporary political
thought. Viewed from one perspective, this sector seems to allow the market principles of individual choice and voluntary action to deal with problems that were previously thought to be primarily the responsibility of
government. The existence of a voluntary third sector gives the lie to the
idea that there can be only two sectors of society: the private market sector in which individuals display their values by making choices in voluntary transactions, and the political/governmental sector in which individuals come together to decide what kind of society they want to live in,
what sorts of things ought to be brought into the public sphere, and how
best government authority and money ought to be deployed to accomplish the collectively desired result. Logically and empirically a third sector exists in which individuals, as part of their effort to live the good life,
can decide to pursue a purpose they think is publicly valuable using only
their own resources or others that can be attracted on a voluntary basis to
pursue them.

In principle, of course, this sector need not be protected, much less subsidized, by government. Indeed, in many countries, voluntary associations
committed to using their own resources for public purposes are regarded as
threats to the existing government and are willfully suppressed. In a liberal
society, however, the rights to use one's own property for public purposes
and to associate on a voluntary basis are usually protected by the state and
facilitated by legal forms of various kinds.

Moreover, as market principles become more influential, it is easy to see
why a voluntary civic sector would be preferred to politics and government

as a way both to satisfy social and political preferences and to achieve social goals. From the point of view of market principles, voluntary civic action has two key advantages over politics and government. First, because individuals contribute only to the social purposes that they, as individuals, think are important to address, we can all be sure that their individual social ambitions are being addressed. In effect, they are voting for social purposes with their money and time, not simply with their political power. Second, because the individuals are contributing their money, time, and material voluntarily, the state is relieved of the burden of having to use its coercive authority to mobilize these resources to accomplish its collective purposes. Individuals are getting the social results they want and are prepared to support; the collective is benefiting from a flow of resources that it does not have to use its authority to amass. It is, apparently, an "efficient" way to define and pursue social purposes.

The Civic Sector as the Privatization of the Definition of Public Value

This all seems so sensible that it is easy to overlook just how important and in some ways breathtaking the idea of a voluntary civic sector really is. In the United States, we have in place a set of public policies designed not only to create a space for, but also to actively encourage, a voluntary civic sector. On one hand, these public policies are rooted in basic first amendment rights to speak and to associate. On the other, they are rooted in the rights of individuals to use their own property for whatever purposes they think appropriate, even if those purposes are to benefit people other than themselves and their families. The policies are also located in tax provisions that encourage individuals to make charitable contributions and exempt from taxes those organizations that have committed themselves to public purposes and renounced the right to enjoy the economic benefits that could flow to them as a result of their activities.

On reflection, what seems surprising about these policies is that they have, in effect, given over to individuals and nongovernmental groups the right to define and pursue public purposes *without subjecting them to the demanding tests of democratic politics*. (More precisely, they have authorized individuals to pursue a very broad set of collectively defined purposes with the means at their disposal, and have given them different kinds of public sanction ranging from tolerance to financial support for doing so.) Put somewhat more provocatively, to some degree, we have both "individualized" and "privatized" decisions about what constitutes the public good.

The charitable exemption of the inheritance tax allows John Paul Getty to decide that what Los Angeles needs is a beautiful art museum rather than a (slightly) better endowed school system. It also allows the millions of individual donors who felt sad when President Kennedy was assassinated to endow a "living memorial" to President Kennedy at Harvard as a way of encouraging young people to go into politics. Resources that otherwise might have gone to collective political processes for decisions as to their use are instead committed by individuals to public purposes that these individuals think are desirable (and are covered by the statutes that define appropriate charitable purposes).

These policies reveal, I think, the U.S. commitment to a broad, liberal individualism. After all, one might think that if there is anything that ought to be considered a fundamentally collectivist decision it would be the decision about what constitutes a widely accepted public purpose. How else could a collective purpose be defined other than through some process of collective discussion? Yet the United States has policies that allow *individuals* to decide what a public purpose is (subject to some broad statutory restrictions), and to act to achieve such purposes to the limit of their own resources and others they can recruit to the cause. This is the privatization of the definition of public purpose in almost the same sense that vouchers are. The main difference is that in philanthropy and volunteerism the choice about what is a public purpose is made by the person supplying the resources, while in the case of vouchers, the decision about the public purpose is made by the individual to whom the collective provided resources.

Institutional Arrangements Supportive of the Voluntary Sector

Once one accepts the idea that individuals have social and political preferences that they would like to see achieved and recognizes the civic sector as a protected social space in which such activity can be carried out, one can see some other important implications of these ideas for the arrangement of social institutions. The most obvious, of course, is one I have already mentioned: the need for policies that create the social, political, and economic space that allows civil society to flourish. As noted, these already exist in the United States, though not necessarily in other parts of the world.

But there are conditions other than explicit policies that might be important to create if a society wanted to take full advantage of the potential of the voluntary sector. For example, if one wanted a vibrant voluntary sector, one can imagine that it might be important to reduce the claims that the state made on individual private resources, or the extent to which it tried to monopolize and control the society's efforts to deal with social problems. Presumably, if the state takes private resources for public purposes, and if it allows or favors its efforts to solve public problems over those offered by voluntary associations, then some of the resources and some of the urgency that private actors might have and feel motivated to use for solving public problems will be lost. The idea that the state might compete with the voluntary sector as a device for defining and responding to social problems provides an additional reason for preferring a small rather than a large government. In this view, a small government is important not only to allow a private economy to flourish but also to allow a vibrant civil society to exist. Of course, one can have some skepticism about the extent to which voluntary action in dealing with social problems could be relied upon exclusively to deal with significant social problems. And one can easily imagine that society's overall ability to define and deal with social problems might well be enhanced through partnerships between the voluntary sector and government as well as through the independent action of the voluntary sector alone. But it is worth paying attention to the ways in which the voluntary and governmental sectors interact; and more specifically, whether (in economic terms) they act as "substitutes" for one another, or as "complements."

One could go even further to form an argument in favor not only of small governments in general but also in favor of highly decentralized federal governmental systems. In this view, a society that imposed few general restrictions on its citizens, decentralized what little authority it retained to small geographic units, and both allowed and encouraged citizens to develop their own voluntary associations would end up creating a world in which much of the collective work that happened in society would be accomplished through voluntary associations rather than government. Moreover, individuals would be able to "shop" among different combinations of voluntary associations and governments to find the ones that most closely approximated their own ideas about what constituted a good society. It is for this reason that those who favor market principles often prefer voluntary associations over politically mandated communities, and decentralized structures of governmental power over centralized ones. These institutional arrangements allow individuals more "choice" in the kinds of societies they want to be a part of than institutional arrangements in which centralized governmental units are the only places where social and political preferences can be realized.

Thus those who prefer the market principles that celebrate individual choice tend to have strong preferences for the kinds of social institutions that are constructed to meet the social and political ambitions of individuals as well as those that meet their material desires. They would like to leave as much as they can to the market and limit government to a few "core functions." To the extent that there remain unsatisfied social and political ambitions after this society has been constructed, they would prefer that those be expressed through voluntary civic efforts rather than through politics and government. They would prefer a thin government that created room for many voluntary organizations over a thicker government that dominated the public space. And to the extent that governments were required at all, they would prefer a federal system of government in which many different regimes were offered to individuals who could then vote with their feet by moving to the regimes they liked best (for either individual material or social and political desires).

Now, the image conjured up by a world in which most social and political ambitions are met by voluntary contributions, civic associations, and "boutique governments" that compete for citizens who like their particular style of governing is, to many, a horrendous one. Insofar as such a society would allow individuals to segregate themselves from one another in homogeneous groups, and to escape the need to test their views about what constitutes a good life and a good and just society with individuals differently situated in society, it seems to be a recipe for the kind of human impoverishment that comes from living with people too much like oneself. Living in highly homogeneous communities may be as bad for idealistic altruists as for materialistic egoists—at least as we understand what goes into "human flourishing."

Such a set of social arrangements might also make it difficult to define and achieve a good and just society. For example, it might turn out that the amount of resources that would be voluntarily contributed to such important purposes as sheltering the homeless, feeding the hungry, healing the sick, enlightening the ignorant, protecting the oppressed, and inspiring the downcast would fall well short of what was required to achieve this goal. (Lester Salamon has called such a possibility the threat of "charitable failure" that parallels concerns about "government failure.") Or it could easily turn out that individuals might act strategically to maximize their own welfare and seek out jurisdictions where the cost of being a citizen was low (say, a suburb or a gated community), but the advantages of being a citizen of a more pluralistic, culturally enriched community (say, a neighboring city) were still available to them.

These, of course, represent important reasons why one might prefer a more centralized, thicker governmental structure. But to find virtue in the creation of a stronger collective instrument, one must again celebrate what market principles find abhorrent: namely, the importance of public as against individual purposes, and the capacity of a "we" to form that would recognize what those public purposes were.

Conclusion

The extension of economic markets throughout the world has brought important changes in material welfare—mostly but not all good. The extension of the markets has been accompanied by increased commitments to market principles or market ideology. These principles are important not only because they have created the room for markets to spread in previously hostile social and political terrain, but also because they have begun to influence social and political thought and the construction of social relations and public institutions outside the boundaries of markets.

At the core of market ideology is the idea that individuals are the only social entities that should be relied upon to assign value to material goods and services on one hand and to social and political conditions on the other. Equally important is the notion that individuals ought to be able to choose. In the economic sphere, they ought to be able to choose how to use their own property, skills, and time to participate as producers in the economy and to spend their own money on the products and services they value. In the civic sphere, they ought to able to decide what social and political causes they hold dear, with whom they will associate, and how they will use their property, time, talents, and energy to advance their social and political causes. In the political sphere, they ought to be allowed to express their views about what constitutes a good and just society and to vote for candidates and lobby for public policies that encode their ideas.

These market ideals turn out to have important implications for a great many aspects of individual and social life. They tend to emphasize individual life at the expense of social and political life. They tend to make material preferences more important than ideas about achieving individual virtue or social justice. They tend to discourage people from having ideas that would make claims on the resources and convictions of others. They tend to make voluntary associations formed by agreements more important than the more demanding associations that are created by having to decide how the collectively owned assets of the state will be used to accomplish public purposes. They make the private economy a more important social sector than the public sector. Within the public sector, they make voluntary associations and nonprofit organizations more important than politics and government. And within the government sector, they confuse us about whose values are most important in guiding the use of the money and the authority of the state.

In the end, what market ideology threatens is the loss of confidence in any collective capacity to decide, to will, and to accomplish things together. At a fundamental level, it attacks the forum and seeks to put the market in its place. Because I take the forum to be the essence of governance, it is hard not to see the market ideology as potentially hostile to the capacity of communities, nations, and the world to govern themselves.

Contributors

All contributors, except for Guido Schaefer, are at the John F. Kennedy School of Government, Harvard University.

Jean L. Camp
Assistant Professor of Public Policy

Akash Deep
Assistant Professor of Public Policy

John D. Donahue
Raymond Vernon Lecturer in Public Policy and the Director of the Visions of Governance in the 21st Century Project

José A. Gómez-Ibáñez
Derek C. Bok Professor of Public Policy and Urban Planning

Anna Greenberg
Assistant Professor of Public Policy (on leave)

David M. Hart
Associate Professor of Public Policy

William Hogan
Lucius N. Littauer Professor of Public Policy and Administration and the Research Director of the Harvard Electricity Policy Group

Viktor Mayer-Schönberger
Assistant Professor of Public Policy

John R. Meyer
James W. Harpel Professor of Capital Formation and Economic Growth, Emeritus

Mark Moore
Daniel and Florence Guggenheim
Professor of Criminal Justice
Policy and Public Management
and the Director of the Hauser
Center for Nonprofit
Organizations

Joseph Newhouse
John D. MacArthur Professor of
Health Policy and Management

Joseph S. Nye Jr.
Don K. Price Professor of Public
Policy and the Dean of the
Kennedy School

Paul Peterson
Henry Lee Shattuck Professor of
Government and the Director of
the Program on Education Policy
and Governance

Guido Schaefer
Assistant Professor, Department of
Economics, Vienna University of
Economics and Business
Administration

Frederick Schauer
Frank Stanton Professor of the First
Amendment and the Academic
Dean of the Kennedy School

Richard Zeckhauser
Frank Plumpton Ramsey Professor of
Political Economy

Index